The Comintern and Early Indian
Communism: 1921-1928

The Comintern and Early Indian Communism: 1921-1928

Panchali Majumdar

TOWARDS FREEDOM

The publication of this book (The Comintern and Early Indian Communism: 1921-1928) has been financially supported by the Indian Council of Historical Research. The responsibility for the facts stated or opinions expressed is entirely of the Author and not of the Council.

TOWARDS FREEDOM

AH-202, Sector II, Salt Lake
Kolkata - 700 091
Phone : 2321 2902, 9331030579
E-mail : towardsfreedom@gmail.com

This edition first published by
TOWARDS FREEDOM
© Author

ISBN : 81-8206-029-X
First Published – 2012

Typesetting & Printed by
The Hallmark
68/1B, Sikdar Bagan Street
Kolkata - 700 004

Published by :
M.K. Bagchi
Towards Freedom
Kolkata - 700 091

Price :   Rs. 295.00

TABLE OF CONTENTS

ACKNOWLEDGEMENT

My personal effort alone could never have completed the venture that I undertook. From the very inception of the work till the closing date, the support that I received from various quarters helped me to complete the work. I had worked on Indian communism before, while working on a similar research project of the UGC under the IXth Plan. It was then that I realised that it could be developed into a doctoral thesis. But it was primarily the fellowship that I received from the UGC under the Teacher Fellowship Scheme of its Faculty Improvement Programme under the Xth Plan that helped me immensely to complete the work. At the very outset therefore I wish to thank the UGC helping me in conducting the research that that was necessary for the thesis. I am also very grateful to the Indian Council of Historical Research, New Delhi, for their grant that made it possible to publish the doctoral thesis into a book.

Professor Kunal Chattopadhyay, my supervisor, not only provided me with inspiration, ideas and encouragement, he also patiently helped in moulding my unformed thoughts into concrete ones. His criticism helped me in infinite ways to improve my work and add the dimensions that were often missing. Although I have not been able to do justice to all his criticisms and suggestions, I am grateful to Professor Kunal Chattopadhyay for all the mental support he gave me in finalising the work. His keen sense of historical thought and invaluable suggestions about the sources that I need to look up helped me in the final phase of evolution of the project. Without his contribution, this work would never have been possible.

The comments of two eminent scholars, Dr. Sobhanlal Dattagupta and Dr. Paul Le Blanc have been invaluable while shaping the thesis into a book. I am indeed indebted to them for the same.

Several institutions have extended much support in the course of writing the thesis. Of them, the National Library, Kolkata, Centre for Social Sciences Library, Kolkata, the Muzaffar Ahmad Pathagar, Kolkata, the Ganashakti Library, Kolkata, the library run by the Ramakrishna Mission Institute of Culture, Kolkata, the Nehru

Memorial Museum and Library, New Delhi, The National Archives
of India, New Delhi, the Central Library and the Archives of
Contemporary History of India of the Jawaharlal Nehru University,
New Delhi deserve special mention. Without the help that the staff
of these institutions, research work would never have been possible.
I am also enormously grateful to the staff of the Central Library,
Jadavpur University and the Departmental Library of the History
Department, Jadavpur University for all the help that they granted to
me.

The help and inspiration that I received from my friends Dr.
Nandini Bhattacharya and Dr. Sibasis Chatterjee deserve special
mention. They were always there when I needed them. I would also
like to thank my colleagues, Dr. Soma Marik and Dr. Sunetra Mitra,
for the help that they have rendered to me. I am grateful to the
authorities of my college Ramakrishna Sarada Mission Vivekananda
Vidyabhavan for granting me two years leave under the Teacher
Fellowship Scheme of the UGC and all my colleagues for being a
constant source of support during the writing of this work.

Lastly, I would like to say that I have always counted upon the
affection, cooperation and support extended by the members of my
family. Among them I have to mention my mother, who did not let
me rest till I completed my work, and my small son, Pushan who
suffered in silence all the neglect that I bestowed upon him.

INTRODUCTION

When communism first started influencing Indian minds, it had been a purely European phenomenon, catering to the industrialised societies of Europe. India was then a British colony, a consequence of its exploitation, its society and economy periled under severe British domination. Freedom fighters had emerged, making tremendous efforts to achieve freedom from foreign rule, and the nationalist movement was in its full swing.

The Russian revolution had occurred in Europe in 1917, a fact that bore tremendous significance not only in Europe, but the rest of the world as well. It was the first success of communism, and a society had, for the first time, been established in pursuance of communist doctrines. Within a couple of years the Comintern or the Communist International had been established, avowed to foster the communist cause in the world. Soviet Russia, being the only example of communist success, gave it leadership, and the Comintern became very active in pursuing its cause.

Gradually ideas of communism began to infiltrate into the colonies of the east, bringing with them images of freedom, images that had never been sought for before. Radical Indian nationalists, dissatisfied with the strategies their leaders proposed, were groping for answers to the existing situation. Soviet Russia, as an ideal to be cherished, loomed large before them as communist ideas slowly began to superimpose upon their nationalist visions and goals. This image of freedom that Soviet Russia presented to the world was very new to the Indians who had for the first time been influenced by socialist doctrines. This freedom was not confined merely to freedom from foreign domination as the nationalists were aiming at. It sanctioned much more. Communism came with incredible hopes about a life free from the abuse of exploitation of all kinds, a life of dignity and freedom, one where the toilers would rule, where the masses would be the leaders, and above all, a life that had never been dreamt of before. They realised, despite their conventional nationalist backgrounds and their limited knowledge of communist principles, that the attainment of socialism was the alternative that they were searching for.

India, unlike Europe, was not just a tool of capitalist exploitation. It was steeped in several layers of exploitation that were both native and foreign. The early communists dreamt of ushering communism into India. Influenced deeply by whatever little communist literature they could procure from Europe, and whatever little help they could obtain from the Comintern, they had sought for an alternative to the nationalist movement, their goals overstepping the visions that the nationalists were seeking. The image of Soviet Russia lurked in their minds as they began their crusade for the emancipation of the toiling masses. At the same time, their non-communist and more often than not, their nationalist backgrounds kept surfacing time and again in their thoughts and ideas. It was, in this background, that communism established itself in India, and even after the fall of the greatest communist state, that of the Soviet Union in 1991, and consequently, the end of the cold war, communism has existed in India, unhampered and undeterred. Its nature has undergone a metamorphosis over the years, but its existence still remains unchallenged.

If Indian communism was totally the creation of Moscow or rather the Moscow led Comintern, as earlier historiography would have us believe, then how can the strength of communism in India be explained, even now, that is after more than a decade has passed after the fall of communism in Soviet Union? This calls for a re-evaluation of earlier literature. The answer too is perhaps that Indian communism, from the very outset, had an indigenous background. It was never totally dependent upon the Comintern and its guidelines, its concepts and strategies being uniquely Indian despite all external influences. External influences, especially Russian, were undeniably there; but the basis of the movement, its leadership, and the ideas conceived by it were absolutely Indian. Possibly this is the reason that Indian communism has survived despite the fall of communism in the Soviet. And this indigenous movement was in existence in India from the very beginning, until the Meerut arrests were made that crushed the movement somewhat and opened the way for the Comintern to directly interfere into the communist movement in India. It is the indigenous communist movement of the second decade of the twentieth century, led by the Indians themselves and that which ran parallel to the one that the Comintern was trying to promote, is the point that this book aims to explore.

It is also important to note that after the fall of the Soviet Union; its archives were opened up, thereby leading to the study and publication of several documents that were unknown to the researchers before. These documents have thrown new light on the history of the Comintern and its activities. This too calls for a reassessment of earlier literature on this period.

One book that needs to be mentioned is Sobhanlal Datta Gupta's "Comintern and the Destiny of Communism in India: 1919-1943 Dialectics of a Real and Possible History". It exhibits marvellous scholarship. However, the perspective of the author differs from mine. Whereas he has examined the early Indian communist movement from the standpoint of the Comintern and its theories on the colonial question in the east and in India, this work has analysed the policies of the Comintern and has juxtaposed them with the theories and activities of the Indian communists themselves, both in India and abroad, before coming to a conclusion.

The first chapter in the book is about the attitude of classical Marxism towards revolution in the backward countries. Marx and Engels shunned the exploitative nature of imperialism, but believed simultaneously that in order to bring about revolution in the colonies, their economies had to be modernised on European terms. The bourgeois order had to be made to emerge because only that could bring about the victory of the workers against the imperialists and at the same time, act as the first step towards the establishment of the socialist order throughout the world. There was undoubtedly ambivalence in their attitude towards the economy of the colonial world. This attitude has led to much conjecture among scholars and a discussion has been made on it. Colonial liberation remained to Marx and Engels, a necessary precondition if the establishment of socialism in the world was at all to be given any consideration. Meanwhile efforts were on in Europe to give shape to an international movement of the workers.

The First International was formed in 1864. Like Marx and Engels the First International, as an international organisation for the workers, supported the liberation movement in the colonies and felt the need for involving the workers' movements with these movements of liberation. The International considered that the involvement of the workers in politics was necessary, as only that could guarantee the success of their goals. It was from here that Lenin and many others began to formulate their theories on the question of the emancipation of the toiling masses in the colonies.

The Second International emerged in 1889 on the hundredth anniversary of the French revolution. The ideas propounded at the Second International were based primarily on orthodox Marxism. But a more practical approach to the problems was sought. Leaders like Lenin, Rosa Luxemburg and Karl Kautsky rose during this time. The existing Marxist notions were modified in order to suit different situations. Vollmar, Karl Kautsky and others were among the first to try and theorise on these lines. Another point that needs mention is that the Second International saw the emergence of revisionist debates, which aimed at reforming Marxist ideas and strategies. Bitter struggles resulted for the need to revise Marxist theories.

It is interesting to note that Bhikaji Cama made an appearance in one of the Congresses of the Second International. He had demanded a solution to British exploitation of the Indians, though nothing much came out of it. The Second International, like its predecessor, displayed the same ignorance about the colonial countries of Asia and Africa.

Lenin had grasped the importance of the colonies ever since the Second International. He began to formulate from then onwards that a rational policy for uprooting the imperialists from the colonies was of utmost importance. But like Marx, he too believed that without the growth of capitalism there could be no victory over it. Hence the development of capitalist forces was necessary if the question of overthrowing it arose. Lenin's theories on self-determination led to much controversy between him and Rosa Luxemburg, a point that has been elaborately discussed in Chapter 1. Internationalism was another issue that Lenin was very concerned about. Here too he was in tune with Marx and Engels who had realised the importance of the Asian colonies in the question of the ultimate conquest of the socialist revolution.

The first chapter also discusses the formation of the Third International or the Communist International, better known as Comintern and its achievements in the first two years of its existence. The Lenin-Roy debate at the Second Congress has also been considered. Another point that the first chapter has examined, is the Congress of the Toilers of the East at Baku.

The Indians were meanwhile gaining much importance among the Comintern leadership. One reason for this was because M.N.Roy's efforts to bring India into the forefront, so as to secure all the help that the Comintern could provide. Another reason, this being more important, was that India was the most precious colony of the British, and its liberation would mean a severe loss for the British imperialists. Strategies involving India were hence of primary importance in the Comintern.

The second chapter examines in detail the theoretical formulations and debates in the Comintern regarding the colonial question from the Third Congress of the Comintern to the Sixth Congress of the Comintern, representing a time period of a little more than seven years. It examines the evolution of doctrine on the colonial question both before and after the death of Lenin in 1924.

The chapter has also discussed how, after the emergence of Stalin, the question of internationalism that orthodox Marxism propounded, slowly began to get the backseat in Comintern circles. As Stalin assumed more and more power, the nature of the Comintern leadership also began to change. It has been discussed how Stalin began to suppress opposition of all kinds in the Comintern, and how bit by bit, and much to the displeasure of veteran communist leaders of the world, the Communist Party of the Soviet Union began to dominate the Comintern's policy making with a singularity of purpose, especially in regard to the colonial question. And by the time the Sixth Congress had occurred, Stalin had already managed to remove much of his opposing forces from the ranks of the Comintern. Trotsky, Kamenev and Zinoviev were some examples.

A discussion has also been made on the evolution of M.N.Roy's notions on the prospects of revolution in India. It has been analysed how, since the Fifth Congress, Roy was proposing a more radical approach towards the question of revolution in India. He refused to brand India with other European colonies and felt that the time had come when the breach with the bourgeois order had to be made so as to bring about the success of the revolution. This was contrary to what the Second Congress had advocated, this was also contrary to what Stalin was advocating during the Sixth Congress. Debates regarding the question of revolution arose during this time particularly after the failure of the Chinese revolution of 1926-1927, one that had been guided by the Comintern leadership from the very beginning.

Meanwhile the Khilafat Movement had petered out and the Non-Cooperation Movement had been withdrawn. The abandonment of the Non-Cooperation Movement at a time when it had just begun to move with spontaneity set many radical nationalists thinking. It was around this time, that is in 1920-1921, that some Indian nationalists for the first time began to think in terms of communism. Another group of communists came from the muhajirin community, who had participated in the Khilafat movement, and had gone to Afghanistan with the purpose of going to Turkey. But with the waning away of the Khilafat movement, they fell at a loss. During this time several Indian communists were busy trying to set up a Communist base in Afghanistan. The Mujahirin came into contact with them, became influenced by their ideas, and then later on, turned into communists. Chapter 3 has tried to analyse individually the environment in which these early Indian communists grew up, how they responded to the changing political milieu, and how ultimately they became inclined towards socialist ideas, while keeping in mind the fact that socialist ideas were unknown to the Indians before the Russian Revolution took place.

The last chapter is a long narrative about what the Indian communists were doing in India. The thrust of this analysis is based on certain points. First, the role of the Comintern in facilitating the advent of communism in India has been noted. Secondly, analysis has been made on how far the early Indian communists were in compliance with the guidelines of the Comintern. Thirdly, the relationship of the communists to the burgeoning nationalist movement and the trade union movement has been examined. Depending on all these points the fourth and the last chapter has examined in details the following:

1. The establishment and the activities of the émigré Indian Communist Party and later that of the Communist Party of India.

2. The establishment of the All India Trade Union Congress, its constitution and its activities and its relationship with the labour movements in other countries till the end of 1928.

3. The involvement of the communists in the strike movements of the 1920's and their effects on the masses and the communist movement as a whole. The reaction of the labour movements in Europe to these strike movements has also been discussed.

4. The establishment and the activities of the Workers' and Peasants' Parties in different parts of India and the role that the communists played in these Parties.

5. M.N.Roy's approach to the Indian question both as a representative of the Comintern and in opposition with its policies.

6. The attitude of the Communists regarding the activities of the Congress, and their own initiatives about radicalising Congress policies.

7. Internal rivalries among the Indian communists, on the question of power, ideology and strategies to be followed in India.

8. The role of the Communist Party of Great Britain in assisting the Indian communist movement.

I have been asked as to why I did not extend this work beyond the Meerut arrests. The answer is simple. I have examined the character of the Indian communist movement, when it was emerging and slowly shaping and consolidating itself. This period of Indian communism is marked by a distinctive indigenous quality despite foreign influence. The nature of communism in the post Meerut years is clearly at variance with that of the pre Meerut days. This is because direct intervention of the Comintern and the Communist Party of Great Britain in the Indian communist movement became rampant, a characteristic that had been absent so far. This new aspect began a new chapter in the Indian communist movement, the reason why I have ended the work before the Meerut arrests were made.

Documents regarding the details of communist activity in India and abroad are many. Added to these are documents about the theories and policies of the Comintern in India and the colonies of the east. These documents have been analysed in the light of earlier works on the same subject before reaching a conclusion on the nature of the early Indian communist movement and its relationship with the Comintern.

CHAPTER - I

DEVELOPING A NEW DOCTRINE FOR THE EAST: THE SECOND CONGRESS AND THE CONGRESS AT BAKU

MARX, ENGELS AND THE NATIONALIST QUESTION

The origin of Marxist ideas on nationalism and colonialism dates back to the nineteenth century when Marx and Engels began constructing their ideas on communism. Imperialism, with colonialism as one of its corollaries in its advanced stages, had then been rampant in several European states, the most powerful of them being England. These imperialist states were colonising not only the states of Asia and Africa, but had already long colonised weaker European countries like Poland and Ireland. Marx and Engels evaluated in details the political and economic manifestation of colonialism, its relationship with imperialism, and above all, its social implications. At times, their erudite and critical observations resulted in certain judgements regarding the imperialist rule over colonies that were being ruthlessly exploited for financial gains and power accumulation. Yet, at the same time, they felt that these colonies, despite their experiences of continual exploitation and consequent impoverishment, would develop as adversaries of their colonial masters, a fact that would help ultimately in the overthrow of capitalism and the advancement of socialism in the world. They felt that it was necessary to expose the colonies to the capitalist world in order to modernise their native socio-economic system, a stage that had to be crossed, so that they could act as tools against the looming capitalist forces and hence expedite the final revolution that is the proletarian revolution.[1]

Marx and Engels realised quite early that in order to bring about the end of capitalism and the establishment of communism, what was desired was, as Marx pointed out, the brotherhood of the workers of all nations. Engels too was saying the same thing. He felt that since "...the condition of workers of all countries is the same, they must also fight together, they must oppose the brotherhood of the bourgeoisie of all nations with the brotherhood of the workers of all nations..."[2] Internationalism had been one of the basic tenets of their theories on proletarian revolution. But at the same time, Marx's attitude to colonialism was distinct, and while he condemned colonial exploitation, he did not see revolutions in colonies as leading directly to working class rule. In the years to come all these ideas matured and diversified with more and more theorists, theorising on the same set of problems over and over again. Controversies in theory mounted, as questions on nationalism, colonialism, imperialism and revolution became more and more pressing with each passing decade.

Among other nations, Marx and Engels harboured certain definite and conclusive views about the Indian political and socio-economic situation. The picture that the Indian society presented to them was one of total stagnation. As early as 1853, Marx had severely criticised the Indian life pattern as "undignified, stagnatory and vegetative life... contaminated by caste and by slavery...and thus brought about a brutalising worship of nature, exhibiting its degradation in the fact that man, the sovereign of nature, fell down on his knees in adoration of Hanuman, the Monkey, and Sabbala, the cow."[3] Indeed, these notions about India reflected the general European outlook towards the Orient. To Marx, these nations, in the absence of capitalist development, were doomed to imperialist and colonial influences— influences that were justified, as they were, in themselves steps to the advancement of these nations towards the role that they were to play in bringing about the final revolution. It was a historical process that could not be denied, and that which would ensure the triumph of the proletariat over the bourgeoisie. Despite the fact that the English capitalists were being guided by the "vilest of the interests", Marx was still propounding that "... English interference ...dissolved these small semi-barbarian, semi-civilised communities, by blowing up their economic basis, and thus produced the greatest and, to speak the truth, the only social revolution ever heard of in Asia."[4] He even commented that "...whatever may have been the crimes of England she was the unconscious tool of history in bringing about the revolution."[5] Irfan Habib has said that in the analysis of the pre-colonial Indian socio-economic situation, Marx was following the assessment of Hegel because it "… happened to be the accepted one among the best bourgeois thinkers of his day. What is of signal importance is how he revised it and set in a totally different analytical framework"[6]. The English after coming to India, said Marx, had "no alternative but to break the power of the native princes by force or by intrigue."[7] The native industry was consequently ruined. Marx has said, "England has to fulfil a double mission in India: one destructive and the other regenerating—the annihilation of old Asiatic society, and the laying down of material foundation of Western society in Asia."[8] It can be seen that Marx was constantly emphasising one point— the establishment of the Western order in the East was imperative, even at the cost of destruction of the indigenous life pattern, if the final revolution was to be sought. David McLellan has said that "Marx was certainly well aware of the importance of colonial exploitation for the coming revolution."[9] But at the same time, in the same article, he was severely criticising the capitalist order. He said:

"The profound hypocrisy and inherent barbarism of bourgeois civilisation lies unveiled before our eyes, turning from its home, where it assumes respectable forms, to the colonies where it goes naked. They are the defenders of property, but did nay revolutionary party ever originate agrarian revolutions like those in Bengal, in Madras, and in Bombay? Did they not in India, to borrow the expression from the great robber, Lord Clive himself, resort to atrocious extortion, when simple corruption could not keep pace with their rapacity? While they prated in Europe about the inviolable sanctity of the national debt, did they not confiscate in India, the dividends of the rajas, who had invested their private savings in the Company's own funds? … The bourgeois period in history has to create the material basis of the new world… Bourgeois industry and commerce create these material conditions of a new world in the same way as geological revolutions have created the surface of the earth…"[10]

In another article, Marx was saying:

"…However infamous the conduct of the sepoys, it is only a reflex, in a concentrated form, of England's own conduct in India, not only during the epoch of the foundation of her

Eastern Empire, but even during the last ten years of a long settled rule. To characterise that rule, it suffices to say that torture formed an organic institution of its financial policy. There is something in human history as retribution that its instrument be forged not only by the offended, but by the offender himself... The Indian revolt does not commence with the ryots, tortured, dishonoured, stripped naked by the British, but with the sepoys, clad, fed, petted, fatted, and pampered by them..."[11]

Marx in fact justified the reaction of the Indian peoples against the British. He said:

"... In view of such facts (British tortures), dispassionate and thoughtful men may perhaps be led to ask whether a people are not justified in attempting to expel the foreign conquers who have so abused their subjects. And if the English could do these things in cold blood, it is surprising that the insurgent Hindus should be guilty, in the fury of revolt and conflict, of the crimes and cruelties alleged against them?"

Marx has also criticised the double standards in European ideology, when it came to the treatment of the colonial peoples. Their ideal of democracy as related to their own land was not similarly suited to that of India. While on the one hand the Europeans criticised the luxurious living of their aristocracy, they maintained at the same time that the Indian aristocracy were to be preserved. "...Now is it not a strange thing that the same men who denounce the 'barbarous splendours of the Crown and the aristocracy of England' are shedding tears at the downfall of Indian Nabobs, Rajahs, and Jagirdars, the great majority of whom possess not even the prestige of antiquity, being generally usurpers of a very recent date, set up by English intrigue!"[12] In the absence of the industrial revolution, the development of capitalism had not occurred in the countries of Asia and Africa. These countries were being targeted by the imperialist ambitions of the capitalist countries of Europe. Colonialism had become rampant. Marx denounced colonial expropriation by capitalist countries. Yet, at the same time he felt that capitalism was essential in order to bring about the revolution as capitalists, for the cause of their own profits, would bring about the industrialisation of the colonies, though at the expense of the destruction of their own economies. This was essential. "... Bourgeois industry and commerce create these material conditions of a new world in the same way as geological revolutions have created the surface of the earth ..."[13]

The notions that Marx harboured about the Indian society, economy and politics were, as Edward Said felt, a result of an image that the so called "Orient" had in the West. This image was, according to Said, "a system of ideas" or a "...system of knowledge about the Orient, an accepted grid for filtering through the Orient into Western consciousness..."[14] He has branded Marx as an "Orientalist" and claimed that in the identification of an Asiatic economic system, "...Marx's economic analyses are perfectly fitted thus to a standard Orientalist undertaking, even though Marx's humanity, his sympathy for the misery of the people, are clearly engaged. Yet, in the end it is the Romantic Orientalist vision that wins out, as Marx's theoretical socio-economic views become submerged in this classically standard image..."[15] He has also said that like any other Orientalist, Marx too believed in the inequality between the East and the West, where the West assumed a distinct superiority over the East. In his opinion, Marx was, like any other Orientalist, "...neither interested in nor capable of discussing individuals..." but "...conceived of humanity either in large collective terms or in abstract generalities..."[16] Said's views have been scathingly criticised by Marxists. Aijaz Ahmad, is of the opinion that Said's remarks about the Orientalist system of thinking is mistaken, uncertain and neglectful of several facts, those that have led to his "...careless remarks about such key figures as Dante and Marx; his astonishing levelling of all kinds of European knowledges under the singular heading of Orientalism, whereas, for example, anyone who knows anything about India would find it scandalous that William Jones and Macauley are so easily called 'Orientalist', and so on...."[17] Debates on this issue can be endless, but one point was very clear in Marx's understanding of the Indian situation. He identified that India had to be freed from colonial exploitation so as to make it possible for the ushering in of the socialist revolution.

In the early 1860s there was a labour revival in Europe, especially in Britain and France. Though the Chartist movement in England had weakened somewhat, enthusiastic labour leaders proliferated, and ardently preached the doctrines of emancipation of the workers. In March 1846, a society called the Fraternal Democrats was set up. It corresponded with the Democratic Association in Brussels, and was organised on the basis of one general secretary for each of the member nations, Germany, France, Scandanavia, Hungary, Switzerland and Poland— a system later incorporated in the statutes of the First International. The formation of this society coincided with the Cracow uprising in Poland, a social revolt aimed at land reforms and the abolition of the feudal privileges. These organisations can be called as the precursors to the establishment of the First International. In 1864, the First International was established. It was, one can say, the first international organisation of the workers on such a large scale. Marx played a very important and active role in the International. Collins and Abramsky have said that at the outset, "Marx's task was to reconcile the irreconcilable. The International had at its inception, five national groups— English, French, Italians, Germans and Polish... For a brief period, however, all agreed on the basic aim of establishing a workers' international. This gave Marx a platform and an opportunity..."[18] to voice in the intellectual sphere, his own views, those that he had been nurturing for several years.

The labour movements that had generated in Europe during this time "responded generously to the struggles for freedom developing in Italy, North America and Poland"[19]. The support for Poland, however, was confined to the working class alone[20]. And in 1865, the International fell into a debate regarding the inclusion of the demand for Poland's independence in the agenda of the forthcoming Geneva Congress. Engels during this time, at the request of Marx, wrote a series of articles regarding the necessity of the working classes to become involved in the liberation of Poland, which was under the domination of Russia, Prussia and Austria. He felt that the issue of Polish independence did deserve the involvement of the workers as it would help to waken the imperialist forces dominating the country and hence in the long run serve the interests of the final revolution, which would usher in a world order, dominated and ruled by the proletariat.

In 1866, Engels wrote, "What Have the Working Classes to Do in Poland?[21]" In this article he clearly said, "... we perceive the difference between the 'principle of nationalities" and the old democratic working class tenet as to the right of great European nations to separate and independent existence. 'The principle of nationalities' leaves entirely untouched the right of national exist-ence for the historic peoples of Europe; nay, if it touches it, it is merely to disturb it..."[22]. Engels criticised sharply the occupation of Poland by Russia, Prussia and Austria. "But why do we name Russia alone in connection with Poland? Have not the two German powers Prussia and Austria shared in the plunder?"[23] He further commented that, "...this same Russian government came soon upon Poland in the name of religious toleration, because Poland was said to oppress the Greek Catholics; in the name of principle of nationalities, because the inhabitants of these Eastern provinces were *Little* Russians and ought, therefore, to be annexed to *Great* Russia; and in the name of the right of revolution by arming the serfs against the masters. Russia is not at all scrupulous in the selection of her means..."[24]

Both Marx and Engels had in fact always supported the cause of freedom of the colonies from the clutches of the imperialists. They felt that though exposition to colonial domination helped a society to transcend to the capitalist order, yet, advancement and revolution were possible only after capitalism was routed—a fact that the colonies could achieve only after they liberated themselves from the hold of the imperialists. The idea that the native bourgeoisie had a tacit alliance with the colonial masters, and that they would try under all circumstances, to preserve their positions against the impending revolution; is also clearly manifested in their works. This view was shared by Marx and Engels even before the establishment of the International[25], and was later enunciated clearly by Lenin in his formulations on colonialism.

The First International too, from the very beginning, supported the movements of colonial liberation. The members with a few exceptions[26] were constantly theorising and improving upon them at the same time, in order to solve among other things, the problems faced by the colonies. In its Foundation Meeting at St. Martin's Hall on September28, 1864, it was discussed that the British foreign and colonial policies were at least as bad as those of the continental autocracies. In Beesely's presidential address it was said "England wrongfully held possession of Gibraltar from Spain, and her conduct in China, Japan, India, and elsewhere was cowardly and unprincipled". He also criticised Britain's policy towards Ireland.[27]. The secretary of the London Traders Council, Odger too pointed out in the context of Polish colonisation that "... the occasion of the meeting ... was the decision of the English and French workers to protest jointly against the 'insults and cruelties' inflicted on Poland"[28].

Even at the next conference at London in 1865, as also in future conferences, colonialism remained one of the main issues of discussion. "It was not the wisdom of the ruling classes, but the heroic resistance to their criminal folly by the working classes of England that saved the West of Europe from plunging into an infamous crusade for the perpetuation and propagation of slavery on the other side of the Atlantic"[29]. Russia too was scathingly criticised. "The shameless approval, mock sympathy, or idiotic indifference with which the upper classes of Europe have witnessed ... heroic Poland being assassinated by Russia; whose head is at St. Petersburg, and whose hands are in every cabinet of Europe, have taught the working classes the duty to master themselves the mysteries of international politics..."[30]. Another incident proves once again that the First International was quite intent on promoting the cause of the colonies. In 1871, there was an application from a branch of the International at Calcutta, which hoped to destroy privileges on colour and caste. It also wanted to help the workers win their political and social rights. In answer to this, it was advised on behalf of the International that there was the "necessity of enrolling natives in the Association" who obviously did not have any native membership before[31]. Internationalism was woven into the policies regarding the empowerment of workers. Just as Engels deemed it the duty of the workers to become involved in the question of Polish independence, the International too felt the need for supporting liberation movements in the colonies from its very inception. There were objections, but the general trend was always in favour of it.

S. F. Bloom has said that Marx had always condemned colonial exploitation by imperialist nations. Marx scorned the idea that in return for enormous tribute, England exported a 'good government' to India.[32] Bloom said that Marx was also an internationalist. "He was an internationalist, not in the sense of advocating a system of co-operative world relations, but in the more specific system of conceiving that system as a resultant or function of the friendly interaction of large nations which were organised harmoniously within"[33]. It can be said that the theories regarding nationalism and colonialism and also those regarding liberation from imperialist clutches, were initially laid down by Marx and Engels. They even propounded that the bourgeois order that was dominating in the West, had to be established in the Asiatic countries, a fact, which would at first, destroy the Asiatic mode of production—which they said, was primitive and hence needed to be abandoned. The new order, they said, would actually ensure the triumph of the workers against the imperialists, as the first step towards the establishment of the proletarian order throughout the world. It was from here that Lenin took up, and it was actually these ideas and theories that dominated several communist individuals and organisations for the years to come.

COLONIALISM AND ANTI-COLONIALISM IN THE AGE OF THE SECOND INTERNATIONAL

The First International came to an end in the mid 1870s. After a decade and a half, when mass socialist parties had developed in several countries, the Second International was set up in 1889, on the hundredth anniversary of the French revolution[34]. The Second International too was a workers' international, bent on preserving their interests and bringing about ultimately their victory over the capitalists. It can be seen that the theories that Marx and Engels had proclaimed, and which found an institutional support in the form of the First International, underwent some evolution during the tenure of the Second International. Orthodox Marxism remained the basic component of ideas formulated at this time. However, revisionist debates regarding its validity also began to emerge at this time. On the other hand, many theorists of this time, improvised upon certain tenets of Marxism in order to suit the demands of different situations. But here too, disagreements loomed manifold. The Second International also saw the rise of many new leaders like Karl Kautsky, Rosa Luxemburg and Lenin.

During the 1870s and 1880s, after the demise of the First International, the Anarchists had become quite active. And by the end of the 1880s and 1890s the Socialist parties had begun to face several difficulties. In fact, the Congresses of the Second International of the nineties somewhat accepted the notion that though the bourgeois order was doomed by "...the inexorable process of the Dialectic..."[35], yet, political actions within the order was perhaps needed, especially in order to preserve the existence of the socialist parties. The socialist parties began to seek practical solutions on the basis of Marxist ideology, to the existing problems in contemporary European society.

Vollmar was among the first to realise and point out the necessity of an "immediate practical programme in the interest of electoral success. 'If you want to win the people and educate them politically, your political behaviour must be comprehensible to them'"[36]. The pressure that was created by the idea that theoretical pedagogy was not enough, and that practical solutions were necessary in order to win the support of the working class; moved Karl Kautsky, "the official party theorist" (as labelled by James Joll)[37], in the 1890s, to formulate a programme, which was agrarian, and which would appeal to the peasant, and at the same time, remain within the sphere of Marxist orthodoxy. Marxist theories however, did not remain conformed to these reformist notions of experienced leaders and bitter struggle ensued for the cause of revisionism in Marxist theory for a long time to come.

The Stuttgart Congress of 1907 had been by far, the most impressive of the Congresses so far. Sixty thousand people attended the open-air rally, which was the first event of the Congress. Eight hundred and eighty- four delegates were registered, of which Germany, Britain and France contributed the largest number of delegates. The first point that was put into debate was the colonial question. Now this question had been on the agenda of the International since its inception. But what can be particularly noticed is the fact that this question underwent a tremendous evolution over the years, thereby depicting different opinions, thoughts and ideas— often very contradictory and revisionist in the analysis of a point. The London Congress of 1896 and the Paris Congress of 1900 had vouched against the colonial policy of the imperialist nations, its exploitative role and its aim at profit maximisation of the imperialist bourgeoisie. But at the next congress at Amsterdam in 1904, the Dutch socialist, Hendrick van Kol put forward an amazingly different view. His resolution said:

"The new needs that will be felt after the victory of the working class and its economic emancipation will make the possession of colonies necessary, even after the future socialist system of government ... Can we abandon half the globe to the caprice of peoples still in their infancy, who leave the enormous wealth of the sub- soil undeveloped and the most fertile parts of our planet uncultivated?"[38]

Eduard David was not in favour of capitalist exploitation of the colonies. He was however not against colonialism as such, if the rights of the colonial peoples were protected[39]. He said:

"...We must condemn the kind of exploitation carried out today by the bourgeois world. At the same time, we must use all our influence both the colonies' population and their natural resources from capitalist exploitation, in the same way that we struggle against capitalism for laws to protect workers in the civilised countries..."[40]

It can be seen that David's attitude was based more reforming the existing situation than actually trying to come out of it altogether. He also said, "Europe needs colonies. It does not have enough of them. Without colonies it would be comparable from an economic standpoint to China"[41]. The colonial policy of David was criticised and condemned by and George Ledebour from Germany[42]. He said, "...Comrade David has missed the main point. As long as we have a capitalist world, colonial policy will exhibit the same abominable characteristics that we all condemn. David appears to believe that these atrocities are avoidable and characteristic only of present day colonial policies. That is a fundamental error."[43] But the Belgian delegate, Modeste Terwagne did not quite agree with Ledebour, and when the draft resolution on the colonial question was introduced, he in fact, proposed an amendment, "The Congress therefore does not reject in principle every colonial policy..."[44] What he said next was very significant. "...Under a Socialist regime, colonialism could be a force for civilisation."[45] He said that if the colonial production came to an end, industries would be damaged very seriously. And since "men utilised all the riches of the globe, wherever they may be situated...", he did not want the Congress to reject every colonial policy in principle[46]. This means that a justification for the policy of colonialism was being forcefully pushed so much so that it was being turned into a favourable policy under the socialist rule. Another amendment of a similar nature was introduced by David. He said, "Whereas socialism aims to put the productive forces of the entire world in the service of humanity and raise the peoples of all colours and languages to the highest level of civilisation, the Congress regards the colonial idea as such an integral part of the Socialist movement's universal goals for civilisation"[47]. It was however rejected, although

Terwagne's resolution was incorporated into the draft. The draft was submitted to the Congress by the majority of commission members whose reporter was van Kol. But the draft was once again debated upon. A minority of the commission comprising of George Ledebour and Emanuel Wurm of Germany, Henri de la Porte and Alexandre Bracke of France, and Karski [Julian Marchlewski] of Poland wanted the removal of the first and the last paragraphs of the draft and introduce instead, a substitute insertion[48].

The first paragraph read:

"Socialism strives to develop the productive forces of the entire globe to lead all the peoples to the highest form of civilisation. The Congress does not therefore reject in principle every colonial policy. Under a Socialist regime, colonisation could be a force for civilisation"[49].

The last paragraph read:

"The deputies of the Socialist parties should propose to their governments that they conclude a treaty and create a colonial law that would protect the rights of the native peoples and be guaranteed by all the treaty signatories"[50].

The insertion that the minority of the commission wanted to make in the place of the first paragraph was:

"The Congress considers that by its inherent nature, capitalist colonial policy must lead to enslavement, forced labour or the extermination of the native populations of the colonised regions.

The civilising mission that the capitalist claims to serve is no more than a veil for its lust for conquest and exploitation. Only Socialist society will offer the possibility to all peoples of developing fully to civilisation.

Capitalist colonial policy, instead of increasing the world's productive forces, destroys the wealth of those countries where this policy is carried out by enslaving and impoverishing the native peoples as well as by waging murderous and devastating wars. It thus slows down and hinders even the development of trade and the export of industrial production of the civilised states.

The Congress condemns the barbaric methods of capitalist colonisation. In the interests of the development of the productive forces it demands a policy that guarantees peaceful, cultural development that puts the natural resources of the earth at service of the further development of all humanity"[51].

It is clear through the above statements that the two views were totally contradictory an ay the same time, irreconcilable in nature. Hence debate was inevitable. Hendick van Kol called the view of the minority negative utopian and theoretical. On the contrary, the majority view, aiming at the improvement of the living conditions of the colonial peoples, was positive, practical and action- oriented.[52] Besides, he said that it was because of the capitalist colonial policy that the productive forces of the colonies were being developed. He contradicted Ledebour, saying that the resources offered by the colonies should be expropriated for the maintenance of modern society. The overpopulation of Europe too needed to be catered to, and emigration to the colonies was perhaps the best answer to this problem.[53]

Eduard Bernstein said, "...The colonies are there; we must come to terms with that. Socialists too should acknowledge the need for civilised peoples to act somewhat like guardians of the uncivilised"[54].

The inherent chauvinism that was revealed by these thoughts was condemned by Karl Kautsky. He put forward a bitter criticism of these revisionist ideas. He said that there was no arguing the fact that the condition of the colonies needed to be improved with appositive outlook. He also said that the European countries did have a civilising role to play in the colonies for the sake of preserving their own interests regarding socialism. But at the same time he said that "conquest and seizure of foreign lands" was not compulsory in order to achieve this. He said:

> "...If we come to oppress and enslave them, they are to be brought under the tutelage of some despotism, no matter how benevolent, they will be mistrustful. Then they will reject foreign despotism along with the foreign domination. Then it will come to wars and devastation. Everywhere we see this colonial policy practiced, it produces rebellion and degradation of the people"[55].

Hendrick van Kol once again scorned Kautsky. He said:

> "The learned Kautsky made matters even worse with his advice on how to develop the colonies industrially. We are supposed to take the machines and tools to Africa! A theoretical pipe

dream. That's supposed to civilise the country! Suppose that we bring a machine to the savages of central Africa, what will they do with it? Perhaps they will start up a war dance around it (Loud Laughter) or increase by one their innumerable holy idols. (Laughter) Perhaps we should send some Europeans to run the machines. What will the native peoples do with them, I do not know. But perhaps Kautsky and I will make the attempt. Perhaps theory and practice will then go hand in hand into that savage land with tools and machines. Perhaps the natives will destroy our machines. Perhaps they will kill us or even eat us and then I fear that (Rubbing his belly) given my superior corporeal development I will have precedence over Kautsky. (Laughter). If we Europeans go with tools and machines we would be defenceless victims of the natives. Therefore we must go there with weapons in hand, even if Kautsky calls that imperialism"[56].

The debate was tremendous, as none of the parties would relent. But the amendments proposed by the minority were adopted 127 votes to 108.

Meanwhile, Bhikaji Kama, a member of the British delegation and a representative of the Indian National Congress, had introduced a resolution, "On British Rule in India". He had said "...The Congress declares it the duty of all friends of freedom throughout the world to aid the liberation movement of that fifth part of humanity who inhabit this unfortunate land"[57]. He had spoken at the debate too, demanding rights for the Indians. He had commented:

"...India pays a heavy price for British capitalist rule. Much has been said about economic questions. What then is the economic situation of India? Each year India must pay thirty-five thousand pounds sterling to Britain, and not a penny of it finds its way back to India. This economic relationship causes the hunger and desperate poverty of an immense population, countless epidemics, and a death rate that has risen to an unspeakable level.

I address here the tribunal of human justice. What is socialism, if not justice? And if there is justice, why must millions of unfortunate Indians endure such agony? (Loud applause) India is a possession of the British crown, a subjugated country ruled by despotism and unbearable tyranny, inhabited by a fifth of the world's population. I call on the congress to raise its protest against this vicious tyranny. (Applause)... I call on you to adopt our resolution. (Applause) Indians demand their human rights and their autonomy. We want the right to self-determination, we demand justice and the right to govern ourselves"[58].

Though Bhikaji Kama made a clear appeal to the Congress to solve the Indian problem, nothing was done about it. Paul Singer, the chairman at the meeting said, "We cannot consider the resolution on British rule in India because it was not previously submitted to the international bureau. But I believe I can say that both the bureau and the Congress agree with the general direction of this resolution"[59]. The Indian question thus remained unsolved despite the support.

One thing is very clear. Whatever theories the socialists were propounding, they had little or no understanding of the life and culture of the countries of Asia and Africa. Even Kautsky, who was so very against colonialism as it entailed slavery and impoverishment of the people at large, called the colonial people "savages", who needed to be civilised in the European way of life.[60] It is strange that none of them took into any notice of civilisations, which had already occurred in these unknown lands much before that in Europe. They failed to take into consideration that these places with their varied climates developed different but parallel means of life. Just because industrialism had not found its way in these places before the colonisers, civilised though they were, they became doomed to the civilising mission of these Europeans, socialists or otherwise.

Lenin made a break in comprehending the situation in the colonies. He refused to accept the need to civilise the colonial peoples. After condemning the Dutch and the German revisionists as opportunists, Lenin said in an article, "The International Socialist Congress at Stuttgart" that the "Congress was to discuss present day colonial policy, which was based on downright enslavement of primitive populations."[61] Regarding the opportunist point of view, that the Europeans were actually performing a civilizing mission in the colonies, Lenin said that the "...bourgeoisie were ... subjecting the native populations to unprecedented outrage and violence, 'civilising' them by the spread of liquor and syphilis. And in that situation, socialists were expected to utter evasive phrases about the possibility of accepting the colonial policy in principle!"[62] He also said:

"The non-propertied, but the non-working class is incapable of overthrowing the exploiters. Only the proletarian class which maintains the whole of society, can bring about the social revolution. However, as a result of extensive colonial policy, the European proletarian partly finds himself in a position when it is not his labour, but practically enslaved nations in the colonies, that maintains the whole of society. British bourgeoisie derives for example, more profit from the many millions of populations in India and other colonies than from the British workers. In certain countries this provides the material basis for infecting the proletariat with colonial chauvinism"[63].

This idea, that the British imperialists were gaining more profits from the colonies than that from their own industries was later elaborated in the discussions on the national and colonial questions at the Second Congress of the Communist International.

Horace B Davis has said that the debates in the Second International could not produce a "...carefully reasoned, compact position on questions affecting nationalism, especially as the representatives came from parties which were after all national and might have been expected to defend the position of their respective countries in international gatherings...Nevertheless the positions taken were frequently in advance of those in the majority countries; and certain of the leaders, especially of the left wing (Lenin et al.) came to attach considerable importance to the sessions of the International and worked hard for the adoption of a correct position..."[64]

The Second International collapsed in 1914. But the seeds of Lenin's later formulations on the national and colonial questions can be traced from this period itself.

Like Marx, Lenin too believed in the beginning that without the growth of capitalism, the emancipation of the working classes was not possible.[65] Colonialism, an aspect of imperialism, had divided the world, said Lenin, "...into countries owning colonies, the colonies themselves, the semi- colonies and the commercial colonies".[66] Even before the Russian revolution, Lenin wrote to Maxim Gorky:

"It would be quixoticism and whining if Social Democrats were to tell the workers that there could be salvation somewhere apart from the development of capitalism. But we do not say this. We say: capital devours you, will devour the

Persians, will devour everyone and go on devouring until you overthrow it. That is the truth. And we do not forget to add: except through the growth of capitalism there is no guarantee of victory over it."[67]

Capitalism was hence absolutely necessary in order to bring about the revolution.

The significance of national wars of liberation against capitalist forces was to Lenin, of utmost importance at this time. He felt that even if the imperialist policies of colonisation and exploitation were resisted by "the means of organising the proletariat", capitalist forces would not be retarded. On the contrary, it would only accelerate the development of capitalism, thereby forcing it to "resort to more civilised, technically higher methods of capitalism".[68] Lenin was of the opinion that the wars of liberation that were brewing in the colonies were wars that were basically aimed against imperialism He was writing:

"... national wars waged by colonies and semi- colonies in the imperialist era are not only probable, but inevitable. About 1000 million people, or over half the world's population, live in the colonies and the semi-colonies (China, Turkey, Persia). The national liberation movements there are already very strong, or are growing and maturing. Every war is a continuation of politics by other means. The continuation of national liberation politics in the colonies will inevitably take the form of national wars against imperialism..."[69]

In the same article, he was harping on the same point again and again. He was optimistic that national wars of liberation would inevitably occur and take the form of revolutionary and progressive forms. Their success however, would depend on several factors. There should either be the participation of a huge number of people, or the international political conditions should be such that would prevent the interference of the imperialist nations, or there should occur an internal revolt by the proletariat against the bourgeoisie in the oppressor nation. He complemented the latter factor to be by far the most desirable.[70] Lenin however, at this stage, was talking only about wars of national liberation against the imperialist powers. There was, at this stage, no mention of another separate war against the native bourgeoisie before the final emancipation of the workers could take place—a fact, which was to assume a significant role in the future strategies of Lenin.

In 1908-1909, Lenin's theories, although based on a standard Marxist position, especially those on the right of nations to self-determination, led to much controversy. Rosa Luxemburg, a Polish socialist, however, who was taking an unusual position, was among the first to contradict Lenin on several points in his "Programme of the Social-Democratic Workers' Party"[71] regarding the right of nations to self determination— a point especially emphasised in the seventh, eighth and ninth clause of Lenin's programme. The seventh point demanded the "Abolition of social estates, and complete equality of rights for all citizens, regardless of sex, religion, race, and nationality". The eighth clause talked of the "Right of the population to receive education in their native language, to be ensured by the provision of schools needed for this purpose, at the expense of state and the organs of self-government; the right of every citizen to express himself at meetings in his own language; use of the native language on an equal basis with the state language in all local, public and state institutions". The ninth clause was "Right of self-determination for all nations included within the bounds of the state"[72]. The third clause was another point in the controversy. It pointed the need for "Extensive local self-government; regional self-government for all localities which are distinguished by special conditions in respect of mode of life and make-up of the population"[73].

Rosa Luxemburg firmly objected to this type of formulation of nationalist principles. She said, "What is especially striking about this formula is the fact that it doesn't represent anything specifically connected with socialism nor with the politics of the working class. The right of nations to self-determination is at first glance a paraphrase of the old slogan of bourgeois nationalism put forth in all countries at all times: the right of nations to freedom and independence."[74] She was saying quite categorically that the workers' parties were not aiming to achieve abstract social ideals, but that they were actually striving to formulate "practical social and political reforms which the class- conscious proletariat needs and demands in the framework of bourgeois society to facilitate the class struggle and their ultimate victory."[75] She emphasised that political formulations were made with the aim to secure a practical solution to the problems of political and social life, especially those that were related to the sphere of class-struggle of the proletariat. This would, she said, "serve as a guideline for everyday politics and its needs; to initiate the political programme of the workers' party and to lead it in the right direction; and finally to separate the revolutionary politics of the proletariat from the politics of the bourgeois and the petit bourgeois parties."[76] She argued that Lenin's thoughts about the right of nations to self-determination were devoid of such principles or guidelines, and that they were avoiding the question altogether.[77]

Rosa Luxemburg felt that it was sheer "utopia" to hope that all nationality questions could ever be solved within the given capitalist framework. All nations, races and other ethnic groups could never be assured of self- determination.[78] To her, the contemporary world, so greatly dominated by the capitalist order little or no chance for self- determination of nations except those few "most powerful nations, the leaders in capitalist development, which possess the spiritual and material resources necessary to maintain their political and economic independence, 'self-determination', the independent existence of smaller and petty nations, is an illusion, and will become even more so..."[79] She felt that the programme of national self-determination was a type of "...an opportunism which tied socialism to the chariot of the class enemy... To this extent Rosa Luxemburg invented the concept of modern Socialist opportunism, its characterisation and its identification as a bourgeois (i.e. hostile) influence within the socialist movement."[80]

It was Rosa Luxemburg's idea that the Austrian Social Democratic Party would "...solve the nationality question not by a metaphysical formula which leaves the determination of the nationality question up to each of the nationalities according to their whims, but only by means of a well defined plan."[81] She then outlined her plan in detail as to how the rights of the different socio- political groups could be protected. When Karl Kautsky, the noted Austrian socialist refused to agree that such a plan would be a fool-proof remedy to the problem of nationalities, and that the plan itself might not be equally acceptable to all individuals or sections of society, she had arrogantly answered, "...Nonetheless, it does represent an attempt to provide a practical solution of these difficulties by the party of the proletariat..."[82]

Regarding colonies, Luxemburg was of the opinion that colonial struggles for liberation did not always lead to independence in the true sense of the term. She has clarified that the gaining of independence of the United States, Brazil and Argentina, not as a removal of national dependence, but only as a transfer of it to another nationality. It was the redskin natives in the case of the United States, controlled by the white immigrants who gained independence whereas the Negroes of Brazil and Argentina were subjected to Spanish and Portuguese immigrants. She expected a same situation to prevail in India as well. She said that since several nationalities were co-existing in India at the same time, and since each differed from the other in social and political development; it was not a simple social construction at all. Hence, she said that a "hasty evaluation" of the nationalist movement in India might lead to erroneous conclusions, which should be avoided.[83]

Rosa Luxemburg forcefully denied the fact that there could be national self-determination within a capitalist system. International socialism she said "recognises the right of independent nations with equal rights". If capitalist nations were colonising other nations so much so that their national existence became dependent on those colonial peoples, even those nations could not be called free. "...So long as capitalist states exist, i.e., so long as imperialist world policies determine and regulate the inner and outer life of a nation, there can be no national self-determination either in war or in peace."[84] On the other hand, the right of nations as a formula, was "...inadequate to justify the position of socialists on the nationality question, not only because it fails to take into account the wide range of historical conditions existing in each given case and does not reckon with the general current of the development of global conditions, but also because it ignores completely the fundamental theory of modern socialism— the theory of social classes."[85]

It was not only Rosa Luxemburg, who was criticising Lenin. Lenin himself was writing in 1914, that the "Russian liquidator Semkovsky, in the St. Petrsburg liquidationist newspaper, and the Bundist Liebman and the Ukranian nationalist-socialist Yurkevich, in their respective periodicals have violently attacked this clause and have treated it with supreme contempt."[86] Lenin labelled them as opportunists and said that they were saying nothing new but merely repeating something that had already been formulated by Rosa Luxemburg earlier. In order to calm down the confusion, he said that he would go into a detailed examination of her theories, and in the process, produce a defence for his own theories as well.

From the very beginning of the article, Lenin wrote in an

aggressive tone, more so when he was eliminating his own criticism. He made a clear expression of his thoughts, never deviating for a moment from his earlier ideas. He said that in order to grasp the true meaning of self- determination of nations, "juggling" with legal definitions, or inventing new ones would certainly not come of any help. There should be a detailed examination of "the historico-economic conditions of the national movements" to reach the conclusion that self- determination of nations means "the political separation of these nations from alien national bodies, and the formation of independent national state."[87]

Lenin said in agreement with Kautsky that the national state was a feature of capitalism and that the multi- national state "represents backwardness, or is an exception. From the standpoint of national relations, the best conditions for the development of capitalism are undoubtedly provided by the national state."[88] At the same time, he also said that such a state, which was based on bourgeois relations, could actually wipe out exploitation and oppression of nations. Hence, self- determination of nations in the Marxist Programme could not, "...from a historico-economic point of view, have any other meaning than political self- determination, state independence, and the formation of a national state."[89]

Lenin analysed at length Rosa Luxemburg's attitude on the demand for the independence of Poland. On the one hand, Rosa Luxemburg was totally against the demand for Polish independence. Yet, on the other hand, she wanted a rather speedy industrial development of Poland, which however would be facilitated by the marketing of Polish manufactures in Russia. Lenin pointed out that in her refutation of the need for Polish independence, Luxemburg was actually unwilling to see the rise once again, of the landed gentry in Poland[90]. But, at the same time, her desire to unite Russia with Poland was based on "purely economic factors of modern capitalist relations"[91], which again, she was thoroughly against. Lenin commented, "...Rosa Luxemburg does not get her arguments to hang together even on the question of the social structure of the government in Russia with regard to bourgeois Poland; as for the concrete, historical, specific features of the national movements in Russia— she does not even raise that question." [92]

Horace. B. Davis has said:

"Lenin as an internationalist was fighting against Great

Russian chauvinism. Luxemburg as a Polish (German) internationalist was, fighting against Polish social patriotism (chauvinism). Paradoxically, they arrived at exactly contrary positions on self- determination."[93]

Peter Nettl has said that this debate actually hinted at the historical limitation of the concept of nationality and nation. He commented: "...Orthodox Marxism, Kautsky's as well as Lenin's, preferred to *equate* the national interest with that of the proletariat than, like Rosa Luxemburg, *subsuming* the one by the other. In any case, events proved Rosa Luxemburg's prognosis incorrect— at least in its application to the immediate future; the outbreak of war showed clearly that when the crunch came class antagonisms were swept aside by national solidarity. Perhaps this is why Lenin preferred to equate rather than subsume, and why in 1914 Rosa Luxemburg felt that so much of her view of the world had shattered into a thousand fragments."[94]

Even when Lenin was summing up his discussion on the question on self- determination in 1916, he was saying that "...the demand for liberation in the colonies is nothing more than 'the recognition of the right of nations to self- determination'".[95] Lenin wrote, says Sobhanlal Dattagupta, that the "in the oppressed colonies...because of retarded growth of capitalism with native feudalism as its mainstay objective conditions for a socialist revolution were not yet mature, and in these countries, what was awaited, was a bourgeois democratic revolution"[96]. Lenin further wrote that in the bourgeois democratic revolution, the motive forces would not necessarily be the national bourgeoisie, despite the fact that it was always the bourgeoisie that exercised hegemony at the beginning of every national movement. Lenin was therefore, aware of the dual role played by the bourgeoisie in the colonial countries. While this class played an anti-imperialist role against imperialist oppressors on the one hand; yet, on the other, when this class come to the forefront, its action would be characterised by compromise and back stepping when the class question would arise. Lenin even marked the point that the working class, while formulating its policies, must take into account, this ambivalent character of the bourgeois nationalist movement.

He said that since the colonies had no capital of their own, nor could they borrow any, without accepting the condition of political submission, capitalist development was not being made possible among the colonial peoples. Hence there was no other way than to liberate them "immediately and unconditionally", in order to facilitate the further advancement of capitalism in the colonies.[97] He also said:

> "To imagine that a social revolution is conceivable without revolts by small nations in the colonies and in Europe, without revolutionary outbursts from a section of the petty bourgeoisie *with all its prejudices*, without a movement of the politically non- conscious proletarian and semi- proletarian masses against oppression by the landowners, the church, the monarchy, against national oppression, etc.— to imagine all this is to *repudiate social revolution*".[98]

Lenin by this time had clearly conceived the notion that colonial exposition to capitalist influences was not enough. There should be revolts from all the disgruntled sections of the society at large against all forms of exploitation and oppression in order to smoothen the way for the final upheaval. What was ultimately desired was the development of capitalism in the colonies itself, independent of the West, so as to arrive at the final stage, when capitalism would be routed and dictatorship of the proletariat established. This time the proletariat would be politically conscious of its rights and would aim to destroy capitalism once and for all. Lenin was very soon to elaborate on this point at the Second Congress of the Communist International.

Internationalism was a very important issue where Lenin was concerned. He felt that the revolution would not be complete until it took an internationally all-encompassing shape. Hence it was necessary to educate the masses in the spirit of internationalism, which was impossible until the oppression of colonies was not eliminated. "…If we are to be faithful to socialism we must even now educate the masses in the spirit of internationalism…"[99] he said. As early as 1908, Lenin was saying:

> "And this step forward of the whole of international socialism, along with the sharpening of the revolutionary democratic struggle in Asia, places the Russian revolution in a special and especially difficult position … Reaction against the mounting proletarian struggle is inevitable in all capitalist countries and it is uniting the bourgeois governments of the whole world against every popular movement, against every revolution both in Asia and, particularly, in Europe…"[100].

That socialism was not possible in an isolated state and that the Asian countries were needed to partner with in the revolutionary process, was clearly stated in Lenin's theories long before the Russian revolution actually occurred. In fact the potential role of the countries of Asia against capitalist forces had been advocated by Marx and Engels as well.[101] Even afterwards, Lenin was saying again and again that the liberation of the Eastern countries was essential if victory was to be achieved. This feeling became all the more emphatic in the months preceding the Second Congress of the Communist International, when the colonial nations had started showing active interest in communist doctrines, perhaps as an alternative means to freedom. A couple of months before the Second Congress of the Communist International Lenin was saying, "...Only when the Indian, Chinese, Korean, Japanese, Persian, and Turkish workers and peasants join hands and march together in the common cause of liberation— only then will decisive victory over the exploiters be ensured. Long live a free Asia!"[102]

Lenin knew however, that revolution and the subsequent empowerment of the workers would not be achieved so easily. The bourgeois forces would always try to resume power through counter-revolution. "Dictatorship of the proletariat, the only consistently revolutionary class, is necessary to overthrow the bourgeoisie and repel its attempts at counter-revolution", unless of course the bour-geoisie surrendered on it own after realising the futility of resistance[103]. It was during this time, that Lenin perhaps clearly grasped the dual role that was to be played by the bourgeoisie in this struggle for revolution. He said that there were two periods of capitalism, "...which differ radically from each other as far as the national movement is concerned. On the one hand there is the period of the collapse of feudalism and absolutism, the period of the formation of the bourgeois- democratic society and state, when the national movements for the first time become mass movements and in one way or another draw all classes of the population into politics... on the other hand there is the period of fully formed capitalist states with long established constitutional regime and a highly developed antagonism between the proletariat and the bourgeoisie— a period that may be called the eve of capitalism's downfall".[104] His enunciations on the theme were however, still to be made more direct and more comprehensible— a fact, which was to occur within a couple of years at the Second Congress of the Communist International.

Michael Lowy has analysed in details the leftist theories of Marx, Engels, Trotsky, Luxemburg, Lenin and several others. He has said that it was actually Lenin, who could best understand the dialectical relationship between internationalism and that of national self determination. According to Lowy, Lenin could comprehend that until the nations were freed from their oppressors, and national identities established firmly, free and voluntary union, cooperation, association and ultimately, the fusion of nations into an internationalist whole was not possible.[105]

After the Bolshevik revolution in 1917, another factor began to assume significance especially for the Eastern countries— the peasantry. The peasantry formed the bulk of the population in the countries of Asia— where dwelt the majority of the world's population. This was a fact that the communists could never ignore and Lenin led the way in emphasising this. He was saying in 1919:

"...Here contact with the peoples of the East is particularly important, because the majority of the people are the typical representatives of the working people—not workers who have passed through the school of capitalist factories, but typical representatives of the working and exploited peasant masses who are victims of medieval oppression...Our Soviet Republic must muster all the awakening peoples of the East and, together with them, wage a struggle against international imperialism"[106].

This awareness of the necessity to adapt to specific conditions was quite characteristic of Lenin. The role of the peasantry began to be analysed in great detail in his writings especially on China. He said that "relying upon the general theory and practice of communism, you must adapt yourself to specific conditions, such as do not exist in the European countries; you must be able to apply that theory and practice to conditions in which the bulk of the population are peasants, and in which the task is to wage a struggle against medieval survivors and not against capitalism"[107]. When Lenin was asked about his plans regarding Asia in February 1920, he had said that it was the same as that in Europe, which was "peaceful coexistence with all peoples; with the workers and the peasants awakening to a new life— a life without exploiters, without landowners, without capitalists, without merchants..."[108]

The impact of the Russian revolution was felt worldwide, and the colonies of Asia and Africa were no exceptions. These colonies, where modern thoughts and ideas had already begun to infiltrate from the West, now came under the spell of yet another novel idea—that of communism. This new influence was laden with ideas of liberty and emancipation and it made an enormous impact on the radical nationalist movements that had developed against imperialist forces in these colonies. Freedom from foreign rule now no longer remained the ultimate goal. The concept of freedom now began to stretch to the emancipation of the poor masses of workers and peasants, who, in the end, were to gain control over the state as the representatives of the producing masses. This process would achieve completion only when this new concept of freedom became established all over the world and narrow national barriers were erased in favour of a wider international co-existence.

Thanks to Marx and Engels, all these ideas had already been developed in the First and Second Internationals. Since the colonies and colonial policies of the imperialist nations of the West formed a major point of discussion in these Internationals, especially in that of the Second, Europe too had begun to think and formulate regularly on the colonial policies of the imperialist nations, the problems faced by the colonies, the probable solutions to them, and above all, the role of the colonies in bringing about the revolution.

The Second International collapsed with the outbreak of the First World War. And ever since then, preparations began for the establishment of the Third International. Links were being formed with the Spartacus group in Germany and the Communist Party of German Austria. A letter written by Trotsky and published in the Pravda on January 5, 1919, addressed to both the groups, and signed by the Russian leaders, Lenin, Trotsky, Sverdlov, Stalin and Bukharin, clearly expressed hopes that the revolution was soon to occur in Germany and Austria. "And our party", they said, "the party of the proletariat— which at the beginning of the revolution, was considered a 'bunch of madmen', and which now has held state power with a firm hand for more than a year— sees with joy that in both Germany and Austria fraternal parties are growing and marching toward our common goal, socialism, along our common road, the dictatorship of the working class"[109]. Soon afterwards on January 21, the

Bolsheviks convened a meeting of revolutionary leaders from several countries then living in Russia to draft a call for the International Communist Congress. Thus began the preparations for the Communist International or the Third International.

An appeal was drafted by Trotsky and submitted to Lenin on December 31 for editing. The final draft was read out in the meeting and was discussed and agreed upon, and finally published on January 24, 1919[110]. Trotsky started by saying that in the wake of the fact that the world revolution was making tremendous advancements, more and more challenges from the counterrevolutionary alliance of capitalist governments was emerging. The League of Nations was one of them. Hence the necessity of calling an international congress of the revolutionary proletarian parties had arisen. The principles of the programme were based on those of the Spartacus League in Germany and the Communist Party (Bolsheviks) in Russia.

He then outlined the goals and tactics of the Communist International. It was said that the "present period is one of disintegration and collapse", a fact which would soon lead to the collapse of the European civilisation as a whole. In such a situation the working classes were to immediately seize power and establish the rule of the proletariat and that of the semi proletariat, as Lenin preferred to call it, comprising of the poor peasants in the countryside. This government should be represented by the toiling masses and which should systematically suppress and expropriate the exploiting classes. The draft then declared the names of several parties and groups, whom the Third International would grant full rights. It was proposed that the Communist International should take the shape of an overall fighting body and subordinate the interests of the revolutionary movement in each country, if need be, for the cause of the common interests of the revolution on an international scale[111].

Meanwhile the Bolshevik leadership in Russia was becoming increasingly aware about the need to set up an international movement in order to stall the capitalist advancement in the world. It was on this accord that Gregory Zinoviev drafted a set of theses[112] that outlined the programme of the Third International. Lenin wrote critical notes on it and the final draft was published in the Pravda on March 2, the day the Third International was convened. These theses outlined the background and the necessity of the Third International, the strategies of which were to correspond to that which had been published before by Trotsky in January 1919.

THE COMMUNIST INTERNATIONAL

With the setting up of the Communist International or the Comintern in 1919, Lenin started becoming all the more conscious about the revolutionary potential of the colonies and semi-colonies, regarding their role in bringing about world socialism. He said that these colonies could be used as effective allies of the socialists in Europe, and with whose help, socialism that was facing a temporary lull in Europe would be reinvigorated. Reference to India and the colonial question had been made in the inaugural Congress of the Comintern itself. "The Comintern considers it its obligatory task to establish a permanent and close bond between the struggle of the proletariat in the imperialist countries and the national liberation movements of the oppressed peoples in the colonies and semi-colonies and to support the struggle of the oppressed peoples 'to facilitate the final breakdown of the imperialist world systems'"[113]. In the Manifesto of the Inaugural First Congress of the Communist International, the colonial policy of the imperialist nations was severely criticised. The participation of the colonial peoples in the war was condemned in the Manifesto. It highlighted the "revolutionary ferment" that developed in the colonies as a consequence. It also said that "... If capitalist Europe forcibly dragged the backward sections of the world into the capitalist whirlpool, then socialist Europe will come to the aid of liberated colonies with its technology, its organisation, its spiritual forces, in order to facilitate their transition to a planned and organised socialist economy"[114].

It is said by several scholars that Lenin turned to the East only when the revolutionary spirit had petered out somewhat in Europe after the liquidation of several Soviet regimes like Finland and the Baltic states. Sobhanlal Dattagupta has argued otherwise[115]. He has said that Lenin had been occupied with the colonial questions, long before the 1920's. Ever since the Stuttgart Congress of the Second International in 1907, Lenin had been making clear pronouncements about his ideas on the colonial question. His criticism of the revisionist approach towards colonialism, his prolonged argument with Rosa Luxemburg, in defence of his own ideas on national self-determination, show that most of his ideas were developed before 1920 and that they only "developed, detailed and concretised" during the time of the Second Congress of the Comintern[116]. However, despite Lenin's notions of the colonial potential in the advancement of socialism, even at the time when Rightists like Van Kol, Eduard David and Berkstein were regarding imperialism as a part of the civilising mission as well as a necessary component in the economy of the imperialist nations of Europe, Lenin actually presented a concrete thesis on the problems concerning national liberation in the colonies only in 1920 at the Second Congress of the Comintern.

Another point needs mention here. The concept of the difference between the two classes of the bourgeois order, reformist and revolutionary, a fact that was emphasised in the Second Congress, is amiss in the Manifesto of the Inaugural First Congress of the Communist International. This Manifesto had been drafted by Trotsky. Hence, authors like Dipak Das[117], Shobhanlal Dattagupta[118] and Glunin[119] have remarked that to Trotsky colonial emancipation was still a subordinate function of socialism in the West. Kunal Chattopadhyay has argued here:

"...No theory can however be built on this. Between 1917 and 1925, the positions that were developed in the Comintern were sufficiently ambiguous...As long as a revolution did not actually become a likely prospect, there was little problem in arguing for positions like maintaining class independence, building class organisations, propagating the construction of worker-peasant soviets, and supporting bourgeois radicals."[120]

This point is important in so far as the fact that this concept of reformism in the bourgeois order and the "ambiguity" surrounding its role in the revolution was to raise, in the next few years after the Second Congress, a furore, that would be hard to control in the Comintern. Kunal Chattopadhyay has rightly said in this context, "What was an unresolved tension in the early 1920s could become a major contradiction in the later half of the decade, and subsequently, throughout most of the twentieth century."[121]

THE SECOND CONGRESS

The Indian delegation at the Second Congress was represented by Abani Mukherjee and Tirumal Pratibadi Bhayankar Acharya. But challenge came from the Indian born young Mexican delegate, M.N. Roy. He made a sharp criticism of Lenin's theses and eventually submitted a set of theses of his own. The Lenin-Roy debate holds an important place in the history of the Comintern's relationship with the colonies and its policies regarding them. Lenin had the text of Roy's theses modified in some ways, changed some of his own and ultimately, at the plenary session of the Congress, the amended texts of both were debated and the problem finally solved through the adoption of both texts.

The colonial question, as usual was, from the very beginning, marked with tremendous controversy. It was discussed for two days, 26th and 28th July 1920. And Lenin, as the Chairman of the colonial commission in the Second Congress of the Comintern (July-Aug., 1920), paid much attention to the question of national liberation in the East. Lenin was very concerned about the division of the world into the oppressor and the oppressed. He said, "...This idea of a division, of dividing the nations into oppressor and oppressed, runs through the theses, not only the first theses published over my signature but also those submitted by Comrade Roy..."[122]. He was also concerned about the role that the peasants were to play in the colonies in bringing about socialism. This is because he knew that since industrial revolution had not touched the colonies of the east, agriculture still remained the basis of these economies. Hence the role of the peasantry was very important. He said, "...It would be utopian to believe that the proletarian parties in these backward countries, if indeed they can emerge in them, can pursue communist tactics and communist policy without establishing definite relations with the peasant movement and without giving it effective support"[123]. This idea that the peasants needed to be involved in the struggle against the imperialists; was however, not new. Lenin had advocated it earlier in his speeches before the Second Congress[124]. He simply concretised those ideas in the Congress.

In Thesis 2 of his original draft Roy said:

"The fountainhead from which European capitalism draws its main strength, is no longer to be found in the industrial countries of Europe, but in the colonial possessions and dependencies. Without the control of the extensive markets and vast fields of exploitation in the colonies, the capitalist powers of Europe cannot maintain their existence even for a short time. England, the stronghold of imperialism has been suffering from overproduction since more than a century ago.

But for the extensive colonial possessions acquired for selling her surplus products and as a source of raw-materials for her ever growing industries, the capitalist structure of England would have crushed under her own weight long ago. By enslaving the hundreds of millions of inhabitants of Asia and Africa, English imperialism succeeded so far in keeping the British proletariat under the domination of the bourgeoisie[125] ".

In challenging this viewpoint, Lenin remarked that Roy went "too far" in assessing the significance of the revolutionary movement in the East. He said that there was nothing to prove that the future of the West depended exclusively on the level of development in the colonial countries. The first sentence was hence changed as "one of the main sources from which European capitalism draws its chief strength..."[126] One can say at this point that the post World War II history validates Lenin in the long run.

In Thesis 3 of his original draft, Roy said, "By exploiting the masses in the colonies, European imperialism would be in a position to give concession after concession to the proletariat at home." This word, "proletariat" was substituted by the phrase, "labour aristocracy". Besides, a subordinate clause was added that "European imperialism seeks to lower the standard of living of the home proletariat by bringing into competition the production of the lower paid workers in the subject countries"[127]. This idea, once again, was not new. Lenin had already propagated it in the Stuttgart Congress of the Second International in 1907, when he said that the proletariat were facing the danger of imbibing "colonial chauvinism"[128].

In Thesis 4, Roy said that "...without the breaking up of the colonial empire, the overthrow of the capitalist system in Europe does not appear possible. Consequently, the Communist International must widen the sphere of activities..." The colonial commission changed the spirit of the opening sentence. In the final draft it read, "The breaking up of the colonial empire, together with the proletarian revolution in the home country, will overthrow the capitalist system in Europe..." and that, ".... These two forces must be coordinated, if the final success of the world revolution is to be guaranteed"[129].

In Thesis 7 of his original draft Roy said, ".... The bourgeois democratic nationalist movements are limited to the small middle class, which do not reflect the aspirations of the masses. Without the active support of the masses, the national freedom of the colonies will never be attained..." He also said:

".... There are to be found in the dependent countries, two distinct movements, which everyday grow farther from each other. One is the bourgeois democratic nationalist movement, with a programme of political independence, and the other is the mass action of the ignorant poor peasants and workers. The former endeavours to control the latter and often succeed to a certain extent, but it would be a mistake to assume that the bourgeois nationalist movement expresses the sentiments and aspirations of the general population. For the overthrow of foreign imperialism, the first step towards revolution in the colonies, the co-operation of the bourgeois nationalist elements may be useful. But the Communist International must not find in them, the media through which the revolutionary movement in the colonies should be helped..."[130]

In Thesis 9 of his original draft Roy said:

"The supposition that, owing to the economic and industrial backwardness, the peoples in the colonies are bound to go through the stage of bourgeois democracy is wrong. The events and conditions in many of the colonies do not corroborate such a supposition"[131].

The Adopted Text however said:

"...Indeed it would be extremely erroneous in many of the oriental countries to try to solve the agrarian problem according to pure communist principles. In the first stages the revolution in the colonies must be carried on with a programme which would include many petty-bourgeois reform clauses, such as division of land etc. but from this it does not follow at all that the leadership of the revolution will have to be surrendered to the bourgeois democrats"[132].

Lenin however said in Thesis 11 of his original draft, that the Communist parties must assist the bourgeois democratic liberation movement in those countries, and that the duty of providing the most active assistance, rested primarily on the workers of those countries on which the backward peoples were dependent colonially and financially. He also called for a determined struggle against attempts to give a communist colouring to bourgeois liberation trends in backward countries. Lenin said that the Comintern should support the bourgeois-democratic movements in the backward and colonial countries, "only on the condition that in those countries, the elements of future proletarian parties, which will be communist not only in name, are brought together and made to understand their special tasks ...", which were struggles "...against the bourgeois democratic movements within their own nations." The communists must enter into a ".... temporary alliance with the bourgeois democracy in the colonial and backward countries, but should not merge with it ..." and that they must, under all circumstances, uphold the organisational and ideological independence of the proletarian movement if it was in its most embryonic form[133].

Dipak Das has said, "Unlike his predecessors, Lenin duly stressed the need for unity in the revolutionary struggle of the proletariat of the West and the oppressed peoples of the East." For, he said, that the main objective policy of the Comintern on the national and colonial questions must be the achievement of ".... closer union of the proletarian and working masses of all nations and countries for a joint revolutionary struggle to overthrow the landowners and the bourgeoisie, as ".... this alone would ensure the victory over capitalism and the abolition of national oppression and inequality". Lenin said that without helping the revolutionary struggles in the colonial and dependent countries, words of sympathy for the oppressed nations and colonial peoples would come to nothing and remain a false signboard of internationalism[134].

S. Dattagupta has highlighted the point that Lenin had realised at this stage that the peasantry of the eastern colonies had a revolutionary potential that needed to be used in the struggle to bring about socialism. He said, "it may not perhaps be an exaggeration to suggest that Lenin's direct encounter with the peasant question in an incredibly complex post-October period led to his growing conviction that unless due recognition was given to the peasant masses constituting the predominant form of social labour the process of socialist transformation would be severely jeopardised in a backward country— a deep theoretical understanding leading to the formulation that the best ally of the proletariat remained the peasantry and that without this alliance the question of socialist transformation would forever remain an enigma in a backward country..."[135] Lenin had undoubtedly understood, especially after the Russian revolution that the peasantry had a definite role to play in the revolution. And though they were not to proceed as leaders in the revolution, yet they could not be simply ignored. Lenin wanted to adapt Marxist theories to the existing situations, which would always vary from place to place.

d'Eucausse and Schram have said that it was because of his conviction that the revolutionary movements of the East were working without the help of the proletarian parties of the West that Roy's theses were transformed from his "categorical profession of faith the Asian revolution as the key to everything into the much less sweeping claim the revolution in Asia was important and could play a role in the worldwide victory over imperialism." They also said that Roy's position in a way was "...the clearest prefiguration of the... asiocentricism of the Chinese"[136].

On the other hand, Allen S. Whiting has said that Lenin modified Roy's stand for yet another reason. Whiting has said that Lenin was not at all keen to tell his European comrades that unless the vast masses of Asia accomplished their revolutionary tasks, their revolutionary activities made no sense[137]. He said, "...While the Russian was anxious to emphasize the importance of the colonial struggle, he was loath to tell his European comrades that their efforts were futile unless the amorphous masses of Asia first achieved their revolution..."[138]

The theses on the national and colonial questions were put to vote and they were adopted with three abstentions. Among those who abstained, one was the Italian socialist Serrati. Serrati had always been against alliance with the bourgeois-democratic movements of liberation in the colonies. On the second day of the debate on the colonial question, when the theses were put to vote, he had thus abstained. He had said:

"In the 'Theses on the National and Colonial Questions' proposed to the congress by comrades Lenin and Roy, I find not only certain contradictions but also in particular a grave danger for the position of the communist proletariat in the advanced countries, which must remain hostile to any class- collaboration, especially in the period before the revolution.

The definition of 'backward' countries is too vague and imprecise not to be open to chauvinist interpretations.

In general, campaigns by bourgeois-democratic groups for national liberation are not revolutionary, even when they resort to insurrectionary methods. They are undertaken either to benefit a nascent national imperialism or to serve the interests of a competitor of the country's former imperialist ruler. National liberation campaigns can never bring revolutionary results unless the working class remains clearly separate. Even in the so called backward countries, the class struggle can advance only by preserving the absolute independence of the proletariat toward all its exploiters, even bourgeois democrats called 'revolutionary nationalists'"[139].

When Roy had charged Serrati of calling his and Lenin's theses counterrevolutionary, Serrati had protested fervently, and Roy had answered:

"I am sure that no proletarian can regard the assistance rendered to the oppressed peoples in their struggle against foreign oppression as being reactionary. Every national revolution in a backward country is a step forward. It is unscientific to distinguish the various forms of revolution. The peoples of the exploited countries, whose economic and political evolution has been hampered, must pass through the stages, which the European peoples traversed long ago. One who regards it as reactionary to aid these people in their national struggle, is himself reactionary and advocate of imperialism"[140].

Distinct nationalist overtones can be detected in Roy's answer. This spirit of nationalism was often to be detected in the ideas of the newly emerging communist leaders of the colonies[141].

Serrati had defended himself. He had said quite categorically, "Comrade Roy did not understand my statement. I say that he did not understand it, because I think I was clear enough. I said that the theses as proposed are not clear enough and could lend themselves to chauvinist and nationalist interpretations..."[142] He further explained:

"The thinking behind this is very clear. Instead of saying that the Communist Party and the proletarian classes can unite with the petty bourgeois movement to some extent and with certain guarantees, I say no, the working class can utilise a bourgeois-revolutionary movement for the purpose of a social revolution, but it cannot support the bourgeois class, even in backward countries. Otherwise it runs the danger of losing its class position and class orientation. The masses in the backward countries can lose their orientation more easily than those in the advanced countries; since the proletariat there has as yet no firm class consciousness and often blindly follows its leaders"[143].

In the Second Congress, a resolution was made on the Eastern Question, which outlined the tasks of the Comintern. The Resolution is as follows:-

1. The Congress considers that without the participation of the East - a definite social and economic power - the problems of the World revolution cannot be solved.

2. The Russian Communist Party (Bolsheviks), which by virtue of its international status at present, occupies the position of a leader of the world communist movement, must take specific and genuine measures to living revolution to the East.

3. The Communist Party's revolutionary work in the East must proceed in two directions: one stems from the Party's basic class revolutionary programme, which enjoins it gradually to create communist parties—sections of the Third Communist International in the Eastern countries; the other is determined by the political and of course, historical, social and economic situation of the present movement in the East, which makes it necessary for it to give support for a certain length of time to local, western, European imperialism, always provided, that these movements do not conflict with the world proletarian class revolutionary aspiration to overthrow world imperialism.

4. To achieve these aims, it is essential immediately to take most earnest and thorough steps to organise party work and anti-imperialist propaganda in the East.

5. This work must be directed by the central organ of the organisations of the peoples of the East, which should set up regional branches and executive departments and itself work directly under the leadership of the Central Committee of the Russian Communist Party.

6. In order to concentrate all this revolutionary energy, which is to be transmitted to the East, where it will be absorbed into the system and awaken the revolutionary instinct, revolutionary work must be centralised in the already existing or potential Soviet Eastern republics.

7. To these ends, it is essential to work out immediately, the particular form of union and the kind of relationship to be

established between the republics, as they become the focal point of revolution in the East.

8.   ...The Congress considers first and foremost that the following particular measures should be undertaken urgently:

i) that the training party and Soviet workers for the East be accelerated,

ii)   that a body of Soviet Orientalists be established in the East,

iii) that an Eastern, international working class red army be established as a part of the international Red Army,

iv) that the training of Red army commanders be intensified"[144].

All these principles talked of the advancement of national revolutionary movements in the colonies on the basis of Soviet experience in the East. But if a detailed examination of the strategies to be pursued in the colonies is made, it will be found that it was here that Roy and Lenin had their major differences. Roy who was more to the left than Lenin said that the people in the colonial countries would have to go through all the stages that the workers had gone through in the West. Hence, communism could be reached only after capitalist development had occurred. However, on the other hand, there was an argument in the adopted text of the Supplementary Theses that "...the foremost and necessary task is the formation of communist parties which will organise the peasants and workers and lead them to the revolution and to the establishment of Soviet republics. Thus, the masses in the backward countries may reach communism, not through capitalistic development, but led by the class-conscious proletariat of the advanced capitalist countries."[145] It was being said that with the help of the workers of the Western countries, the backward countries "may" skip the stage of capitalist development. The use of the word "may" is very significant as it was a matter of correct strategy and tactic— both of which needed to be developed. This was Lenin's idea. He realised that the colonies had a very different economic background when compared to that in the West. And if a practical solution was sought to this problem, it had to be sought accordingly.

Sanjay Seth has jeered at Roy's interpretation of the existing social classes in India— classes that were meant to play a significant role in the revolutionary process. He has said that Roy's analysis of the national liberation movement; his analysis of the movement of the workers and the peasants that was incorporated in the same movement; his analysis of the bourgeois order that prevailed in India as a hindrance towards the achievement of socialism were "...not closely argued or free of ambiguities..."[146] He has also pointed out that despite Lenin's recognition of the "...different types of nationalist movements and parties in the East, some of which were willing to compromise pursuit of the nationalist goal by reaching an 'understanding' with imperialism...", yet, the "...question, however, was still under what conditions to support bourgeois nationalism— a gap, even with Roy's theses as amended, had not been significantly bridged..."[147]. The points that Seth has raised was not just regarding the conditions of support regarding the support that the Comintern was to lend towards the revolutionary elements of the nationalist movement. He has also said that in coming to the decision of supporting the revolutionary elements within the bourgeois led nationalist movement, which also harboured a stronger group of nationalists with a tendency to come to a compromise with the imperialists against the interests of the rising masses, did not mean Lenin's "...capitulation to Roy..."[148]. This was because Lenin, unlike Roy, did not separate the two movements. He said that one was incorporated within the other. Shobhanlal Dattagupta, in his recent book, has wholeheartedly supported Seth's arguments regarding the duality in the sphere of the nationalist movement in India as well as the attitudes of both Lenin and Roy towards it[149]. But the last part of Seth's argument regarding the gap in the policies of Roy and Lenin on the conditions of support to be lent to bourgeois nationalism, has been avoided in Dattagupta's arguments.

Lenin realised that strict adherence to the system of development of socialist consciousness in Europe could not simply be imposed on the eastern colonies since their criteria for economic development was very different from that in the West. Hence he laid greater emphasis on peasant soviets than the organised proletariat while considering the role that was to be played in bringing about socialism in the east. He also realised that in the Eastern colonies had to be freed first from the clutches of imperialism before emancipation of the toiling masses could be made possible. Thus initial cooperation with the bourgeois order was necessary so as to overthrow the imperialists, and before a final split was made and the revolutionary mass movement directed itself solely against exploitation of all kinds and lead the path to socialism. That this cooperation of the revolutionary elements within the nationalist movement with the compromising bourgeoisie was necessary and at the same time temporary, had been highlighted by Lenin from the beginning. The question regarding the bridging of the gap between the ideas of Roy and Lenin also needs to be analysed here. Thesis 8 and Thesis 9 of the Supplementary Theses did formulate a policy regarding the support that was to be lent to the bourgeois nationalist elements. Roy himself read out the theses in the Congress and said in his report that he had agreed to the alterations made by Lenin in his original set of theses[150]. In the Supplementary Report too, one that he made soon afterwards, Roy had said:

"Naturally, a revolution started by the masses will not, in the first stage, be a communist revolution, for revolutionary nationalism will play a part. But at any rate this revolutionary nationalism is going to lead to the downfall of European imperialism, which would be of enormous significance for the European proletariat."[151]

It is obvious from these statements that Roy and Lenin had undoubtedly come to an agreement.

The fact that Lenin conceded to substitute the term "bourgeois-democratic" by "national-revolutionary", and the fact that he consequently accepted the reformist and revolutionary trends in the bourgeois led movements in the colonies was definitely not a "capitulation to Roy" as Seth and Sobhanlal Dattagupta have commented. They have suggested that Lenin stuck to his original bourgeois democratic movement, and only added a "distinction" between the two types of the "(still) bourgeois-democratic"[152] movements. Now why should Lenin concede to use a particular term, recognise the dual character of a particular movement that was of signal importance in the colonies and at the same time, maintain his own original earlier supposition, as these two scholars seem to have suggested? Lenin was certainly not doing it in order to patronise Roy, he had already altered and scrapped many parts of Roy's theses. Had he wanted to do it again, he could have easily done it. The point that he did not, was because he accepted Roy's position about the nature of the bourgeoisie in the colonies, especially in India. In his "Report on the National and Colonial Questions" he said so very clearly. The quotation that follows is the same that has been used by Seth and Adhikari to establish their respective points.

1

"However, the objection has been raised that if we speak of the bourgeois-democratic movement we shall be obliterating the distinctions between the reformist and the revolutionary movements. Yet that distinction has been clearly revealed of late in the backward and colonial countries, since the imperialist bourgeoisie is doing everything in its power to implant a reformist movement among the oppressed nations too. There has been a certain rapprochement between the bourgeoisie of the exploiting countries and that of the colonies, so that very often— perhaps even in most cases— the bourgeoisie of the oppressed countries, while it does support the national movement, is in full accord with the imperialist bourgeoisie, that is, joins forces with it against all revolutionary movements and revolutionary classes. This was irrefutably proven in the commission, and we decided that the only correct attitude was to take this distinction into account and, in nearly all cases, substitute the term *national-revolutionary* for the term *bourgeois-democratic.*

"The significance of this change is that we, as communists, should and will support bourgeois liberation movements in the colonies only when they are genuinely revolutionary, and when their exponents do not hinder our work of educating and organising in a revolutionary spirit the peasantry and the masses of the exploited. If these conditions do not exist, the Communists in these countries must combat the reformist bourgeoisie, to which the heroes of the Second International also belong. Reformist parties already exist in the colonial countries, and in some cases their spokesmen call themselves Social Democrats and Socialists. The distinction I have referred to has been made in all the theses with the result, I think, that our view is now formulated much more precisely."[153]

This statement clearly shows that Lenin accepted Roy's notions about the bourgeoisie in the colonies and he gave it serious consideration. Adhikari has aptly summed it up as "...Lenin's keen sense for the concrete, his respect for practical experience made him see a positive contribution in what Roy was saying, and that was the question of the compromising tendency of the national bourgeoisie in the liberation movement..."[154] Adhikari has also studied the minutes of the commission on the national and colonial question of the Second Congress to show that Lenin actually engaged in a discussion with Roy regarding the changes that were to be made in his theses. So Lenin's attitude about changing the term from bourgeois-democratic to national-revolutionary, was neither a capitulation and nor a sense of patronisation. It was the acceptance of a fact that he had himself not considered before. Just because Roy was young and quite new to the Comintern circles, it did not mean that Lenin accepted his proposal just to pat him on the back.

The next point that Sanjay Seth has made and Sobhanlal Dattagupta has seconded, is that "...for Lenin, nationalism was the main project in the East, Roy pointed to two— more or less anti-thetical— projects in the colonies..."[155] Out of the two that Roy envisaged, one was the bourgeois-democratic nationalist movement that did not include the masses, and the other was the revolutionary movement, comprising of the toiling masses, its goal though not quite clear[156]. Sobhanlal Dattagupta has said:

"...The central difference between them has been aptly summed up by Sanjoy Seth, when he argues that for Lenin the project in the East was one, namely, national liberation; for Roy the projects were multiple in the sense that, notwithstanding his acceptance of Lenin's position, for him, a distinction had to be made between bourgeois-democratic movements and mass revolutionary movements led by the Communist Party..."[157]

This too is a misrepresentation of Lenin. If Lenin's Report on the National and Colonial Questions is considered, it will be seen that Lenin attached utmost need to the formation of the peasant soviets in the colonies. He said that since capitalism had not yet matured in the colonies and semi-feudal relationships still remained, the organisations of the peasants could be used as an effective weapon. He also said:

"Our experience in this respect is not as yet very considerable. However, the debate in the commission, in which several representatives from colonial countries participated, demonstrated convincingly that the Communist International's theses should point out that the peasants' soviets, soviets of the exploited, area weapon that can be employed not only in capitalist countries but also in countries with pre-capitalist relations, and that it is the absolute duty of the Communist parties and of elements prepared to form Communist parties everywhere to conduct propaganda in favour of peasants' soviets or of working people's soviets. This includes backward and colonial countries. Wherever conditions permit, they should at once make attempts to set up soviets of working people"[158]

Another lengthy quotation is needed to prove the point. Lenin said in the same speech:

"...If the victorious revolutionary proletariat conducts systematic propaganda among them[159], and the soviet governments comes to their aid with all the means at their disposal, in that event it will be a mistake to assume that the backward peoples must inevitably go through the capitalist stage of development. We should create independent contingents of fighters and party organisations in the colonies and backward countries and at once launch propaganda for the organisation of peasants' soviets and strive to adapt them to the pre capitalist conditions. In addition, the Communist International should advance the proposition, with the appropriate theoretical grounding, that the backward countries, aided by the proletariat of the advanced countries, can go over to the soviet system and, through certain stages of development, to communism, without having to pass through the capitalist stage."[160]

If these two quotations and the ninth thesis of the Supplementary Theses that followed soon afterwards are considered, it will become clear that Lenin's notions about the colonial question were not based merely on the attainment of national independence. Indeed Lenin had a firm belief about the soviet system, one that he fervently wanted to introduce in the colonies, independent of and parallel to the progress of the national movement. Had it not been so, and had Lenin's standpoint been merely to advance the cause of the national movement in the colonies, he would never have urged the formation of peasants' organisations for their subsequent emancipation.

Adhikari has made a thorough examination of the debate, both from Lenin and Roy's points of view. In doing so he has taken into consideration M.N.Roy's *Memoirs*, the documents of the Communist International and the works of other scholars like Overstreet and

Windmiller, E.H.Carr and others. He has, in fact, expressed doubts regarding the authenticity of what was said in Roy's Memoirs. In Adhikari's opinion, which is based entirely on the juxtaposition of Roy's memoirs with the Second Congress documents; Roy was being arrogant and was rejecting Lenin's policy of self-determination—a policy, which, according to Adhikari was a "...wise policy of supporting the national liberation struggle of the oppressed peoples as a whole as an anti-imperialist movement and a part of the world revolutionary process"[161]. He also said that "... Roy is distorting Lenin's position as formulated by him even in his preliminary draft, by attributing to him a view which without reservation ascribed to the national bourgeoisie of the colonial and the oppressed countries a historically revolutionary role"[162]. Adhikari has claimed that "Roy was contraposing the spontaneously developing workers' and peasants' economic struggles to the general national liberation movement, and proposed that the CI and the communists should support the former and not the latter as it was a bourgeois democratic movement. This dichotomy pervades the positions and formulations of Roy..."[163]

Adhikari has made detailed quotations of Roy's *Memoirs* in his discussion. He has concluded that Roy's claims of actually making Lenin doubtful of his own theses was totally wrong and that in fact, Roy's original draft had to undergo several alterations, whereas in Lenin's case it was only one. After quoting heavily from the Second Congress documents and the memoirs of Roy, Adhikari has finally explained that Lenin wanted the inclusion of Roy's final draft as well as his own in the proceedings, not because he was influenced by Roy's theories. He had made several alterations in Roy's theses so that the general arguments remained in line with those of his own. He felt that Lenin was actually seeking to incorporate the element of concrete experience of the colonies, a fact that was amiss in the strategies that were being devised for the colonies regarding their role in bringing about the fall of capitalism and the emergence of the socialist order[164]. The only positive contribution of Roy, said Adhikari, was the identification of "... a compromising bourgeois democratic trend in the national liberation movement as well as a potentially revolutionary trend of workers' and peasants' movement and posed the question of the attitude and relation of the CI and the communists towards both..."[165]. But despite this contribution to knowledge about the Indian situation in the Comintern, it can be said that there was an element of exaggeration in Roy's ideas about the revolutionary trend in the movement of the working masses. His emotional attachment to the nationalist movement which he had joined at the beginning of his career as a revolutionary was clearly manifested in his theses. Lenin realised this and consequently scrapped off both small and large portions of his theses in order to make it more rational, practicable and divested of sentimental links with Roy's past. He wanted to devise a systematic and practical solution to the problems faced by the colonies in the east on the basis of what the situation demanded, rather than depending on imitating the European experience there. However, the Second Congress marked the beginning of the development of new ideas regarding the significance of the East and its role in bringing about world socialism. The colonial question in the East, which had so long been discussed at the previous Internationals mainly by the Europeans, now saw, for the first time, the active representation of the Eastern countries. It set the way for more debate and discussions in the years to come. Though these ideas had in them an element of vagueness, yet they reflected a strong desire to comprehend the objective conditions in the east— so long neglected in the West.

THE BAKU CONGRESS

One important decision resulting from the Congress was the agreement to hold a conference composed of the near, middle and Far East at Baku in Azerbaijan. The Baku Congress was organised by a committee based in Baku that included Azerbaijan communist Nariman Narimanov and M.D. Guscinov, said Said Gabiev of Dagestan and the Turkish communist leader, Mustafi Subhi. The Central Party of the Communist Party of Russia was represented by G.K. Ordzhonikidze and Yelena Stasova[166].

The total number of registered delegates at the Congress was about 2050. Among them, as the congress records lists 55% as communist party members, another 20% as supporters and 25% as non-party members. Representatives from several nations attended the Congress. M.N. Roy, despite his reputation as a committed leader, which he achieved at the Second Congress, refused to attend the Baku Congress[167]. He has said in his memoirs, "Evidently, it could serve only the purpose of agitation, which alone was not enough to bring about a revolution. On that ground, I opposed the idea. It could not possibly be a Congress, competent to plan action on the basis of a deliberation by accredited representatives from the countries concerned. As a matter of fact, on such a short notice, revolutionary organisation even in the adjacent countries could not be expected to send delegates to the Congress"[168]. He called it "Zinoviev's Circus at Baku"[169] and sent Abani Mukherjee there as the leader of the Indian delegation. Roy hardly ever conformed to the discipline that was a general feature in the communist circles, and this was only another such instance. Much of the ideas that were propagated at Baku were those that had already been discussed at the Second Congress. The representation at Baku was one of a heterogeneous nature. Out of 2050 delegates, there were 576 workers, 495 peasants, 437 professionals and educated workers and others[170]. An emotional appeal lined the speeches, which, in general, discussed the struggle to be carried on before a new future could be welcomed.

The Indian representation at Baku was very small, comprising of only fourteen members, as against two hundred and thirty-five Turks, one hundred and ninety two Persians, hundred Georgians, eighty two Chechens, forty Afghans and so on. The Chinese delegation was smaller with only eight members[171]. Yet, the Indian and the Chinese problems of colonialism were given much importance, for they represented the two greatest colonies of Asia where nationalist sentiments had already made headways. Enver Pasha, the former leader of the Young Turk movement, and of the Turkish government, attended the Congress, ".... seeking Soviet arms and money to build an international Islamic revolutionary organisation with the stated goal of driving the Allied invaders from Turkey... But among Congress delegates, Enver was widely despised for his government's role in driving the Turkish workers and peasants into World War I and for inciting the slaughter of Turkey's Armenian population." About fifty-five women delegates took part in the Congress and the cause of women's struggle for liberation was also addressed on many occasions. In fact, despite strong objections three women were elected to the Presiding Committee, and once elected, ".... the entire Congress role to greet them in a thunderous ovation[172]".

Lenin, Trotsky and Zinoviev were elected as honorary chairmen of the Congress of the Peoples of the East. The members of the Presiding Committee were Quelch from Britain, Rosmer from France,

Shablin from Bulgaria, Jansen from Holland, Reed from the USA, Bela Kun from Hungary, Hodo Yoshiharo from Japan, Steinhardt from Austria and Stalin from Russia[173]. It is strange that in the Congress of the Peoples of the East, where the colonial question remained a very significant issue, not a single representative of the colonies were elected to the Presiding Committee.

The Indian and Chinese delegations, as mentioned earlier, were quite small. Yet they attracted much attention for being colonies where anti-imperialist nationalist movements had already developed. The significance of these two nations to the delegates of the Baku Congress is clearly highlighted in Zinoviev's speech. "…. I will not speak to you about the peoples who are particularly well-represented here…. I will say a little more only about those countries that are poorly represented here— India and China…"[174] Zinoviev stated quite starkly as to how the British were exploiting the Indian masses and crushing their resistance with ruthless fervour. He even went on to state the Jallianwallahbagh massacre. Imperialist exploitation of China was also mentioned soon afterwards. He emphasised that this exploitation was easily made possible, as the masses were ignorant. And hence, what was essential was to educate the masses so that they could at least begin to grasp the intention of the imperialist powers, which could, by no means be called benign.

On the next day, Radek outlined the tasks of the Congress. He spoke more or less on the same lines as that of Zinoviev. His desire for an anti-capitalist alliance, reflected strongly in his speech. He said that the worst exploiters of mankind were the capitalists and that they were likely to ruin to whichever place, they settled for sometime[175]. He also spoke about the tremendous power that the British imperialists could wield in order to maintain their stronghold over colonial economy.

Radek said that the colonial people were faced with a two-fold system of exploitation, which made their existence very vulnerable. He said, "… For the peasant in the East it means that, where previously he had to pay tribute in order to maintain the Sultan's clique and all manner of shahs, emirs and khans, now he has to pay twice as much. He must pay for his own exploiters and pay for the bayonets of the French and British forces, who will defend his exploitation by the local exploiters"[176]. According to Radek, there was a solution to this problem, and that the World War had made the solution possible.

For the imperialist powers of Europe directly involved in the War, were facing a tremendous economic crisis, so much so that "... their spines too must crack ..."[177] Debts had mounted and they were still grappling in the dark to solve these problems. Consequently, the general masses of these countries were suffering. The Eastern markets too, at this time, could not provide any help as they too had been deeply affected by the War and that their purchasing power had dwindled manifold. Hence, commented Radek, "... As a result the whole of world imperialism is choking in the process of a tremendous crisis, gripped by powerful convulsions..."[178] The more the crisis deepened, the more recalcitrant the general masses became. "And never in its long history has Britain seen such a huge wave of strikes and mighty worker's demonstrations as we are now witnessing... In America we also see a wave of strikes...we see Italy on the threshold of a revolution..."[179]. On the other hand, he also emphasised the rising trends of workers' and peasants' movements in India, Egypt, Ireland and so on. And by juxtaposing these two situations, one, that of the weaning economies of the imperialist countries and the other, that of the rising trends of revolution of the workers and peasants, both in these countries and the colonies, Radek arrived at his solution. He said:

"If the workers and the peasants of the East want to be free from exploitation, they too can win victory because their adversary is breaking up, is suffering economic collapse, and because their adversary has been beaten by the Red workers' and peasants' Soviet Russia. Victory for the workers and peasants of the near East depends only upon their own consciousness and will. No enemy will daunt you, no one will hold back the workers and peasants of Persia, Turkey and India, if they unite with Soviet Russia. Soviet Russia was surrounded by enemies, but now it can produce weapons with which to arm not only its own workers and peasants but also the peasants of India, Persia and Anatolia, all the oppressed, and lead them to a common struggle and common victory". Records say that he was applauded at this point[180].

It can be noticed here that the theory of internationalism still dominated the policies of the Comintern. Hence, what was advocated was not independent struggles of nations against imperialism but the necessity of an anti-capitalist alliance in order to overthrow capitalism and establish international socialism. So keen was Radek about bringing about the success of his theory that he kept on reassuring the colonial people about the surety of Russian help. He felt that the way he was propagating in order to overthrow the capitalists was sure to bring success to the world revolution and hence an alliance was needed.

Radek explained that the workers and peasants of Soviet Russia would never betray the colonial peoples. For they depended solely on the resources their own land provided. Besides, they were also aware that capitalism and socialism could never co-exist peacefully and hence, if the capitalists were not crushed, Soviet Russia would be crushed by them "... And the Eastern policy of the Soviet government is therefore no diplomatic manoeuvre, no pushing of the peoples of the East into the firing line so that the Russian Soviet Republic may gain some advantage by betraying them"[181]. In this straightforward reassurance of loyalty, the Russians were clearly calling upon the Eastern peoples to join them in their struggle against imperialism. The Eastern peoples, he felt, could not be groomed for a successful venture against capitalism until they joined hands with Russia. This perception influenced Russian policies for a long time, until a shift was made at the Sixth Congress. And in awakening the East from their slumber against their imperialist oppressors in "... their common struggle against a common enemy...", a new civilisation would be created, one that would be "... a hundred times better than the one created by the slave owners of the West"[182]. The enemy was "common" and therefore, so had to be the "struggle" against it. This was the basic principle that was being advocated by the Comintern at Baku, for the cause of which a new necessity had arisen— the indoctrination of the colonial masses. The speech was lucid and undoubtedly very expressive and moving in content. But there was also an element of coaxing the Eastern peoples to join the fray, so as to achieve victory over the capitalists.

The colonial masses, so long, had been given leadership only by nationalist leaders, intent only upon freedom from imperialist powers. These nationalists, both radical and moderate had attributed all the causes of misery of the masses to the exploitative rule of the capitalists. The exploitation by the native capitalists had been totally ignored. The Comintern leadership proposed to ally with the revolutionary leadership of the colonies and the colonial masses and strategise on the basis of the new idea, one that had been generated by the Lenin-Roy debate at the Second Congress. This was the role that the bourgeoisie were to play in bringing about revolution in the colonies. The Congress at Baku saw repeatedly the discussion of this topic— the national bourgeoisie.

Another speech, that of Bela Kun, too discussed in details the colonial question and the strategies to the adopted there. Bela Kun, the Hungarian delegate read out a detailed set of theses. His speech too was lined with concepts on internationalism. At the very beginning he commented that the Russian revolution had "smashed" the "former structure of government" and that it strove "to carry the struggle forward until no possibility was left of any sort of oppression. It aimed at establishing the "authority of the workers and the poorest peasants". Bela Kun said:

"In another sense, too, this revolution did not step halfway. It was not checked at the frontiers of the state but spread both westward and eastward like a devouring flame. The revolution's extension to West and East threatens to bring about the final downfall of the system that, not content with exploiting the working people of its own countries, came to flower in imperialist colonial policy and bore fruit in world war"[183].

Bela Kun then went on to say how the imperialists were using the native bourgeoisie in order to foster their own interests. He said that even the workers of their own nations were being used for the same purpose. "In order to subjugate the colonial peoples, the imperialist exploiters have mobilised the European workers, trying to win them over by means of bribes— crumbs from the superprofits extorted from the colonial peoples... In this way it was hoped to deflect the workers from their revolutionary vocation". They were even using the colonial troops "... in order to defend their shaken state power against the working class"[184].

Apart from all these measures, the European imperialists had another very strong way to restrain the rise of the workers and the peasants. It utilised the aid of the ruling class of the colonies. He said, "This aid makes its exploiting policy less difficult and less expensive— and also less costly in blood— than it would otherwise be. Once their own resistance has been broken, the sultans and emirs— and the ruling strata associated with them in the Eastern countries— have always readily agreed to become collectors of tribute for the imperialist oppressors"[185]. The capitalists would make promises about empowering the masses, but they would make reforms only to suit their own interests and the preservation of those interests. Bela Kun also said that it was not necessary to undergo the process of capitalist development in order to bring about the establishment of socialism. He said, "... This idea is maintained for the sole purpose of prolonging the power of the emirs, pashas, beys and foreign colonialists over the poorest peasantry of the East" and that ".... Only imperialist colonialists argue like this"[186]. As to the point that the Eastern peoples were not yet mature enough to handle the state, Bela Kun said, "... The ability to rule, like the ability to use a weapon, demands that you make a start and get in some practice: those who never handle a rifle will never learn to shoot"[187]. This notion that the colonial peoples were not fit to govern themselves had been a pretext during the days of the Second International that the revisionists had used in order to justify colonial expansion of European nations. The point had been a source of a tremendous debate at that time. The revisionists had lost, but only with a small margin. The situation, as can be seen, had changed ever since, especially after the Bolshevik revolution.   Bela Kun constantly assured the meet that an anti-capitalist alliance between the Eastern colonies and the Soviet Russia was certain to bring about the demise of capitalism and the victory of the exploited toiling masses of producers. He then went on to present another set of theses. Here too, he outlined the situation in the Eastern colonies and highlighted the necessity of a united anti-capitalist struggle against the imperialist powers. However, in the last section of these theses he clearly made a mention of the impending goals.

"The victory of the Communist Party in the West will put an end of the exploitation of the Eastern peoples. But such a victory in the West will not mean that East and West can then get on without mutual economic links. On the contrary, the victory of the revolution in the East and in the West will mean that relations between different countries will be based not on exploitation but on reciprocal support and aid. After the victory of the Communist revolution, economic intercourse will take place between states. Thus the economic relations of the Eastern states that have not adapted the Soviet system would serve the interests of only a small group of capitalists....

"Complete liberation from imperialist exploitation, transfer of land to the toilers, and emancipation from the power of speculator-exploiters requires the removal of power of the networking element, all foreign colonialist elements (generals, officials and so on), and all privileged persons. It also requires organisation of the rule of the poor on Soviet principles. And all the other interests of the working people demonstrate to the East that it is imperative to establish Soviet power"[188].

Regarding the agrarian question, Bela Kun said:

"The Russian peasantry carried on their agrarian revolution with the support of the industrial workers under the leadership of the Communist Party. Wielded together in soviets, these peasants are now defending the land they took from the landlords and the power they took from the exploiters. In the same way the oppressed peasantry of the East will count in their revolutionary struggle upon the support of the revolutionary workers of the West, and the Communist International, and the present and future Soviet states"[189].

Bela Kun's theses were accepted unanimously. They were also in tune with the policies of the Second International. Moreover the expressiveness that marked the speeches in general at Baku, characterised his speech as well.

The agrarian question was discussed next by Skachko. He delivered a long speech before presenting his "Theses on the Agrarian Question". He said that the Eastern countries were basically "peasant countries", where peasants formed the main productive force, unlike that in the West, where the industrial workers were the chief producers. And all these peasants lived a miserable life because of their poverty due to exploitation. Moreover, their condition was in a state of constant deterioration. Several peasants had been reduced to agricultural labourers, especially in countries like India. As a solution to the problem, he said:

"All the land belonging to the landlords and feudalists, shahs and khans must be taken from them and given to the peasants, without any payment, without any compensation to the former owners. Together with the land, all the animals and farm implements belonging to the estates of feudalists and landlords must be taken, for the peasant must receive not only land but also the possibility of working it. For this purpose he must seize all the instruments of production and all the wealth that his landlord oppressors possessed"[190].

Skachko attacked the clergy as well. For they had, he said, in many cases, appropriated "waqf" lands for their personal use. And in doing so, they had defied the "shariat". He also said, "... Of course the clergy who have concentrated huge tracts of land in their hands and exploit peasant labour on this land, declare that it belongs to God. It is therefore inviolable, they say, and the peasant dare not reach out to take it. But this is all lies and fraud, comrades!"[191] Skachko called upon the delegates with vigour, to end this exploitation of the peasants. He said:

"Now comrades, we must turn to a scourge of the peasants of all the countries of the East— one that beats sweat and blood out of them and devastates their holdings: the fearful burden of taxes borne by the peasantry of Turkey, Persia and India for hundreds of years ... The scourge of taxation and the tyranny of officials and administrators associated with it must be destroyed; all taxes must be cancelled. The peasants must be freed from exploitation not only by the landlords but also by the state"[192].

Skachko's ideas for the future did not end here. He visualised further and once again fervently called upon his comrades to execute these ideas. He felt that the peasants should at first, overthrow the rule of the imperialists and the local oppressors and then move on to form soviets. And since the peasants were unaware about this system of existence, Skachko said:

"And it is for you, comrades, to use every means to show the peasantry the need to go over from scattered labour to joint labour. It is for you to show that the way of life based on separate little economic cells, separate households, has always led the peasants— and will lead them in future— to disintegration, making possible their enslavement and oppression. For the peasants to become a mighty force, they must merge into a close, organised unity such as that achieved by the proletariat of the industrial countries of the West... To achieve such a complete liberation from all the oppressors and parasites who feed at their expense, the peasantry will have to wage a protracted struggle against not only the foreign capitalist conquerors but also their own landlords and feudalists, their own bourgeoisie"[193].

Skachko then submitted his theses on the agrarian question.

The theses on the agrarian question outlined the poor and miserable condition of the peasants of the East. It said that the peasants were in such a state because the feudal society of the East made them economically dependent on the landlords who often seized their lands and reduced them to bondage. Besides, the imperialist governments also seized lands in order to grant them to the privileged classes and the capitalists, hence obliging the peasants to become subtenants and labourers. Hence, the exploiters needed to be wiped out and peasant Soviets formed, which would introduce reforms to cater to their own needs[194]. Another point, stressed greatly at the Second Congress, was made once again:

"The peasants of the East, now marching arm in arm with their democratic bourgeoisie to win independence for their countries from the Western European imperialist powers, must remember that they have their own special tasks to perform ... When independence is won, the local landlords and bourgeoisie will certainly try to take the place of Western European capitalists in the exploitation of these peasants"[195].

The theses were unanimously adopted.

In the seventh session of the Congress at Baku, Zinoviev, as the chairman, clearly pointed out that small groups were often neglected and hence he wanted to remedy such an action, in case it had been committed. Besides, he also called upon the representatives of the women to speak[196].

Two speeches were delivered as a result. One was made by Najiye Hanum, a member of the Communist Party of Turkey. She insisted on equality of women in all respects. "The women of the East are not fighting merely for the right to walk in the street without wearing the chador ... the question of the chador, it can be said, comes last in priority. If the women, who form half of every community, are set up against the men and do not enjoy the same rights, obviously it is impossible for the society to progress; the backwardness of Eastern societies is irrefutable proof of this"[197]. She said that the classless society, which was to be delivered with the coming of Communism, should free the women from being subjects to the despotism of their

menfolk. She even put forward a list of her demands.
1. Complete equality of rights
2. Ensuring to women unconditional access to educational and vocational institutions established for men.
3. Equality of rights of both parties to marriage. Unconditional abolition of polygamy.
4. Unconditional admission of women to employment in legislative and administrative institutions.
5. Establishment of committees for rights and protection of women everywhere, in cities, towns and villages.

She went on to promise that since "…. the communists have reached out their hand to us, and we women will prove their most loyal comrades"[198].

Another delegate, Bibinur, from Turkestan made a short speech at the Congress at Baku. She addressed the Congress, "You represent the very best forces of the toiling and the oppressed masses"[199] and felt that the future that would be ushered in through the joint efforts of the Congress and the oppressed peoples of the East would be one of peace and happiness. But the struggle would be a tough one and that the women would certainly play a significant role in it[200].

She highlighted the fact that the women of the East were exploited to a great extent. "We, the women of the East, are exploited ten times worse than the men, and are more closely affected by the ugly sides of secluded led by the Muslim women of the East…"[201] However, in the list of inequalities, the question of gender inequality was yet to be given a serious thought. The inequalities of nations, races and above all, classes loomed large and dominated the policies of the Comintern.

The mood at Baku was generally one of hope, high spirits and aspirations for the imminent future. The ideas were in tune with those advocated at the Second Congress and not many new ideas were propounded. The delegates outlined their problems as well as those of others with much details, clarity and understanding. But it fostered an interaction among the delegates and provided each of them with a platform to voice their grievances and formulate strategies to encounter them. The Congress at Baku actually carried the ideas advocated at the Second Congress, a step further; an effort was made to analyse the problems of the colonies of the East from a practical standpoint, taking into account their respective cultural backgrounds.

It sought to find solutions to the problems regarding the application of theories on nationalism and colonialism to diverse socio-economic and cultural situations. The Indian problems formed one of the core issues in the discussions and debates on the colonial question, despite their meagre representation. This was because the prosperity of the leading imperialist nation, England, depended to a large extent on India, her greatest colonial stronghold. The representatives of the various countries discussed that the struggle of the colonies against their imperialist masters and the local bourgeoisie, one after another, would not be an easy task. For the imperialists were rich and powerful. Yet, they understood that the struggle was essential and were hopeful about its culmination— one that would usher in the revolution that would sanction the victory of the workers over the capitalists and lead to the establishment of a new social order.

NOTES AND REFERENCES

1   Karl Marx, The British Rule in India, (New York Daily Tribune, No. 3805, 25 June, 1853), *Collected Works*, Moscow, 1979, Vol.12, pp. 125-133.

2   Karl Marx and Frederick Engels (On Poland), Speeches at the International Meeting held in London on November 29, 1847 to mark the 17th anniversary of the Polish Uprising of 1830,*Collected Works*, Vol. 6, op.cit. pp. 388-392.

3   Karl Marx, The British Rule In India, *Collected Works*, Vol.12, p. 132.

4   Ibid.

5   Ibid.

6   Irfan Habib, *Essays in Indian History, Towards a Marxist Perception*, New Delhi, 1995, p. 18.

7   Karl Marx, The East India Question, July, 25, 1853, (New York Daily Tribune, No. 3828), *Collected Works*, Vol.12, p. 197.

8   Karl Marx, The Future Results of the British Rule in India, (New York Daily Tribune, No.3840, August 8, 1853), *Collected Works*, Vol. 12, op. cit. pp.217-218.

9   David McLellan, *The Thought of Karl Marx: an introduction*, London, 1971, pp. 201.

10 Karl Marx, The Future Results of the British Rule in India, (New York Daily Tribune, No.3840, August 8, 1853), *Collected Works*,

Vol. 12, op. cit. pp. 221-222.

11 Karl Marx, The Indian Revolt, September 4, 1857, (New American Cyclopedia, Vol. 1), 1858, *Collected Works*, Vol. 15, p. 353.

12 Karl Marx, The East India Question, July, 25, 1853, (New York Daily Tribune, No. 3828), *Collected Works*, Vol.12, p. 198.

13 Karl Marx, The Future Results of the British Rule in India, (New York Daily Tribune, No.3840, August 8, 1853), *Collected Works*, Vol. 12, op. cit. pp. 222.

14 Edward Said, *Orientalism*, Penguin Books, New Delhi, 2001, p.6.

15 Ibid. p.154.

16 Ibid.

17 Aijaz Ahmad Interviewed II, Issues of Class and Culture, Ellen Meiksins Wood and John Bellamy Foster eds. *In Defense of History, Marxism and the Postmodern Agenda*, Aakar Books for South Asia, Delhi, 2006, p.106.

18 Henry Collins and Chimen Abramsky, *Karl Marx and the British Labour Movement: years of the First International,* London, New York, 1965, pp. 39.

19 Ibid. pp.14

20 Ibid. (The Italian cause was supported by all sections of the society, the Northern States of America was supported by the radical labour movements).

21 Frederick Engels, What Have the Working Classes to do in Poland? *Collected Works*, Volume 20.

22 Ibid.p. 157.

23 Ibid. p. 153.

24 Ibid. pp. 160-161. (The Greek Catholics in Poland comprised of only the serf community).

25 See the respective speeches of Marx and Engels on the occasion of the second anniversary of the Cracow insurrection, *Collected Works* Vol. 6, op. cit. pp. 545-552.

26 The French Proudhonists were not in favour of the workers becoming involved in political issues like the liberation of the colonies. This, they felt, would divert them from their main goal of educating the working classes so as to achieve victory in the revolution.

27 Henry Collins and Chimen Abramsky, *Karl Marx and the British Labour Movement: years of the First International,* p.34.

28 Ibid. p. 35.

29 The General Council of the First International, 1864- 1866, The London Conference 1865 Minutes, Moscow, 1964, p. 287.

30 Ibid.
31 General Council Minutes, August 15, 1871, Quoted from Collins and Abramsky, *Karl Marx and the British Labour Movement: years of the First International*, p. 222.
32 Solomon. Frank. Bloom, *The World of Nations*, New York, 1941, pp. 44-45.
33 Ibid. p. 207.
34 Strictly speaking, only an International Socialist congress had been called in 1889. When in 1893, the Congress decided that it would be a regular affair, only then did they date it back retrospectively to 1889.
35 James Joll, *The Second International: 1889-1914*, London, 1955, p.76.
36 Quoted from James Joll, *The Second International: 1889-1914*, London, 1955, p. 91.
37 James Joll, *The Second International: 1889-1914*, London, 1955, p. 91.
38 John Riddell ed. *Lenin's Struggle for a Revolutionary International, Documents: 1907- 1916, The Preparatory Years*, New York, London, Sydney, 1986, p. 5.
39 Ibid. pp. 5-6
40 Ibid. p.5.
41 Ibid. p.6.
42 Ibid.
43 Ibid. p.6.
44 Ibid. pp.6-7.
45 Ibid. p.7.
46 Ibid. pp. 6-7.
47 Ibid. p. 7.
48 Amendments by the Commission Minority, Ibid. pp.8-9.
49 Draft Resolution on Colonialism, Commission Majority Proposal, Ibid. p.7.
50 Ibid. p.8.
51 Amendments by the Commission Minority, Ibid. pp.8-9.
52 Ibid. pp. 9-10.
53 Ibid. p.10.
54 Ibid.
55 Ibid. pp.11-12.
56 Ibid. p.14.
57 Ibid. p. 9.
58 Ibid. pp. 14-15.

59 Ibid. p. 15.
60 Ibid.
61 The International Socialist Congress at Stuttgart, Ibid. p.38.
62 Ibid.
63 Ibid. p. 39.
64 Horace. B. Davis, *Nationalism and Socialism: Marxist and Labour Theories of Nationalism to 1917*, Monthly Review Press, New York, 1973, pp. 127-128.
65 See Karl Marx, The British Rule in India, The Future Results of the British Rule in India, *Collected Works*, Vol.12.
66 V.I.Lenin, Imperialism, the Highest Stage of Capitalism, *Collected Works*, Vol. 22, Moscow, 1977, p. 263.
67 V.I.Lenin, Letter to Maxim Gorky, January 3, 1911, *The National and Liberation Movement in the East*, Progress Publishers, Moscow, pp. 50-51.
68 Ibid. p. 50.
69 V.I. Lenin, 'The Junius Pamphlet', written in July 1916, *Collected Works*, Vol. 22, p, 310.
70 Ibid. p. 311.
71 Programme of the Social-Democratic Workers' Party, adopted at the Second Congress of the Party, 1903, Minutes of the Second Congress of the RSDLP, London, 1978, pp. 3-9.
72 Ibid. p. 6.
73 Ibid.
74 Horace. B. Davis ed. *Rosa Luxemburg, The National Question and Autonomy, The National Question; selected writings*, London, New York, 1976, p. 102.
75 Ibid. p. 109.
76 Ibid.
77 Ibid. pp. 109-110
78 Ibid. p. 123.
79 Horace. B. Davis ed. *Rosa Luxemburg: The National Question, Selected Writings of Rosa Luxemburg*, London, New York, 1976, p. 129.
80 Peter Nettl, *Rosa Luxemburg*, Oxford University Press, London, Oxford, New York, 1969, p. 503
81 Horace. B. Davis ed. *Rosa Luxemburg: The National Question, Selected Writings of Rosa Luxemburg*, p.103.
82 Ibid. p.104.
83 Ibid. p.132.
84 Ibid. p.290.

85 Ibid. p.135.
86 V.I.Lenin, the Right of Nations to Self- Determination, *Collected Works*, Vol. 20, p.395.
87 Ibid. p.397.
88 Ibid. p.400.
89 Ibid.
90 Ibid. p.403.
91 Ibid.
92 Ibid. 404.
93 Horace. B. Davis ed., *Rosa Luxemburg, The National Question and Autonomy: selected writings*, p. 20.
94 Peter Nettl, *Rosa Luxemburg*, p. 507.
95 V.I. Lenin, The Discussion of Self- Determination Summed Up, *Collected Works*, Vol. 22, p.337.
96 Shobhanlal Dattagupta, *Comintern, India and the Colonial Question, 1920-1937*, K.P.Bagchi, Calcutta, 1980, pp.7.
97 V.I. Lenin, The Discussion of Self- Determination Summed Up, *Collected Works*, Vol. 22, p.338.
98 Ibid. p.355.
99 Ibid. p.353.
100 V.I.Lenin, Inflammable Material in World Politics, Proletary, No. 33, August 5, 1908, *Collected Works*, Vol. 15, pp. 187-188.
101 "The question is, can mankind fulfil its destiny without the fundamental revolution in the social state of Asia?" See Karl Marx, The British Rule in India, *Collected Works*, Vol.12, p.132.
102 V.I.Lenin, To the Indian Revolutionary Organisation, Pravda, No. 108, May 20, 1920, *Collected Works*, Vol.31, p. 138.
103 V.I.Lenin, A Caricature of Marxism, and Imperialist Economism, *Collected Works*, Vol. 23, p. 69.
104 V.I.Lenin, The Right of Nations to Self- Determination, *Collected Works*, Vol.20, p.401.
105 Michael Lowy, Marxists and the Nationalist Question, *New Left Review 96*, pp.86-100.
106 V.I.Lenin, Address to the Second All Russian Congress of the Communist Organisations of the Peoples of the East, November 22, 1919, *Collected Works*, Vol.30, p.161.
107 Ibid.
108 V.I.Lenin, In Reply to Questions put by Weigand, Berlin correspondent of Universal Service, February 1920, *Collected Works*, Vol. 30 , p. 365.
109 Lenin, Trotsky, Sverdlov, Stalin, Bukharin, "Letter to the Spartacus

Group in Germany and the Communist Party of German Austria",
John Riddell ed. *The German Revolution and the Debate on Soviet
Power, The Communist International in Lenin's Time*, New York,
1986, pp. 445-447.

110   Letter of Invitation to the First Congress of the Communist
International, Ibid. pp. 448-452.

111   Ibid.

112   Gregory Zinoviev, 'The Hour of a Genuine Communist International
Has Struck', Ibid. pp. 459-466.

113   *The Communist International—A Short Historical Outline*, pp.63-
64, Quoted from Gangadhar Adhikari ed. *Documents of the History
of the Communist Party of India, Vol. I, 1917-1922*, Peoples
Publishing House, New Delhi, 1971, p. 105.

114   Manifesto of the Inaugural First Congress of the Communist
International, Quoted from Gangadhar Adhikari ed. *Documents of
the History of the Communist Party of India, Vol. I, 1917-1922*,
pp. 108-109.

115   Shobhanlal Dattagupta, *Comintern, India and the Colonial
Question*, 1920-1937, pp. 7-8.

116   Ibid. p. 7.

117   Dipak Kumar Das, article, "The Colonial Question: Lenin- Roy
Debate, An Overview", *Society and Change*, Vol. 5, No. 2 and 3,
January – June, 1988, p.109.

118   Sobhanlal Dattagupta, *Comintern, India and the Colonial Question:*
1920-1937, Calcutta 1980.

119   G.I Glunin, The Comintern and the Rise of the Communist
Movement in China 1920-1947, in R. Ulyanovsky ed., *The
Comintern and the East, Moscow, 1979.*

120   Kunal Chattopadhyay, *The Marxism of Leon Trotsky*, Progressive
Publishers, Kolkata, 2006, p.146.

121   Ibid.

122   John Riddell ed., *Workers of the World and Oppressed Peoples
Unite! The Communist International in Lenin's Time: proceedings
and documents of the Second Congress, 1920, Vol. I*, New York,
1991, p. 212.

123   Ibid. pp. 212-213.

124   See V.I.Lenin, Address to the Second All Russian Congress of the
Communist Organisations of the Peoples of the East, November
22, 1919, and V.I.Lenin, In Reply to Questions put by Weigand,
Berlin correspondent of Universal Service, *Collected Works*, Vol.
30.

125 Gangadhar Adhikari ed. *Documents of the History of the Communist Party of India, Vol. I, 1917-1922,* pp. 180-182.

126 Ibid.p.181.

127 Ibid. p. 180.

128 John Riddell ed. *Lenin's Struggle for a Revolutionary International, The Communist International in Lenin's Time*, New York, 1986, p. 39.

129 Gangadhar Adhikari ed. *Documents of the History of the Communist Party of India, Vol. I, 1917-1922*, p.80.

130 Ibid. p. 184.

131 Ibid. p. 186.

132 Ibid. p. 187.

133 V.I.Lenin, *Collected Works*, Vol. 31, p. 150.

134 Dipak Kumar Das, article, "The Colonial Question: Lenin- Roy Debate, An Overview", *Society and Change*, Vol. 5, No. 2 and 3, January – June, 1988,p. 114.

135 Sobhanlal Dattagupta, *Comintern, India and the Colonial Question, 1920-1937*, p.11.

136 Stuart Schramm and Helene Carrere d' Encausse, *Marxism and Asia: an introduction with readings*, The Penguin Press, London, 1969, p. 28.

137 Allen. S. Whiting, *Soviet Policies in China, 1917-1924*, Columbia University Press, New York, 1954, pp. 54-55.

138 Ibid.

139 John Riddell ed., *Workers of the World and Oppressed Peoples Unite! The Communist International in Lenin's Time: proceedings and documents of the Second Congress, 1920, Vol.1*, pp. 276-277.

140 Ibid. p. 279.

141 Even in China, Chen tu Hsiu's ideas as late as 1924, in his "Two Mistaken Ideas that We Have About the Boxers" were lined with nationalist feelings. See Stuart Schram and Carrere d'Encausse, *Marxism and Asia*, p. 223.

142 John Riddell ed., *Workers of the World and Oppressed Peoples Unite! The Communist International in Lenin's Time: proceedings and documents of the Second Congress, 1920, Vol. I,* p. 280. His defence belied a sense of impatience at Roy's outburst. In fact, before going into the theoretical explanation, he first justified his stand regarding his disagreement about the theses.

143 Ibid. p. 281.

144 Schram and Carrere d' Encausse, *Marxism and Asia*, p. 169.

145 G.Adhikari, *Documents of the History of the Communist Party of*

India, Vol. I, p. 185.

146 Sanjay Seth, *Marxist Theory and Nationalist Politics: The Case of Colonial India*, Sage Publications, New Delhi, 1995, pp.62-63.

147 Ibid. p.66.

148 Ibid.

149 Sobhanlal Dattagupta, *Comintern and the Destiny of Communism in India, Dialectics of a Real and Possible History*, Kolakta, 2006, pp.66-67.

150 John Riddell ed. *Workers of the World and Oppressed Peoples Unite! The Communist International in Lenin's Time*, Volume 1, New York, 1991, p.222.

151 Ibid. p.224.

152 Sanjay Seth, *Marxist Theory and Nationalist Politics: The Case of Colonial India*, p.66.

153 John Riddell ed. *Workers of the World and Oppressed Peoples Unite! The Communist International in Lenin's Time*, Volume 1, p.213.

154 G.Adhikari, *Documents of the History of the Communist Party of India, Documents of the History of the Communist Party of India*, Vol. I, p.160.

155 Sanjay Seth, *Marxist Theory and Nationalist Politics: The Case of Colonial India*, p.63.

156 Ibid.

157 Sobhanlal Dattagupta, *Comintern and the Destiny of Communism in India, 1919-1943Dialectics of a Real and Possible History*, p.66.

158 John Riddell ed. *Workers of the World and Oppressed Peoples Unite! The Communist International in Lenin's Time*, Volume 1, p.214.

159 'them' refers to the masses of peasants and workers.

160 Ibid. p.215.

161 G.Adhikari, *Documents of the History of the Communist Party of India*, Vol. I, p. 157.

162 Ibid. p.158.

163 Ibid.

164 Ibid. pp. 156-171,

165 Ibid. p.163.

166 John Riddell ed. *To See the Dawn, Baku 1920, First Congress of the Peoples of the East*, New York, 1998, p.20.

167 Ibid. p.22.

168 M.N.Roy, *Memoirs*, Bombay, 1964, p. 391.

169 Ibid. p.392.

170   John Riddell ed. *To See the Dawn, Baku 1920, First Congress of the Peoples of the East,* p.243.
171   Ibid. p. 242.
172   Ibid. p. 25.
173   Ibid. p. 62.
174   Ibid. p. 76.
175   Ibid. pp. 80-88.
176   Ibid. p. 88.
177   Ibid. p. 88.
178   Ibid. p. 89.
179   Ibid. p. 90.
180   Ibid. pp. 92-93.
181   Ibid. p. 93.
182   Ibid. p. 95.
183   Ibid. pp. 172-173.
184   Ibid. p. 173.
185   Ibid. p. 173-174.
186   Ibid. p. 177.
187   Ibid. pp. 177-178.
188   Ibid. pp. 182-183.
189   Ibid. p. 182.
190   Ibid. pp. 183-188.
191   Ibid. p. 188.
192   Ibid. p 189.
193   Ibid. pp. 191-192.
194   Ibid. pp. 194-199.
195   Ibid. p. 198.
196   Out of 2050 delegates, only 55 were women, Ibid. p. 242.
197   Ibid. pp. 204-205.
198   Ibid. pp. 206-207.
199   Ibid. p. 207.
200   Ibid.
201· Ibid. p. 207.

THE COMINTERN AND INDIA: 1921-1928

THE THIRD CONGRESS

The Third Congress of the Communist International took place in June- July 1921. Delegates from forty-eight countries, twenty-eight youth associations and other proletarian organizations were present in it. "...In all there were 605 delegates from 103 organisations from 52 countries"[1]. The Third Congress also discussed the national and colonial question, although the thrust on these issues was less than that in the Second Congress. In fact, the European issues were the major points of discussion in the Third Congress. The question however arose from time to time in the process of discussion of other issues and that is how the evolution of ideas on the national and colonial questions can be ascertained. The Indian communists had, by this time, assumed much importance in the communist circles, though many strands of thought prevailed among different groups, all of which wanted itself to be heard. Lenin on the other hand, always kept trying to disentangle the confusions in these new ideas. He wanted to apply communist principles and theories to different situations as demanded by the situations themselves, instead of adhering to the dogmatic principles of execution of communist theories, or being influenced by nationalist sentiments of several communist leaders of that time. Lenin also ascribed an important role to the peasantry in the Third Congress, and it formed a major part of his discussions— a point that was further detailed in the Fourth Congress of the Comintern.

Despite the fact that the national and colonial question did not form the major part of the discussions in the Third Congress, yet it figured quite often during these very discussions. Even before the Third Congress began, the ECCI Circular on the Agenda of the Third Comintern Congress in May 1921 said, "The Third Congress will first of all have to satisfy itself in regard to the extent to which each of the affiliated parties has in fact carried out all the conditions advanced by the Second Congress..."[2] The circular clearly stated that the Comintern was assuredly making headways into the East, the success of the Congress at Baku being one proof for it. Besides, the revolution in Asia was essential and that without which the world proletarian revolution was not possible[3]. It said, "...This too must be firmly grasped by every proletarian communist. Only then will the worker communist be adequately armed ideologically against the 'European' opportunism of Herr Hilferding and other heroes of the Two-and-a-Half International, who have in stock nothing but disdainful smiles for the oppressed peoples of the East"[4].

However, the spirit of the Third Congress was more or less attuned to the immediate needs in the countries of Europe, especially Germany and Italy. Both Adhikari and Jane Degras are of the opinion that the world situation of that time demanded such a policy[5]. When Russia was in the throes of a tremendous crisis both in the economic and political spheres, only a revolution in Europe could prevent its downfall. And revolution in Germany seemed imminent. The colonies were significant during this time only in as much as their role in the destruction of the capitalist order of Europe was concerned.

Lenin realised and was in fact very conscious that the situation of Russia was very delicate as far as its socialist existence was concerned. That was because Russia as a socialist state was totally isolated, as Europe was dominated entirely by the capitalist order. Since socialism as propagated by Marx and Lenin, was an international concept; hence its existence in isolation was very precarious— a fact that needed to be remedied so as to foster that very existence. In his Theses for a Report on the Tactics of the R.C.P. Lenin said:

"The international position of the R.S.F.S.R. at present is distinguished by a certain equilibrium, which, although is extremely unstable, has nevertheless given rise to a peculiar state of affairs in world politics.

"This peculiarity is the following. On the one hand, the international bourgeoisie is filled with a furious hatred of, and hostility towards, Soviet Russia, and is prepared at any moment to fling itself upon her in order to strangle her. On the other hand, all attempts at military intervention, which have caused the international bourgeoisie hundreds and millions of francs, ended in complete failure, in spite of the fact that the Soviet power was then weaker than it is now and that the Russian landowners and capitalists had whole armies on the territories of the R.S.F.S.R.... the conflict of interests between various imperialist countries has become acute, and is growing more acute everyday. The revolutionary movement among the hundreds of millions of oppressed peoples of the East is growing with remarkable vigour. The result of all these conditions is that international imperialism has proved unable to strangle Soviet Russia, although it is far stronger, and has been obliged for the time-being to grant her recognition or semi-recognition, and to conclude trade agreement with her. The result is a state of equilibrium which, although highly unstable and precarious, enables the Socialist Republic to exist— not for long, of course—within the capitalist encirclement"[6].

One can see from the use of Lenin's language that he was quite aware of the fact that the preservation of the socialist order in Russia amidst capitalist countries was very temporary, and that entertaining any notion of permanence about it would be a mistake. Side by side, the overthrow of capitalism entailed the inclusion of the colonies into the struggle as they formed a major source of power for the capitalists. In the Theses on the World Situation and the Tasks of the Comintern, as adopted by the Third Congress, the idea was the same. In Thesis 26 it said:

"The vigorous development of capitalism in the East, particularly in India and China has created new social bases for the revolutionary struggle. The bourgeoisie of these countries tightened their bonds with foreign capital, and so it became an important instrument of its rule. Their struggle against foreign imperialism, the struggle of a very weak rival, is essentially half-hearted and very weak in character. The growth of the indigenous proletariat paralyses the national revolutionary tendencies of the capitalist bourgeoisie..."[7]

The Theses had been originally prepared by Trotsky as "International Situation and the Tasks of the Comintern"[8]. He had presented it in the Third Congress of the Comintern, and was also its main reporter. Kunal Chattopadhyay has juxtaposed this part of the theses with the analyses of Trotsky's ideas in the First Congress of the Comintern[9]. He has then quite aptly concluded, "...It is evident that even though the First Congress Manifesto had a different approach, Trotsky was perfectly capable of learning from the 2nd Congress debate."[10] However, the ambivalence of ideas about the relationship between the masses and the bourgeoisie was still not quite clear to him. This becomes evident from yet another speech, "Prospects and Tasks in the East", where Trotsky said that though they approved of the support of the Kuomintang by the communists in China, there still remained the risk of a national-democratic revival[11]. Kunal Chattopadhyay has said:

"These speeches and reports indicate a complex picture. On one hand they show that Trotsky was absorbing the lessons of class struggle in the colonies and the semi-colonies. On the other hand they also reveal a substantial adherence to his old position, and the beginnings of a general theory, and also, a considerable degree of Comintern acceptance of the same. So far, Trotsky had not resolved the ambiguities any more than Lenin. It would require a class struggle experience comparable to 1905 to force him to elaborate the general theory. This experience came in the shape of the rise and decline of the Second Chinese Revolution."

This vagueness was a major feature in the deliberations that took place and the strategies that were adopted regarding the ushering in of a permanent revolution in the colonies. This vagueness remained for some time until the Chinese Revolution of 1926-27 failed because of strict adherence to earlier principles that were undefined in so many ways. And since the Fifth Congress of the Comintern in 1925, when the "class struggle experience" had actually occurred, serious debates resulted on these issues— debates that could not just be controlled under the veil of discipline. No amount of coercion could actually quieten the arguments that were raging in the minds of the Comintern members, and eventually many of them had to be expelled from the Comintern so that the views of Stalin were preserved unchallenged.

Lenin actually "…defined three main forces of the international revolutionary movement: the country of the victorious proletariat, the revolutionary movement in the capitalist countries and the liberation struggle of the oppressed peoples"[12]. Hence the question of the colonies in their role against the capitalist order emerged continuously in Lenin's speeches. In his Report on the Tactics of the R.C.P. on July 5th, he said, "… Much inflammable material has accumulated in the capitalist countries which up to now have been regarded merely as the objects and not as subjects of history, i.e., the colonies and semi-colonies. It is quite possible therefore that the insurrections, great battles and revolutions may break out there sooner or later, and very suddenly too… Inasmuch as the attempts of the international bourgeoisie to strangle our Republic have failed, equilibrium has set in, and a very unstable one it is, of course"[13]. It can be pointed out here that when Lenin was propagating about the impermanence of the socialist order in isolation, he was at the same time, making pronunciations regarding the impermanence of the capitalist order as well. It was here that the role of the colonies loomed. In the same article, he was saying:

"... The movement in the colonial countries is still regarded as an insignificant national and totally peaceful movement. But this is not so. It has undergone great change since the beginning of the twentieth century: millions and hundreds of millions, in fact the overwhelming majority of the population of the globe, are now coming forward as independent, active and revolutionary factors. It is perfectly clear that in the impending decisive battles in the world revolution, the movement of the majority of the population of the globe, initially directed towards national liberation, will turn against capitalism and imperialism and will, perhaps, play a much more revolutionary part than we expect. It is important to emphasise the fact that for the first time in our International, we have taken up the question of preparing for this struggle. Of course there are many more difficulties in this sphere than in any other, but at all events the movement is advancing. And in spite of the fact that the masses of toilers— the peasants in the colonial countries— are still backward, they will play a very important revolutionary part in the coming phases of the world revolution. (Animated approval)"[14].

Lenin was conscious of yet another fact. There had been a rise of a left-sectarian tendency in the Congress, which aimed at amending the tactics of the Comintern by adopting offensive strategies as against those advocated at the Second Congress. Lenin sharply criticised their move and said that in Europe the proletarians were mostly organised, but that the majority of the working class had to be won over before any offensive step could be taken and that "... anyone who fails to understand this is lost to the communist movement"[15]. Adhikari has said, "Lenin not only exposed the mistakes of the 'left' tendency at the congress but won over the comrades representing the same so that the congress adopted the theses on tactics unanimously"[16]. The Congress had said:

"The parties of the Communist International will become revolutionary mass parties only if they overcome opportunism, its survivals and traditions, in their own ranks by seeking to link themselves closely with the working masses in their struggle, deriving their tasks from the practical struggles of the proletariat, and in these struggles rejecting both the opportunist policies of self-deception, of hushing up and smoothing over the unbridgeable contradictions, and view into the relation of forces and ignore the difficulties of the struggle"[17].

The theses said that the task of the communists was to deepen and unify the struggle in order to achieve concrete demands. This was because every positive action of the communists would mobilise the bourgeoisie against the workers and that consequently, the party should always aim at defeating the enemy[18]. In the Manifesto of the ECCI on the conclusion of the Third Comintern Congress on 17th July 1921, there was a great emphasis on internationalism. It was said that the bourgeoisie were not only very powerful, but that it also had centuries of experience in holding power. This was to serve as a warning against underestimation of their policies[19].

In the Theses on the Structure of the Communist Parties and on the Methods and Content of their Work, as adopted by the Third Congress of the Comintern on July 12, 1921, it was clearly laid down:

"1.The organisation of the party must be adapted to the conditions and purpose of its activity... 2. There can be no one absolutely correct and unalterable form of organisation for the communist parties. The conditions of the proletarian class struggle are subject to change in an increasing process of transformation and organisation of the proletarian vanguard must always seek the appropriate forms that correspond to these changes. Similarly, the parties in the different countries must be adopted to the historically determined peculiarities of the country concerned..."[20]

The Third Congress took note of the fact that the situation was different in every country and that each country had to be dealt with separately if the final success of the revolution was to be guaranteed. This idea was in tune with the policies of the Second Congress.

There was one thing that Lenin was becoming increasingly conscious at this time. This was the question of the role of the peasantry in perpetrating the revolution. Lenin felt that the peasants, who formed the bulk of the population in several countries needed to be educated on communist lines so that they could facilitate the revolutionary process. This idea had already been propagated at the Second Congress and it was further developed during the Fourth Congress.

In his Theses for a Report on the Tactics of the R.C.P., he clearly mentioned that a firm alliance between the proletariat and the peasantry was needed in order to achieve the revolutionary goal in the true sense of the term. Although he was talking specifically in terms of Russia, yet he mentioned:

"...this was one of the most difficult tasks of socialist construction, with perhaps the sole exception of Britain. However, even in regard to Britain it must not be forgotten that, while small tenant farmers constitute only a very small class, the percentage of workers and office employees who enjoy a petty-bourgeois standard of living is exceptionally high, due to the actual enslavement of hundreds and millions of peoples in Britain's colonial possessions"[21], He also said, "The alliance between the small peasants and the proletariat can become a correct and stable one from the socialist standpoint only when the restoration of transport and large scale industry enables the proletariat to give the peasants, in exchange for food, all the goods they need for their own use and for the improvement for their farms..."[22].

In the Report on the Tactics of the R.C.P. on July 5th, Lenin was saying, "... And in spite of the fact that the masses of toilers— the peasants in the colonial countries are still backward, they will play a very important revolutionary part in the coming phases of the world revolution"[23].

Lenin even tried to formulate a strategy in order to bring about the alliance of the proletariat and the peasantry. In his Report on the Tactics of the R.C.P. he "...analysed the problem of the relation between the proletariat and the peasantry..."[24]. He said here, that Russia was the first state in history, where only two classes existed— the proletariat and the peasantry. The peasantry here formed the bulk of the population, but was very backward in itself. It was here that the relationship between the peasants and the proletariat came into question. Lenin analysed it. He said:

"... How do the relations between the peasantry and the proletariat, which holds political power, find practical expression in the development of the revolution? The first form is alliance, close alliance. This is a very difficult task, but at any rate it is economically and politically feasible.

"How do we approach this problem practically? We concluded an alliance with the peasantry. We interpret this alliance in the following way: the proletariat emancipates the peasantry from the exploitation of the bourgeoisie, from its leadership and influence, and wins it over to its own side in order jointly to defeat the exploiters"[25].

Lenin understood the difficulties that lay behind fulfilling such a task. In his Theses for a Report on the Tactics of the R.C.P., he was saying:

"... In the transition period, the small farmer class is bound to experience certain vacillations. The difficulties of transition and the influence of the bourgeoisie, inevitably cause the mood of this mass to change from time to time. Upon the proletariat, enfeebled and to a certain extent declassed by the destruction of the large scale machine industry, which is its vital foundation, devolves the very difficult task of holding out in spite of these vacillations, and of carrying to victory its cause of emancipating labour from the yoke of capital"[26].

He felt that the dictatorship of the proletariat would not bring about an end of the class-struggle. It would continue until communism could be established on an international scale. Until the completion of the task, the bourgeoisie would always gear up its own forces by allying with their counterparts in other countries, against the proletariat in bringing down communism. Since the bourgeoisie had been in power for such a long time, their experience in handling power would come into use at this stage and help them always, in their attempts to restore the bourgeois order once again. "That is why", he said, "we must continue our relentless struggle against these elements (bourgeoisie, feudal groups etc). Dictatorship is a state of intense war. That is just the state we are in..."[27]. Sobhanlal Dattagupta has aptly remarked, "This is an evidence of how Lenin hinted at the possibility of the growing fusion of the anti-imperialist and the anti-capitalist struggle in the colonies"[28].

The Indian point of view was as always, highly diversified in nature. Three sets of theses were submitted to the Comintern by three groups of professed communists on the occasion of the Third Congress. One was presented by Virendranath Chattopadhyay's group, one by M.N.Roy, and another by Bhupendranath Datta. All the three sets of theses are now available thanks to the efforts of Purabi Roy, Sobhanlal Dattagupta and Hari Vasudevan[29]. All three sets however, had little in common, hence once again betraying the lack of unity among them— a fact which was quite well-known. The authors have commented that "... the viewpoints were irreconcilable and so nothing could be done to consider them..."[30].

Virendranath Chattopadhyay, G.A.K. Luhani and P. Khankoje presented a thesis to the ECCI and the Congress Commission on Oriental Questions in July- August, 1921 on India and the World Revolution. The first part of the thesis is about the analysis of Indian conditions. It says that the proletarian world-revolution had a serious relevance in the Indian context as "... India transcends other parts of

Asiatic and African continents now under the sway of World-capitalism"[31]. But at the same time, the thesis clearly said that the situation in India, regarding its traditions, society and economy were completely different from European conditions. Whereas the linear division of the European society could be easily made, such was almost impossible to apply to Indian conditions. "... but these lines of horizontal cleavage— so sharp and clear— drawn in the industrial West have, in India, been intersected from the very inception of its history, by exceptionally strong vertical lines of social division and, latterly, of religious antagonism"[32]. In a society torn by caste and religious differences, a clear cut distinction between the exploited and the exploiting classes could never be made. Besides, the development of capitalism in India was so highly dependent on British capital that the exploitation of one race by another was another feature of the Indian socio-economic system. The thesis said:

"So long as this foreign character of capitalism remains the exploited masses fail to discriminate with any degree of precision between, on the one hand, the historical World-Bourgeoisie engaged in the misappropriation of wealth produced by the workers, and, on the other hand, a body of foreigners, politically supreme and racially distinct, carrying on a colossal scale the economic exploitation of a vast area"[33].

According to the thesis, as long as foreign domination is present in the colonies, the ideology of proletarian class-consciousness remain merely a potential, which can be invigorated only after the removal of the exploitation by a foreign political order[34].

The second part of the thesis deals with the position of British imperialism. It said that British imperialists were very powerful and were capable of "sabotaging"[35] proletarian revolution. National movements were developing against them as foreigners but not as the leaders of the capitalist order. Besides, the English workers, at the expense of the British colonies, enjoyed a better standard of living than their counterparts in the colonies themselves. Hence, even the enlightened English worker, who does "rise to a sense of solidarity with the proletariat of continental Europe", refused to do so with the proletariat of the English colonies of Asia and Africa. Chattopadhyay has named this stratum as the sub-bourgeois proletariat. He has said that the pressure from British imperialism thus broke the "front of the revolutionary World-proletariat... before that front could be formed into an actual battle line"[36].

In such a situation, Chattopadhyay and his group felt that "The absolute destruction of British Imperialism is an imperative necessity of the world revolutionary situation; and the destruction could be achieved only by detachment of India from the British Empire"[37]. They also objected to the strategy adopted at the Second Congress. They said:

"... here academic objections to rigid communist grounds to giving assistance to and collaborating with the bourgeois-democratic and nationalist revolutionary movements of political liberation in the East show a pathetic and stupid detachment from the realpolitik of the World situation. And so far as India is concerned any danger of the Indian bourgeoisie settling down to the exploitation of the Indian proletariat as a result of the overthrow of the British empire is totally out of the question, as, in the event of destruction of British imperialism, World capitalism would be shattered to pieces, and the Indian bourgeoisie, numerically insignificant and conspicuous for its historic record of decrepitude and inefficiency, will not be able to make any stand against the irresistible match of proletarian revolt all over the World"[38].

M.N.Roy, now famous from the colonial debate with Lenin at the Second Congress, submitted to the Third Congress of the Communist International, his Draft Theses on the Oriental Question. His views differ drastically with those of Chattopadhyay's. While outlining the Indian conditions he has said:

M.N.Roy then defined the line of activity which he felt would be best suited to the East. He said, "Therefore the activities of the Communist International in the economically and industrially advanced countries of the East should consist of the formation of such political parties as are capable of developing and directing the revolutionary movement according to the objective conditions. Such parties will be the apparatus of the Communist International:- through them the peoples of the East will be unified in the respective countries to fight against the foreign imperialism, and they will lead the fight further on for economic and social emancipation of the working class against the native bourgeoisie as soon as it takes the place of the foreign exploiter"[39].

M.N.Roy felt that the forces of the World Revolution in the East were to be found in the "... poor peasantry in those countries where feudalism still exists and among the proletarian and agrarian workers in those countries where machine industry has been introduced and the major portion of the population has been brought directly under the domination of foreign capitalism, either foreign or native"[40].

Bhupendranath Datta, Ebul Hassan and Abul Hassan submitted a Signed Memorandum to the Indian Commission: Scheme of Organisation of the Indian work, to the Mali Bureau (Small Bureau) of the Communist International during the same time. The memorandum said that an organised communist nucleus was of "utmost necessity". This nucleus would facilitate the organisation of a communist party in India and "carry on such propaganda and active work among the Indian labourers in other parts of the world, to help the formation of the party in India"[41]. Its next task would be to "impart training in order to educate the individual workers in the principles and practice of communism and to make various kinds of propaganda among the working classes, to enlist large numbers of sympathisers with the aims and aspirations of the movement"[42]. He also said that in order to bring "... the Indian proletariat in an organised body to the centre of the world revolution ...", the communist nucleus would need the help of "... the experienced Russian and other comrades, specialists in oriental affairs, who will form the permanent Indian commission of the Comintern for the Indian work"[43]. Regarding the overthrow of the British rule in India, Datta was of the opinion that it would have to be the first step towards the revolution. This was because the British rule in India was "the strongest and best organised capitalist rule in the world, which stands on the way to the free development of the social forces". In such a situation, Datta envisaged that the Comintern had to "... therefore help and support the nationalists and other revolutionary forces in India without encouraging any nationalist or chauvinist aspirations..."[44]. The composition of the commission was then outlined in the scheme in a way as to facilitate quick action against the British in times of need.

Another point emphasised in the programme was the role of foreign links. The scheme said:

"All available Indian communists residing outside should be sent by various means to India, to create different nuclei in the existing labour organisations and to form such organisations wherever wanting in the large industrial centres of India, and to work through at least two powerful centres in India, one in Calcutta and the other in Bombay, the unity of which will be the formation of the Communist Party in India"[45].

Datta felt that the help of Indians residing abroad was crucial where the overthrow of the British rule in India and the subsequent success of the communists were concerned.

If all the three sets of theses are taken into consideration, it is really no wonder that the Comintern did not include them in the proceedings. Whereas Virendranath Chattopadhyay was talking about a society with strong feudal ties, very different from that in the West; M.N.Roy was considering one with sharp class differences very like that in the West. When Virendranath Chattopadhyay was proposing to flout the strategies of the Second Congress, Roy proposed to unify the peoples of the East against foreign imperialism, under the aegis of the Comintern. Bhupendranath Datta was, on the other hand, at the same time, devising a policy of uniting the Indians residing abroad in a common struggle against the British. The conditions that were being spoken of were different; the methods of the struggle that were being proposed were different. Only one thing was common. All considered that the overthrow of the British from India should be the primary task of the Comintern. They all felt that the fall of the British would pave the way for the victory of communism in the world—for the British were, in a way, the leaders of the capitalist order in the West, and that their ruin would harbinger the ruin of capitalism as a whole. The next episode, that is the aftermath of the fall of the British, the rise of the native bourgeoisie and their exploitation of the toiling masses was not being given due consideration by any of them. Datta did not bring it into consideration at all. Roy left it vague, and Chattopadhyay felt that the native bourgeoisie was not strong enough to rise on its own after the fall of the British in India. It can hence be said that their primary concern was the ruin of British power. It is clear that all these leaders, with strong nationalist backgrounds found it hard to shed off their sentiments, a fact which surfaced often when they formulated strategies against capitalist-imperialist forces as members of a nation dominated by foreign imperialists.

A problem arises when the reaction of M.N.Roy is taken into consideration. Both Jane Degras and G.Adhikari have reported that Roy was very disappointed about the Congress. On 12th July 1921, the last day of the Congress, Roy was allotted five minutes to speak in the twenty-fourth sitting. And Roy did not like it. Adhikari says that Roy made a short protest against the non-inclusion of the "eastern question in the agenda of the congress"[46]. Degras has commented, "… M.N.Roy, the Indian delegate, used the five minutes allotted to him to make an 'energetic protest' against the opportunist way in which the Eastern question was discussed"[47]. She has also said that he criticised this neglect of the 'national and colonial question' in the proceedings as 'sheer opportunism'[48]. Roy clearly said in his speech:

> "The method by which the eastern question is being discussed in this congress— (is) purely opportunistic and more worthy of the programme of the Second International. There is not even the slightest possibility of arriving at any conclusions from the few words which the delegates from the eastern countries have been allowed to speak here.

> "I protest against their method of discussing the eastern question. It was put on the agenda of the congress at a session of the Executive Committee. But during the whole sittings of the congress, no attention whatsoever was devoted to this question. Finally only yesterday the commission met me in the first session. But it was a pitiable sight. Not even a single representative of European or American countries was present. This commission constituted according to the general opinion, in accordance with the established rules of the congress, decided that on this question there would be no theoretical resolution. But such a decision is not correct and it is proper to change it. Therefore I call upon the congress to entrust the eastern question once again to a properly constituted commission and consider it with all the seriousness it merits"[49].

Roy made no mention of his Draft Theses in his Memoirs. Sobhanlal Dattagupta says that it is strange that Roy's Memoirs is quiet on this point. Though Roy has mentioned his discussions with Lenin and Trotsky before the Congress[50], he had actually put in no effort to explain his frustration at not being allowed enough time to voice his opinion at the Congress. He has devoted an entire chapter to the Third Congress[51], yet the Draft Theses is not mentioned at any point. Nor is his disappointment at being given only five minutes to speak reflected anywhere.

Between the Third and the Fourth Congresses the strategy of the united front became quite dominant. The ECCI took vigorous steps to bring together several working class organisations to primarily defend the immediate needs of the workers. Adhikari has commented that the reformist groups of these organisations were given special consideration by the ECCI[52]. Worldwide campaigns were made in order to instil working class solidarity. On 30th July, 1921, the ECCI called upon the international working class organisations and progressive intellectuals to render "assistance and relief to the famine stricken parts of Soviet Russia"[53]. This was just after the 'Hands off Russia' campaign hoisted by England and France. On 18th December 1921, the ECCI adopted the "theses on the united front of the working class, and on the relations with the workers who supported the Second and Two-and-a Half Internationals, and with those who are organised under the Amsterdam Trade Union International as well as with those who support anarcho-syndicalist unions"[54]. In early 1922, the ECCI even called a meeting of the representatives of these organisations to consider the united actions of the working class in Europe, to achieve the demands of the workers against the capitalists of Europe and America. Soon afterwards the Commission of Nine was set up, composed of three members from each of the three Internationals. The setting up of the Commission of Nine had a powerful impact on the working classes of Europe this led to some difficulties with the reformist leaders of the Second International. But the ECCI was not to be put down so easily. A second plenum was called between 7th and 11th June, 1922 for "carrying forward the tactics of united front"[55].

THE FOURTH CONGRESS

During this time communist strategies were facing setbacks in several countries hence leading to a somewhat demoralising effect on the working class organisations. On the other hand, fascism was making headways in Europe and national liberation movements were surging in the colonies of Asia and Africa. This was the time when the Fourth Comintern Congress was convened. "The decision to convene the Congress was probably taken in the Second extended plenum of the ECCI which met in the beginning of June. In the Inprecor dated 17 July 1922 a brief item appeared inviting the Indian Communist Party to send delegates to the Fourth Congress. In the fortnightly, The Vanguard of Indian Independence, edited by M.N.Roy, in the issue of September 1 1922, there was an article on 'the World Congress', which also invited India to send delegates."[56] The Congress continued for a month between 5th November and 5th December 1922. It was represented by 408 delegates from 66 parties and organisations from 58 countries and the membership of the communist parties was 12, 53,000[57].

Lenin's health had, by this time begun to deteriorate. He could not attend several sessions of the Congress owing to his ill health. But he wrote a few articles from which his attitude can somewhat be made out.

Lenin could not attend the first session of the Congress, for which he wrote a regret note "To the Fourth Congress of the Communist International and to the Petrograd Soviet of Workers and Red Army Deputies", dated 4th November 1922. In this note he clearly mentioned that the winning of support of the workers was the primary goal, which had to be attained at any cost. He also said that the unity of the working class organisations was necessary in order to fulfil this task. He actually said, "The amalgamation of the Second and Two-and-a-Half Internationals will benefit the proletarian revolutionary movement: less friction and less fraud is always to the benefit of the working class."[58] In the last paragraph of the note he said, "... Soviet Russia considered it a matter of the greatest pride to help the workers of the whole world in their difficult struggle to overthrow capitalism..."[59] That Soviet Russia would itself seek to help the workers of all the countries in their struggle against capitalism was now being mentioned more starkly than ever before. This shows that the Soviet experience of the civil war and hostile relations with the capitalist European nations had taught them that the existence of a socialist state amidst countries that were engaged in a zealous pursuit of capitalism would be very very temporary. Hence what was needed was the spread of socialist principles to other parts of the world.

Lenin wrote another article, "Five Years of the Russian Revolution and the Prospects of the World Revolution" and reported it to the Fourth Congress of the Communist International on November 13 1922. This article was mainly a deliberation on the New Economic Policy that had been initiated in Soviet Russia in 1920. Since the policy was a deviation from orthodox socialist principles, Lenin explained its necessity and justified its launch as a means to stabilise the dwindling economic status of Russia and hence strengthen the forces of communism once again. He felt that despite the establishment of a socialist republic in Russia, hasty measures of socialist reforms could not be introduced until the existing bourgeois trends were replaced by new socialist norms in the socio-economic sphere. So, in order to preserve the new socialist state, "...it would be better if we first arrived at state capitalism and only after that at socialism"[60]. Lenin made no bones in admitting the mistakes of this new government. He in fact mentioned them over and over again in the article. "...Undoubtedly, we have done, and will still do, a host of foolish things. No one can judge and see this better than I ..."[61], he said. He also said that mistakes were bound to occur in a government that was being run on socialist lines for the first time. But the important thing was that they had begun to learn from their mistakes, and in the policies of the future these mistakes would always be eliminated and the interests of the toiling masses preserved.

Another important issue was raised in this article. Lenin was conscious of fact that the strategies of revolution that were being proposed, had a heavy influence of the Russian situation—a fact that had to be abandoned as different nations were faced with different situations and were incomparable to Russia in many ways. Hence, they needed to devise new strategies to suit their own ends. Lenin said:

"At the Third Congress, in 1921, we adopted a resolution on the organisational structure of the Communist Parties and on the methods and content of their activities. The resolution is an excellent one, but it is almost entirely Russian, that is to say, that everything in it is based on Russian conditions. This is its good point, but it is also its failing. It is a failing because I am sure that no foreigner can read it. I have read it again before saying this. In the first place, it is too long, containing fifty or more points. Foreigners are not usually able to read such things. Secondly, even if they read it, they will not understand it because it is too Russian. Not because it is written in Russian— it has been excellently translated into all languages— but because it is thoroughly imbued with the Russian spirit. And thirdly, if by way of exception some foreigner does understand it, he cannot carry it out. This is its third defect... I have the impression that we made a big mistake with this resolution, namely, that we blocked our own road to further success... "[62].

Lenin wanted the Russians as well as the foreigners alike, to study the situation accurately, and then devise strategies of revolution for their own countries by assimilating only a part of the Russian revolution. The imposition of the Russian system on all countries, without taking note of their individual necessities, would amount to disaster.

In his speech at the Plenary Session of the Moscow Soviet on November 20th 1922, Lenin once again analysed the policies being pursued by Soviet Russia. He once again justified the need to retain old policies before new and drastic ones could be implemented. He said:

"We still have the old machinery, and our task is to remould it along new lines. We cannot do it at once, but we can see to it that the

Communists we have are properly placed. What we need is that they, the Communists should control the machinery they are assigned to, and not, as so often happens to us, that the machinery should control them. We should make no secret of it and speak of it frankly. Such are the tasks and difficulties that confront us.... We need to take the right direction, we need to see that everything is checked, that the masses, the entire population check the path we follow and say: 'Yes, this is better than the old system'. That is the task we have set ourselves..."[63]

All these documents of Lenin do not as such pertain to the role of the colonies in bringing about the revolution. Yet I mention them because they help in explaining the situation in which the Fourth Congress took place. Lenin, it can be seen from these excerpts, was clearly in favour of rethinking the policies. Though optimistic about the future, he had become very conscious of the mistakes made, and the need to rectify them.

By this time the civil war had ended in Russia. The New Economic Policy had also begun to yield results; thereby rendering some amount of stability to the crisis struck economic situation. The relationship of Russia with other European nations had improved somewhat and tensions on that front had hence dwindled.

The Fourth Congress allotted much importance to the countries in the East regarding their role in precipitating the revolution. M.N.Roy submitted a lengthy "Report on the Eastern Question" to the Congress. He began with his usual alacrity by clearly stating that the countries of the East could not just be divided into the colonial and semi-colonial countries. He said that the perspective needed to be different and that the Eastern countries could be divided into three groups.

"...First, those countries which are nearing to most highly developed capitalism. Countries where not only the import of capital from the metropolis has developed industry, but a native capitalism has grown, leading to the rise of the bourgeoisie with a developed class-consciousness, and its counterpart, the proletariat, which is also developing its class-consciousness, and is engaged in an economic struggle which is gradually coming into its political stage. Second, those countries in which capitalist development has taken place but is still at the lower level, and in which feudalism is still the backbone of the society. Then we have the third grade, in which primitive conditions still prevail, where feudal-patriarchalism is the social order..."[64]

Roy said that revolutionary movements had developed in each of the Eastern countries. But owing to their different social setups, "… the character of the revolutionary movement in those countries is also different. In so far as the social character is different the programme for those movements must be different and the tactics must also be different"[65]. He also felt that the "fundamental principles that were laid down by the Second Congress of the Communist International" needed to be elaborated according to the needs of each country. Hence several generalised strategies had to be rethought.

Roy then went on to analyse the consequences of the World War, which he has called the "great imperialist war".[66] He felt that the war resulted in a "great social upheaval", one that had a lasting influence not only on the foreign bourgeoisie, but on the native ones as well. The foreign bourgeoisie sought imperialist protection, while the native ones "were terrified by its possibilities". Roy explained that the native bourgeoisie of the colonial countries was not yet "developed enough as yet to have the confidence of being able to take the place of foreign imperialism and to preserve law and order after the overthrow of foreign imperialism. They are now really afraid that in case foreign rule is overthrown as a consequence of this revolutionary upheaval, a period of anarchy, chaos and disturbance, of civil war will follow, that will not be conducive to the promotion of their own interests"[67].

It can be said that Roy strongly believed that native capitalism had grown and the bourgeoisie had developed a class-consciousness. On the other hand, he also believed that the native bourgeoisie was not yet strong enough to handle state administration on their own. For that, the help of the foreign imperialists was imperative. Hence capitalism in the colonies of the East was still highly dependent on the foreign imperialists for the advancement of their interests. That was the reason that the native bourgeoisie were compelled to "compromise with the imperial overlord"[68]. This compromise too, was according to Roy, a temporary measure, as it itself bore the seeds of future conflict. He said that the imperialists had to grant concessions to the native bourgeoisie to win them over to their side in the face of mounting national resistance. But those very concessions had opened "a bigger vision" before the bourgeoisie and that with the development of industries a rivalry between both was sure to occur.

M.N.Roy said that the bourgeoisie led nationalist movements in the colonies were "objectively revolutionary". Yet the same bourgeoisie could not be called a "revolutionary factor"[69]. For the bourgeoisie were not engaged in a class war against the feudal order. It was, he analysed, an "internecine war" between the weaker native bourgeoisie against the much stronger and powerful foreign ones. Sobhanlal Dattagupta has said that this was a warning served by Roy about the native bourgeois forces[70]. It was not only a warning. It was also a step further in the broaching of the moot point— whether the bourgeois led nationalist movement was to be further supported.

"So, the nationalist struggle in the colonies, the revolutionary movement for national development in the colonies, cannot be based purely and simply on a movement inspired by bourgeois ideology and led by the bourgeoisie... This problem brings us face to face with a problem as to whether there is a possibility of another social factor going into this struggle and wresting leadership from the hands of those who are leading the struggle so far"[71].

Roy as usual slid to his point very smartly before going once again into the analysis of the existing situation in the countries of the East.

Roy felt that the in countries where capitalism was sufficiently developed, such a "social factor" was already coming into existence. The proletarian class had been created and the agrarian class was also being gradually drawn into the struggle, due to the creation of "a vast mass of poor and landless agrarian toilers" by the penetration of capitalism. In the other countries where capitalism was not yet sufficiently developed, and where feudalism or its remnants still formed the basis of the social order, "there had been the development and growth of the agrarian movements"[72]. Hence the masses according to Roy were slowly becoming enlightened regarding their exploited status. In such a situation, said Roy, a "triangular fight" was developing, one "which was directed at the same time against foreign imperialism and the native upper class which directly or indirectly strengthens and gives support to foreign imperialism"[73].

On the other hand, Roy said that the bourgeois forces would lead the national movement only to a certain level. They would continue the fight until the imperialist restraints to their vested interests were removed. Once it was achieved, they would try to stop the revolution to proceed further. He commented:

"...You know how the movement in Egypt and India has been brought to a standstill by the timidity, the hesitation of the bourgeoisie, how a great revolutionary movement which involved the wide masses of the peasantry and the working class and which constituted a serious menace to imperialism could not produce any very serious damage to imperialism simply because the leadership of this movement was in the hands of the bourgeoisie"[74].

Roy was continuously stressing the fact that the bourgeoisie were not to be depended upon, where the interests of the masses were concerned.

Roy divided the native bourgeoisie into two classes. He said:

"... the upper layer, which was developed industrially and owning big industrial and commercial interests interlinked with imperial capital, found it dangerous for their extension, and therefore went over to the imperialists thus constituting itself a positive obstruction to the revolutionary national movement. The other section with its weak social background did not have the determination, the courage, to put itself at the head of this big revolutionary movement to lead it forward, and the movement consequently, betrayed and misled by these elements, has come to its present period of depression"[75].

Once again Roy made it evident that the bourgeoisie were not to be trusted.

Roy then came to his point. He said that the bourgeoisie could not be trusted upon at all to complete the revolution in order to bring about the emancipation of the masses. Hence what was needed was the training of that social factor which was objectively more revolutionary in character, and which could step into the place of the bourgeoisie and assume leadership, once the national revolutionary struggle was betrayed by the bourgeoisie[76]. He felt that "... They alone will be in a position to lead the colonial peoples and oppressed nationalities to the conquest of complete political and economic independence"[77].

M.N.Roy further said that the communist parties in the East were no more than nuclei organisations, yet they were to play a big part while assuming the leadership of the national revolutionary movement. Sobhanlal Dattagupta has criticised this point very pertinently. He has said:

"... Roy while acknowledging that the communist parties in the colonies were nothing more than nuclei, felt all the same that desertion and betrayal of the revolutionary struggle by the bourgeoisie would witness the assumption of the leadership of the national revolutionary struggle by the communist party and that the communist party alone would be in a position to lead the colonial peoples and oppressed nationalities to complete political and economic independence. But Roy did not elaborate the crucial issue as to how, despite their weakness, the communist parties would achieve hegemony in the national revolution"[78].

The Fourth Congress devoted much time to the national and colonial questions. The representatives of the colonial countries could get time to voice their notions about the problems regarding the colonies, unlike that in the Third Congress. Besides, the Congress prepared a long set of theses— "Theses on the Eastern Question". The theses however, was propounded on the same lines as those developed at the Second Congress.

The theses began by outlining the crises being faced by the capitalist European countries in the post-war period. As a result, the struggle against the imperialists in the colonies had also sharpened manifold. On the other hand, labour movements had begun to generate and communist parties had formed in the Eastern countries. The struggle against the imperialists was no longer in the exclusive control of the compromising feudal or bourgeois elements. The theses at this stage, hinted without quite mentioning the rise of new leadership in the colonies. Imperialist rivalries had also emerged in various spheres, thereby striking another blow to the imperialist forces. With the decrease in imperial pressure on the colonies native capitalism had also begun to grow and seek profits outside the restraints imposed by the imperialists themselves. The theses clearly said:

"... The demand for national and economic independence put forward by the national movements in the colonies serves to express the needs of bourgeois development in these countries. The growth of native productive forces in these colonies, therefore causes an irreconcilable conflict of interests between them and world imperialism, for the essence of imperialism consists in using the varying levels of development of productive forces in various parts of the economic world for the purpose of extracting monopoly super- profits"[79].

The second thesis said:

"The backwardness of the colonies is reflected in the motley character of the national revolutionary movements against imperialism, which in their turn, reflect the varying states of transition from feudal and feudal patriarchal relations of capitalism. The variety of conditions makes its impression upon the ideology of these movements. To the extent that conditions of capitalism arises and develops in feudal bases in hybrid, imperfect and intermediary forms, which gives predominance above all to merchant capitalism, the rise of bourgeois democracy from feudal-bureaucratic and feudal-agrarian elements proceeds often by devious and protracted paths. This represents the chief obstacle for successful mass struggles against imperialist oppression as the foreign imperialists in all the backward countries convert the feudal (and partly also the semifeudal semibourgeois) upper classes of native society into agents of their domination (military governors— Tuchuns— in China, the native aristocracy and tax farmers— the zamindars and talukdars— in India, the feudal bureaucracy in Persia, the agrarian-planter capital formations in Egypt etc.)"[80]

The second thesis pointed out that this was the reason that the upper class led successful mass movements against the imperialists was not possible in countries where the feudal patriarchal system no longer existed. However, in countries like Mesopotamia, Morocco and Mongolia, where the feudal patriarchal system was still in vogue, and the native aristocracy was still not totally separated from the people at large, the national movements were being led by the upper classes of the society itself. In such a situation, the thesis said:

"... The real and consistent solution of this depends on the extent to which the national movement in any particular country is capable of attracting to itself the toiling masses and breaks off all connections with the reactionary feudal elements and includes in its programme the social demands of the masses"[81].

It also said that the Comintern supported all national movements against imperialism. But at the same time, it said that the final victory could be achieved only if the masses joined the movement at large after making a total break with "all advocates of compromise with imperialism in the interest of maintaining class domination"[82].

The third part dealt with the peasant question in the colonies. Taking into consideration Lenin's preoccupation with the peasantry since the days of the Third Congress, this was somewhat expected. The thesis clearly said that the peasantry of the colonies was an exploited class. It also said:

"The revolutionary movement in the backward countries of the East cannot be successful unless it is based on the action of the masses of the peasantry. For that reason the revolutionary parties in all eastern countries must define their agrarian programme which should demand the complete abolition of feudalism and its survivals expressed in the forms of large landownership and tax farming. In order that the peasant masses be drawn into active participation in the struggle for national liberation, it is necessary to proclaim the radical reform on the basis of land ownership. It is necessary also to compel the bourgeois nationalist parties to the greatest possible to adopt this revolutionary agrarian programme"[83].

The fourth section dealt with the "Labour Movement in the East". The thesis said that the labour movement had made much progress in the East. Proletarian class parties had also formed. But they were still suffering from lack of internal organisation, amateurity, sectarianism and other defects.

Regarding the tasks of the Comintern, the theses said that the proletariat should struggle to secure the support of the peasants, without which the revolution would not be complete. The native proletariat should also be able to take up the role of political leadership. Only after this was done could bourgeois democracy be combated. On the other hand, the communists of the colonies should participate in anti-imperialist oppression. "The refusal of the communists in the colonies to participate against anti-imperialist oppression on the pretext of alleged 'defence' of independent class interests is opportunism of the worst kind calculated only to discredit the proletarian revolution in the East"[84]. The theses at this stage were very much in tune with the strategies propounded at the Second Congress. It was also said:

"The communists and the working class parties in the colonial and semi-colonial countries are confronted with a twofold task: on the one hand to fight for the most radical solutions of the problems of bourgeois democratic revolution, directed to the conquest of political independence, and on the other to organise the workers and peasants to fight for their special class interests and to take advantage of the antagonism existing in the nationalist bourgeois democratic camp... The working class of the colonies and semi-colonial countries must know that only by deepening and extending the struggle against the imperialism of the great powers can its role as a revolutionary leader be fulfilled. On the other hand the economic and political organisations and the political training of the working class and the semi-proletarian classes will facilitate and extend the revolutionary scope of the struggle against imperialism"[85].

Another aspect regarding the tasks of the Comintern was, as emphasised in the Second Congress, the need for a united anti-imperialist front. The reason was to expedite the struggle against imperialism by mobilising all anti-imperialist elements and also to prevent the native ruling classes to make compromise with the foreign

capitalists against the interests of the masses. Besides, it would help
"... to develop the revolutionary will and to make more definite the
class-consciousness of the masses of the toilers and bring them into
the front ranks of the struggle, not only against imperialism but against
all survivors of feudalism"[86]. "The Tasks of the Proletariat on the
Pacific Coast" was the seventh thesis. It said clearly that the
communist parties in the colonial and semi-colonial countries of the
Pacific coast should, like that in the East, conduct propaganda among
the masses to take active part in the struggle for national liberation
and to consider Soviet Russia as the "bulwark of all the oppressed
and exploited masses"[87]. It also said that the communist parties of
the imperialist countries "...in view of the threatening danger must
not limit themselves merely to a propaganda against war, but must
exert all their efforts to remove all the disruptive factors from the
labour movement in their respective countries and to prevent the
capitalists from taking advantage of national and racial antagonisms.
These factors are: the immigration question and cheap coloured
labour"[88]. The last thesis highlighted the tasks of the countries
possessing colonies. It said:

"Every communist party in the countries possessing colonies must
undertake the task of organising systematic ideological and material
assistance to the labour and revolutionary movement in the colonies.
They must carry out a persistent and determined struggle against the
quasi-socialist, colonising tendencies prevailing among certain
categories of well-paid European workers in the colonies. European
communist workers in the colonies must strive to rally around
themselves the native proletariats and gain its confidence by concrete
economic demands (equal pay for white and native workers,
protection of labour, labour insurance, etc.)"[89].

Sobhanlal Dattagupta has made a detailed examination of the
theses in comparison to that of Roy's. He said that though the Theses
on the Eastern Question did not directly contradict Roy's
observations, yet it cannot be said that theses were in agreement
with his ideas. He has commented:

"... it is true that at the Fourth Congress Roy's views on the
industrialisation of the colonies and the political and economic
consequences that followed (which were shared by some other
delegates representing the colonial countries) were not directly
criticised. But this cannot make one agree with the conclusion reached
by Robert. C. North and Xenia. J. Eudin that the Theses on the Eastern

question adopted at the Fourth Congress supported Roy's analysis, contending thereby that the Comintern lent support to Roy's viewpoint. A careful scrutiny of the theses would belie this interpretation"[90].

He then pointed out several instances of difference in both the sets of theses.

The major points of difference according to Sobhanlal Dattagupta were these:-

1. The Theses, unlike Roy, did not characterise the development of capitalism in the colonies as industrialisation or as a consequence of "changed economic policy of imperialism. The Theses stressed the objective political conditions that led to a weakening of the imperialist pressure in the colonies".

2. The Theses "rejected" the stand taken by Roy and other delegates from the colonies, which "emphasised the delinking of the communist party from the national movement (as the latter was led by the colonial bourgeoisie) and consequently stressed the exclusive role of the communist party in providing leadership to people's struggles".

3. The Comintern "did not agree with the assessment of the strength of the proletariat and the communist parties in the colonies as given by the Eastern delegates".

4. The Theses "laid particular emphasis on the role of the peasantry in the revolutionary struggle against imperialism in the colonies, an issue that was not at all sufficiently stressed by Roy and the other delegates from the colonial countries in their zeal for securing the hegemony of the proletariat in the national liberation struggle".

The excerpt that Sobhanlal Dattagupta provides from the Theses on the Eastern Question to substantiate the first point, deals with the weakening of imperialist forces as a result of the war, and its subsequent repercussion on the hold that these forces exerted over their respective colonial domains. The excerpt ends at "... It is precisely this weakening of imperialist pressure in the colonies, together with the increasing rivalry between various imperialist groups that has facilitated the development of native capitalism in the colonies and semi-colonial countries which are outgrowing the narrow framework of the domination of the great imperialist powers"[91]. The rest of the paragraph says:

"Hitherto the capitalists of the great powers in maintaining their monopoly rights to secure super-profits from trade, industry and taxation of backward countries have striven to isolate these from the world economic intercourse. The demand for national and economic independence put forward by the national movements in the colonies serves to express the needs of bourgeois development in these countries. The growth of native productive forces in these colonies, therefore causes an irreconcilable conflict of interests between them and world imperialism, for the essence of imperialism consists in using the varying levels of development of productive forces in various parts of the economic world for the purpose of extracting monopoly super- profits"[92].

This is a clear indication that the native forces were trying to develop themselves by encroaching into grounds that had so long been denied to them by the imperialists, who were bent on monopolising their super-profits from trade, industry and taxation of backward countries. This explains the conflict of interests between both the groups. Hence the development of capitalism in the colonies was a result of the development of bourgeois forces—a fact, which originated due to the crises of war. Sobhanlal Dattagupta's point that industrialisation was only a consequence of the slackening of imperialist hold and not the reason behind the rise of capitalism in the colonies, as stated by the Theses against Roy's idea that industrialisation was leading to the development of capitalism in the colonies, can only be called an elaboration of the same point.

The second point of Dattagupta which stressed that Roy and other colonial delegates wanted an exclusive role of the communist party in providing leadership to the mass movement was contradictory to the united-front policy that the Comintern proposed. It can be said here that both Roy's theses as well as that of the Comintern, proposed a temporary agreement between the communist party and the bourgeoisie. The Theses on the Eastern Question said:

"The labour movement in the colonies and semi-colonial countries must first of all secure for itself the positions of an independent factor in the common anti-imperialist front. Only on the basis of the recognition of this independence and the maintenance of complete independence is a temporary agreement with bourgeois democracy permissible and necessary"[93].

Roy too did not just dissociate the communist party from the bourgeois. He also considered the communist parties to be young and undeveloped when the Theses were labelling them to be in their "embryonic stage". He said:

> "Therefore we find the necessity of these communist parties, which at the present moment cannot be called more than nuclei, are destined to play a big role in so far as they will assume the leadership of the national revolutionary struggle when it is deserted and betrayed by the bourgeoisie"[94].

This danger of the bourgeoisie going over to the imperialist side, and the necessity for the mobilisation of other revolutionary forces was mentioned in the Comintern Theses as well. It said:

> "The expediency of these tactics is dictated by the prospects of a prolonged struggle against world imperialism demanding the mobilisation of all revolutionary elements. This mobilisation becomes all the more necessary from the fact that the native ruling classes are inclined to make compromise with the foreign capitalists directed against the fundamental interests of the masses of the people"[95].

This renders doubtful the third point made by Sobhanlal Dattagupta, regarding the Comintern disagreeing with Roy in his assessment of the proletariat and the communist parties in the colonies.

The fourth point of contradiction is regarding the difference in emphasis on the agrarian question and the role of the peasantry in the revolutionary struggle in the colonies. This point can be considered considering the fact that whereas the Theses on the Eastern Question devoted an entire section to the agrarian question, Roy's theses was not that elaborate. Whereas Roy's theses highlighted the "gradual" rise of the peasant movements against the imperialists, who were responsible for the creation of a huge section of "poor and landless agrarian toilers"[96], and the existence of the feudal elements, the leaders of the countryside, who were allied closely with the native as well as the foreign capitalists; the Comintern's theses propounded that the "revolutionary movement in the backward countries of the East cannot be successful unless it is based on the action of the masses of the peasantry"[97].

If both the sets of theses are taken into account, then the major point that had been discussed was the sly character of the bourgeoisie and that how their interests were, in the long run, not conducive to those of the toiling masses. They would always ally with the imperialists even to the extent of deserting the masses in their war for national liberation, once the masses began to rise and their interests began to clash with the former. Hence they were not to be trusted at all. The situation could be combated only by training "the other social-element", the proletariat, to assume leadership of the masses in their revolutionary struggle and carry it to its successful completion.

Another point made by Sobhanlal Dattagupta was "... Although in the concluding portion of his Report he (Roy) referred to the importance of united-front tactics, the whole tenor of his speech was directed precisely towards a negation of this line..."[98] He has also said:

> "The difference between the Theses of the Fourth Congress and Roy's Report basically represented the fundamental difference between the outlook projected by Lenin in the Second Congress, which aimed at dialectically fusing the national and the class question, and one characterised by ultra leftism, which rather unilaterally divorced these two aspects, the premise being that capitalism and industrialization had sufficiently developed in colonies like India and that a revolution under the exclusive leadership of the proletariat was on the anvil in the advanced countries of the East..."[99]

The major part of Roy's theses dealt with the nature of the bourgeoisie, their vacillating tendencies and their lack of loyalty to the revolutionary struggle. The strategy of the united-front tactics of the Comintern as effective and necessary in the revolutionary struggle was brought up very abruptly only in the last paragraph. Despite the point that he continuously made regarding the slippery character of the bourgeois order, especially in its role as the leader of the masses in their revolutionary movement, he was never hinting that the masses should not join the bourgeoisie at all. He was saying that this alliance was sure to be betrayed by the bourgeoisie sooner or later and that the proletariat should be trained so as to takeover from the place from where bourgeoisie would leave the movement. He also said that that it was the proletariat that would ultimately carry the movement to its successful completion.

Roy himself was not free from the nationalist spirit that shook his thoughts as his fellow Indian communists, however much he was at variance with them otherwise. His initiation to the national movement as a nationalist was a fact that continuously surfaced in his later communist notions. Perhaps it was this that was reflected when he vehemently characterised with total condemnation, the native bourgeoisie as allies of the imperialists. If Roy's records are given any consideration, it can be seen that he had criticised the Comintern's viewpoint earlier— during the Second Congress, and later too—

during the Fifth Congress. Hence, if the Comintern's theses did not actually conform to his views, there is no reason to suppose that he would let it go without a debate, especially when he was a member of the Eastern Commission, which drew up the Theses on the Eastern Question.

Roy enunciated his ideas further in his books, India in Transition[100] and What Do We Want?, both written in 1922. In these works Roy expressed his views very clearly. He did not believe that India was still in the throes of feudalism. He admitted that feudal elements were still in existence; yet at the same time, he felt that India had very much been drawn into the aegis of capitalism. He said, "It is recognised by all that India is in a state of transition. She finds herself in a position which links the past lived through and left behind, with the dawning future of new activities, new hopes and new aspirations." That perhaps explains the title of the book, India in Transition[101].

The first chapter of the book deals with the emergence and growth of the bourgeois class in India. In doing so it deals elaborately on how the feudal rule came to an end with the failure of the revolt of 1857, and how the country subsequently came under capitalist exploitation. He divided the Indian society into four classes, the landed aristocracy, including the native chiefs; the bourgeoisie and the intellectuals; the petty peasantry; and the working class, including the landless peasants[102]. But while analysing the nature of these classes, he refused to call any of them feudal[103]. He considered their feudal characteristics only as elements of the bourgeois order. He also said that the Indian bourgeoisie was accumulating power and that the British sought to placate them in many ways. He commented:

"The political expression of the British government's reconciliation with the Indian bourgeoisie is in the Montagu-Chelmsford Reform Scheme. Taking advantage of the unexpected opportunity presented to it by the war conditions of 1917-18, the Indian capitalist class acquired such a secure position that it was no longer possible for the government to ignore it. To revive after the war the old policy of obstructing the industrial growth of the country would surely force the Indian bourgeoisie, which had developed its political consciousness and organisation sufficiently, to place itself actively at the head of the revolutionary movement which was spreading wider and wider throughout India. The only way to prevent such a catastrophe was to devise means of divorcing the political ambition of the bourgeoisie from the spontaneous revolutionary upheaval of the masses"[104].

Hence they granted political concessions to the Indian bourgeoisie through reform measures. Besides it allowed the native capitalists to develop, but only by "... conceding it the position of junior partnership in the exploitation of India..."[105]

M.N.Roy also analysed the position of the peasantry and their relationship with the rulers. He said:

> "The secret of the incurable misery of the Indian peasantry lies in the fact that it is being ground between two mill-stones, viz. foreign capital in a higher stage of development and native capital in a lower stage. In the field of exploitation the two depend upon each other, while at the same time, owing to the very historic inevitability of the evolution of capitalism, they cannot help clashing with each other. When they depend upon each other, the native trader brings the farmer directly under the commercial exploitation of the foreign bourgeoisie; when they conflict with each other, it is again the peasantry which perishes in the clash"[106].

He also said that "... nothing short of radical readjustment can improve the situation" and that a revolution was essential in order to bring about such a change[107]. He then went on to say that after being exposed to tremendous exploitation both in the home and foreign fronts, the peasantry had become restive and rebellious. M.N.Roy highlighted the examples of peasant revolts that were occurring in the country, and commented, "So we find the rebellious mood of the peasantry is becoming so manifest that it is causing alarm to the government and the landed aristocracy alike. Both are very much concerned in checking it"[108].

M.N.Roy also analysed the effect that British industrialism had on India and the Indian proletariat. He said that with the coming of the British, the "... political control of the country passed to the bourgeoisie, which, however, happened to be foreign. Under the political rule of the bourgeoisie the economic exploitation of the society could not remain in the fetters of antiquated methods. Gradually the entire production of the land was brought under capitalist exploitation on the one hand, and manufactures of capitalist industries destroyed to a great extent the backward form of craft production, on the other[109]. But the process and method of production, he said, remained the same as before— the exploitation of the workers too remained as much a feature of production in the new set-up as earlier, intensifying in itself as never before. This setting in of capitalism as the new order was however very abrupt. It did not replace the old system of production, it simply eliminated it. The transformation was so swift that the old society suddenly found itself superimposed with the new one, without getting enough time to adjust to it even. He said, "... This method of imperialist exploitation dislocated the social organism..."[110]

M.N.Roy's concept of the proletariat was not limited to the factory workers alone. He talked of the great number of wage earners employed as clerks, ministerial employees in government offices, assistants in large trading firms, teachers etc. They were either residing in the cities or coming from the suburbs to work in the town everyday, with the mounting of the cost of accommodation in the cities. Roy called them the intellectual proletariat. Their economic condition was miserable, yet psychologically they belonged to the bourgeoisie and not the working class. He said:

"Their economic condition was objectively destined to make them revolutionary, but their social prejudices not only prevented the growth of revolutionary class-consciousness, but actually dragged them deeper and deeper into the depths of decay and demoralisation...

... The fundamental thing is that in every sense of social economics, this class has been proletarianised, and the substitution of one capitalist government by another cannot and will not change their position. Their social prejudices must succumb before they realise that their salvation lies in the frank recognition of their social position, and consciously take their stand where they really belong"[111].

The factory workers in the cities, drawn mainly out of the agricultural proletariat, in their quest for a more comfortable life in the cities, had suffered a total disillusionment. Roy says that the same worker, who had some time back, meekly accepted his condition as fate, could not be kept content any longer. Not only was city life much more demanding, it was also one that very pointedly exposed the inequalities of wealth and the intensity of their exploitation. Very few of the workers actually opted to return to their native villages, he said, after enumerating several reasons for it. Instead, as the capitalist organisations developed further, along with the improvement in the scale of industrial production, the workers began to organise themselves.

The strikes began in 1918, and soon swept the whole country. Trade unionism had made progress and "side by side with the national struggle, class struggle had also been developing"[112], said Roy. He also said that before long the nationalist leaders "suddenly found in it a very good weapon to be used for the purposes of demonstration"[113]. They did not understand the actual significance of the struggle and rendered it a political colour. The leadership too passed into the "control of conservative reformists and government agents"[114]. Roy commented that the nationalists were "more interested in turning out a popular demonstration than to develop the revolutionary consciousness of the masses by participating in their struggle for everyday life"[115]. By 1922 however, when "India in Transition" was published, he said that the first stage, "which was marked by a mad wave of spontaneous strikes" was over and the next stage, "organisation and preparation for continuing the struggle"[116] had begun. This unerring faith of Roy in the advancement of the proletariat in the colonies, especially in India, can be marked ever since the days of the Second Congress. In fact, his distrust of the nationalist elements was also not new. It had forever been a strong basis of his arguments. The idea that national freedom had to be gained did hold place in his ideas. To him the national struggle that would end at the achievement of freedom from foreign rule was not enough. The struggle would end only after the ultimate emancipation of the working classes. The fervency of his appeal was, as always, directed towards this second part of the struggle, one that would lead to the victory of the workers that Roy seemed to concentrate on more— a fact which led to the interpretation that Roy was averse to the united-front strategy. Perhaps the first part of the revolution, the struggle for national liberation was to him, a necessary yet a trivial step in the revolutionary process as a whole. It was the break-up with the bourgeoisie after the gaining of national freedom, and after the unmasking of their true nature, that was of more significance to Roy. The ultimate goal of the revolution could be visualised only from that point onwards. "The national liberation of India is but a prelude to a greater thing— the social emancipation of the working class. National struggle and class struggle are going on side by side; the noisiness of the former cannot conceal the existence of the latter"[117].

Although the question of the united-front was not sufficiently taken up in "India in Transition", it was given much importance in "What Do We Want?" This book, in the form of a manifesto, was rather propagandist in nature, but nevertheless analysed the Indian problems and its possible solutions more or less in accord with his earlier ideas as propagated in the Fourth Congress. The same intent is present, only the style is rather flashy. The peasant question also has been given much importance. In this work too, Roy has analysed the reasons as to why capitalism should be destroyed, and why, at the same time, it was futile to depend on the native capitalists and the native bourgeoisie as well. This analysis is fully in tune with that made in the Fourth Congress and in "India in Transition." The only difference is that here the necessity of the united-front strategy is very clearly enunciated.

Regarding the peasant question Roy said that the peasant problem could never be solved, and the peasants drawn into the sphere of the revolutionary struggle unless their lands could be appropriated without compensation from the landlords and the usurers. Nothing else, he felt, would convince the masses of the true aims and objectives of the revolution, those that promised the emancipation of mankind from all sorts of exploitation. Roy said that along with the toiling masses of the country, the upper classes of India were also facing oppression from foreign rule as their economic ambitions were being held in a strong leash by them. This made them clamour for independence from foreign rule. Herein lay the importance of this class to the masses of workers and peasants. He said:

> "These classes have a part to play in the general scheme of our social revolution. Their free development will break down all the old bondages of social conservatism and religious prejudice, bonds which can only be broken by the free development of economic forces by the rise of higher means of production. Therefore, we must lead the masses of our people to support the progressive upper and middle classes in their struggle against imperialist domination. But we must never for a moment confuse our goal with theirs"[118].

He then repeated as before that these classes would stop the struggle once they had achieved political control over the country. But the masses under the guidance of the communists should carry the struggle further and secure substantial economic improvement for the working classes. Besides, it was from here that the struggle was to be led on to its culmination, when the victorious working classes would attain total power.

S.Dattagupta's comment is,

> "A careful reading of *India in Transition* does in fact show Roy's consistent inclination towards making a case for explaining the course of the anti-imperialist struggle in terms of polarisation of the bourgeois and proletarian class interests. The case for

industrialisation, which in effect meant a reversal of imperialism's economic policy, provided the rationale behind his argument... A careful study of the programme enumerated in this book (*What Do We Want*) would suggest that Roy, while lending cautious support to the bourgeois-nationalist movement against imperialism was however putting forward a programme for the liberation of the working class and the peasantry which would be relevant only in relation to the proletarian revolution..."[119]

The polarisation of class interests involved between the bourgeois and the proletarian classes in terms of the anti-imperialist struggle was not a new phenomenon. It was always this factor that prompted the theoreticians of the Comintern to formulate a united-front policy in which the proletariat was always supposed to retain its independent existence. This was because the class interests of the two classes, the bourgeois and the proletariat were bound to clash— a fact that would either provoke the bourgeoisie to beckon to the capitalists for compromise, or force them to bring the proletariat under control. Right from the Second Congress, this theory had been in vogue[120]. The situation too was very fluid. The same ideas were being discussed upon since a long time, the same theories and the same strategies seemed to appear in the deliberations over and over again only with shifts in the emphasis of several points.

THE FIFTH CONGRESS

The Fifth Congress was held from 17th June to 8th July 1924, two years after the Fourth Congress was held. Regarding the number of delegates and the number of countries that were represented in the Congress there are several opinions. It can be said that around five hundred delegates representing forty to fifty parties attended[121]. Adhikari has said:

"... Against India we find noted 'two delegates' and '10 mandates'. These two delegates are 'with decisive vote' and India had no delegates 'with consultative vote'. According to the information Chinmohan Sehanovis got from the Institute of Marxism-Leninism in Moscow, the two delegates at this Congress were M.N.Roy and Mohammad Ali"[122].

Regarding the three delegates from India in the commission for the national and colonial question, Adhikari has commented that the third person might have been Clemens Dutt, who then had close connections with Roy and Mohammad Ali.

Meanwhile Lenin had died and tributes were paid to him at the very beginning. It was only then that Zinoviev made a report on the activities and the tactics adopted by the ECCI between the Fourth and the Fifth Congresses. Jane Degras has said that Zinoviev's tone from the very opening was not very optimistic. He said, "After five years of the International we have to state that the movement has not developed as quickly as we expected. We can all remember the time when Lenin thought... that the victory of the revolution in all countries was a matter of months"[123]. However, he also said that despite the fact that the bourgeois forces might unfold more counter-revolutionary measures in the West, the objective situation was still revolutionary— a fact that would guide their future tactics. This was felt at a time when the revolutionary surge had settled down to some extent in Europe. Counter-revolutionary forces had become unexpectedly successful in gentling the fervour which had surged not only in Europe but in the countries of the East as well, especially in their struggle against imperialism.

Zinoviev had retained the spirit of the Second Congress, saying that the united front was necessary. But the point that can be argued upon is that he advocated for a united front only from below, a fact that changed the very essence of the Leninist doctrine as proposed in the Second Congress. Duncan Hallas has said, "...'Only from below' was the substance of Zinoviev's line, meaning that united-front action should be proposed only to the rank and file of other parties and workers' organisations, not to their leaderships."[124] This was not what Lenin had advocated. This was only a caricature of united front. For a real united front is always from above, in the hope of influencing the masses below. If the masses are already willing to leave their leaders and work with the communists then no united front is necessary.

Duncan Hallas has made an analysis of the situation quite clearly. He has commented:

"... A united front means united in action and is meaningless if the revolutionaries have no real forces to commit such an action.

If the united-front tactic is judged inappropriate, then it is politically necessary to say so. The whole thrust of the political line given at the fifth congress of the Comintern was that the offensive was the order of the day in a number of countries, especially in Germany. This was grotesquely wrong, but if it had been true, then the united front tactic— which, remember, is a defensive tactic— should have been seen by the congress as at least secondary and, in particular cases, definitely wrong.

But this was not done. Instead, the line of the united-front 'only from below' was proclaimed. It was a nonsense. The essence of the united front tactic is that the appeal for united action is made to the leadership of another workers' organisation as well as the rank and file, although, of course, everything depends on the response of the rank and file. Unity in action will then prove to the rank and file of that organisation that revolutionary politics are superior to that of their own leadership. To make the appeal for united action only to the rank and file is not a united front at all— it is merely an appeal to individuals to work with or join the party, an appeal which revolutionaries should make in all circumstances anyway."[125]

The speech of Zinoviev aroused much controversy because its generalisations regarding the policies to be followed in the countries of Europe. Besides, Russian dominance was very evident in the authoritative tone of the speech. Bordiga, one of the founding members of the Italian Communist Party objected to the tactics that the Comintern had adopted so far. He said that the report of the ECCI should be analysed and examined. He also said that the national speakers in the Congress spoke mainly about those parts of the Report, which concerned their respective countries. Hence the speeches were rarely international in nature. Bordiga also challenged, for the first time, the overriding authority of the Russian Party. He felt that each country had its own special situation to deal with, and that it was not necessary that it would always be right. Radek too supported the move against the practice of promoting artificial unanimity. Criticisms continued unabated. The German, Bulgarian, Polish and Italian delegates put in scathing criticisms of several policies of the Comintern. Zinoviev defended himself saying that the methods of agitation might be different in different nations, but the basic questions like the proletarian dictatorship would always remain the same in the West. Zinoviev felt that all these events marked the "beginning of the second wave of the international proletarian revolution".[126] He also said that the time factor was very important. Capitalism would undoubtedly break down. At the same time, it was possible that the communists might have to enter a prolonged period of democratic pacifism when capitalism would either vegetate or disintegrate rapidly. The peasant question in the colonial countries also came up along with those on the Peasant International or the Krestinstern.

Eleven sessions of the Congress were needed to discuss the ECCI Report. Radek and Bordiga disagreed to the resolution, but it was ultimately passed in the Congress against eight votes. The tendency to suppress all voices of dissent in order to maintain the supremacy of the line that was being advocated by the Soviet Union, had become a feature of the discussions in the Comintern. It was soon to assume a much greater role by the time the Sixth Congress took place.

Two paragraphs were devoted to the national and colonial questions in the Resolution of the Fifth Congress on the Report of the ECCI. Though the language of the paragraphs varies in two different books, the meaning remains more or less the same. The two paragraphs are as follows:-

"17. On the national question, the executive had frequent occasion to remind many sections for whom this question is one of the greatest importance that they were not carrying out the decisions of the Second Congress satisfactorily. One of the fundamental principles of Leninism, that communists should constantly and resolutely fight for self-determination, rights of nationalities (secession and formation of independent states), has not been applied by all sections of the Communist International in the desired manner.

"18. In addition to winning the support of the peasant masses and of the oppressed minorities, the executive committee in its instructions always emphasised the necessity for the winning over of the revolutionary movements for the emancipation of the colonial peoples of the east so as to make them the allies of the revolutionary proletariat of the capitalist countries. This requires not only the extension of the direct contact between the executive and the national emancipation movement of the orient, but also very close contact between the sections in the imperialist countries with the colonies of those countries, and in the first place a constant struggle against imperialist colonial policy of the bourgeoisie in every country. In this respect the activities are everywhere still very weak"[127].

It has been commented by several scholars that the position of Roy and that of the Comintern began to diverge tremendously from the Fifth Congress onwards. "By the time of the Fifth Congress then Roy's position was in complete contradiction to that of the Comintern"[128]. Adhikari has pointed out theoretical problems in the assertion of Roy, saying that the socio-economic emancipation of the masses was possible only after the attainment of political freedom[129].

Roy said at the very outset that the colonial question was an important issue where the revolution was concerned and that it had to be understood theoretically before proceeding to formulate policies on it. He reiterated his position in the Second Congress and raised the issue of the rejection of his amendment in the Congress. It was the 10th paragraph that Lenin omitted entirely. It said:

"The bourgeois national democrats in the colonies strive for the establishment of a free national state, whereas the masses of workers and poor peasants are revolting even though in many cases unconsciously, against the system which permits such brutal exploitation. Consequently, in the colonies, we have two contradictory forces; they cannot develop together. To support the colonial bourgeois democratic movements would amount to helping the growth of the national spirit which will surely obstruct the awakening of class-consciousness; whereas to encourage and support the revolutionary mass action through the medium of a communist party of the proletarians will bring the real revolutionary forces into action which will not only overthrow the foreign imperialism, but lead progressively to the development of Soviet power, thus preventing the rise of native capitalism in place of the vanquished foreign capitalism, to further oppress and exploit the people"[130].

This was in July 1920. When Roy was deliberating in the Fifth Congress, it was four years later in 1924. Roy situated this point while arguing to justify the content of Paragraph 10 in his original draft in the Second Congress. Roy said that his amendment was "totally mistaken when considered in the light of the events that have taken place since the Second Congress"[131]. He said that the communists should have connections with the nationalist movements, while asserting at the same time that "...it seems to have been overlooked that these connections have not always been successful... For instance, a movement which might have a revolutionary significance in 1920 is not in the same position in 1924. Classes which might have been allies of the revolutionary proletariat in 1920 will not be allies in 1924. Here is the danger of rigid formula and the cause of our inefficiency, futility and lamentable lack of any activity in this sphere. If we are to improve we must rectify this fundamental error"[132]. He said that the Second Congress itself showed the way by pointing to the significance of the class movement when it called for the organisation of the peasantry into soviets and uniting it with that of the West.

Despite his earlier pronouncements, Roy now said that capitalism was not well developed in the colonial countries and that it would be mere romanticism to speak of a revolutionary proletariat in those countries. But there was the existence of a vast mass of peasantry and hence arose the significance of the revolutionary movement, one that needed to be nurtured and supported. He said that a direct connection with the masses was required to foster such a need, but then the ECCI Resolution advocated the need for a direct connection with the national-liberation movement. Since, he said, "These include all sorts of classes and aims"; the revolution would never progress and fall prey to theoretical confusion once again[133].

Roy felt that the connection of the communists with the national–liberation movement had hardly yielded any results. He explained further:

"… It is not true to say that I am in favour of self-determination of the toiling masses and not of self-determination of nationalities. The self-determination of all oppressed nationalities must be advocated, but we must find out how they can realise self-determination. By admitting the self-determination of oppressed nationalities we must not admit the self-determination of the bourgeoisie without admitting that of the masses. But neither has the proletariat alone a right to self-determination. All classes have a right to it. But we must analyse social conditions in order to understand what class is going to play the most important part in obtaining it. The Communist International must support national-liberation movement, but for practical purposes it must find out what class is leading them, and must have its direct contact with that class"[134].

M.N.Roy criticised Manuilsky's comment that the national-liberation movement in British India had revived greatly in the past one year, that is, 1923. The national-liberation movement did indeed prosper in 1920-1921, but by 1923 the movement had slowed down. He said, "As a matter of fact last year was a period of the worst depression in the nationalist movement there"[135]. He also criticised Manuilsky's remark regarding the recent struggles of the peasantry in India as representations of the furtherance of the nationalist movement. Roy said:

"But these are signs of decomposition in the national movement the form of which— the united-front against foreign domination— is dead. The struggle of the peasantry is the struggle of the exploited peasantry against the Indian landlords. It is parallel to the struggle of the Indian town workers against Indian capitalists. Thus the national movement is split. In 1920-21 the revolting peasantry and the proletariat were led by the bourgeois and the petty-bourgeois who, however, failed to understand the significance of the revolutionary forces they have called into action. Now this nationalist movement is split by a class-struggle. With which class are we to have our 'direct contacts'?[136]"

Roy also said that the Indian bourgeoisie had been won over by the British imperialists. He said that the Indian bourgeoisie demanded that foreign relations and military power should remain in the hands of the British because "the Indian bourgeoisie knows better than anyone else that the discontent of the masses is economic and not nationalistic, and exploiting class in India demands protection from the exploited. Indian capitalism is running straight into the arms of British imperialism and the same tendency will soon be seen in other countries"[137].

Roy concluded:

"...The direct contact of the Comintern should be with that social class which is most revolutionary, and the separate condition of each country must be analysed from this point of view. Every section of the Comintern must be given its special task, in order that national sections may not be reproached again with negligence which has not been their fault"[138].

Manuilsky attacked Roy very harshly in his concluding speech on the national question. He said that Roy was "exaggerating the social movement in the colonies to the detriment of the national movement"[139]. He remarked, "He (Roy) goes so far as to say the national movement has lost its character of the united front of all classes of an oppressed country, the new period is beginning in which the class-struggle is becoming transported into the colonies"[140]. He said that even if the Indian situation saw a relative development in the sphere of class-struggle, it would "mean to lose sense of reality" if the point was generalised. And in doing so Roy was committing the same error as that of Bukharin, even more so because it was a "question of the backward countries"[141]. At the same time, said Manuilsky, Roy in regard to the colonial question, "reflects the nihilism of Rosa Luxemburg"[142]

Roy's disagreement regarding the united-front tactics of the Comintern had surfaced for the first time in the Second Congress, when he had engaged in a protracted debate with Lenin on the national and colonial question. Lenin had then simply scrapped those parts of his original draft, which were not in consonance with the theories and tactics as proposed by the Comintern. Roy had accepted it then without further ado, and the policy could be executed. What he had retained then was only a complete distrust about the bourgeoisie, a fact which he made very clear in his Report in the Fourth Congress. But despite this distrust of bourgeois ideology, which he felt was bound to recoil the moment the interests of the bourgeois class were hurt, a fact that would jeopardise national and mass interests; he did not oppose the united-front tactics of the Comintern. In fact, he expressed his solidarity with it, that too in the same Report. Two years later, his attitude changed dramatically— a fact that needs to be examined in detail before corroborating with the dictums of different scholars.

Adhikari has commented that Roy's view regarding the direct contact of the Comintern with the most revolutionary class was necessary and that the conditions of each country were to be analysed separately, was not in keeping with the spirit of Lenin at the Second Congress, as Roy claimed to be. He strongly criticised Roy's views:

"This is incorrect. The position of the Comintern has always been in the spirit of Lenin, viz to support the national liberation movement as a whole in as much as it acts and struggles against foreign imperialist rule, at the same time striving to keep direct contact with the revolutionary elements. If this were done in the spirit of contraposition, it could only create insurmountable difficulties for the revolutionary element, i.e. for the communists, in the task of building the broad united anti-imperialist front for ensuring final victory"[143].

Sobhanlal Dattagupta too has maintained a similar outlook. He said:

"Interestingly, Roy tried to defend his position in terms of the Theses on the National and colonial Questions adopted at the Second Congress. Citing the authority of the Theses, he pointed out that the Resolution of the Executive was in clear contradiction with the main direction of the Colonial Theses since the latter, in envisaging united-front tactics, had called for not direct contact with the bourgeois nationalists but only with the revolutionary workers and peasants. This interpretation of the Theses, was, however, a complete travesty of truth... Roy's interpretation of the Colonial Theses reveals once again that he could not grasp, even at the time of the Fifth Congress, the dialectical quality of Lenin's flexible formulation of united-front tactics. For Roy, a united front would mean exclusively an alliance of workers and peasants, since he could not, like Lenin, dialectically fuse the national and the class question in the colonial countries. For Roy it was an either-or issue and accordingly, since for him it was the class question that unilaterally determined the course of the liberation movement in India, he contested Manuilsky's position…"[144]

Shashi Joshi has on the one hand, criticised the validity of Lenin's theses of the Second Congress. She said, "After 1923, when the expected world revolution failed to materialise, Lenin's theses of 1920 lost their relevance even for the Comintern. Consequently, clinging to the Leninist legacy of the colonial theses was quite fruitless and even misleading"[145]. "The Irrelevance of Leninism" is an entire chapter that she has devoted to it. In its conclusion, she has said:

"In conclusion it bears emphasis that 'Royism' that Indian communists often tried to counterpose to 'Leninism' actually cohered together in their shared Marxist logic of the insurrectionary paradigm a la State and Revolution. This paradigm was only relevant for the violent overthrow of an Absolutist State. Moreover, Lenin's formulations on imperialism were based purely in economic terms. They were devoid of any conception of the varied political nature and specific form of colonial states in different countries. Therefore, the Leninist paradigm had no room for evolving a political strategy and forms of effective struggle that could undermine a modern hegemonic state through peaceful mass movements. Thus Leninism was not only irrelevant in Indian conditions but also misleading"[146].

However, Shashi Joshi has, on the other hand, at the same time, in the same chapter, criticised Roy's denial of the nationalist ideology, which he considered to be oriented for protecting the interests of the bourgeoisie alone[147].

Two questions arise from the evaluation of these comments. One, whether Roy could never accustom himself to the Comintern tactics of the united-front and that his position at the Fifth Congress was only a continuation of his earlier point, and two, whether, and to what extent was Roy's condemnation of the united-front tactics in the Fifth Congress justified. Before going into the explanation of these points, more documents need to be seen.

The first document to be cited is the Draft Resolution of the presidium, ECCI dated 4.4.24. on proposed plan of work in India. This Resolution called for the creation of a well-knit illegal Communist Party in India. This Party would mobilise all "…available revolutionary elements into a legal mass party which will be called the PEOPLES PARTY. The composition of the legal party will be all the scattered and demoralised forces of national-revolution, namely the petty-bourgeoisie, the poor peasantry and the town proletariat..."[148]

The 6th point of the same Resolution states among other things: "The C.P., moreover, will issue a manifesto through the neutral organisations... calling for the organisation of the united anti-imperialist front embodied in the People's Party. In the manifesto the respective revolutionary significance of the various classes of the Indian society will be clearly analysed, the inevitable weakness of the anti-British struggle based purely on the class interests of the bourgeoisie will be pointed out, the unwillingness of the upper classes to undertake a revolutionary fight will be exposed, the role of the workers in the national revolutionary movement will be brought to the foreground and it will be shown how the petty-bourgeois nationalists cannot play an important political role, nor achieve their own liberation, unless they make the closest possible alliance with the revolutionary masses"[149].

This document clearly shows a deviation from earlier principles. The composition of the People's Party is an unmistakable indication towards the change of intent in the principles of the Comintern. It mentions only the "petty-bourgeoisie, the poor peasantry and the town proletariat". The big bourgeoisie and the landowning classes—the leaders of the national liberation movement in India are deliberately excluded.

Next, the work of this so called People's Party would now be directed towards exposing the "unwillingness of the upper classes to undertake a revolutionary fight" and the indispensable revolutionary role of the workers and the peasants in bringing about their own liberation. The primary interest of the united-front as advocated by Lenin in the Second Congress was to "secure the co-operation of the bourgeois nationalist revolutionary elements", in order to overthrow foreign capitalism, as the first step towards revolution. Hence, once again, a distinct shift can be noted in the Comintern's policies.

The second document that needs mention is the Draft Resolution on the Colonial and Eastern Question (Draft by Comrade Bricke) for the Fifth Congress of Comintern, 1924. The second point in this Resolution states that a compromise had already been arrived at in several colonies, between the imperialists on the one hand and the native bourgeoisie and landowners on the other. Hence the "process of decomposition in the national liberation movement of these countries" had already begun. It also said that "the national movement in India is at present passing through a period of unmistakable decline, accompanied with a corresponding strengthening of the position of British imperialism in India..." Records mention that this part of the Resolution is crossed out by pen in the archive copy[150].

The Second Congress had said, "So to help overthrow the foreign rule in the colonies is not to endorse the nationalist aspirations of the native bourgeoisie, but to open the way to the smothered proletariat there"[151]. It had also proclaimed:

"For the overthrow of foreign capitalism which is the first step towards revolution in the colonies the co-operation of the bourgeois nationalist revolutionary elements is useful.

But the foremost and necessary task is the formation of communist parties which will organise the peasants and the workers and lead them to the revolution and to the establishment of Soviet republics.

Thus the masses in the backward countries may reach communism, not through capitalistic development, but led by the class conscious proletariat of the advanced capitalist countries"[152].

The Second Congress, as is evident here, was advocating the fact that the overthrow of the imperialist powers from the colonies had to be brought about with the help of the revolutionary bourgeois elements. But that communism could not be achieved with their help is also tacitly acknowledged in the same theses. Though not directly mentioned, this was definitely a hint at the ultimate split between the upper classes and the toiling masses. The theses further explained that communism could be reached under the leadership of the "class conscious proletariat of the advanced capitalist countries". The amended Supplementary theses of the Second Congress, however, did not mention what policy was to be followed if the bourgeois elements came into a compromise with the imperialists, and then refused altogether to co-operate with the masses in their struggle against the imperialists.

In such a case, if the Draft Resolution on the Colonial and Eastern Question for the Fifth Congress is to be considered, which said that compromise between the imperialists and the native upper classes had actually been made, then going by the dictates of the Second Congress that did not provide any solution to such a case, another shift in policy was undoubtedly being envisaged by the Comintern itself. It is no wonder therefore that the part had been crossed out. The deviation from the Leninist policies of the Second Congress is further confirmed by the same Resolution. The 6th point of the Resolution said:

"...The Communist Parties in the Eastern and colonial countries must strive to establish a UNITED ANTI-IMPERIALIST FRONT COMPOSED OF NATIONAL REVOLUTIONARY FORCES OF ALL COUNTRIES. This watchword must serve as a means for drawing the widest possible masses of the proletariat, the peasantry, the petty-bourgeoisie and the intelligentsia into the active struggle against imperialism and its allies, native feudalism and its bureaucracy..."[153]

The 8th point said:

"... The Communist Parties must determinedly and persistently oppose the half-heartedness and vacillation of the bourgeoisie in this question, expose their hesitation and indecision to the masses, and in those cases where the bourgeoisie by means of the compromises with the imperialists strives to avoid open struggle, the Communist Parties must themselves mobilise the toiling masses for the fight against the particular bourgeois government..."[154]

The concluding part said:

"WHILE PRESERVING A LEGAL OR ILLEGAL COMMUNIST APPARATUS—ACCORDING TO THE POLITICAL CONDITIONS PREVAILING IN THE COUNTRY—WE MUST STRIVE TO SECURE THE DIRECT LEADERSHIP OF THE WORKERS' AND THE PEASANTS' PARTY"[155]

An interesting remark that Sobhanlal Dattagupta has made is in connection with Stalin's attitude. He has said, with corresponding evidence from several documents, that at this stage, Stalin's views somewhat conformed to those of Roy's. There were differences, but then, there were differences with formal ECCI position too, and hence the latter refused to endorse his point of view.[156] S. Dattagupta has said:

"... while Stalin's position was not in agreement with the official Comintern position as reflected in the ECCI Resolution of 6th April, 1925, it virtually echoed and thereby vindicated the position of M.N.Roy. On one level, the understanding seems valid in the sense that, following Roy, Stalin too rejects the notion of a homogenous concept of colonialism and embraces the idea of differentiation of colonies. On another level, however, Stalin's position on the role of the nationalist bourgeoisie apparently seems identical with Roy's position and stands in contrast with the position of the ECCI, especially with regard to his analysis of India, a closer analysis would suggest that Stalin's outlook was somewhat different from that of Roy, notwithstanding their striking similarities (i.e. endorsement of the idea of the People's Party, while highlighting the importance of the Communist Party). For Roy, bourgeois nationalism in countries like India was already a spent force. But in Stalin's understanding the nationalist bourgeoisie had split into a revolutionary and a compromising wing, demanding concentration of fire on the compromising wing and its isolation; however, on the question of leadership in the liberation struggle in countries like India, Stalin's position was very close to Roy's understanding, as it underscored the necessity of securing the hegemony of the proletariat by building up the Communist Party..."[157]

This inclination to create an alternative power base of the workers and the peasants under the leadership of the communists, and one that would fight against the bourgeoisie if they hesitated in fighting the imperialists had not been proposed so directly ever before. Besides, the united-front between the national revolutionary forces of all countries, as advocated here, comprising only of the "proletariat, the peasantry, the petty-bourgeoisie and the intelligentsia" and not the bourgeois class as a whole, and posed against "imperialism and its allies, native feudalism and its bureaucracy" is a clear transgression of the principles of the united anti-imperialist front as advocated in the Second Congress.

In such a situation, the answer to the first question, that is whether Roy's denouncement of the united-front tactics in the Fifth Congress was a continuation of his thoughts as expressed in his original Draft Theses in the Second Congress, would be "No". He had made his point in the Second Congress, but after the debate, the point had not been raised again until the Fifth Congress. He had in fact, zealously followed the theory during the Non Co-operation movement in India. He had merely retained his distrust for the bourgeoisie, and kept harping on the point that the bourgeoisie were engaged in the anti-imperialist fight only for the preservation of their own capitalist interests, and were bound to betray the national-liberation movement before its completion. This would occur the moment they would be able to visualise that their success was close at hand and that this success would give them the power that they had craved for always. Hence they would then try to guard this success and betray the national-liberation movement, the continuation of which would mean bringing the interests of the masses to the forefront, as the next step of the struggle. Now mass interests would always be detrimental to that of the bourgeoisie. In such a situation, strangely enough, the theories so far propagated by the Comintern did not have an answer.

The Non Co-operation movement began in 1921 and was withdrawn by Gandhi in 1922, when it was still in its full swing. Industrial strikes that had also spread all over the country, and especially in Bombay, in 1918-1920 too were suppressed and lockouts made. Moreover, the communists were being arrested and prosecuted in the Kanpur Conspiracy case. The surge of the revolutionary spirit in Europe had also been stemmed, with the failure of the greatly expected revolution in Germany.

It is this situation that served as a background to Roy's formulations in the Fifth Congress, and his stand has to be analysed in this perspective as well. It was soon after the Second Congress that the Non Co-operation movement began. This was a totally bourgeois led nationalist movement. It began in the cities, but soon spread to the countryside as well. A huge population became engulfed in the spirit of movement. If the Comintern doctrines were to be followed, then this situation provided the ideal opportunity—a bourgeois led nationalist movement that could reach the masses and involve them quite actively in the movement. It was apparently a spontaneous movement of the masses led by the bourgeoisie against the imperialist order. The Comintern theory of a united-front simply fit. But the abrupt withdrawal of the movement after the Chauri-Chaura incident, even when it was in its full swing was enough to prove to the Comintern led communists like Roy, that it was not what they had thought it to be. Roy felt that the mass upheaval was being used by the nationalist bourgeoisie for the furtherance of their own interests. In fact, it proved as disillusionment to him. Yet, he did not oppose the doctrine.

Meanwhile the strikes had abated, and the revolutionary upsurge in Europe had also petered out, hence rendering the belief that the revolution was imminent in Europe, almost impossible. But Roy continued to adhere to the Second Congress doctrines. It was not before the Fifth Congress that he demanded a re-examination of the previous theories in the context of the contemporary situation, which he felt, had changed since the time of the Second Congress. Such a situation had perhaps left Roy at a loss regarding his linking of theory and practice.

Besides, it was not just Roy who was vouching for a rethinking of the whole procedure. The Draft Resolution of the presidium, ECCI dated 4.4.24. on proposed plan of work in India and the Draft Resolution on the Colonial and Eastern Question (Draft by Comrade Bricke) for the Fifth Congress of Comintern, 1924, clearly show that the Leninist doctrines were being imposed upon or rather modified with new doctrines of mass participation in the revolutionary process. These theories were almost devoid of the role that was being assigned to the native bourgeois class in bringing about the revolution. Instead, they advocated the need for the exposition of the true character of the native bourgeoisie, that is, their inclination to compromise with the imperialists even against mass interests, the moment their interests were threatened to be hampered by the demands for reform from the masses.

A significant point that is indicated in these documents is that the generalising of theories for all colonial nations too required modifications. That the situation in Java, Egypt and India were different, and that the formation of the workers' and peasants' party was "PARTICULARLY NECESSARY" in these countries, for the securing of power for the workers and the peasants[158], had also been mentioned.

Another point that needs mention here is that Lenin undoubtedly advocated the anti-imperialist united-front strategy. But he was, at the same time, clearly mentioning that the communist parties in the colonies, however embryonic, should always retain their independent character. He also said that communism would be achieved "not through capitalist development", but only under the guidance of the "class-conscious proletariat of the advanced countries". Hence, the germs of the final breach between the bourgeoisie and the proletariat were always there. Like Roy, he too did not intend to "smother" the proletariat in the process of sanctioning "the nationalist aspirations of the native bourgeoisie". It is that he wanted the breach to occur only after the attainment of liberation in the colonies. But the future strategies of the Comintern in the colonies, in case the liberation movement was betrayed by the bourgeoisie before its completion, had not been provided by the theories of the Second Congress. It is a matter of extreme hypotheses as to what Lenin would have done in the changed circumstances. And it is here that Roy's role came into play. He wanted to place an alternative theory regarding a situation that would arise if the national liberation movement was betrayed by the bourgeoisie before its completion. He felt that the united-front tactics were not helping in the progress of the revolutionary process as the situation had changed.

Roy's views answered a situation that had not been dealt with in the Second Congress. And looking at the failure of the Chinese revolution a couple of years later, when the rigid Comintern dictates for the united front prevented the revolution's spontaneous progress, a fact that caused its collapse; it can be said that viewed in the long run, the opposition was justified.

BETWEEN THE FIFTH AND THE SIXTH CONGRESS

When the Fifth Congress came to an end, the debate regarding the colonies was still over the united-front tactics. But gradually the dimensions of this debate began to change. Between the Fifth and the Sixth Congresses there was a gap of four years. By the end of this span, Stalin entered into opposition with Trotsky, Zinoviev, Kamenev and others— whom he labelled as ultra-leftists and whom he refused to tolerate. He said that they were pursuing policies which were most anti-Leninist in nature and that it could not hence be compromised with. He then gradually accumulated much power and began to influence the strategies of the Comintern.

The situation in China had meanwhile become very crucial. The working classes had become organised to some extent under the aegis of the Chinese Communist Party (CCP). They had begun to rebel against imperialist oppression. China being branded as a semi-colony by the Comintern, the Communist Party of China had to conform to the principles of the united-front strategy from the very beginning. Accendingly the CCP had allied with the nationalist party called Kuomintang. But the situation that had made the united-front tactics possible began to change with rise of Chiang Kai Shek, the right wing Chinese leader. He began to assume tremendous powers, he even staged a coup de'tat and soon the agreement between the allied forces disappeared. At that time, when most Chinese as well as Russian leaders and the representatives of the Comintern were vouching against the maintenance of the united-front, Stalin made a great show in favour of supporting the cause for the maintenance of the front. Leaders like Trotsky, Zinoviev, Kamenev, Radek, Rakovsky etc. made strong protests against such policies of the Comintern.

They felt that supporting a regime under Chiang, who was conducting the massacre of the workers and peasants on a very large scale, would tantamount to the betrayal of the cause of the revolution. But Stalin remained unperturbed and refused to budge. On the other hand, in order to crush criticism of his strategies, he took drastic measures. He began to expel opposition from all fronts— the Comintern and the CPSU. Trotsky, Zinoviev and many others became a prey to his absolutism. Those who remained were too weak to oppose.

China was not the only point of discontent. The KPD in Germany too was facing several problems. Here too a tussle developed between the right and the left wing communists. Stalin was once again in favour of the right. In Poland, the communists had supported Pilsudski's government in the hope for transformation of the existing order. But when Pilsudski began to assert his own powers against them, they had to turn back. In America the party membership had decreased from 16,000 to 12,000. In Bulgaria, the Communist Party had been nearly obliterated. The opposition now became very critical of the stand taken by the Comintern in several cases. In the July meeting of the CC of the CPSU Stalin was blamed for the mistakes of the Polish Communist Party. Trotsky felt that the support of the allied nationalists and the communists in China would also end in the same way as that in Poland. But once again, as usual, a deaf ear was turned to him. Stalin's authoritarianism began to increase further and he refused to comply. Instead he began to cut down the power of the opposition either by cancelling their memberships or by expelling them from the various posts that had been assigned to them.

With Chiang Kai shek coming to power through a coup de'tat and with the assertion of his absolutist tendencies, Trotsky's criticism of Stalin's policies had become vociferous. In March 1926, Zinoviev drafted the Theses on the Current Questions of the International Communist Movement. The theses were put forward in the name of the CPSU delegation and were passed unanimously. Bordiga who was already at much variance with the Comintern tactics, had wanted to vote against them but he was not present when the vote was taken. The theses firmly vouched for the continuation of the united-front tactic. It said, "...now as before the Communist International is of the opinion that the united front tactic is but a method of conducting revolutionary agitation among the masses, mobilising them and winning the majority of the workers for the Communist

International..."[159] The theses also warned against the reformist tendencies that were trying to crush the working class movement[160]. On the whole they were in complete support for the Comintern line.

By April, however, Zinoviev's ideas had undergone a change. He entered headlong into a fight against the Stalinist line of action. There were two opposition lines in the CPSU by now. One was the old faction led by Trotsky, while a new faction under the leadership of Zinoviev and Kamenev also emerged. In fact Zinoviev, at this time, openly stated that his fight against the Trotskyist opposition had been a great mistake[161].

Jane Degras has said that by August-September, Stalin had begun to take drastic steps against them. She has commented, "... the campaign in the Russian and Comintern press against Trotsky, Zinoviev, Kamenev, and their supporters grew more bitter"[162]. Trotsky, on the other hand felt that despite the faults that were being committed by the communist parties of Poland and Great Britain, their members escaped without harm as they supported Stalin in the in the CPSU question. He felt that the CPSU too was becoming more and more dominant in the Comintern day by day, almost in fact suffocating opposing opinions. But Stalin refused to democratise the working of the Comintern. He considered the leading role of the CPSU in the Comintern to be a necessary step in the progress of the revolution.

On 25th October 1926, Zinoviev was removed from the post of the President of the Comintern. The ECCI resolution dismissing him from his post said:

> "Considering the anti-Leninist line of the opposition bloc in the CPSU, considering the leading part which comrade Zinoviev, as President of the Comintern, played in carrying out this incorrect line, considering the opposition bloc's disruptive fraction work, unprecedented in the history of the Bolshevik party, and considering the transference of these fractional machinations by comrade Zinoviev into the ranks of the Communist International, the ECCI delegation attending the joint plenum of the CC and the CCC of the CPSU, in accordance with the decisions of the most important sections of the Comintern, considers it impossible for comrade Zinoviev to remain and continue to work at the head of the Comintern"[163].

The expulsion of Zinoviev was not enough. As if to encourage collective leadership in the Comintern, the post itself was sought to be abolished in the Seventh Plenum of the ECCI. The ECCI was to meet thrice a year. The membership of the presidium was increased to 18 plus 7, which was to meet in Moscow fortnightly. Besides the organisational bureau was to be dissolved, to counteract the separatist tendencies that were developing. The report was adopted unanimously[164].

The Eighth Plenum of the ECCI put in a severe warning for Trotsky and Vuyovich as members of the ECCI. It is evident from the Resolution that the criticism of the policies of the Comintern had become much sharper during this time. Trotsky had condemned the leadership of the Comintern as a body of bourgeois-liberals, as being conservative and "spokesmen of the national bloc" and for pursuing a policy that was "shameful"[165]. The ECCI Resolution on the other hand, said, "The policy advanced by comrades Trotsky and Vuyovich at the present plenary ECCI session, and with which Zinoviev and Radek are in complete agreement, is in glaring, irreconcilable, and fundamental contradiction to Comintern policy as laid down by Lenin"[166].

Regarding the Trotskyist criticism of the nature of the Chinese revolution, the ECCI resolution said, "Their evaluation of the nature of the Chinese revolution is basically false, contradicting all Lenin's fundamental ideas on the tasks of the communists in a bourgeois-democratic revolution in backward semi-colonial countries". The resolution also said, "Comrade Trotsky tried in vain to screen his Menshevik attacks behind a veil of pseudo-radical left phrases, hypocritical assertions of his desire to submit to the resolutions adopted, and dishonest proposals to 'regulate the conflict' in order to conceal his desertion from the communist workers..."[167] The Comintern leadership also said that "... Precisely at this moment the Trotskyists fling accusations of treachery against the world party of communism, and charge the state of the proletarian revolution with degeneration. Objectively this attack of the Trotskyist opposition follows the same line as the attack of the bourgeoisie and their agents, designed to annihilate the decisive power centres of the proletarian world revolution..."[168] And after this harsh and detailed criticism of the Trotsky led opposition forces, Trotsky and Vuyovich were issued a warning. The resolution said:

"1. The ECCI observes that both the principles and the conduct of comrades Trotsky and Vuyovich are incompatible with their positions as member and candidate of the Executive Committee of the Communist International.

2. The ECCI categorically forbids comrades Trotsky and Vuyovich to continue their fractional struggle.

3. The Plenary session of the ECCI empowers the presidium of the ECCI, in agreement with the ICC, formally to exclude comrades Trotsky and Vuyovich from the ECCI if this struggle should not cease.

4. The ECCI proposes to the CC of the CPSU to take decisive steps to protect the CPSU from the fractional struggles of comrade Trotsky and Vuyovich."[169]

In a few months' time Trotsky and Vuyovich were formally expelled[170].

Now looking at all the incidents, from the expulsion of Zinoviev as the Comintern president to the expulsion of Trotsky and Vuyovich as ECCI members, it can be said that the opposing voices in the Comintern were sought to be choked, especially when they were against the Comintern policies that were increasingly being formulated by the Russian side in most non-democratic ways and the looming figure of the CPSU as the leader of the Comintern and its absolutist tendencies.

The question that arises here is about what it was that prompted Stalin to take such drastic action against the Trotskyist opposition. Kunal Chattopadhyay has summed it up quite appropriately. He has said:

> "In later years, particularly after the Chinese revolution changed the terms of the debate, Trotsky made it clear that he did not believe in the existence of any revolutionary bourgeoisie. He denounced the 'search' for a revolutionary national bourgeoisie as a hoax, a Menshevik strategy of running revolution to the ground. As we have seen, when he elaborated and extended the strategy of permanent revolution as a general theory of contemporary revolutions in backward countries, he did so precisely because in his eyes, there could exist no revolutionary, anti-imperialist (and anti-feudal) movement that was not led by the proletariat. In such a movement, he expected no significant role by any section of the bourgeoisie. Even before 1925, his line differed from that of Zinoviev etc. unlike them, he opposed the Chinese Communist Party's joining the Kuomintang..."[171]

This was the basic point of disagreement between Stalin and the Trotsky led opposition. And this was a point which negated the strategies that Stalin adopted for the colonies. Stalin used the "ambiguities in Lenin's formulation"[172] to show just how much he adhered to the principles of Lenin, and how much Trotsky did not. He used this argument as a pretext to depose Trotsky and his supporters.

By the beginning of 1928 most opposing members had been expelled and those who remained were too weak to make themselves heard. And in the Ninth Plenum of 15th February 1928, the ECCI was satisfied with its job of bringing into check all opposing voices.

"The ECCI plenum notes with satisfaction that the fifteenth congress of the CPSU has decisively put an end to Trotskyist opposition by placing it outside the party. The plenum expresses its complete solidarity with the decisions of the CPSU and with the measures taken by the Soviet organs to stop anti- Soviet activities of the opposition. The ECCI plenum believes that the decisions of the fifteenth congress are of utmost importance for the further strengthening of the proletarian dictatorship and the construction of socialism in the Soviet Union..."[173]

What emerges from this is not just the urge to smother opposition in the ECCI of the Comintern. Another deviation can be noted. There is the desire to deviate from the theory of internationalism as well. From this time on it began to be formulated that socialism could be established in one country. Stalin was the main perpetrator of this line of thought. Hence, what now became important was the need to secure some strong allies, who could be used as a guard against the increasing pressure from the west. He tried to mould China, an important eastern nation, in the clutches of imperialism, into one such ally. To Stalin's increasingly bureaucratic mind, making deals with the Chinese nationalist strongman seemed more practical than placing hopes in the revolutionary workers and peasants of China.

THE SIXTH CONGRESS

The Sixth Congress was held in Moscow from 17th July to 1st September 1928. Jane Degras mentions two records regarding the representation in this Congress. She says, "It was attended, according to one source, by 532 delegates of whom 347 had voting powers; according to another, by 575 delegates of whom 375 had voting powers... Fifty-eight parties were represented, six without voting powers"[174]. In India meanwhile the trade union movement had developed further. Workers and Peasants' parties also began to be formed in several parts of the country. The revolutionary spirit that had been crushed with the withdrawal of the Non-Co-operation movement, had, by now, risen once again and was influencing the fervour of the working masses. Among the Indian delegates, a new face emerged— that of Saumyendranath Tagore. He made a speech in the Sixth Congress in which he criticised the moves that the Comintern proposed in regard to the colonies[175].

The period immediately preceding the Sixth Congress saw a huge controversy over the question of "decolonisation". This theory was intended to show that the capitalist countries, which had been exploiting the masses of the colonies for a long time, changed their attitude after the war, especially towards countries like India. They were executing reform programmes that catered to the industrialisation of the colonies that promoted economic development, a fact that would culminate in the establishment of the socialist order. Otto Kuusinen perhaps used the term to identify the analyses of the cotemporary situation by the Indian communists. The word raised a controversy and began to be constantly used within quotes by the Indian communists, who were trying to explain their respective stands on the given question.

Kuusinen had admitted in October 1928 that the industrial development had proceeded rapidly in the preceding twenty years. At the same time he said:

"...But if even several communist comrades have been induced, on the strength of this fact, to assume that British policy is following an entirely new course in regard to the industrial development of India, I must say that they have gone too far... Some of these comrades went even the length of holding out the prospect of a decolonisation of India by British imperialism. This was a dangerous term. The comrades who have represented and partly still represent this—in my opinion— false theory are comrades who otherwise deal very seriously with the problems of our movement— comrades Palme-Dutt, Roy and Rathbone. A certain wrong conception made its appearance even in comrade Rajan's speech in the discussion of the first item on the agenda. I consider it my duty to elucidate this question. If it were really true that British imperialism has adopted the course of the industrialisation of India which leads to its decolonisation, we would have to revise our entire conception of the character of the imperial colonial policy. I think the facts show that this is not the case"[176].

Even earlier in the same year, G.A.K.Luhani had explained himself. He too had agreed that the post-war economic policy of the

British had undoubtedly increased the pace of industrialisation in India. But at the same time he had said, "The term is a misnomer, if it is taken to signify more than it is meant to signify. It is certainly not meant to signify the 'de-revolutionisation' of India. It does not certainly signify a permanent liquidation of the contradiction of interests between British imperialism and the social forces comprising the Indian population. Most emphatically, it does not signify the exclusion of India from the Asiatic revolution against imperialism. On the contrary, it signifies an enormous intensification of the proletarian masses of India in the latest capitalist forms in the big urban centres, and the expropriation of the vast peasant masses in the 'hinterland'..."[177] His idea was that the post war British policy of industrialisation, enhanced the social contradictions existing in India.

M.N.Roy's Draft Resolution on the Indian Question too is more or less based on the same idea[178]. In his theses "On the Indian Question in the Sixth World Congress", he however reacted very sharply to Kuusinen's comments. He accused Kuusinen of not having sufficient knowledge of the Indian conditions and that he was presenting a picture of India that was much older. He then said quite categorically:

"... British imperialism does not wish to lose an iota of power in India. This is the subjective factor which has very great significance; but it alone is not decisive. The objective factor, that is, what, in the given situation, is possible for the British bourgeoisie to do maintain their domination in India and the effects of what they do, reacts upon the subjective force. If the subjective were the decisive factor, there would never be a revolution for the ruling class would never want to abdicate its power"[179].

Roy further elaborated that the advancement of industrialisation of India was only a manifestation of the fact that there had been a weakening of the imperialist forces, which prompted them to change their earlier policies. But India still remained a British colony. "She will never cease to be a colony until the British power is overthrown by revolutionary means. No compromise (however far-reaching) between the Indian bourgeoisie and the British imperialists will give real freedom to the Indian people..."[180]

One can see that the evaluation of the contemporary situation in India by the Indians were being harshly criticised by the Comintern line. The practical experience factor, which had been so important in the formulation of policies during the Second Congress, was no longer to be seen. Even then there had been disparities, views had often crossed; but such a gross denunciation of the ideas of the native communists of the colonial countries had not been there. This new trend of making itself established with force, without discussion, and with the elimination of the opposing factors, can be considered as the background to the deliberations in the Sixth Congress.

On close examination of the Theses of the Agitprop of the ECCI, further details concerning the Stalinist line can be discerned. In Thesis 4 it was clearly outlined:

"... The Communist Manifesto was merely the programme of a handful of progressive individual workers of the period of the bourgeois revolution; the Communist Manifesto was only a grand scientific prophesy of the doom of capitalism. The programme of the CI constitutes the programme of the International Communist Party which is fighting in the period of social revolution, the programme of the party which has already one of its detachments engaged in carrying out the building of socialism".[181]

This is an indication that the principles formulated were not completely in tune with classical Marxist principles. This point becomes evident when in Thesis 8 there is a clear mention of the necessity to construct socialism in one country. It says:

"The programme bases the tasks of proletarian dictatorship upon ten years experience of the USSR... the programme points to the peaceful, planned building of socialism in the USSR, demonstrating to the oppressed mankind that it is possible and necessary to build socialism even in one country in which power has passed into the hands of the proletariat, and in which the dictatorship of the proletariat prevails".[182]

The Stalinist line that refuted the internationalist approach of classical communism can be clearly seen manifested here.

On the other hand, there was the increasing supremacy of the CPSU in the Comintern that had to be contended with. The Comintern had suddenly turned into an absolutist structure by itself. In the Programme of the Communist International adopted at its Sixth Congress, the intention is explored further. It becomes evident from this programme that the intention of the Communist International had now transformed dramatically. Whereas once it had been the champion of the interests of the working classes, it now became a propagator of the interests of the Soviet Union. The Soviet Union had been glorified for its achievements before going into the true motive. It said:

"The existence side by side of two economic systems— socialist in the Soviet Union and capitalist in other countries— imposes on the workers' State the task of warding off the attacks of the capitalist world(boycott, blockade etc.). at the same time it has to manoeuvre in the economic field and to make use of its economic connections with capitalist countries (with the aid of foreign-trade monopoly, one of the pre-requisites of successful socialist construction, and by means of credits, loans, concessions, etc.). The guiding line to be followed must be that of establishing as wide contacts as possible with foreign countries, but only in so far as they prove useful to the Soviet Union, i.e. help to strengthen Soviet industry by creating a basis of heavy industry, electrification, and finally for a socialist machine building industry. Only in so far as its economic independence of capitalist environment is made secure, can the Soviet Union withstand the danger that its socialist achievements will be destroyed and the country transformed into an appendage of the capitalist world system"[183].

It is only after this candid admission did the theses go into the details of how it would promote the revolutionary struggle of the toiling masses of the workers and peasants.

This was the basic deviation— one of guarding the national interests at the face of the collective interests of the Comintern. This deviation representing the Stalinist version had become quite prominent and it had begun influencing all the strategies of the Comintern. Opposition, as usual, was harshly put down or eliminated entirely. In order to fulfil these demands, the powers of the ECCI were increased manifold[184]. As a result, earlier ideas were greatly modified, often destroyed, to make place for the emergence of the Soviet Union as a looming figure in the Comintern, a guardian international communism with tremendous powers to override all opposition, where its own national interests were concerned.

A detailed set of theses, "Revolutionary movement in the Colonies and Semi-colonies", was presented at the Sixth Congress of the Communist International. It said in its introduction itself that the policies of the Second Congress as formulated by Lenin were still valid and that "they should serve as a guiding line for the further work of the Communist Parties"[185]. It said that there had been a rise in the mass movements in the colonies and semi-colonies, a fact that was beginning to pose a great danger for the imperialist powers. But despite these admissions, those which had also been made in earlier Congresses, the general tone of the theses cannot be said to be quite in keeping with that of the earlier ones.

The introductory section deals with the analysis of the contemporary international situation. It elaborated on the rising trend of nationalist movements in the colonies and semi-colonies in Asia, Africa and Latin America and their relationship with the imperialist powers. It highlighted the contradiction between the imperialist and subject countries and the role of the communists in bringing about the emancipation of the colonies and semi-colonies. It also mentioned the support that that was to be rendered to these movements by the proletariat of the U.S.S.R and the proletarian movement of the capitalist countries that were being led by the Communist International. This was criticised by Saumyendranath Tagore in the speech that he delivered at the Congress. He was of the opinion that despite the fact the Communist parties of India and England were closely tied up, yet, the idea of the British Communist Party leading that of India would tantamount to the "...subordination of the colonial party to the leadership of the imperialist home country..."[186] He also said that though the Indians welcomed the guidance of the Comintern, yet the only leadership acceptable to them was the "...leadership of the Communist International..."[187]

The second section was on "The Characteristic Features of Colonial Economics and of Imperial Policy"[188]. This section dealt with the nature of imperialism in the colonies. It said that the imperialists were instruments of oppression and exploitation of the colonies and semi-colonies, and that they were pursuing their objectives in the name of civilising the colonial and semi-colonial nations. It was said that despite the reform measures that were being introduced in the colonies for the improvement of the situation, were in actuality, unable to control the "devastating consequences everywhere brought about by capitalist development"[189].

Thesis 11 of the same section highlighted the parasitic nature of imperialism. It said that the imperialist nations were securing a twofold advantage from their colonies. On the one hand they were putting undue economic pressure on the colonies; while on the other hand, they were securing an "extra-economic" monopoly. This monopoly helped them to secure tremendous economic advantages along with other advantages like "the preservation and development of the conditions" of their "own existence" and the enslavement of the colonial masses. The same thesis said:

"... The profits obtained in the colonies are, for the most part, not expended productively, but are sucked out of the country and are invested either in the metropolis or in new spheres of expansion on the part of the imperialism concerned. Thus the fundamental tendency of colonial exploitation acts in the direction of hindering the development of productive forces in the colonies, of despoiling them of their natural riches, and, above all, exhausting the reserves of human productive forces in the colonial countries"[190].

Thesis 12 dealt mainly with the character of development that the colonies experienced with the coming of imperialism. It said:

"Inasmuch, however, as colonial exploitation presupposes a certain encouragement of the development of production in the colonies this development, thanks to the imperialist monopoly, is directed on such lines and accelerated only in such a degree as corresponds to the interests of the metropolis and, in particular, to the interests of the preservation of the colonial monopoly..."[191]

It also said:

"... Real industrialisation of the colonial country, in particular the building up of a flourishing engineering industry, which might make possible the independent development of the productive forces of the country, is not accelerated, but, on the contrary, is hindered by the metropolis. This is the essence of its function of colonial enslavement: the colonial country is compelled to sacrifice the interests of its independent development and to play the part of an economic (agrarian raw material) appendage to foreign capitalism, which, at the expense of the labouring classes of the colonial country, strengthens the political power of the imperialist bourgeoisie in order to perpetuate the monopoly of the latter in the colonies and to increased its expansion as compared with the rest of the world"[192].

Thesis 13 was about the impoverishment of the peasantry of the colonial and semi-colonial nations. It was said that the condition of the peasantry in the subject countries was deteriorating day by day under the control of the imperialist regimes.

"The pitiful attempts at carrying through agrarian reforms without damaging the colonial regime are intended to facilitate the radical conversion of semi-feudal land-ownership into capitalist landlordism, and in certain cases to establish a narrow stratum of kulak peasants. In practice, this only leads to an ever-increasing pauperisation of the overwhelming majority of the peasants, which again, in its turn, paralyses the development of the internal market. It is on the basis of these contradictory economic processes that the most important social forces of the colonial movement have their development"[193].

Thesis 14 too explored the exploiting nature of the imperial powers. It was mainly on the role of finance capital. After highlighting the fact that imported capital was used in the subject countries primarily for the "extraction and supply of raw material, or for the first stages of their utilisation", the thesis explained further, "Another basic feature in the mutual relations between the capitalist states and the colonial countries is the endeavour of various monopolist groups of finance capital to monopolise the whole external trade of the separate colonial and semi-colonial countries, and in this way to subordinate to their control and regulations all the channels which connect the colonial economy with the world market ..."

In Thesis 15, the last thesis of this section, the imperialist economic policy on the whole has been analysed. It said:

"The entire economic policy of imperialism in relation to the colonies is determined by its endeavour to preserve and increase their dependence, to deepen their exploitation and, as far as possible, to impede their independent development. Only under the pressure of special circumstances may the bourgeoisie of the imperialist states find themselves compelled to co-operate in the development of big industries in the colonies"[194].

This thesis was otherwise a mild critique of the decolonisation theory. It said:

"All the chatter of the imperialists and their lackeys about the policy of decolonisation being carried through by the imperialist Powers, about co-operation in 'the free development of the colonies, reveals itself as nothing but an imperialist lie. It must be of the utmost importance that the Communists, both in the imperialist and the colonial countries, should completely expose this lie"[195].

There is a controversy regarding the nature of industrial expansion in India during the post war years. There were two basic points of debate. One, whether industrialisation was on the rise and if so, whether it could be called an advancement in industrialisation at all; and second, whether this industrial policy of the British imperialists did actually lead to the subsequent decolonisation of India. Sobhanlal Dattagupta has gone into it in great details in both of his books[196]. In the book *Comintern, India and the Colonial Question 1920-1937*, he has depended primarily on Varga's statistics in analysing the contemporary conditions. To him the explanation rendered by Varga was much better than those made by contemporary Indian communists like Roy and British communists like Palme-Dutt. "However, a far more detailed and very sophisticated criticism of the 'industrial thesis' was put forward by Varga", he has said[197]. He has also gone into a detailed discussion on the debate that had ensued between Varga and Palme-Dutt, once again proclaiming that Varga's analysis was superior to that of the others.

Varga pointed out with statistics that the post-war period saw an increase in the agrarian population and a contrasting decline in that of the working class. This he said implied the agrarianisation of the working class for the lack of work[198]. S.Dattagupta feels that there was "a general regression of industry" in India—a fact that was responsible for the given statistics. He also feels that the new Colonial Theses "categorically rejected the new industrialisation thesis and, consequently, the theory of decolonisation"[199]. He himself is quite in agreement with the Comintern's dictates on this line[200].

In the book, *Comintern and the Destiny of Communism in India: 1919-1943*, S.Dattagupta has not gone into the details of the level of industrialisation that had occurred in India. He has however, made a thorough examination of the different viewpoints on the "decolonisation" issue that had emerged at that time.

The first point that ought to be mentioned is whether Roy should be judged in the context of his belief in benevolent imperialism, as propounded in imperialist historiography. It can be said here that Roy could never be labelled as a supporter of imperialist strategies at this stage. He has mentioned Kuusinen's evaluation of himself in his theses "On the Indian Question" several times and at the same time he has offered an explanation of his views as well. In all these discussions, Roy never once conferred support on the imperialist powers. What he wanted was a change in strategy of the Comintern regarding India and other colonies. He felt that the bourgeoisie had been almost completely won over by the imperial forces in India, and that they could never be trusted upon in future. Hence what was needed was a strong proletarian led mass movement against the imperialist order that would secure power for the working classes once and for all and help in the establishment of socialism[201]. S. Dattagupta has revised his earlier opinion here. He has quoted Roy and has clearly mentioned that Roy was never in support of the imperialist policies of the British in India[202].

Roy also felt that the exigencies of war had necessitated the British to evolve a new economic policy for India— one that was in keeping with the needs of the time. They were promoting industrialisation in India not because they wanted to "decolonise" India on the whole but that they had their own economic and political considerations in mind. This could be done by promoting the growth of Indian industries under their own surveillance, one that would yield results to sustain their own economic interests, harmed severely with the outbreak of the war. On the other hand the bourgeois class in India that had become more vociferous by time, needed to be stalled before they could resort to drastic steps. This too could be achieved through the promotion of industrialisation in India. On the other hand, this policy of the British to foster industrialisation marked in some ways the maturing of the proletariat, a fact that enhanced their role as leaders of the revolutionary movement for the establishment of socialism. Hence, the coalition between the communists and the native bourgeoisie was no longer necessary as the bourgeoisie had already been sold out to the imperialists and the time had come for the workers to assume independent leadership of the movement against the imperialists[203].

The next part of the debate is whether industrialisation had occurred at all in India in the given period, so as to be able to promote the advancement of the workers as leaders of the nationalist movement, now directed not only against imperialist forces but also their allies. Regarding this point S. Dattagupta has argued (once again on the basis of Varga's documents) that there had hardly been any industrialisation at all. Varga's statistics indicate that the working class population was falling rapidly, with the rise of agricultural population on the other hand. This signified shortage of work in the industries—a fact which denoted crisis in the industrial sphere[204]. It can be said at this point that Varga's statistics cannot be accepted as final. There are other statistics as well. Amiya Kumar Bagchi's records show that the labour population ratio was not that bleak[205]. But the discrepancies in the statistical observations are tremendous. Varga's records regarding the industrial population are over fifteen times that of Bagchi[206]. In the case of a universally accepted fact of India being primarily an agricultural country, with industries that could be considered nascent when compared to those of Europe, thirty-three million industrial population was certainly not that minuscule a population at all.

Another bunch of statistics has been provided by G.K. Shirokov. He has said that there was a rise in the number of small and middling industries. But at the same time the percentage of small industries in the total number of enterprises was only 11.1 in 1917, and rose to only 16.9 in 1929. He has also provided statistics on the working class population, those which tally somewhat with those of A.Bagchi's. He has mentioned in his table that the percentage of workers involved in small industries rose from 1% to only 1.9%[207]. Hence if statistics are to be given any consideration at all it becomes obvious that the industrial population in the 1920s had not shown any drastic fall, one that would suddenly impair the livelihood of the workers and consequently push them towards the countryside to pursue agriculture once again as their primary source income.

Meanwhile, the British had begun to offer protection to several industries like cotton, jute, sugarcane, iron and steel and so on. There was in fact a spurt of industries in the small and middling sectors. Several doubts remain unsettled in this sphere too, regarding the point whether true industrialisation was actually taking place under the tutelage of the British. It can be mentioned here that there had been advancement in the industrial sector, not only in those of cotton and jute, but in the iron and steel industry as well[208].

It is worth mentioning here that Saumyendrananth Tagore too had made certain comments on this issue, in the speech that he made at the Congress. Clearly disagreeing to the generalising tendency of the Comintern leadership, especially where the industrial development of the colonies was concerned, he said, "...I consider this formulation also not a very valid one. To lump together different countries at different levels of industrial development is methodologically wrong and illogical..."[209] Saumyendrananth Tagore was of the opinion that industrialisation had developed greatly though "...it was still inadequate for socialist construction..."[210] What Saumyendrananth felt was that each colony had attributes that were different from those of the others, except that all of them were being ruled by capitalist powers. Hence, each needed to be treated separately, and policies were to be made accordingly.

The third section is on "Communist Strategy in China and Similar Colonial Countries"[211]. The failure of the Chinese revolution must have raised quite a few questions regarding the role of the Comintern in China. It can be seen that from the Sixth Congress onwards there was continuous reference to the Chinese question during the deliberations in the Comintern. It appears that the Comintern was constantly trying to justify its manoeuvres in China. Besides, the Chinese experience began to taint all the policies that were being formulated regarding the colonies and the semi-colonies. This section dealt basically with the strategic questions regarding the progress of revolution in the colonies. It analysed the role of the bourgeois-democratic revolutions as well as the attitude of the national bourgeoisie. Here too, once again the role of the peasantry was given much importance. Thesis 17 said:

"Along with the national emancipatory struggle, the agrarian revolution constitutes the axis of the bourgeois democratic revolutions in the chief colonial countries. Consequently the Communists must follow with the greatest attention the development of the agrarian crisis and the intensification of class contradictions in the village, they must from the very beginning give a consciously-revolutionary direction to the dissatisfaction of the workers and to the incipient peasant movement, directing it against imperialist exploitation and bondage, as also against the yoke of various pre-capitalist (feudal and semi-feudal) relationships as a result of which peasant economy is suffering, disintegrating and perishing"[212].

This was more or less in tune with the attitude of the Second Congress.

Then there is the analysis of the character of the native bourgeoisie. It was said that the national bourgeoisie of the subject countries was not uniform in character. The trading bourgeoisie was always in support of the imperialist forces, while the rest, who were in support of the liberation movement, were also not consistent in their actions. Unlike China, said Thesis 18:

"In India and Egypt we still observe, for the time being, the typical bourgeois-nationalist movement—an opportunist movement, subject to great vacillations, balancing between imperialism and revolution"[213]. This tendency of the native bourgeoisie has been termed in the Thesis as "national reformism" as against "bourgeois-democratic", the term used in the Second Congress proceedings[214].

In Thesis 19, "Proletarian Leadership in Colonial Emancipation"[215], certain new ideas can be noted. It begins with the idea that improper evaluation of the nation-reformist tendency of the national bourgeoisie in the colonial countries gives rise to mistakes. It also said that insufficient attention had been given to the tasks that the Second Congress had laid down as the

"basic tasks of the Communist parties in the colonial countries, i.e. the task of struggle against the bourgeois-democratic movement inside the nation itself. Without this struggle, without the liberation of the toiling masses from the influence of the bourgeoisie and of national-reformism, the basic strategic aim of the Communist movement in the bourgeois-democratic revolution— the hegemony of the proletariat— cannot be achieved. Without the hegemony of the proletariat, an organic part of which is the leading role of the Communist Party, the bourgeois-democratic revolution cannot be carried through to an end, not to speak of the socialist revolution"[216].

This is something new. So long the most important task of the communists was to foster an alliance with the bourgeois-democratic movement, without merging with it totally, and preserving at the same time their own independent thoughts and ideas. The "liberation of the toiling masses from the bourgeoisie and of national reformism" was the basic aim undoubtedly. But it came only after the imperialists were overthrown. The basic aim until then was liberation from foreign imperialist control. In this thesis however, it has been clearly said that without the hegemony of the proletariat, even the bourgeois-democratic revolution could not be achieved.

This is corroborated by a point mentioned in Thesis 21. In this thesis, the labour movement in the colonial and semi-colonial countries has been divided into two phases— the first phase was between 1919 and 1923, and the second phase followed it. For the second phase it was said:

"The most important characteristic of the second period of rapid growth of the Labour movement in the colonies, on the other hand, the period which began after the Fifth Congress of the Communist International, was the emergence of the working class of the colonies into the political arena as an independent class force directly opposing itself to the national bourgeoisie, and entering upon a struggle with the latter in the defence of its own immediate class interests, and for the hegemony in the national revolution as a whole. The history of the last few years has clearly confirmed this characteristic of the new stage of the colonial revolution, first of all in the example of the Chinese revolution, and subsequently the insurrection in Indonesia. There is every ground to believe that in India the working class is liberating itself from the influence of the nationalist and social reformist leaders, and is being converted into an independent political factor in the struggle against British imperialists and the native bourgeoisie"[217].

This is a clear expression of Roy's thoughts as expressed in his theses in the Second Congress. He had been admonished by Lenin then. Even as late as the Fifth Congress, the strategy of the united-front with the bourgeoisie had been defended with vigour. The failure of the Non Co-operation movement, owing to its sudden and unforeseen withdrawal had occurred then. But when the nationalist bourgeois forces had once again geared up to oppose the British policies, and had forcefully boycotted the Simon Commission, the Comintern was speaking differently. Clearly, it was not just the developments in the colonies that were shaping the policies of the Comintern. The increasing authoritarianism of Stalin and his followers in the Comintern, a faction which refused to formulate any policy that would clash with the interests of the Soviet Union as a nation, had begun to gain grounds.

In Thesis 23, a danger regarding the leadership of the national movement has been cited. It has been said in the thesis that unless the faith of the toiling masses in the "bourgeois national-reformist leadership of the national movement" was shaken, it would begin to pose as a danger to the revolutionary cause. The bourgeois led nationalist movement has been severely criticised here.

"Consequently it is necessary, by means of correct Communist tactics, adapted to the conditions of the present stage to help the toiling masses in India, Egypt, Indonesia and such colonies to emancipate themselves from the influence of the bourgeois parties. This is not to be achieved by any noisy phrases, however radical they may sound superficially, about the absence of any distinction between the oppositional national-reformists (Swarajists, Wafdistys, etc.) and the British imperialists and their counterrevolutionary allies...."[218]

In the same thesis however, it has also been said:

"The masses see the chief immediate enemy of national emancipation in the form of the imperialist-feudal bloc, which in itself is correct at this stage of the movement in India, Egypt and Indonesia (as far as one side of the matter is concerned). In the struggle against the ruling counter-revolutionary force, the Indian, Egyptian, and Indonesian Communists must proceed in advance of all, they must fight more determinedly, more consistently and more resolutely than any petty-bourgeois section or national-revolutionary group. Of course, this fight must not be waged for the organisation of any kind of 'putsch' or premature attempt at rising on the part of the small revolutionary minority, but for the purpose of organising the widest possible strata of the masses of toilers in demonstrations and other manifestations so that in this way the active participation of these masses can be guaranteed for a victorious uprising at a further stage of the revolutionary struggle"[219]

Ambivalence can once again be traced here. Whereas in Thesis 19 and Thesis 21, it was argued that the hegemony of the proletariat was an utmost necessity even for the completion of the bourgeois-democratic revolution, Thesis 23 was against it for the time being.

.   Another piece of information that catches attention is the point within parenthesis in the second paragraph of the same thesis— "as far as one side of the matter is concerned". It has been mentioned in the context of the justification of the antagonism of the masses for the imperialist-feudal bloc. The question that arises is "Why should mass antagonism against the imperialist-feudal bloc be justified 'as far as one side of the matter is concerned'?" And if so, then which "side" does not quite justify it? If the Theses on the National and Colonial Question of the Second Congress are to be given any consideration, then it can be said that first part of the revolutionary process was against the imperialist-feudal bloc. So the question would be justified if the policies of the Second Congress were to be taken into account—a fact which had been harped upon at the very outset in the Revolutionary Movement in the Colonies and Semi-colonies. In that case what would the other side be— the side which did not justify? If the Chinese question is considered, then Chiang Kai shek's establishment of an area of control, and the support rendered to it by the Comintern, totally under the influence of Stalinist forces, would somewhat explain the matter. In such a case, the movement against the imperialist-feudal bloc need not be supported if a strong anti-nationalist camp could be formed, a camp that would loyally support the Soviet line. And Stalin was, at this time, actually looking for power bases that would strengthen the forces of Soviet Union as a nation. In doing so, the resources and the influence of the Comintern were also being used.

In the last paragraph of Thesis 23, it has been said that there was a necessity to reject all types of blocs that could be formed between the communists and the national-reformist opposition, to the extent that even temporary blocs were to be rejected. The Communist Party, it said, was to maintain complete political independence. This too was against the formulations of the Second Congress which had categorically supported temporary agreements between the communists and the nationalist forces. Another point that deserves mention here is that a certain amount of vagueness prevailed regarding the two stage theory of revolution, consisting of liberation by overthrowing the imperialist forces and then marching on towards the establishment of the dictatorship of the proletariat after defeating the native bourgeois elements that had arisen after the fall of the imperialists. The demarcating line between the two stages, so clearly pointed out by Lenin in the Second Congress; cannot be found in the theories of the Sixth Congress.

The last section of the theses on the Revolutionary Movement in the Colonies and Semi-colonies was about "The Immediate Tasks of the Communists"[220]. This portion dealt with the role of the imperialists and the necessity for their overthrow from the subject countries. It also analysed once again the vacillating role of the native bourgeoisie and the part that the communists were to play in such a situation. Apart from India, the problems of other colonies and semi-colonies have also been discussed separately in this section, though most of it had already been discussed in the earlier part.

The Second Congress as well as those following it had vouched strongly for the united-front strategy. A twofold stage of revolution had been visualised, where the first part would ensure the fall of the imperialists and attainment of liberation that were to be brought about by the coalition of the communist and bourgeois elements. The next stage would guarantee the fall of the native bourgeoisie, who would come to power after the achievement of liberation from the imperialists and would soon afterwards, for the preservation of their own economic interests, resist the assumption of power by the working masses. The completion of this stage would open the way for the establishment for the rule of the proletariat.

The Sixth Congress was rather vague on several prospects of this policy of revolution in the colonies and semi-colonies. For example, in the seventh thesis, Contradictions to Imperialism, it was said:

"The objective contradiction between the colonial policy of world imperialism and the independent development of colonial peoples is by no means done away with, neither in China, nor in India, nor in any other of the colonial and semi-colonial countries; on the contrary, the contradiction only becomes more acute and can be overcome only by the victorious struggle of the toiling masses in the colonies. Until this contradiction is overcome, it will continue to operate in every colony and semi-colony as one of the most powerful and objective factors making for revolution"[221].

The two stages of revolution have not been clearly demarcated in the theses.

Roy's theoretical position like several of his fellow Indian communist counterparts was thoroughly against the continuation of lending support to the bourgeois led nationalist movement. The Indian communists felt that industrialisation was on the rise in the post war period. Despite the fact that this was under the total control of the British, the working class was maturing and that it would soon be able to assume the role as the leaders of the revolution. They vouched for an early break with the bourgeois led nationalist movement. Stalinist views on the contrary, paid little or no importance to the rising proletariat in India. It either proposed the continuation of the earlier strategy of supporting the bourgeois led nationalist movement or hinted at the formation of an anti-nationalist bloc that would be controlled by the Soviet through the Comintern.

S.Dattagupta is of the opinion that this was an attempt at reconciliation of the two attitudes[222]. The Comintern ever since the Second Congress had never aimed at reconciliation. Lenin had strongly opposed what had appeared incorrect to him as long as he was alive. He had in the Second Congress, simply cancelled certain points made by Roy. But then he had also absorbed what he could learn from Roy's theses as well. In the Sixth Congress, it can be seen that the views of the native communists of India were simply shrugged off. The views of Soviet Russia were being pushed continuously from this time onwards. Stalin had by this time become very powerful and was continuously using the Comintern to air his own thoughts. It was not the reconciliation of views, but the establishment of a Soviet line of action that the Comintern was actually aiming at. Had it really wanted reconciliation, Roy would certainly not be dropped soon afterwards, a fact that cannot be ignored.

NOTES AND REFERENCES

1   G. Adhikari, *Documents of the History of the Communist Party of India*, Volume 1, New Delhi, 1972, p. 262.

2   Jane Degras, Extracts from an ECCI Circular on the Agenda of the Third Comintern Congress, May 1921, *The Communist*

International 1919-1943 Documents, Vol.1, 1919-1922, London, 1960, pp. 222-223.

3   Ibid. p. 223.

4   Ibid.

5   G.Adhikari, *Documents of the History of the Communist Party of India*, op.cit. pp. 262-267; Jane Degras, Extracts from an ECCI Circular on the Agenda of the Third Comintern Congress, May1921, *The Communist International 1919-1943 Documents*, Vol.1, 1919-1922, pp. 229-239.

6   V.I. Lenin, *Collected Works*, Volume 32, Moscow, 1977, pp.453-454.

7   Jane Degras, *The Communist International 1919-1943 Documents, Vol.1*, 1919-1922, p. 234.

8   Apart from a few changes in the words not much change can be noticed in the representation of the theses in Jane Degras, *The Communist International 1919-1943 Documents,.Vol.1*, 1919-1922, p. 234 Leon Trotsky, *The First Five Years of the Communist International*, Volume 1, New York, 1972, pp.250-251. The meaning too remains unaltered.

9   Kunal Chattopadhyay, *The Marxism of Leon Trotsky*, p.146.

10   Ibid.pp.150-151.

11   *Leon Trotsky Speaks*, p.202, Cited from Kunal Chattopadhyay, *The Marxism of Leon Trotsky*, p.151.

12   G.Adhikari, *Documents of the History of the Communist Party of India*, Vol.1, p. 265.

13   V.I. Lenin, *Collected Works*, Volume 32, op.cit. pp. 478-479.

14   Ibid. pp. 481-482.

15   Ibid. p. 470.

16   G.Adhikari, *Documents of the History of the Communist Party of India*, Vol.1, p. 264.

17   ane Degras, *The Communist International 1919-1943 Documents, Vol.1*, 1919-1922, p. 247.

18   Ibid. p. 249.

19   Ibid. pp. 281-285.

20   Ibid. p. 257.

21   V. I. Lenin, *Collected Works*, Vol.32, pp. 455-456.

22   Ibid. p. 487.

23   Ibid. p. 481.

24   Ibid. p. 485.

25   Ibid.

26   Ibid. p.460

27 Ibid. p. 495.
28 Sobhanlal Dattagupta, *Comintern, India and the Colonial Question*, Kolkata, 1980, p.51.
29 Purabi Roy, Sobhanlal Dattagupta and Hari Vasudevan ed. *Indo-Russian Relations 1917-1947*, Part 1, Kolkata, 1999.
30 Ibid. p. 125.
31 bid. p.116.
32 Ibid. p. 118.
33 Ibid. p. 120
34 Ibid. p. 121.
35 Ibid. p. 122.
36 Ibid. p. 124.
37 Ibid. p. 125.
38 Ibid.
39 Ibid. p. 130.
40 Ibid.
41 Ibid. p. 134.
42 Ibid.
43 Sobhanlal Dattagupta, *Comintern, India and the Colonial Question*, op.cit. p.53.
44 Ibid. pp. 134-135.
45 Ibid. p. 135.
46 G.Adhikari, *Documents of the History of the Communist Party of India*, Vol.1, op.cit. p. 266.
47 Jane Degras, *The Communist International 1919-1943 Documents, Vol.1*, 1919-1922, op.cit. p. 226.
48 Ibid. p. 227.
49 G.Adhikari, *Documents of the History of the Communist Party of India*, Vol.1, op.cit. pp. 266-267.
50 M.N.Roy, *Memoirs*, Bombay, 1964, p. 499.
51 Ibid. p. 510-516.
52 G.Adhikari, *Documents of the History of the Communist Party of India*, Vol.1, op.cit. p. 518.
53 Ibid. p. 519.
54 Ibid.
55 Ibid.
56 Ibid. p. 120.
57 Ibid.
58 V.I.Lenin, *Collected Works*, Vol.33, Moscow, 1973, p. 417.
59 Ibid.
60 Ibid, p. 420.

61   Ibid. p. 428.
62   Ibid. p. 430.
63   Ibid. p. 442.
64   G.Adhikari, *Documents of the History of the Communist Party of India*, Vol.1, op.cit. pp. 535-536.
65   Ibid. p. 536.
66   Ibid. p. 537.
67   Ibid.
68   Ibid. p. 538.
69   Ibid. p. 539.
70   Sobhanlal Dattagupta, *Comintern, India and the Colonial Question*, op.cit. p.53.
71   G.Adhikari, *Documents of the History of the Communist Party of India*, Vol.1, op.cit. p. 539.
72   Ibid. p. 540.
73   Ibid.
74   Ibid. pp. 540-541.
75   Ibid. p. 541.
76   Ibid. pp.542-543.
77   Ibid. p. 543.
78   Sobhanlal Dattagupta, *Comintern, India and the Colonial Question*, op.cit. pp. 53-54.
79   G.Adhikari, *Documents of the History of the Communist Party of India*, Vol.1, op.cit. p. 547.
80   Ibid. pp.547-548.
81   Ibid. p. 548.
82   Ibid. p. 549.
83   Ibid. p. 550
84   Ibid. p. 553.
85   Ibid. pp. 553-554.
86   Ibid. p. 555.
87   Ibid. p. 557.
88   Ibid.
89   Ibid. pp. 558-559.
90   Ibid. p. 56.
91   Ibid.
92   G.Adhikari, *Documents of the History of the Communist Party of India*, Vol.1, op.cit. p. 547.
93   Ibid. p. 555.
94   Ibid. p. 543.
95   Ibid. pp. 554-555.

96   Ibid. p. 540.
97   Ibid. p. 550.
98   Sobhanlal Dattagupta, *Comintern, India and the Colonial Question*, op.cit. p. 53.
99   Sobhanlal Dattagupta, *Comintern and the Destiny of Indian Communism: 1919-1943*, p.89.
100 India in Transition was co-authored with Abani Mukherjee
101 M.N.Roy, *India in Transition*, Bombay, 1971, p. 15.(The book was first published in Geneva in 1922)
102 Ibid. p. 21.
103 See Chapter 1, The Growth of the Bourgeoisie, M.N.Roy, *India in Transition*.
104 Ibid. p. 37.
105 Ibid. pp. 39-40.
106 Ibid. p. 72.
107 Ibid. p. 85.
108 Ibid. p. 87.
109 Ibid. p. 93.
110 Ibid. p. 94.
111 Ibid. pp. 105-106.
112 Ibid. p. 136.
113 Ibid.
114 Ibid.
115 Ibid. p. 140.
116 Ibid. p. 140.
117 Ibid. p. 142.
118 What Do We Want?" Geneva, 1922, p. 263.
119 Sobhanlal Dattagupta, *Comintern, India and the Colonial Question*, p. 62.
120 See Thesis 7 of the Supplementary Theses on the National and Colonial Question of the Second Congress, Adhikari, p.185, and the General Tasks of the Communist Parties in the East in The Theses on the Eastern Question of the Fourth Congress, Adhikari, pp. 554-556.
121 See Jane Degras, Extracts from an ECCI Circular on the Agenda of the Third Comintern Congress, May 1921, *The Communist International 1919-1943 Documents, Vol.2*, 1923-1928, p. 94. Also see G.Adhikari, *Documents of the History of the Communist Party of India, Vol.2*, p. 349.
122 G.Adhikari, *Documents of the History of the Communist Party of India*, Vol.2, p. 349.

123   Jane Degras, Extracts from an ECCI Circular on the Agenda of the Third Comintern Congress, May 1921, *The Communist International 1919-1943 Documents, Vol.2*, 1923-1928, p. 98.

124   Duncan Hallas, *The Comintern*, Bookmarks, London, 1985, p.106.

125   Ibid. p.107.

126   Jane Degras, Extracts from an ECCI Circular on the Agenda of the Third Comintern Congress, May 1921, *The Communist International 1919-1943 Documents, Vol.2*, 1923-1928p. 102.

127   See Jane Degras, Extracts from an ECCI Circular on the Agenda of the Third Comintern Congress, May 1921, *The Communist International 1919-1943 Documents, Vol.2*, 1923-1928, p. 106. Also see G.Adhikari, *Documents of the History of the Communist Party of India*, Vol.2, pp. 350-351.

128   Sobhanlal Dattagupta, *Comintern, India and the Colonial Question*, p. 70.

129   G.Adhikari, *Documents of the History of the Communist Party of India, Vol.2*, p. 353.

130   Ibid. Vol. 1. pp. 186, 188.

131   Ibid. Vol. 2. p. 358.

132   Ibid. pp. 358-359.

133   Ibid. p. 359.

134   Ibid. p. 360.

135   Ibid.

136   Ibid. pp. 361-362.

137   Ibid. p. 362.

138   Ibid. p. 363.

139   Ibid.

140   Ibid.

141   Ibid.

142   Ibid. p. 364.

143   Ibid. p. 353.

144   Sobhanlal Dattagupta, *Comintern, India and the Colonial Question*, pp. 66- 68.

145   Shashi Joshi, *Struggle for Hegemony in India 1920-1947, Vol.1*, New Delhi, 1992, p.45.

146   Ibid. p.60.

147   Ibid. p.52.

148   Purabi Roy, Sobhanlal Dattagupta and Hari Vasudevan ed. *Indo-Russian Relations 1917-1947, Part 1*, p.183

149   Ibid. pp.183-184.

150   Ibid. p.191-192.

151 G.Adhikari, *Documents of the History of the Communist Party of India, Vol.1*, p.185.

152 Ibid.

153 Purabi Roy, Sobhanlal Dattagupta and Hari Vasudevan ed. *Indo-Russian Relations 1917-1947, Part 1*, p.192.

154 Ibid.

155 Ibid. p.193.

156 Sobhanlal Dattagupta, *Comintern and the Destiny of Communism in India: 1919-1943*, Kolkata, 2006, pp.118-114.

157 Ibid. p.113.

158 Ibid.

159 Jane Degras, *The Communist International 1919-1943 Documents, Vol.2, 1923-1928*, p. 253.

160 Ibid. p. 256.

161 Ibid. p. 308.

162 Ibid. p. 309.

163 Ibid. p. 310.

164 Ibid. p. 319.

165 Ibid. p. 374.

166 Ibid.

167 Ibid. p.376.

168 Ibid.

169 Ibid. p. 377.

170 Extracts from a Decision of the ECCI Presidium and the ICC expelling Trotsky and Vuyovich from the ECCI, ibid. pp. 403-407.

171 Kunal Chattopadyay, The Marxism of Leon Trotsky, pp. 449-450.

172 Ibid. p.146.

173 Extracts from the Resolution of the Ninth ECCI Plenum on the Trotsky Opposition, Ibid. p.425.

174 The Sixth Congress of the Communist International, ibid. p. 446.

175 Saumendrananth Tagore, The Nature of the Social Revolution in the Colonial Countries, *Against the Stream*, New Delhi, 1977.

176 The Revolutionary Movement in the Colonies by Otto Kuusinen, G.Adhikari, *Documents of the History of the Communist Party of India*, Vol.3C, op.cit. p. 477.

177 G.A.K.Luhani, Developments in the Political Situation of India, Ibid. p. 512.

178 G. Adhikari, *Documents of the History of the Communist Party of India* Vol. 3C, pp. 572-606.

179 Ibid. p. 632.

180 Ibid.

181   Ibid. p. 609.
182   Ibid. p. 612.
183   Jane Degras, *The Communist International 1919-1943 Documents,* *Vol.2,* 1923-1928, p. 512.
184   See Statutes of the Communist International Adopted at the Sixth Congress, Ibid. pp. 464-471.
185   Revolutionary Movement in the Colonies and Semi-colonies, People's Publishing House, p.1.
186   Saumendrananth Tagore, The Nature of the Social Revolution in the Colonial Countries, *Against the Stream,* p.2.
187   Revolutionary Movement in the Colonies and Semi-colonies, People's Publishing House, Ibid.
188   Ibid. p. 10.
189   Ibid.
190   Ibid. pp.13-14.
191   Ibid. p. 14.
192   Ibid. p. 15.
193   Ibid. p. 18.
194   Ibid. p. 20.
195   Ibid. p. 21.
196   Sobhanlal Dattagupta, *Comintern, India and the Colonial Question1920-1937,* Calcutta, 1980, *Comintern and the Destiny of Communism in India: 1919-1943,* Kolkata, 2006
197   Sobhanlal Dattagupta, *Comintern, India and the Colonial Question,* p. 81.
198   Ibid. p. 74.
199   Ibid. p. 153.
200   "Decolonisation, therefore, was a very real issue. The Comintern's criticism of this theory was directed towards a reaffirmation of the Marxist position that the that the idea of the industrialization of the colonies under imperialism is a myth. The rebuttal of this theory was particularly important because objectively the advocates of industrialization thesis were lending support to the typical imperialist historiographical literature which preaches the very myth of industrialization of British India under the 'benevolent' supervision of imperialism. This should be particularly emphasized because attempts are made by some scholars in admiration for Roy and crude intolerance of Marxism to pass off the Comintern's criticism of Roy's position as purely a reflection of what they call a Russian distortion of the whole issue, or a kind of mysterious 'Stalinist intrigue', which they suggest led ultimately to Roy's

expulsion; in other words, the import of these interpretations is the refusal to admit the crucial theoretical importance of the stand taken by the Comintern on the decolonization question, and appreciate the importance of the discussion in relation to a Marxist understanding of the colonial question ". Ibid. p.156.

201 "On the Indian Question" G.Adhikari, *Documents of the History of the Communist Party of India*, Vol.3 C, pp.630-671.

202 Sobhanlal Dattagupta, *Comintern and the Destiny of Communism in India: 1919-1945*, Kolkata, 2006, p133-134.

203 See "Draft Resolution on the Indian Question" ,"On the Indian Question", G.Adhikari, *Documents of the History of the Communist Party of India*, Vol.3 C, and M.N.Roy, *The Future Results of the British Rule in India*, London, 1926.

204 Sobhanlal Dattagupta, *Comintern, India and the Colonial Question*, p.74.

205 Whereas Amiya Bagchi's statistics show the population of 1921 as 306 million, those of Varga's show 316 million. Whereas A. Bagchi's statistics show the employment in the industrial sector in the same year as 2,681,125, those of Varga's show 33 million. This population had decreased in comparison with his statistics of 1911, whereas in Bagchi's records it had increased somewhat.

206 Industrial Population of India as estimated by Varga and Bagchi.

Year	1921	1911
Varga	33000000	11300000
Bagchi	2681125	2105824

See E. Varga, *Economics and Economic policy in the Second Quarter of 1925*, Inprecor, 5(66), 26 August 1925, pp. 76-78 as quoted in Sobhanlal Dattagupta Comintern, India and the Colonial Question, *op.cit, and Amiya Kumar Bagchi,* Private Investment in India 1900-1939,*New Delhi, 1980, p,122.*

207 G.I.Shirokov, *Industrialisation of India*, New Delhi, 1980, p.19.

208 See Amiya Kumar Bagchi, *Private Investment in India 1900-1939*, Rajat Kanta Ray ed., *Entrepreneurship and Industry in India 1800-1947*, New Delhi, 1992 and A.I.Levkovsky, *Capitalism in India: basic trends in its development*

209 Saumendrananth Tagore, The Nature of the Social Revolution in the Colonial Countries, *Against the Stream*, p.2.

210 Ibid.

211 Revolutionary Movement in the Colonies and Semi-colonies, People's Publishing House, Ibid. p. 22.

212 Ibid. p. 24.

213   Ibid. p. 25.

214   Ibid.

215   Ibid. p. 27.

216   Ibid. p. 28.

217   Ibid. pp. 31-32.

218   Ibid. p. 34.

219   Ibid. pp.34-35.

220   Ibid. p. 44.

221   Ibid. p. 7.

222   "Thus in a report on India released by the Comintern one cannot afford to miss the rather unsuccessful attempt to reconcile the two trends", Sobhanlal Dattagupta, *Comintern, India and the Colonial Question*, op.cit. p.89.

THE ORIGINS OF COMMUNISM IN INDIA

It has been established in the previous chapter that the Indian communists had become quite active during the twenties of the previous century. They had come into contact with the Communist International and had begun to formulate theories of their own as well. With these theories they expected to cater to the objective conditions prevalent in India and bring about the much wanted liberation of the Indian masses not only from their colonial masters but also from the native exploiting classes. But the question as to who these communists were, and how they came to embrace communism especially in the absence of any previous foundational work done by earlier theorists has to be analysed. Unlike Europe, socialist theories had not made any headway in India and in other countries of Asia prior to the First World War. Socialist influence began to be felt only after the Bolshevik Revolution of Russia in 1917, when India was already in the throes of its nationalist movement. In fact, it was from here that the communist movement emerged.

In order to analyse the emergence of communism in India the immediate political background has to be seen. After coming to India in 1915, Gandhi had become quite active in the political sphere. He involved the masses in his struggle against the British. His system of struggle was through satyagraha, a non-violent struggle. Yet it had managed to procure much of his demands from the British. He had attracted several people to this new movement all over India. By 1919 the Khilafat movement[1] had begun. By 1920, Gandhi called upon the Indians to join the Khilafat movement through the Non-Cooperation movement. On the other hand, the Bolshevik Revolution had occurred in 1917 and the Communist International had been established in 1919. In 1920, the Communist International was holding its Second Congress and India was in the midst of the Khilafat- Non Co-operation movement. The Comintern was advocating the cause of the colonies as elements of imperial oppression, whereas the nationalists were busy tracking down communal harmony for protesting against British strategies. When the Comintern was campaigning for the cause of freedom from exploitation, both imperial and native, the nationalist leaders were fighting against British policies. By 1921, the Khilafat movement had waned[2], and soon afterwards, when the Non-Cooperation movement was in its full swing, Gandhi suddenly withdrew the movement after the Chauri-Chaura incident[3]. This shocked several nationalist leaders. They felt that the spontaneity of the Chauri-Chaura incident had been deliberately ignored. Those believing in nationalism of the militant type of the Tilak kind were thoroughly disillusioned. In fact, the compromising nature of Gandhi's movement had already frustrated several of them, and now some more joined the fray. Many of them started searching for a new alternative to the Gandhi led nationalist movement. The Russian Revolution had occurred, bringing in new hopes and aspirations for the exploited masses. It began to attract these disgruntled nationalists towards communism.

The implications of the Russian Revolution were tremendous. When the colonial masses were being exposed constantly to intense exploitation both from the imperial and native overlords, the idea of a state which was free from exploitation and inequality, turned into a dream that had to be pursued at all costs. Young impressionable minds became attracted to communism, as it offered more than what they had ever thought of.

The most outstanding among the emerging communists of India was Manabendranath Roy. He was the first to engage attention of the Russian communists towards the Indian situation. The famous Lenin-Roy debate at the Second Congress of the Comintern shows clearly that he had begun formulating on his own, and his formulations depended much more upon his own experiences than upon the theories and dictates of the Comintern. He too began as a nationalist fighting for freedom from British rule before he actually turned into a communist. Hence the concept of attaching primary importance to freedom from imperialist rule as the key to the solution of Indian problems stems from here.

Roy was born in a small village, Urbalia, in the 24 Parganas district of Bengal. Born to a Bhrahmin family, he had been named Narendranath Bhattacharya, one which he changed to

Manabendranath Roy in course of time. However, this adopted name remained with him till his end and even afterwards. He is hardly ever referred to with his original name.

Roy joined the revolutionary movement in Bengal when he was in his early teens and still in school. This was at a time when the First World War had already started. Soon afterwards, he was entrusted with the task of procuring arms from the Germans, which they were supposed to deliver at the Dutch East Indies. He said in his *Memoirs* that it was his "…first trip out of the country. I returned within two months, with some money, not much; but as regards arms, the coveted cargo of the Golden Fleece— it was a wild goose chase."[4] This did not however put an end to the hopes of the Indian revolutionaries. They planned again with the Germans for their help, and Roy was once again sent abroad for the purpose. This time too, the plan failed. Roy then went to Japan and then to China, where he was arrested by the British police. However, he was soon set free because of lack of evidence. It was after this that Roy left for America. Here he adopted his new name and began to work anew. Here he also met and married his first wife Evelyn Trent, who played a very important role in shaping the future ideas of Roy[5].

Roy himself said, "I had come to America as an emissary of 'revolutionary nationalism' actually in alliance with Germany in the fight against British Imperialism"[6]. Moreover, it was perhaps here, in America, that Roy first began to critically analyse the policies and prospects of the Indian nationalist movement. In fact, he was still in search for German help in organising an insurrection in India. His *Memoirs* say clearly that he "…wanted to go to Germany in quest for help for raising an army to liberate India" and that he was "frustrated" and "disappointed" as things had not worked well in those directions[7]. He said that it was his experiences in America that helped him to turn back "…upon a futile past, futile because it was narrow-visioned, and to peer, still hesitatingly, into the unknown future of a new life which happened to be full of worthwhile adventures, rich experiences and ultimately disappointments also. It was the beginning of an exciting journey in a new world."[8]

While staying in New York, Roy had made the acquaintance of Lala Lajpat Rai. He often went to listen to his talks. At the end of one of these talks Lala Lajpat Rai was asked by a listener whether it would make any difference to the Indian masses if the exploitation of the foreign imperialists was replaced by that of the Indian capitalists. According to Roy's *Memoirs*, Lajpat Rai had answered that it did indeed make a difference in being kicked by one's own brother on the one hand, and foreigners on the other. This answer, Roy said, made him rather "uncomfortable". He also said:

"... there was something wrong in our case. Suddenly a light flashed through my mind; it was a new light.

I left the hall alone, still quite confused in my mind, but vaguely visualising a different picture of freedom. Keeping away from Lalaji and other friends, I frequented the New York Public Library to read the works of Karl Marx and discovered a new meaning in them. It was not long before I accepted Socialism, except its materialist philosophy. That was my last ditch, which I defended still for quite a long time"[9].

If this quote from Roy's *Memoirs* is given any consideration, it can be said that it was like this for almost all the early Indian communists. They all began by hating the British for their imperialist hold over India. They wanted to free India from the clutches of British imperialism. This was their primary aim. They felt that this would put an end to the miseries of the Indian masses. The notion of exploitation by the native feudal elements was not present in their earlier formulations. Nor were they aware of any danger that could be posed by the emerging native bourgeoisie, in the absence of their foreign counterparts. Very few actually read Marxist literature before they began to feel the first doubts about the existing system of struggle. It was almost always some person influencing the other, or some dramatic experience, like Roy's that set them thinking otherwise. Unfortunately all these persons are now dead, and the actual stories, in their true forms, cannot be totally unfolded. This is mainly because these early communists censored their own works of emotions that they had once felt. It can only be assumed therefore, as to what it was, that influenced these young radical minds.

Roy's political connections and inclinations had brought him more than once into confrontation with the police in the United States. But he managed to escape. He went to Mexico after the war broke out in America. It was in Mexico that Roy's future theories began to concretise. Roy's early literary works clearly reveal his nationalist bent of mind. In his *The Way to Durable Peace*, he highlighted the evils of British colonisation of India in all spheres of life, among which, he has specifically mentioned economy, education and public health.[10] He defended the cause of Indian revolutionaries who were seeking German help with the intention to oust the British. He clearly spelt out that the American policy of denouncing the Indian struggle for freedom as sedition and rebellion was a misconception on the part of the Americans and that their "…hatred of the enemy (Germans) had clouded the clarity of your (America's) vision".[11] Roy also claimed in the Letter that there had indeed been no benevolence on the part of the British while they were colonising India on the pretext of carrying on a civilising mission in the colonies. He said, "… we might clarify that the Indian people have not in any way been benefited by the English administration; on the contrary, her progress has been aimed at making them recede"[12]. The entire essay is based on the notion that liberty of the colonies from imperialist stronghold was the answer to all problems. The emphasis on liberty is tremendous, so much so that the American concept of human liberty has been constantly cited in defence. In fact, the essay betrays a longing for acquisition of American support as well. In the last section of the essay it has been said:

"We have indicated to you, through the preceding lines, the few historic facts, that, we suppose, are already well known to your Excellency, with the object of calling your attention to a place where exists and flourishes 'the organised abuse' that ought to be eliminated, if your intention to promise and establish real and lasting peace in the world was to be fulfilled sincerely and effectively. Because it is not in Europe, but in the weak people of Asia and Africa, where the germs of modern wars are incubated by the imperialistic greed of the European nations, whose fighting and insatiable ambition, very often throws the world into convulsions so horrendous, causing many innocent people to suffer, in order to bring about these catastrophes. The panacea that can only rip out from its root, the innumerable wrongs of these wars, is the complete liberation of all countries and subjected people, not only in Europe, but also in Asia and Africa. Therefore, our desires towards the end of making India independent, not only propose to win for one fifth of the world population their freedom,— that is, without any doubt, an inherent birth right— but they are also destined to prepare the road by which, some day, all Mankind will be able to travel toward the sole goal of Peace and Brotherhood…"[13]

This quote sums up the feeling of Roy during this time. What is interesting is that the desired goal was still not equality or end of exploitation or the capture of power by the workers and peasants. It was still "Peace and Brotherhood"— understandable because Roy was still not yet a communist.

Roy's *India: Her Past, Present and Future* was published in Mexico in 1918.[14] This book is also a representation of Roy's nationalism. The book first deals with the past Indian heritage, then it analyses how this rich heritage was tarnished by the coming of the British, and then it suggests how India would ultimately liberate and emancipate herself. The book highlights in detail the conditions that existed before the British came and then it points out by comparing both situations, how the situation worsened manifold after the British set foot in India. In doing so, the past has been highly glorified. For example, he commented that:

"...Together with their religion, philosophy and literature, the Hindus formulated a well-defined social system at least 1,500 years before Christ. This system contained many of the principles of modern socialism, such as the concept of state and government elected by the people. By about 2000 B.C. the whole country was united in the kingdom of the Hindu emperor Yudhishthira."[15]

The book also says that Indian trade too was very prosperous in the ancient times.

After establishing the fact that India's ancient past was one to be cherished for its glory and efflorescence, Roy went on to analyse that the British had brought much harm to the Indian society and economy. Thousands were impoverished beyond hope. Famines became a regular feature thereby dooming the already impoverished even further. Indigenous industries were ruined and British goods replaced the local ones. A huge amount of money was constantly drained out to Britain, a fact which made matters worse. This money was used, Roy pointed out, to maintain a huge army and other expenses of the British. It did not in any way serve Indian interests. Coupled with this the British held the Indians at a very low esteem and unchecked racial discrimination prevailed[16].

Roy said, "Indians are traditionally peaceful"[17]. They incorporated various alien cultures if the need arose and "In their long history of political power and economic prosperity, they did not once conquer and oppress other nations".[18] His language while describing the intentions of the European colonisers speaks volumes about his feelings that were so overtly inspired by nationalism at this time. He said that the "fertility of the earth and the dexterity of the people" left them with a bounty which could satisfy their needs and provide them with enough leisure to pursue spiritual, intellectual and moral matters. However, when British imperialism, "… obeying its national instinct, brought cruel devastation which threatened to destroy the traditional socio-economic structure of peaceful India, the people found themselves, for the first time in their lives, forced to concentrate all their energy on the political condition of their country"[19]. They began to organise with the hope of overthrowing the British from India.

The British tried to curb the nationalist movement in every possible way. But it could not quite crush the movement altogether. The last chapter, "The Future" is an elaboration on the theme of how the reform programmes of the British were futile in satisfying the revolutionary Indians in the long run and that India's independence, despite British manoeuvres was inevitable. What is amiss here, if Roy's later works are brought into comparison, is a concrete programme of the struggle that he had envisaged. For instance, Roy said:

"… Nevertheless, India will be free sooner or later, not through the kindness of English rulers, but though her own energy. India is destined to play a prominent role in the future of humanity. No one will be able to prevent the successful and dignified carrying out of her duty in time to come. Unfortunately to achieve this goal, India will have to go against the teachings of the prophets and temporarily the glorious tradition of her history. A war for true liberty will have to be initiated. The aim of this conflict will be the final termination of the arrogant rule of one part of humanity over another; an incredible belief that one part is essentially inferior to the other, which has the right to impose its guidance and rule in the name of civilisation…"[20]

Certain terms and expressions in this excerpt are very significant. "True liberty", "termination of one part of humanity over another" do express a certain influence, very different from nationalism, yet perhaps betraying at the same time, an incompleteness of perception. Roy's reading of Marxist works, his association with the socialists (he had been a member of the Mexican Socialist Party) were beginning to show in his thoughts. However, it was perhaps only the beginning and concretisation of these thoughts were still a far way off. It was not before the Second Congress of the Comintern that Roy could actually express his thoughts as a communist. Samaren Roy has said that this work "…is more concerned with denying the spirituality of India and emphasising the British exploitation of India than with postulating a thesis on class war..."[21]

In August 1919 Roy wrote an article, "Hunger and Revolution in India"[22]. This article too was an exposition of the nature of British exploitation of Indian resources and the ensuing calamitous consequences. It also said that the nationalist struggle against the British had begun and that the British were using repressive measures to curb its progress. Nevertheless what Roy has said towards the end of the article is very interesting. It was written in italics for emphasis. Roy said:

"...They (British), and the rest of the world have still to learn that *the struggle for Indian independence is not a local affair, having for its end and purpose the creation of another egoistic nationalism; the liberty of the Indian people is a factor in world politics, for India is the keystone of imperialism which constitutes the greatest and most powerful enemy of the Social and Economic Revolution that exists today...*"[23]

In the very next paragraph it was said:

"And English capital is more than mere English capital— it represents at once the epitome and bulwark of the capitalistic system throughout the world. Seen in this light, it becomes self-evident that the liberation of India is more than a mere act of abstract justice; it signifies a long step towards the redemption of the world from the jaws of the capitalistic system..."[24]

These two excerpts show clearly that they bore the seeds of Roy's future formulations. The idea that British capitalism was primarily dependent on its colonies was developed further in the Second Congress. That India was the most important of all those colonies, and that its liberation would tantamount to the collapse of British imperialism was another notion that was elaborated upon later. Moreover, the concept of "Social and Economic Revolution" was being introduced for the first time. It is clear that Roy had begun thinking on the lines of capitalism, imperialism and their relationship with the colonies, their relationship with the nationalist movements operating in the colonies, those which he has termed "Social and Economic Revolutions". It can also be said that India's place and the role that it was supposed to play in the international scenario was also being given a thought for the first time.

Despite the fact that new ideas had begun to creep into Roy's theories, the element of vagueness was still very strong. Marxist influence though evident, was yet to be assigned a proper role in his theoretical deliberations. The role of the proletariat and the peasantry was still being totally ignored. The concept of the bourgeoisie, both foreign and native, was also missing. Only the communist spirit can be discerned, that too at a very preliminary stage. It was more of a socialist influence that marked the thoughts of Roy during this time. A clear representation of his communist principles cannot be traced before the Second Congress of the Comintern. Samaren Roy has said that "...the proletariat was small when he left India, and he had hardly any acquaintance with it. One of the exaggerations of his early Marxist study was to think of Indian liberation in terms of simultaneous liberation of the workers and peasants. This might have been provoked by his American experience but was largely built on his later reading of Marxist texts."[25] When Roy came to Moscow, communism had already made deep imprints on him. But his communist ideas were still not totally free from his initial influence of nationalism, a fact that kept appearing frequently in his future ideas for quite some time to come.

Another nationalist turned communist was Dange. He too had been attracted by the prospects of the Russian Revolution, and had begun to educate himself in the doctrines of communism immediately after his disillusionment with the Non-Cooperation movement. Shripat Amrit Dange was born in 1899. His mother died when he was still very young. He spent his childhood among the railway workers in Nasik at the Nasik Railway Station village[26]. A few years later his family moved on to Bombay from where he passed his Matriculation examinations in 1917 and started his political life as a nationalist and follower of Tilak. Tilak however, died in 1920 and Dange joined the Non-Cooperation movement soon afterwards under the leadership of Gandhi. But, from the very beginning, he could not quite accustom himself to the Gandhian way of thinking and differences began to emerge. He became critical of Gandhi and in 1921 he brought out his book, *Gandhi vs. Lenin* and soon afterwards started his paper, *The Socialist*, in which he began to write regularly. Dange later on became one of the main communist leaders in western India.

Dange's early works are clear reflections of his feelings of that time. That he had lost total faith in Gandhi, and that communist ideas were having a deep influence on him becomes very evident through these works. Although *Gandhi vs. Lenin* is influenced more by radical nationalist ideas[27] than by Marxist economic ideas, yet it was full of new ideas regarding the contemporary problems and the solutions that had been envisaged for them[28]. The book had tremendous appeal for the younger group of radical nationalists, especially those who were dissatisfied with the Gandhian means of struggle. In fact, many communists later admitted that *Gandhi vs. Lenin* and Dange's *The Socialist* had been a major source of inspiration for them, and had encouraged them to adopt communism as the only means of struggle for the future. He expressed in this book his dislike for the Gandhian attitude of attacking the modern industrial civilisation as the root of all discontent and upholding the earlier economic structure as the answer to it. He also felt that there was over-emphasis on moral reform and extreme faith in the goodness of human nature. Besides, its system of political struggle was, according to Dange, rather weak in nature[29]. But on the other hand, like Gandhi and other nationalists of the time, Dange did advocate the need for liberty from foreign yoke. "...We are convinced of the necessity of freedom..."[30] he said. He even highlighted the way it could be achieved. He felt that the British could be ousted only when the army refused to co-operate, when taxes were not paid, and when the workers and the peasants resorted to mass action[31]. It can be noted that he could not quite totally reject the nationalist ideas to which he had originally been initiated to.

Dange's writings in *The Socialist* show undoubtedly that he was not just thinking in terms of national liberation from the imperialist yoke, but that he wanted the freedom of the masses from exploitation of all forms, foreign or native. Dange shunned all early texts that advocated contentment with the existing situation. He felt that contentment was the tool the rich used in order to stall the discontented from rebelling. He said:

"But why do not men get up and ask, 'Why do ye hammer out always the song of contentment? Does it not show that ye are afraid, that if we be discontented, we will snatch at something that will remove our misery and bring it down on the head of another, who feeds on the sweat of our brow? To hell with your philosophy, the creation of our oppressors' brain...'"[32]

This shows that Communist ideas were indeed having a deep influence on Dange.

Dange also said that the masses could not be united in terms of freedom from foreign rule; they had to be educated in terms of freedom from exploitation. As early as August 1922, he was saying, "The foreigner is the cause but not the only cause. No foreigner rules England, no foreigner rules America, France and the so called 'free nations'. Yet the same plaintive cry is heard there too. The people there too are not happy. So we say the foreigner is not the only cause"[33]. In the same editorial he said that the success of the movement would not come unless the masses were incorporated into it. He therefore wrote:

"We set to work. We had programmes and programmes. We went even to the length of civil disobedience but hastily hurried back. We thought we were fulfilling God's wish in the retreat, while we only aided the Devil, who chuckled. We did not succeed, and now we are dull and deadened.

"The truth is that we had not reached the real people, while we deluded ourselves with the belief that we had convinced the masses of our needs. But we had convinced only a few classes."[34]

This clearly reveals that the dual scale of exploitation that was in operation in the colonies under imperialist domination had been comprehended by Dange at this stage, hence expressing in the process, an inclination towards similar thoughts that were being vigorously explored in the Communist International, ever since its Second Congress in 1920. The strategy of mass involvement in the struggle against exploitation was another idea that was being systematically propagated by the Comintern at this time. Dange was undoubtedly imbibing these ideas.

Dange also said:

"In swaraj and out of swaraj, it is the same to them. The peasant toiling today is not the master of his corn. He sees no government. He knows his landlord and his moneylender, who rob him of his fruits. Them he hears crying for Liberty, and the peasant only sighs at the irony of it! Liberty to rack-rent him the more! The worker bears the patriot of huge donations, vigorously appealing to do away with the oppression of poor India and next day finds the patriot mill-owner kicking him for short work or sickness.

"With nothing to offer the toiling masses we cannot move forth.

"The peasant worker must have land to himself. The worker must own that with which to work...The real people of India shall own the land, capital and instruments of production. Then alone will the people fight for swaraj and win it, quite a different kind of swaraj from the bourgeois raj"[35].

Coming not long after the withdrawal of the Non-Cooperation movement, this was quite an outburst. Not only did it demonstrate his lack of faith in the Gandhian way, it also displayed Dange's attitude regarding the bourgeois led nationalist movement in India. It is worth mentioning here that it was not very long ago that Dange had written in his *Gandhi vs. Lenin*, that in order to end the miseries of the workers and the peasants, "...We cannot accept the communist plan, in all details, because it is too much fraught with coercion and violence..."[36] When radical nationalists were turning communists, their theories too underwent an evolution from nationalism to communism, one that could be applied to the Indian soil. Hence these variations and discrepancies were common occurrences of that time. L.P.Sinha however says that "... These elements of the formative stage of Dange's communism have to be carefully noted, in view of the fact that though Dange became, and has remained ever since, a devout communist, yet certain element of non-conformism and angularities have always been Dange's trait"[37].

Despite the fact that the withdrawal of the Non-Cooperation movement had been severely criticised by Dange, yet, he was not in favour of small skirmishes against the British. He felt that the nation had to undergo a process of preparation before it could make an attack against imperialist domination. He said:

> "...We must not be aggressive and even sometimes refuse to be drawn in a defensive skirmish on a front which has our best troops, till we have organised all fronts uniformly....Our opposing forces are interested in getting out our best men on the best front before they organise all over for concerted action. As a tactic of war, let us not be drawn into it for some time. Let us first prepare the state of the people to match the state of the rulers, then alone will disobedience and all have their effect."[38]

This question of adequately preparing the forces before the attack is made is evident in the ideas of almost all the leading Indian communists of the time.

What is significant is that even after his total disillusionment with the Non-Cooperation movement; Dange could not actually tear away from the Congress. He sharply criticised the activities of the Congress on several occasions, but he could not do away with it altogether[39]. In 1922 he formed the Indian Socialist Labour Party within the folds of the Congress itself. It is evident that despite being highly critical of several of the moves made by the Congress, he was still not thinking in terms of breaking away from it. On the one hand he was saying:

"...Unfortunately our leaders having been leavened with the ideology of our capitalist ruling class (which fact they will indignantly repudiate) have simply shut their eyes to the real needs of the country, needs of organising the lower strata of our society which by far form a major part of our population"[40].

On the other hand he was advocating the formation of a Socialist party by the radical members of the Congress within the Congress. The ambivalence becomes very obvious when he said:

"...the radical men of the Congress should have pursued one cardinal objective of introducing in the Congress politics an element of strong opposition to vested interests in and outside of it. The blind acceptability of the infallibility of an individual or an institution, found wanting in rationality however great popular and commanding he or it be due to great sacrifice or age long service, will lead nowhere but to inaction and create out of a spirited nation a dotard, depending upon influences and suggestions foreign to its reason and falling into a dead mass when the supply of single individual or external inspiration is cut off.

"...We suggest to the radical minded men of the Congress who have not grown superstitious and have not taken to counting heads in the over-hot spiritual furnace, a programme of the Party suited to our present conditions."[41]

This was not just an attack on the following of Gandhi. It also shows that he was calling for the use of alternative principles by the Congress, when the Comintern was presenting a rather different viewpoint by advocating the need of an independent communist faction operating within the nationalist party. This was at a time when the Second Congress of the Comintern had long been over in 1920, and the Third Congress too had taken place in 1921. In fact, preparations were already being made for the Fourth Congress when Dange was still formulating within the Congress. This shows that he could not yet shake off his nationalist influence altogether even when he was seriously thinking on communist lines.

Dange however, was conscious that the interests of the workers should be related to the international movement of the workers. He felt that the party should

"...recognise the interests of the workers throughout the world, of whatever race, colour or creed, are one and that war imperialism and the exploitation of the native races the socialist commonwealth must ultimately be international and the prevention of these evils can only be secured by a world organisation of free peoples cooperating in the production and distribution of the world's goods. With this end in view it should work for the development, to its fullest extent, of the international labour and socialist movement in the prevention of war, the abolition of conscription and militarism in all their forms and the liberation of the subject peoples."[42]

To him, the spreading of socialism was not the work of a separate communist party, operating within the folds of the nationalist party, as the Comintern wanted it to be. He felt that the nationalist party itself could engage in the spreading of socialist consciousness.

Dange had utmost faith in the democratic order. He said, "The party must recognise that circumstances may arise when a government or reactionary class might attempt to suppress liberty or thwart the national will and that to defeat such attempts democracy must use to the utmost extent its political and industrial power."[43] It is ironical that when on the one hand Dange was advocating socialism, he was, on the other, propagating its development within the democratic order itself. The nationalist in him had still not been totally replaced by his communist ideals, however radical they might have been. This trend can be noticed in several of the earlier communists.

This can be explained by the fact that when Dange became communist, the ideological environment in India was very mixed in nature. Coupled with the nationalist urge to get rid of the British rule, was the flow of socialist ideas from Europe, especially Russia. Socialist theories offered an alternative to the existing system of nationalist struggle, and Russia loomed as a large example of this. The inflow of Marxist ideas to India was very limited at this time due to constant British vigilance. And this prompted these early communists like Dange to seek these ideas even more, to imbibe them, so as to provide an alternative basis of struggle which would rout imperialism, foreign domination and mass exploitation once and for all. This was their basic idea, when they became communists. But even then they could not quite totally shake off their initial experience as nationalists, fighting in order to gain freedom from the British. This dichotomy prevailed almost always in the ideas of the early Indian nationalists, in fact, sometimes even after the Comintern had made inroads into the sphere of communism in India.

Dange's writings were forceful and novel in content. They managed to influence several young radicals of the time like

S.V.Ghate, R.S.Nimbakar, K.N.Joglekar and others. C.G.Shah, another communist intellectual, became very close to Dange during this time. Ranchoddas Bhavan Lotwala, a Gujarati businessman, had been highly influenced by communist doctrines after he became disillusioned with the Non-Cooperation movement. He was instrumental in helping the early communists in and around Bombay. He helped Dange too in advancing his ideas further. In fact, Lotwala and C. G. Shah were instrumental in funding *The Socialist*. Muzaffar Ahmad, the noted Bengali communist has said in his memoirs, "He was the first person in Bombay to help the communists of our time."[44] Lotwala helped not only Dange, but also C.G.Shah in the early stages when they were maturing into communists.

It can be seen that almost all the early communists of Bombay came under the influence of Dange at some part during their early career as communists. Moreover, most of them had also been disheartened at the withdrawal of the Non-Cooperation movement and Gandhi's method of struggle as such. Ghate, a Maharashtrian Brahmin by birth, joined the communists after the Musli satyagraha. Dange's *The Socialist* too seemed to have influenced him. Besides, he was also quite friendly with C.G.Shah, who had turned to communism from the very outset and had shunned the nationalist means of struggle against the imperialists from the very beginning.

C.G.Shah had been influenced by the life of Mazzini while he was still in college. His father had wanted him to become a civil servant. But C.G.Shah sacrificed his brilliant academic career and other lucrative prospects, left his home at Ahmedabad and settled in Bombay. The Russian Revolution had only just occurred and C.G.Shah was very highly impressed by the implications it had to the existing order. Though the news about the revolution was often distorted by the British press, yet it could not totally prevent the attraction that it posed to the young Indian radicals of the time. The early Indian communists, "... the pioneers of the Marxist movement in India were fascinated with such humanist slogans of the Revolution as, 'Private property is abolished', 'None shall have the cake unless all have bread', 'Each for all, all for each', 'Religion is the opium of the masses' and others".[45] Apart from these influences, C.G.Shah secured another form of help, which made his sailing through much more comfortable than it would otherwise have been. He came into contact with R.B.Lotwala, "a wealthy flour mill magnate and at that time an ardent socialist, who made him his private secretary and became his close friend".[46] Lotwala also helped him to procure and read much Marxist literature of the time. He worked independently until he made his contact with Dange in 1922.

Another important figure of the time was R.S.Nimbakar. He joined the communist movement while still in college. He too had been disillusioned by the Chauri-Chaura incident and the withdrawal of the Non-Cooperation movement. On the other hand Dange's *The Socialist* also made a profound impression on him and he consequently decided to build working class organisations, especially trade unions. He was elected as the General Secretary of the Bombay Municipal Workers' Union and he subsequently played a big role in the Girni Kamgar Union of Bombay[47]. K.N.Joglekar was another communist who had been a brilliant scholar, influence initially by the nationalist activities of the period. He admitted to have been influenced by Dange's *Gandhi vs. Lenin*. But like many others of the time, his loss of faith in the nationalist activities became absolute after the Chauri-Chaura incident and the calling back of the Non-Cooperation movement. The Russian Revolution also influenced him greatly, and he became actively involved in the communist movement of the time. Besides, Roy's works too had a profound impact on him and very soon he became one of the communist leaders during the formative phase of communism[48]. B.T.Ranadive, another brilliant scholar of economics from Bombay University, became actively associated with the communist movement in the early twenties. He became involved in the Girni Kamgar Union and the railway workers' movement and rose to prominence in the late twenties.

Bengal saw the emergence of several communist leaders. Of them, mention has already been made of M.N.Roy. Apart from him there were Bhupendranath Datta, Abani Mukherjee, Virendranath Chattopadhyaya, Nalini Gupta, Muzaffar Ahmad, Soumyendranath Tagore and several others. If the history of the life of these communists are taken into consideration it can be seen that here too, like that in Bombay, nearly all of them rose from nationalist beginnings.

Bhupendranath Datta was initially a member of the revolutionary organisation, "Yugantar". He had been convicted for a year for pursuing anti-British activities. After his release he went to the United States to further his education. It was from there that he established contacts with Indian revolutionaries in Germany. By 1916 he had been elected General Secretary for Indian Independence, which continued until the committee itself was dissolved after Germany's defeat in the world war. During this time, Bhupendranath Datta came into contact with the Bolsheviks. He went to Moscow as a member of the Indian delegation in 1921 and had discussions with the leaders of the Comintern on Indian political issues.

On August 9th, 1921, Bhupendranath Datta, with Ebul Hasan and Abul Hasan, submitted to the Mali Bureau, a signed memorandum to the Indian Commission regarding the scheme of organisation of Indian work. Datta wanted to form a communist nucleus. The memorandum said, "The object of the communist nucleus will be to organise a communist party in India and to carry on such propaganda and active work among the Indian labourers in other parts of the world, to help in the formation of the party in India."[49] Its next task would be to "impart training in order to educate the individual workers in the principles and practice of communism and to make various kinds of propaganda among the working classes, to enlist large numbers of sympathisers with the aims and aspirations of the movement"[50].

B.N.Datta then went on to say that in order to bring "… the Indian proletariat in an organised body to the centre of the world revolution …," the communist nucleus would need the help of "… experienced Russian and other comrades, specialists in oriental affairs, who will form the permanent Indian commission of the Comintern for Indian work…"[51]

Regarding the overthrow of the British rule in India, Datta says that this would be the first step towards the revolution. Regarding the role of the Comintern he said:

"… help and support the nationalists and other revolutionary forces in India without encouraging any nationalist or chauvinist aspirations. The nucleus of the Communist Party will form a part of the revolutionary council consisting of well known revolutionaries which should specially be created to overthrow the British rule in India, and the relation of this revolutionary council to the Comintern should be realised through the Indian Commission and not through the medium of the communist nucleus alone"[52].

The scheme emphasised to a great extent the importance of the overthrow of the British rule in India. And in order to facilitate quick action and other needs, the scheme proposed the setting up of two secretariats or general centres in Moscow and in Western Europe, under the supervision of the Indian commission, yet with much power and autonomy in times of need[53].

The scheme also highlighted the role of foreign links. It said: "All available Indian communists residing outside should be sent by various means to India, to create different nuclei in the existing labour organisations and to form such organisations wherever wanting in the large industrial centres of India, and to work through at least two powerful centres in India, one in Calcutta and the other in Bombay, the unity of which will be the formation of the Communist Party in India."[54]

The plan also gave importance to the labour organisations in the colonies of America, Africa and other islands. It further recommended. the use of the Ghadar Party to promote the interest of the communists regarding the formation of the Party. It also said that the Indian labourers working abroad should be encouraged to form strong nuclei of their own and function anonymously under the loose guidance of the Indian commission and maintain regular links with the Comintern. All this, the scheme said, should be used to facilitate the Communist Party of India and in propaganda work among Indian labourers.[55]

Three appendices were attached to the memorandum. The first highlighted the rise of strikes in Bengal, the second stated the rising tendency to strike among "Hindu" labourers in Fiji and the third showing a diagram of a plan of organisation and connections of Indian work to be made by the Comintern.

If these theses are analysed in the light of Lenin's and M.N.Roy's draft theses on the colonial question and the Supplementary theses on the colonial question as submitted to the Second Congress of the Comintern, several differences seem to emerge. Besides, another point to be considered is that Lenin wrote a letter to B.N.Datta regarding his theses, where he said that Datta should abide by his theses on the colonial question and on the other hand, "...gather statistical facts about Peasant leagues if they exist in India"[56].

In the theses of Datta, there is no mention of the peasantry at all. But the peasantry formed a very important social class in the colonies, without which, as Lenin said, revolution could not be imagined[57].

Secondly, the relationship between the proletariat in the colonies and that of the imperialist countries has not been considered. This has been dealt with in details in the Supplementary theses and had formed an important part in the Lenin-Roy debate in the Second Congress of the Comintern[58].

Another point, so grossly neglected in Datta's memorandum was the role of the bourgeois democratic forces in bringing about the revolution. It has been mentioned in B.N.Datta's theses that "... The Comintern should therefore help and support the nationalists and other revolutionary forces in India without encouraging any nationalist or chauvinist aspirations."[59] Yet, the amount of support that should be rendered or the point of time to which the support could be extended and the nature of such support remains rather vague. At one point the memorandum says, "Each decision for the non-communist work should be sanctioned by the Indian Commission in consultation with the communist nucleus or Party"[60]. Here too the nature of non-communist work" has not been analysed at all. Compared to the Lenin-Roy debate, the Supplementary theses or even the Draft Theses on the Oriental Question presented to the Third Congress of the Comintern by M.N.Roy, Bhupendranath's memorandum remains rather quiet on the question of alliance with the native bourgeois democratic forces.

Lastly, the concept of internationalism or of world revolution too is somewhat amiss in the memorandum of Datta and his associates. There is repeated mention in the theses of how the Indian proletariat should be brought into relationship with the Indian workers employed in other colonies and how this alliance would help in the consolidation of the Party. But the concept of alliance with the proletariat of the advanced imperialist nations and their role in bringing about the fall of imperialism and in ushering the revolution has been ignored. In fact no strategy has been mentioned that would uproot imperialism once and for all. The development of revolutionary strategies among the Indian workers at home and abroad has been hinted at through the first two appendices attached to the memorandum. But the question of their role in bringing about world revolution remains unanswered. On the one hand, Datta's memorandum says that the first step towards revolution should be the overthrow of British rule in India. The consequent steps however, have not been dealt with. This is very unlike what had been propagated in the Second Congress[61].

It can bee seen that the early Indian communists were still not quite familiar with the theories that were in vogue in the Comintern. Whereas M.N.Roy had already secured a place in the Comintern, others were still quite far off. When Lenin refused to agree with Roy on certain issues in the Second Congress, Roy entered into a prolonged debate with him. But despite the fact that several other communists were vying with Roy to secure a foothold in the Comintern, they interestingly, appreciated Lenin in a different light altogether. In his *Aprakashito Rajnaitik Itihas*, Bhupendranath Datta constantly refers to Lenin as "Mahatma Lenin"[62]. And when Lenin asked him to stick to his own theses on the colonial question, and work instead to gather facts about peasant leagues in India, Datta was not at all put down by it. He felt that it was "like a comradely order" (*ekti comradegoto karjer hukum chhilo*[63]), one that he intended to follow. An element of being rather overawed by the Russian Revolution and its leaders is evident in Datta's writings like several other communists of the time. The nationalist fervour too had not died down in him like other contemporary Indian communists, and kept surfacing from time to time in whatever theoretical formulations he made.

One important, but highly ignored communist leader of the time was Abani Mukherjee. Gautam Chattopadhyay's research on his life brings forth another nationalist turned communist. He was born in 1891 in Jabalpur from where his family soon shifted to Calcutta. Abani was initiated into nationalist ideals from Sakharam Deuskar, who lived in the ground floor of his house. Later on he was greatly influenced by the extremist leader, Bipin Chandra Pal.

Abani Mukherjee got himself involved in the politics of the anti-partition movement of 1905-06. But the political situation became very alarming at this time, and Abani was sent to Japan to pursue his academic career there. Afterwards he went to Leipzig to complete his education, and returned to India ultimately in 1912 after achieving his degree. This time he came under the spell of Jatindranath Mukherjee. He was, like Roy, assigned the task of securing arms for the revolutionaries from China and Japan. He did manage to secure the arms, and while returning with a shipload of them, he was caught by the British police at Penang in 1915. He was then taken to Singapore, court-martialled, and eventually sentenced to death. But he escaped by a very daring act of adventure[64].

Abani surfaced again at Berlin in 1921. It was after this incident that a dispute arose regarding his identity and his loyalty towards the communist movement. Cecil Kaye has said with his characteristic alacrity, "...Thus the Communist International added a second string to their bow, by supporting the revolutionary Nationalism of the India Independence Party as well as Roy's 'Indian Communist Party'. With characteristic duplicity, they agreed to despatch Abani Mukherjee to India on behalf of the 'India Independence Party'...with a letter of recommendation signed by Barkatullah and B.N.Dutt dated October 13th, 1922, stating that Abani Mukherjee was a 'member and Joint Secretary of the Indian Committee for Russian relief' while, on practically the same date (October 2nd, 1922) they issued an official warning against him..."[65] A circular of the Comintern, dated sometime in early 1923, actually deposed him from his rank in the Comintern. It said:

"The Executive Committee of the Communist International hereby notifies all its national sections as well as all other parties, groups and individuals concerned that reports have been received to the effect that one Abani Mukherjee, who attended the II Congress of the Communist International and sometimes worked as a member of the Indian Communist Group, has been engaged in activities which makes serious reflections on his political honesty. In view of this fact it is quite impossible for him to remain in the ranks of the Communist International."[66]

However, another document from the British records has stated that despite the fact that the Comintern actually disowned Abani, he continued to correspond with Zinoviev. The document further states:

"...It is not at all impossible that the C.I., while publicly condemning Abani Mukherjee, were secretly supporting him as a second string of their bow, as an emissary of the anti-Roy party— the 'Indian Independence Party'of Chatto, Barkatullah and B.N.Dutt....Abani Mukherjee's record seems to show definitely that— whether his publicly stated views— he is a definite advocate of violence and in touch with the Communist International: and that if he was allowed to come to India, he would do so as a propagandist of revolutionary and Bolshevik ideas...."[67]

This explains to a great extent, the role that Abani was playing as a member of the Comintern. This perhaps also explains why he was exonerated later on and given responsible positions by the Comintern in future.

Bhupendranath Datta and Muzaffar Ahmad have expressed strong doubts about the integrity of Abani, who according to British records, made a statement to the British, only after which he was freed. This statement has been a subject of much controversy[68]. Even Roy, who went to the extent of co-authoring *India in Transition* with him, called him "a fortune-hunter" who could not be trusted[69]. He has also said that he had entrusted him with the job of collecting statistical material for "his" book, *India in Transition*[70]. It is highly doubtful whether Roy actually entrusted Abani with the job and then made him his co-author for the book. Roy himself, though called Abani pompous, was no less so himself and it is highly improbable that he would co-author a book with someone whom he had merely employed. Besides, this was not the only case. Abani once again co-authored with Roy several other letters and articles among which was the manifesto that was sent to the Ahmedabad Congress.

Gautam Chattopadhyay has shown several instances by which the fantastic story of Abani can actually be confirmed[71]. G.Adhikari has endorsed this view[72]. Gautam Chattopadhyay has also provided a reason as to why Muzaffar Ahmad was so highly against Abani.

"The truth is that Muzaffar Ahmad and his entourage do not possess one iota of solid evidence against Abani that can be accepted by any historian. On the other hand, once Abani's revolutionary bona fides are accepted, the credit for establishing the Communist Party of India, in October 1920 at Tashkent, goes to him, as well to Roy and Shaffique. Also, Abani came back to India in 1922, with a warrant over his head, made many contacts and established the nucleus of the Communist Party in India too. In this entire episode, Muzaffar Ahmad played an insignificant role. Naturally, once these historical facts are established firmly, the myth of Muzaffar Ahmad being the founder of the Indian communist movement gets blown up sky-high."[73]

The evaluation of Abani Mukherjee's career is very difficult. The dearth of his writings and the constant criticism of him by his fellow communists make it confusing. However, owing to the efforts of Purabi Roy, Sobhanlal Dattagupta and Hari Vasudevan[74], some of Abani's letters and writings have been unearthed, which help somewhat in constructing the ideas that he upheld during his early years as a communist. Most of his letters and articles that can be found have been co-authored with Roy. This shows that not only was he working together with Roy, he must have been working at par with him too.[75]

Abani Mukherjee had attended the Second Congress of the Communist International and was instrumental in forming the émigré Communist Party of India in Tashkent on 17th October 1920. He was, in fact, one of the founding members of the Communist Party of India in Tashkent, along with six others, of whom two were M.N.Roy and his wife Evelyn Trent-Roy[76]. But what is significant is that Abani, like Roy, and unlike several of his communist counterparts like Bhupendranath Datta and Virendranath Chattopadhyay, could actually comprehend very early, the strategy that the Comintern envisaged for the colonies in its Second Congress. In fact, it was perhaps at this juncture, that he shed his nationalist image and adopted communism in its place. He wrote in a letter to Shiv Prasad Gupta of Benares:

"You may disagree with me, but I tell you that I am a Communist today... As a Communist, my fight is not ended with the freedom of India from British rule— it will end only then, when the entire capitalist system of the world will fall down. You may understand by this that I am no longer a nationalist— to make it clearer to you. I tell you that I am anti-nationalist and Internationalist..."[77]

In the same letter, he criticised the nationalist policies for catering to only a limited section of the society. The vast masses hence remained largely indifferent when they were asked to revolt against the British. Abani felt that the masses needed to be educated and made conscious of their own interests before they rose in revolt. At the same time, he has however acknowledged that the overthrow of the British was necessary, and that "... we Communists and you nationalists must work hand in hand for the overthrow of British rule which is our common enemy..."[78] The idea of the two-pronged Revolution so as to achieve the desired goal, becomes very apparent in the letter. This was actually what was propagated at the Second Congress of the Communist International, and what many failed to comprehend for a long time to come. Besides, his conversion into a communist moved his goal further from mere attainment of political independence to that of "...universal peace and happiness by destroying Classes, Private Property and the wage system as it exists under Capitalism..."[79]

If *India in Transition* is taken into consideration, then too the same type of mindset becomes evident. The two-stage theory of the Revolution has been envisaged here too. The book says, "... The basis of the national movement is the rivalry of the weak and suppressed bourgeoisie against its immensely stronger imperialist prototype controlling the state power..."[80] Later on, in the concluding paragraph it says that the native bourgeoisie had the option to ally with the imperialists. But to do so, its demands had to be met.

However, "…The Indian bourgeoisie, by itself, is too weak to make the imperialist government pay heed to its demands. Therefore it must depend upon mass action for imposing its will. This is playing with fire, digging one's own grave. Signs are already to be seen that the workers and peasants, who are steadily emerging from the first confusion of a great social upheaval, do not find the Congress and Khilafat programmes include their interests. The inevitable consequence of this is the eventual divorce of the mass movement from bourgeois leadership…"[81] Even if it is taken for granted that Abani Mukherjee was only involved in collecting statistics for the book, and that he had not penned down the words himself, yet it cannot be denied that there is a very obvious similarity of ideas with the letter that has been quoted above. Hence, it does prove that Roy and Abani were, during this time, thinking on the same lines.

The letter written by Abani Mukherjee to Shiv Prasad[82] is dated December 30, 1920. In this letter it was clearly stated the policies followed by the nationalists would never serve the interests of the masses, even if the nationalists could assume power. He wrote:

"…. I do not think that the driving of the English from India only will bring happiness and freedom to the Indian people. If we put Lajpat Rai in the place of Chelmsford, Ram Tiwari or Lakshman Singh or even Ali Khan in the place of the English ruling class, the masses will not be any happier. The workers of India will go on suffering as they are doing today, if not more…"[83]

The letter also said:

"…Just look at the present day Indian strikes. All the time Mr. Gandhi or someone else is settling their disputes according to their own ideas, and these settlements are not all satisfactory to the workers. Why? Because, Mr. Gandhi and the lawyers and the leaders who do interfere on behalf of the workers, have quite different interests to those of the workers themselves. Revolutions are not brought by a person, by a group or by a sect. facts collect for centuries and then burst forth in a way as is best suited for the majority…."[84]

It is not only ironical but also very significant at the same time, that only five days later, on January 4, 1921, Roy and Abani jointly wrote a letter to Gandhi, inviting him to attend the All-India Revolutionary Congress. He was also told that the Russians were keen to help India achieve her freedom and requested to send "… as many delegates from all parts of the country to attend it…"[85] Moreover, they assured Gandhi that the importance of the Congress would be phenomenal[86]. It is ironical because knowing Gandhi's methods of struggle it would definitely have been obvious to them that Gandhi would not be interested. But the significance lies in the fact that the Non-Cooperation Movement was still in its full swing in India, and Gandhi was its leader. The movement had already gained huge proportions and the masses were also being actively incorporated into it. The contents of the letter become meaningful once they are analysed in such a situation— the proliferation of the nationalist movement in India on the one hand, and the Comintern propagating collaboration with the nationalists for overthrowing the imperialist stronghold— the first step towards the Revolution, on the other. Roy and Abani had indeed grasped the colonial strategy of the Comintern.

Virendranath Chattopadhyay, another communist leader of that time, was the brother of the famous nationalist leader, Sarojini Naidu. He had gone to London to appear in the I.C.S. examination, in which he failed and soon became very deeply involved in political work. He became associated with Shyamji Krishna Varma, while staying in the 'India House' and later joined the 'New League' and 'Free India Society' that had been established by Savarkar. Then he went to Paris and joined Madame Cama in her work for freeing India. Just before the war began he went to Germany and became the spokesperson of the émigré Indian revolutionaries there. He was one of the founding members of the Berlin Committee and also its first secretary[87]. Like Bhupendranath Datta, he too wrote a thesis, dated August 6 1921, on the occasion of the Third Congress of the Comintern. It was titled "Thesis on India and the World Revolution"[88]. He wrote it jointly with G.A.K.Luhani and P.Khankoje. He had already submitted a detailed plan of work concerning India to the Small Bureau around the same time[89]. This too had been a joint effort of Chattopadhyay, Luhani and Khankoje.

The "Thesis on India and the World Revolution" says at the very beginning that regarding the proletarian World-revolution, "India transcends other parts of Asiatic and African continents now under the sway of World-capitalism"[90]. It also said that the peasantry was totally "unorganised" whereas the workers were "loosely organised in general labour unions"[91]. At the same time he felt that the workers were not yet class-conscious. He said:

"...This loosely organised mass of workers is not, in any sense of the term, class-conscious. There have been many strikes in local areas for local ends; there is not a single instance of a class-conscious sympathetic strike on a large scale. There is no proletarian press to fuse the recurring local and sectional discontents into a widening synthesis of class-conscious revolt against capitalist aggression and exploitation. Even if there were a press, there would hardly be anybody in the ranks of the proletariat to read it, as only 6 per cent of the Indian population is literate"[92].

He then went on to analyse the reasons that blocked the rise of a class-conscious proletariat.

The thesis says that India was facing several problems. It was not just economic differences that were dividing the Indian society. India was steeped in a rigid type of caste system which layered the society in terms of caste. Another factor was religion. In an already segregated caste society there was a huge Islamic population that divided the society in terms of religion. "British imperialism", he said, "has not only given a fresh vitality to these causes, but has also in itself been further obstacle to the emergence of India of those conditions which make a revolutionary class-conscious proletariat possible"[93].

The thesis also said that the character of exploitation in India was different form that in the West. Unlike the West, this exploitation was more foreign, and hence different. It said:

"Industrialism to the extent to which it exists in India today under the aegis of British Imperialism loses its identity as the economic exploitation of one class by another and takes on more and more the character of an economic exploitation of one race by another. The development of India along capitalist lines is being carried on principally by and for British capital"[94].

Chattopadhyay was aware of the role played by the native bourgeoisie in the exploitation of the working masses. He said clearly:

"So long as this foreign capitalism remains the exploited masses fail to discriminate with any degree of precision between, on the one hand, the historical World-Bourgeoisie engaged in the misappropriation of wealth produced by the workers, and, on the other hand, a body of foreigners, politically supreme and racially distinct, carrying on a colossal scale the economic exploitation of a vast area"[95].

He also said that in a situation like that in India, where industrialism was still in its early stages and foreign imperialism dominated the economic relations, the environment required for the development of a class conscious proletariat was absent. Regarding the fact that would lead to the coming in of such an environment and the maturing of the workers in the ranks of the World-Proletariat, the thesis said:

"So long as the economic exploitation of a given vast area by and in the name of a foreign political entity is a concurrent dominating factor in the economic exploitation of one class by another, the revolutionary class consciousness of the proletariat remains merely potential. The Indian proletariat can take its rightful place in the ranks of the World-proletariat in its struggle against the bourgeoisie only after the supervening British imperialism has been withdrawn."[96]

In the second section of the thesis, "British Imperialism and World Revolution", it has been said in the very beginning:

"... If the concentration of financial power in the hands of the United States of America be left out of consideration for a moment, it can almost be said that World capitalism is synonymous with British capitalism-- so great indeed is the British sphere of political and economic control over the raw materials and markets of the World..."[97]

At the same time, the thesis was saying that "Industrialism has nowhere a longer tradition than in England, and nowhere, except perhaps in the United States of America, has the capitalist structure of social organisation reached so clearly the penultimate stage of dissolution as in England..."[98] Chattopadhyay was conscious that despite the fact England was very advanced in terms of the growth of a class-conscious proletariat, yet, it still retained tremendous power to keep it under control. "...It is not by a mere accident or chance that the instrument of proletarian revolution in England— the British Communist Party— is one of the weakest of the constituent bodies of the Communist International..."[99]

The concept of "labour aristocracy" that had been formulated in the Supplementary theses at the Second Congress[100] and that of "colonial chauvinism" propagated by Lenin in the Stuttgart Congress of the Second International[101] even earlier in 1907 has however, been comprehended clearly and incorporated into the thesis. The thesis said:

"The British working classes are a product of the industrialism that the British bourgeoisie has so systematically developed in the British Isles, although primarily called into being by the historic process of bourgeois exploitation— the British working classes in contradistinction to the proletariat of continental Europe— live, move and have their being in an atmosphere of relative prosperity created by an efficient and successful capitalist imperialism abroad. The average British working man, particularly the skilled labourer, has had historically a higher standard of livelihood than his copees in other parts of Europe...[102]

The thesis also says that the economically superior working class was gradually evolving into an intermediary class between the workers and the bourgeoisie, and that this class was surviving on the profits made from colonies like India. This class, said Chattopadhyaya, was developing "a kind of sub-bourgeois mentality"[103]. Moreover, this class did "rise to a sense of solidarity with the proletariat of continental Europe, but with the wretched proletariat of England's Asiatic and African dependencies the British working classes have no sense of solidarity"[104]. He said:

"...British Imperialism is already launched on a policy of undermining the nascent revolutionary spirit of the British proletariat, at critical moment of the World-revolution, by admitting it into partnership in a gigantic sweating system which replaces the exploitation of the British working classes by the exploitation of India and other Asiatic and African countries, within the fabric of capitalist circumstances, due directly to British Imperialism are arising, which operate with increasing force towards the conversion of class-cleavage into race cleavage"[105].

This shows that the Comintern's dictates were definitely making inroads into the theories being propagated by the contemporary early Indian communists. On the other hand simultaneously, the concept of racial distinction rampant among the British proletariat for those of the Asian and African colonies is somewhat deliberately being made evident, thereby showing once again the tremendous distrust of the Indian leaders for the British. This feeling, tinted heavily with nationalist fervour, was a common feature among the revolutionary nationalists turned communists of the time. Chattopadhyay obviously was no exception.

The thesis dealt with the tasks of the Communist International in its third section, "The Task of the Communist International"[106]. This part harps basically on one primary point— the "destruction of British Imperialism"[107]. It said that this "can be achieved only by the detachment of India from the British Empire.... Meanwhile the destruction of British Imperialism remains the first charge of the Communist International, and to that end it is incumbent on the

Communist International to exploit to the utmost extent every available revolutionary tendency in and outside India..."[108]

The last part of this section flatly denounced the policy of temporary collaboration of the communist parties with the bourgeois-democratic movements of the colonies, as propagated by the Comintern in the Second Congress. It said:

"...Here academic objections on rigid communist grounds to giving assistance to and collaborating with bourgeois-democratic and nationalist revolutionary movements of political liberation in the East show a pathetic and stupid detachment from the realpolitik of the World Situation. And so far as India is concerned any danger of the Indian bourgeoisie settling down to the exploitation of the Indian proletariat as a result of the overthrow of the British Empire is entirely out of the question, as, in the event of the destruction of British Imperialism, World capitalism could be shattered to pieces, and the Indian bourgeoisie, numerically insignificant and conspicuous for its historic record of decrepitude and inefficiency, will not be able to make any stand against the irresistible march of the proletarian revolt all over the World."[109]

This was not conforming to the spirit of the Second Congress which was very clear about its stand on the nature of the native bourgeoisie, who would always try to assume power once the imperialists were ousted[110].

The plan of work concerning India that was submitted to the Mali Bureau around the same time is also very interesting when the strategies are noted. The plan divided the scheme of work into six parts— work in India, work among emigrant Indian labourers outside India, special propaganda among Indian soldiers stationed outside India, creation of special communist literature for India, work in Europe and technical revolutionary training[111]. Here, certain measures that were suggested for communist propaganda were very new. For example, it advocated the publication of labour newspapers in the five principal Indian vernaculars, establishment of secret schools for the training of communist propagandists and organisers, propaganda by cinema and so on[112]. Chattopadhyaya had realised that educating the illiterate Indian masses to communism would not be an easy job, especially in the absence of systematic propaganda work. The measures that he proposed were not only very novel, they were practical as well. He even advocated the need for the setting up of a bureau for the smuggling of revolutionary literature and arms and ammunition[113].

Like Bhupendranath Datta, Chattopadhyaya too felt that emigrant Indian labourers should be trained[114]. He also advocated intensive propaganda work among emigrant Indian soldiers and students, who would hence, in future, be useful for the "dissemination of communist ideas"[115]. Moreover, he proposed the setting up of technical revolutionary training for the Indian workers in the preparation and manipulation of explosives and the and in the methods of destruction of bridges, railway lines and buildings, etc.[116] All the moves that were being suggested, bore a heavy dependence on violence and clandestine activities— lines that the revolutionary nationalists followed. Besides, much stress had been put on the role of the immigrant Indian workers[117].

The deviation from the Comintern dictates in both the theses and the plan is a clear representation of the fact that the nationalist in Chattopadhyaya was not only alive but very much so. The destruction of British Imperialism was so essential that he did not even allow any time for the preparation for it. Here he also varies with Dange who had insisted on proper preparation before the British were finally attacked[118]. Another point that needs mention here is that the early communists were just being guided by Comintern dictates. They were thinking on their own, they were trying to situate Marxism on Indian soil and then devise policies accordingly.

Among the early communists, apart from nationalists and revolutionary nationalists, there was another group— the muhajirin turned communists. The muhajirin were devout Muslims who had been antagonised with the annexation of Turkey and the deposing of the Khalifa, the religious head of the Muslims. They wanted to start a jihad or the holy war against the British. But in order to do so they had to emigrate to an Islamic state and make preparations to wage such a war. Meanwhile, Afghanistan had become independent and its ruler, Amir Amanullah Khan welcomed to his country all those Muslims who did not want to live under the British. The hijrat movement started and thousands of Muslims began to leave for Afghanistan. However, soon afterwards, he entered into a treaty with the British and ordered the expulsion of the muhajirins, who now prepared to go to Turkey. But the Khilafat movement petered out when an independent democratic government under Kemal Ataturk was established there. The muhajirin were now at a loss and thirty-six of them went to Tashkent. Here they met M.N.Roy and other communist leaders and were for the first time initiated to the concept of communism.

One of the most important of these muhajirins turned communists was Shaukat Usmani. He has made a detailed report of his experiences in Afghanistan and later on in Tashkent and Moscow in his book, *Historic Trips of a Revolutionary*[119]. This book is very helpful in understanding the actual background that led to the evolution of communists from muhajirins.

From Shaukat Usmani's detailed description of his journey to Tashkent from Afghanistan, and his ultimate indoctrination into communism, it is clear that he began from the scratch where communism is concerned. In fact even after arriving at Tashkent and coming into contact with Roy and others, it took him quite some time to turn into a communist[120].

Shaukat Usmani has recorded the formation of the émigré Communist Party of India. But at the same time he has recollected that he himself did not join the Communist Party until "nearly six months"[121]. He says that the reason for this was "... quite simple. I had no knowledge of Marxism. My main aim was to fight like a soldier in the ranks of the fighters for liberation of India."[122] Looking at this statement it can be said that Shaukat Usmani, though a muhajirin turned communist, had unquestionable nationalist influence like any of his fellow communist contemporaries— one, that was as usual, difficult to just shrug off.

Usmani has said that his knowledge increased only after he started studying more and more of the subject, interacting with the local people and working in Andijan with the Kashgar elements[123]. It was while narrating this phase of his life that he has said, "Our knowledge of the practical application of the Leninist doctrine began to increase day by day..." and that he began to study the theories of Marxism as well[124].

Later on, Shaukat Usmani, along with a few other Indian youths, was sent to study in the Communist University of the Toilers of the East in Moscow, where he was subsequently indoctrinated into communism. The impact of this training in Moscow had a profound influence on him. He has said, "My studies in the Soviet Union instilled in me the true lesson of Marxist Leninist teaching. Since then the Soviet Union has become the land of my inspiration; I dream as if I am still living there."[125]

Turning over the facts that Shaukat Usmani has mentioned in his long narrative, it can be said that his initiation into communism too fits into the general trend prevalent among the early Indian communists. He was not a communist from the beginning. He came from a different background altogether, his main influences being those of religion and nationalism, his primary aim being that of ousting the British from India.

Muzaffar Ahmad was born in Sandwip, in the Sundarbans in 1889. He belonged to a poor Muslim family, and spent the first part of his life as a devout Muslim. He never joined the nationalist struggle for freedom. For he felt that as a committed Muslim he could not quite endorse the strong Hindu influences that seemed to dominate the politics of the time. He had felt that the movement, despite being anti-British, was also "Hindu-revivalist"[126] a fact that he could not ignore. Nevertheless, he has also mentioned that the swadeshi movement had, in some way held sway over him. He has said, "I was a very poor student but, as far as possible, I also used swadeshi goods. I also wore mill cloth, purchased from swadeshi stores in Noakhali bazaar. Priyanath Mukhopadhyay, son of the well-known pleader, Kumudinikanta Mukhopadhyay, was its proprietor"[127].

He however, did share the anti-British feelings of his counterparts, a fact that made him search for a new alternative to the nationalist movement in which he had no faith whatsoever. At least that is what his autobiography seems to suggest. Meanwhile, the British government had adopted very strong measures to curb the infiltration of Marxist-Leninist ideas from Russia— a place where the socialist revolution had already occurred. This, in a way, provided a stronger inclination to imbibe socialist ideas as a stronger substitute for the weakened nationalist movement[128]. This tendency to get to know and absorb what was being deliberately suppressed and defamed was yet another contemporary trend[129]. Gautam Chattopadhyay has, however, shown that "...young Muzaffar Ahmad in 1921 might have been independently attracted towards the Russian revolution, but it was Roy and his emissary Nalini Gupta who actually brought him and his friends over to the camp of communism. It is both an act of historical distortion as well as ingratitude for Ahmad to deny his debt to the half-forgotten but courageous Nalini Gupta."[130] One of the documents that Gautam Chattopadhyay has quoted from is a Home Department record of June 1923, which says, "Nalini Gupta achieved a certain amount of success. It was through his efforts that the communist centre at Calcutta came into being... The Calcutta group was started by Muzaffar Ahmad, a journalist who owed his conversion to communism to the visit paid by Nalini Gupta to India at the beginning of 1922. Since with the aim of date, Muzaffar Ahmad has been in direct correspondence with Roy..."[131] The next part of the sentence, where he has stopped is "...and at regular intervals received small sums of money from him..."[132] This shows that ever since he became a communist in 1922, he had not been working independently, but in close coordination with the Comintern via Roy.

Muzaffar Ahmad has said that he was "...directly connected with Bengal"[133] when the attempts to develop communist nuclei in different parts of the country had already begun. He has admitted that initially he did not know any of the communist leaders in other parts of the country. He came to know them in course of time either through the Communist International or other sources. Suchetana Chattopahyay has said:

> "...The early communist network which emerged with Muzaffar Ahmad at its centre was peopled with ex-nationalists and Khilafat activists as well as politically unformed recruits. They had participated in or had observed with interest and sympathy the mass upsurge against imperialism in the 1920s. The abrupt half of the movement in early 1922 had generated a sense of defeatism, disorientation and despondency...Abdur Rezzaq Khan (1900-1984) and Abdul Halim (1901-1966), two of the early communists who were to remain with the movement in all its complexities and vicissitudes throughout their lives, represented this section."[134]

The workers' strikes and other movements that were going on in Bengal also affected the thoughts of Muzaffar Ahmad. Besides, he often visited the sailors in Calcutta, many of whom belonged to his birthplace, Sandwip. Despite the fact that he visited them primarily to be "in touch with his countrymen", yet, at the same time, he was getting concerned by their problems. During this time Muzaffar Ahmad was editing the journal *Navayug*, in which he began to focus on the problems and demands of the sailors.

Another influence on Muzaffar Ahmad was the intellectual scenario of the time. His association with Nazrul Islam and his journal *Dhumketu* had a lasting influence on him. Communist ideas were fast becoming topics of interest among the intellectuals. Even those who had not conceived of these ideas clearly, were eagerly formulating so as to find a new answer to the existing problems. The anti-British policies that were being pursued by Gandhi and the Congress were failing to satisfy the nationalists especially those of the revolutionary type. Marxist-Leninist literature too was slowly seeping in. It was in such a background that the emergence of Muzaffar Ahmad as a communist can be explained.

What is striking about the autobiography of Muzaffar Ahmad, very unlike those of other contemporary communists, is that this autobiography often takes a rather personal stance, where the criticism of individuals is concerned. For example, when documents, as mentioned above, show Muzaffar Ahmad's contact with M.N.Roy through Nalini Gupta, his autobiography says that the Nalini Gupta told him nothing about the organisation of the Comintern[135]. He has criticised almost all his contemporary communists in quite scathing terms. Of them, his attitude regarding Abani Mukherjee has already been mentioned. For Dange and Singaravelu, he said that he mentioned both their names together because both tried to achieve great feats only through smartness[136]. He also said that though these two persons preferred to call themselves communists, they were actually nationalists and did not believe in the unity of the proletariat of all nations. Muzaffar Ahmad felt that despite their feelings, they always welcomed enthusiastically whatever financial support they got from abroad[137]. His description of how all his contemporary communists received money from the Comintern also reveals the same attitude. It appears almost as if he was justifying his own receipt of money from the Comintern, something for which he did not care, yet he was dependent upon so as to nurture the cause of communism in India[138]. It seems that his criticism of the early communists was a way by which he was actually trying to glorify himself. Another point that can be detected in the book is Muzaffar Ahmad's unending efforts to appease Roy during the early part of his career. It did not matter what he exaggerated or whom he criticised in order to prove the significance of his role as an Indian communist in the early 1920s. This attitude about proving the significance of his personal role as a leader of the masses was perhaps one of the reasons that kept Muzaffar Ahmad in touch with communism in the early part of his career.

Another source which too was responsible for the emergence of Indian communists, was the Ghadar Party. This was a revolutionary nationalist party, formed in North America mainly by Sikhs. Members of this party, as a result of their interaction with the socialists of North America and the influence of the Russian Revolution became oriented towards the leftist movement against imperialism. Many of them, in fact, turned into communists. Sohan Singh Josh was one of them.

Sohan Singh Josh was born in a Sikh Jat family in 1896 in the Chetanpura village of Amritsar district in Punjab. His family was poor and debt ridden, yet he did manage to secure an education, a fact that ultimately led to the shaping of his non-rural career[139]. He joined the Akali movement in 1920, when the movement was in its initial stages. He began to edit the paper Akali for some time, and came into contact with the nationalist ideas that were spreading in Punjab after the Jallianwallahbagh incident. The Akalis were leading the Gurdwara freedom movement against the British. They felt that the British, in order to serve their own interests, were using the gurdwaras. Sohan Singh Josh has said, "...Gurdwaras, instead of being places of worship of God, became places of prayer for the everlasting *raj* of British imperialists..."[140]

Sohan Singh Josh was arrested and jailed in 1922. In jail, he came into contact with many nationalist Congress prisoners, and his ideas about freedom from the British slowly began to exceed the limits of the gurdwaras. While still in jail, he read quite a few books on politics. His village friend, Surat Singh, then a student of the Berkley University and editor of the weekly Gaddar, the mouthpiece of the Hindustan Ghaddar Party, sent him several books to read. Sohan Singh has said in his autobiography, how a book "Liberty and the Great Libertarians" had a deep and lasting influence on him, and how after reading it, he began to question all the existing norms of his life[141]. He has said, "Born in the politically backward province of Punjab, I was brought up in a puritan religious atmosphere. But the ideas enunciated in *Liberty and the Great Libertarians* later became a touchstone for me to assess the religious, social, political and cultural values inherited from the past. I cast away a lot of rubbish that I had been carrying in my mind, and the book awakened the critic in me."[142] To him the religiosity that was the basic component of the Akali movement gave way to a more secular nationalist movement against the British imperialists. It took Sohan Singh Josh quite sometime to get adjusted to it. For this idea of Indian independence was a much broader concept than that of the freedom of the gurdwaras. But the change had undoubtedly come by the time he made his statement in the Akali Leaders' Conspiracy Case in the Court of Anderson in January 1925. He said that the Akalis were "...striving to achieve their objective of freedom of the gurdwaras...They have been compelled to start the mass struggles to secure back the gurdwaras. They have taken to direct action and began driving out the *mahants*. The British Government tried its level best to suppress this movement in order to keep their lackeys, the *mahants*, in saddle."[143] He also said at the same time:

> "I have never worked for the attainment of the Sikh *Raj*, the talk of which is a religious sin to me...Those days, long ago, took wings and flew away when the Indians used to work for selfish ends. These are the days of democracy and I fully believe in the democratic form of government. So, all my efforts will be bent on achieving *Swaraj*; that is to say the *swaraj* of the Indians by the Indians and for the Indians, without favouring any creed or colour. I will fight for the freedom of my country which might and will leave no stones unturned to achieve *Swaraj* peacefully (and) as soon as possible."[144]

This was one level of change. The other level of change, that is his initiation into Marxism had also begun although it began to surface a little later.

Sohan Singh's statement in the Akali Leaders' Conspiracy Case had attracted the attention of the Akali leadership and he joined the movement with vigour soon after his release. It had also attracted the attention of Bhai Santokh Singh of the Hindustan Ghadar Party, and Sohan Singh was asked to write articles for its Punjabi monthly magazine, *Kirti*. Sohan Singh has however admitted that the articles that he wrote were "...inspiring, but from the Marxist viewpoint are ideologically weak..."[145] But the Ghadar leadership was impressed and he was asked to join the Kirti as the editor-in-charge. He accepted the offer and joined it on 21st January, 1927. He read whatever material he could find that related to Marxist theories of socialism. The British denunciation of Bolshevism in such a fervent manner also raised question in the minds of the anti-British factions. Sohan Singh Josh has said in his autobiography:

> "...And the Bolsheviks were being slandered day in and day out, as satan incarnates. But we had by then learnt to read an opposite meaning to whatever the Government officials said. Our own view of the Bolsheviks was of good and bold people who had dethroned the Czar and established the rule of the proletariate..."[146]

It was from this time onwards that Sohan Singh Josh's initiation into Marxism began to gradually surface.

The first such example can be found in his drive to change the getup of the title-page of the *Kirti*, soon after he became its editor-in-chief. On top of the title page was printed for the first time the words of Marx, "Proletarians of the world, unite! You have nothing to lose but your chains!" the picture on the top of the title page was also changed into one that depicted the "...the unity of the factory workers and the farm workers for breaking the chains of slavery..."[147]

Sohan Singh Josh has said that the functions of the *Kirti* were not limited to propaganda work alone. It also aimed at the creation of a mass base among the Indian workers and peasants, to make them conscious of their ultimate goal and the significance of the weapons of organisation and class struggle that were needed to attain it. The first Kirti Kisan Conference took place in September 1927 and the Kirti Kisan Party was established on 12th April 1928 in Amritsar. This party, under the leadership of Sohan Singh Josh, soon established contacts with the communists in Bengal and Bombay and became very active in the criticism of the pro-landlord policies of the National Congress. It also aimed at the betterment of the conditions of the peasantry in Punjab set itself to expose that the aim of the Zamindara League (an organisation of the landlords in Punjab) was not to improve the condition of the peasants, but to preserve the interests of the landlord class.

It can be summed up from all these facts that Sohan Singh Josh's political life did not, like most other contemporary Indian communists, begin from a nationalist base. It was rather a path that led from the antagonism of a devout Sikh against the British to that of nationalism and finally communism.

It can be seen from the lives of the early Indian communists that all of them began their struggle essentially as non-communists, fighting against the British. Soon afterwards, however, they were in some way, either disillusioned by the method of struggle, or forced to move out to other countries in order to escape arrest or extradition. This exposed them to communist influences that were raging in Europe at that time, influences strong enough to lure these young minds desperately in search of alternative means of struggle for overthrowing the oppressive British rule. It is however not clear, whether their initiation was purely a result of theoretical influences or whether it involved much more. Young impressionable minds suddenly getting converted from nationalism to communism might have also involved certain more personal experiences. When Dange, for example, was questioning the withdrawal of the Non-Cooperation movement, he was, at the same time, amazed by the impact of the Bolshevik revolution. This drama that the success of the revolution actually brought about, unfolded itself to him in bits in pieces, and that too very secretly, thanks to the attitude of the British. This attraction to forbidden communist literature lured many into reading more and more of it. Human influences also had a big role in the conversion of the nationalists into communists. Dange and Roy had been major sources of inspiration to several early communists. What is noteworthy is that these early communists were, despite their respective influences, trying to think independently and formulate new theories of revolution on their own. Several problems arose as they tried to situate their newly acquired knowledge to the Indian plane, where the nationalist struggle against the British was already in full swing and repression of the communists had become a regular feature. It was amidst all this confusion and a tremendous diversity of ideas that the early communists emerged and began to mature.

NOTES AND REFERENCES

1   The Khilafat movement began in 1919 after Turkey was annexed by the Allied Powers at the end of the First World War, thereby, in a way deposing the Khalifa, the religious head of the Muslim world. Gandhi, who wanted to forge communal unity, found this a good opportunity and started the Non-Cooperation movement in 1920 in support of the Khilafat.

2   After the setting up of an independent democratic government under Kemal Ataturk in Turkey, the Khilafat upsurge died down.

3   When the Non-Cooperation movement was still in its full swing, a crowd of protestors set fire to a police station in Chauri Chaura in Bihar in February, 1922. Twenty-two policemen died as a result. Gandhi called back the movement immediately, saying that the masses were not yet ready to participate in a satyagraha of such a magnitude.

4   M.N.Roy, *Memoirs*, Bombay, 1964, pp. 3-4.

5   It is surprising that Roy has deliberately made absolutely no mention

of her in his *Memoirs*.

6   Ibid. p.22.

7   Ibid. p.27.

8   Ibid. p.23.

9   Ibid. pp.28-29.

10 M.N.Roy, *The Way to Durable Peace*, Calcutta, 1986. This essay was originally written in English and published in New York by the Indian Nationalist Party, as *An Open Letter to His Excellency Woodrow Wilson* soon after Roy fled to Mexico in 1917. Later on in Mexico, he rewrote the essay in Spanish and titled it "*El Camino Para la Paz Duradera del Mundo*" meaning "*The Way to Durable Peace*".

11 Ibid. p.21.

12 Ibid. p.30.

13 Ibid. p.41.

14 M.N.Roy, India: Her Past Present and Future, Sibnarayan Ray ed. *Selected Works of M.N.Roy*, Volume 1, 1917-1922, New Delhi, 1987, pp.85-153.

15 Ibid. p.94.

16 See Chapters 2-7, Ibid.

17 Ibid. p.142.

18 Ibid.

19 Ibid. p.143.

20 Ibid. p.153.

21 Samaren Roy, *The Twice Born Heretic*, Calcutta, 1986, p.76.

22 From Gale's, August 1919, Volume 3, No.1, pp. 9 and 25, Sibnarayan Ray ed. *Selected Works of M.N.Roy*, Volume 1, 1917-1922, pp.155-158.

23 Ibid. p.158.

24 Ibid.

25 Samaren Roy, *The Twice Born Heretic*, p.75.

26 .A.Dange, *Selected Works*, Volume 1, Bombay, 1974, p.12.

27 Mazzini has been quoted plenty of times along with Tilak and Tolstoy. S. A. Dange, *Gandhi vs.Lenin*, Bombay, 1921.

28 Dange himself admitted later on in his statement before the court in the Meerut Conspiracy Case that "the book was written by me in March 1921 when in obedience to the call of non-cooperation movement, I left my college and joined the students' non-cooperation movement. Though I joined the non-cooperation movement I was not in thorough agreement with the Gandhian programme. In this book I have compared Gandhism and Leninism

and have shown preference in favour of the latter. In spite of this, I have to say that the book is not a Leninist work at all. No Marxist literature was available at that time. In the book I have confounded the view of ordinary economic determinism with the historical materialism of Marx and I have in many places shown leanings towards idealist philosophy, which has no place in Marxist materialism. See Dange, *Selected Works, Volume* 1, pp.34-35.

29   See S. A. Dange, *Gandhi vs.Lenin*, Bombay, 1921.

30   Ibid. p.54.

31   Ibid. pp.54-59.

32   Editorial from *The Socialist* dated August 19, 1922, titled "Paradise Lost!" Ibid. p.144.

33   Editorial from *The Socialist* dated August 5, 1922, titled "Probing at the Root", Dange, *Selected Works, Volume* 1, p.137.

34   Ibid. pp. 137-138.

35   Ibid. p. 139.

36   S. A. Dange, *Gandhi vs.Lenin*, p.59.

37   L.P.Sinha, The Left Wing in India, 1919-1947, Muzaffarpur, Bihar, 1965, p.63.

38   Editorial from *The Socialist* dated August 12, 1922, titled "Wasting Heroism", Ibid. p.142.

39   See Editorials from *The Socialist* dated August 28, 1922, titled "Maharashtra Treacherous" and another dated September 9, 1922, titled "The Call of Sat Shri Akal", Dange, *Selected Works, Volume* 1.

40   Editorial from *The Socialist* dated September 16, 1922, titled "Formation of the Indian Socialist Labour Party of the Indian National Congress", Ibid. p.162.

41   Ibid. pp.162-163

42   Ibid. p.165.

43   Ibid. p.166.

44   Muzaffar Ahmad, *Myself and the Communist Party of India*, 1920-1929, Calcutta, 1970.

45   C.G.Shah, Marxism, Gandhism, Stalinism, Bombay, 1963, See Introduction by A.R.Desai, p.ix.

46   Ibid.

47   See Panchanan Saha, *Dictionary of Labour Biography*, Calcutta, 1995, pp.186-188.

48   Ibid. pp.122-126

49   Purabi Roy, Sobhanlal Dattagupta and Hari Vasudevan eds. *Indo-Russian Relations, Part 1*, 1917-1928, Calcutta, 1999, p.134

50   Ibid.
51   Ibid.
52   Ibid. pp.134-135.
53   Ibid. p.135.
54   Ibid.
55   Ibid. pp.135-136.
56   V.I. Lenin, *Collected Works, Volume* 45, Moscow, 1970,p.270.
57   John Riddell ed. *Workers of the World and Oppressed Peoples Unite!* New York, 1991, p.213.
58   See Thesis 3 of Roy's draft and the corrected version in G.Adhikari, *Documents of the History of the Communist Party of India, Volume*1, 1917-1922, New Delhi, 1971, p.180.
59   *Indo-Russian Relations, Part 1*, 1917-1928, pp.134-135.
60   Ibid. p.135.
61   The Thesis 4 of the Supplementary theses clearly said, "The breakup of the colonial empire, together with the proletarian revolution in the home country, will overthrow the capitalist system in Europe. Consequently the Communist International must widen its sphere of activities. It must establish relations with those revolutionary forces that are working for the overthrow of imperialism in the politically and economically subjugated countries. These two forces must be coordinated if the final success of the world-revolution is to be assured" See G.Adhikari, *Documents of the History of the Communist Party of India, 1917-1922.*
62   Bhupendranath Datta, *Aprakashito Rajnaitik Itihas*, Calcutta, 1953.
63   Ibid. p.290.
64   See Gautam Chattopadhyay, *Communism and Bengal's Freedom Movement, 1917-1929*,Volume 1, New Delhi, 1970; *Rus Biplab o Banglar Mukti Andolan (Bengali)*, Calcutta, 1967; *Abani Mukherjee: A Dauntless Revolutionary and a Pioneering Communist*, New Delhi, 1976.
65   Cecil Kaye, *Communism in India*, Calcutta, 1971, pp. 57-58.
66   Circular of W. Kolarow on Behalf of the ECCI (sometime in the beginning of 1923) against Abani Mukherjee, Purabi Roy, Sobhanlal Dattagupta and Hari Vasudevan ed. *Indo-Russian Relations* 1917-1947, Part 1, Kolkata, 1999, p174.
67   Subodh Roy ed. *Communism in India, Unpublished Documents*, 1919-1924, Calcutta, 1997, pp.191-192.
68   According to Gautam Chattopadhyay, the British imperialists always wanted to create disunity among the revolutionary groups. With this intention they often forged documents—Abani's statement was

perhaps such a document. But when the British dispatched a strong worded letter to the Soviet government in 1921, asking them to hand over Abani to them, they were refused. Instead the Comintern kept on assigning important tasks to him. This proves whether Abani was actually a spy or a revolutionary. See Gautam Chattopadhyay, *Rus Biplab o Banglar Mukti Andolan*, p.14. G.Adhikari has said, "Are we to believe all the alleged statements in the Government of India files in the National Archives attributed to political leaders? Are we, for instance, to believe the statement to the police alleged to have been made by Muzaffar Ahmad after his arrest in 1923, which is also in the government files in the archives? Here Muzaffar is supposed to have told the police what Nalini Gupta told him about the CI and which reads unworthy of a communist. Only prejudiced persons will draw unfair conclusions merely on the basis of these alleged statements in the archives." See G. Adhikari, *Documents of the History of the Communist Party of India*, Volume1, New Delhi, 1971,p.25.

69   M.N.Roy, *Memoirs*, p.300.

70   Ibid.

71   Abdur Rezzak Khan has said, "...I was very much impressed by Abani Mukherjee in 1922-23 and can certify that Muzaffar Ahmad never met Abani, nor knew anything about him first hand..."Interview with Abdur Rezzak Khan, p.155; Atul Bose has commented, "Abani Mukherjee struck me as a rough diamond, a man of great integrity but rough and terse..." Interview with Atul Bose, p.152; Satis Pakrasi has said, "...My impression about Abani was good. He was a good looking man and very well read. He also wrote very well and was engaged in writing a Bengali book in 1923, called Gariber Katha (On the Poor). He read out large parts to me and what he wrote on the peasantry impressed me very much. He also recounted to me how he escaped from Singapur jail back in 1917..."Interview with Satis Pakrasi, p.146. See Appendix A, Gautam Chattopadhyay, *Communism and Bengal's Freedom Movement*, 1917-1929,Volume 1.

72   G. Adhikari, *Documents of the History of the Communist Party of India*, Volume1, p.25.

73   Gautam Chattopadhyay, *Communism and Bengal's Freedom Movement*, 1917-1929,Volume 1, p.27.

74   Purabi Roy, Sobhanlal Dattagupta and Hari Vasudevan ed. *Indo-Russian Relations 1917-1947, Part 1*.

75   In Shaukat Usmani's letter to Amita Roy, he has clearly said,

"...Your uncle was an important figure in Tashkent and what others could not do in respect to approach with the authorities, Mukherjee was very much at home with the Soviet commissars." He has also written in the same letter, "Please note on my authority that *India in Transition* was a joint work of Roy-Mukherjee". See Gautam Chattopadhyay, *Abani Mukherjee: A Dauntless Revolutionary and a Pioneering Communist*, Appendix F, Letter from Shaukat Usmani, pp.54-55.

76   G.Adhikari ed. *Documents of the History of the Communist Party of India*, Volume 1, p.231.

77   Purabi Roy, Sobhanlal Dattagupta and Hari Vasudevan ed. *Indo-Russian Relations 1917-1947, Part 1*, Part 1, p.46.

78   Ibid. p.47.

79   Ibid. p.46.

80   M.N.Roy in collaboration with Abani Mukherjee, *India in Transition*, Geneva, 1922, p.204.

81   Ibid. p.240.

82   Shiv Prasad was Abani Mukherjee's co-prisoner at Singapore.

83   Purabi Roy, Sobhanlal Dattagupta and Hari Vasudevan ed. *Indo-Russian Relations 1917-1947, Part 1*, p.47.

84   Ibid. p.49.

85   Ibid. p.51.

86   Ibid.

87   Ibid. p.170.

88   Purabi Roy, Sobhanlal Dattagupta and Hari Vasudevan ed. *Indo-Russian Relations 1917-1947, Part 1*, pp. 116-125.

89   Ibid. pp.105-114.

90   Ibid. p.116.

91   Ibid. p.117.

92   Ibid. pp.117-118.

93   Ibid. p.119.

94   Ibid. pp.119-120.

95   Ibid. p.120.

96   Ibid. p. 121.

97   Ibid. p.121.

98   Ibid. p.122.

99   Ibid. pp.122-123.

100 Gangadhar Adhikari ed. *Documents of the History of the Communist Party of India*, *Volume* I, 1917-1922, pp. 180-182.

101 John Riddell ed. *Lenin's Struggle for a Revolutionary International, The Communist International in Lenin's Time*, New York, 1986, p. 39.

102   Purabi Roy, Sobhanlal Dattagupta and Hari Vasudevan ed. *Indo-Russian Relations 1917-1947, Part 1*, p.123.
103   Ibid.
104   Ibid.
105   Ibid. p.124.
106   Ibid. p125.
107   Ibid.
108   Ibid.
109   Ibid.
110   See Theses 6-9 of the Adopted Text of the Supplementary Theses, G. Adhikari, *Documents of the History of the Communist Party of India*, Volume 1, pp.183-187.
111   Purabi Roy, Sobhanlal Dattagupta and Hari Vasudevan ed. *Indo-Russian Relations 1917-1947, Part 1*, p.107.
112   Ibid. p.108.
113   Ibid. p.109.
114   Ibid.
115   Ibid. pp.110-111.
116   Ibid. p.112.
117   "For the purpose of propaganda and organization, revolution and the ultimate seizure and exercise of political power, the value of the emigrant and the returning Indian proletariat is undoubtedly the highest." Ibid. p.114.
118   See Editorial from *The Socialist* dated August 12, 1922, "Wasting Heroism", Dange, *Selected Works, Volume 1*, p.142
119   Shaukat Usmani, *Historic Trips of a Revolutionary*, New Delhi, 1977.
120   Shaukat Usmani has said, "In one of my meetings with Roy, he asked me to go to the small bureau of the Revcom office and fetch some English books and study them. Following his advice I went to the Revcom office and picked some pamphlets at random in Persian and English, and started reading them.
      "It was quite amusing to come across such terms as bourgeoisie, proletariat, petty-bourgeoisie and dictatorship of the proletariat. Often irresistibly I would laugh while reading such odd terms, and my fellow residents would be amused by my behaviour. On one occasion the laugh was on when Roy asked me to study trade unionism. I replied that I was not interested in trade and industry. Both Roy and his American wife could not suppress their laughter", Ibid. p.46.
121   Ibid. p.46.

122 Ibid.

123 Ibid. pp.46-49.

124 Ibid.

125 Ibid. Preface, p.v.(It should be noted that this was written much later, when he was writing his book).

126 Regarding Vande Mataram, Muzaffar Ahmad has said, "How could a monotheist Muslim youth utter this invocation? No Hindu Congress leader was able to understand this. The terrorist revolutionary movement in Bengal was definitely anti-British, but it was also a Hindu-revivalist movement: its aim was the restoration of Hindu rule..." Muzzafar Ahmad, *Myself and the Communist Party of India* 1920-1929, Calcutta, 1970, p.12.

127 Ibid. p.11.

128 "The British government in India adopted very strong measures to prevent the actual news of the proletarian revolution in Russia from reaching India and along with this started circulating slanders of various kinds against Lenin and other Soviet leaders...But, in spite of this, favourable news would leak through even the adverse newspaper reports. Besides, the common people of India took it for granted that there must be something good in whatever the British government put forth as bad." Ibid. pp.16-17. (It is to be seen whether Muzaffar Ahmad was putting himself in the "common people" category, because how far the common people in the sense of the masses understood the thoughts about proletarian revolution is very debatable and doubtful as well)

129 Dange, C.G.Shah were among other communists to take this path in search for an alternative means of struggle.

130 Gautam Chattopadhyay, *Communism and Bengal's Freedom Movement*, 1917-1929, Volume 1, p.60.

131 Ibid. p.59.

132 Subodh Roy ed. *Communism in India, Unpublished Documents*, 1919-1924, p.118.

133 Ibid. p.79.

134 Suchetana Chattopadhyay, Talking Bolshevism: Muzaffar Ahamd and the first socialist nucleus among the urban intelligentsia in the early nineteen-twenties, *Jadavpur University Journal of History, VolumeXXI,* 2003-2004, p.53.

135 Muzaffar Ahmad, *Aamar Jibon o Bharoter Communist Party,* National Book Agency, Calcutta, 1969, p. 107.

136 Ibid. p.374.

137 Ibid. p.378.

138 Ibid. pp.383-390.
139 Sohan Singh Josh, *My Tryst With Secularism, an Autobiography*, Patriot Publishers, New Delhi,1991, pp.1-17.
140 Ibid. p.26.
141 Ibid. pp.68-69.
142 Ibid. p.75.
143 Ibid. p.82.
144 Ibid. p.84.
145 Ibid. p.98.
146 Ibid. pp.102-103.
147 Ibid. p.110.

CHAPTER – IV

THE EMERGENCE OF AN ALL INDIA PARTY

The Second Congress of the Comintern had advocated for the colonies under imperialist domination, a policy that would require the communists to work in collaboration with the bourgeois nationalist party until the imperialist order was overthrown and the proletariat became powerful and educated enough to carry out a revolution against the local bourgeoisie. Meanwhile, however, the communists were to carry on independent propaganda among the toiling masses of peasants and workers so that they became aware of their rights, their dues and their power[1]. This was one side of the story.

The other side of the story was that the early Indian communists came mainly from nationalist backgrounds. Hence, their main aim was to overthrow the British, which would, they felt, bring an end to all the problems that the colonies were facing. Even when these nationalists became communists, they still nurtured this anti-British feeling in the same way. The overthrow of the British was not always considered as a step towards the final goal— the dictatorship of the proletariat. British domination was to them an evil, which had to be destroyed, so as to solve all or at least almost all the existing socio-economic and cultural problems in India[2]. The internationalist, class struggle oriented and socially egalitarian dimension of the communist movement was still not clear to them and they seemed to feel that many problems of exploitation would be done away with just by defeating the British. This feeling is apparent in different proportions in the early writings of all the Indian communists of the 1920's.

There is yet another side to the story. Despite all these contradictions, a beginning had definitely been made and the communists were making serious efforts to grasp what the Comintern was saying, and then theorising on their own, with respect to the Indian situation. Contradictions, confusions and conflicts did arise; the communists were human after all. But at the same time, from the point of view of the rulers, the communists were beginning to pose a significant threat– so much so that the British took several steps to curb it. The Peshawar Conspiracy case, the Kanpur Conspiracy Case and the Meerut Conspiracy Case are examples of it. The fear that the British held for the communists is evident from the way their agents kept track of them from the beginning. All communist work had to be carried on in a very clandestine manner because of British repression.

The delegates representing India had not been very vocal in the Second Congress of the Comintern. M.N.Roy, who gained much fame in the Second Congress of the Comintern, went to the Congress as a representative of Mexico, though his involvement in it was as an Indian seeking to overthrow the British in order to establish socialism in India. On the other hand, the Second Congress too gave much importance to the question of liberation in the colonial countries. It sought to explore the problems that imperialist domination posed, and then formulate strategies accordingly so that socialism could be achieved. Meanwhile it proposed for the Indians a strategy that meant for the Indian communists an infiltration into the Congress leadership, it being the principal bourgeois-democratic, anti-imperialist organ. The Comintern also said that the communists should support only the revolutionary elements within the nationalist movement, which was also represented by the reformist bourgeoisie. At the same time, it suggested that the communists should retain their independence of thought and continue to propagate their thoughts and ideas among the Indian masses. The basic question that confronts anyone at this point is whether the early Indian communists were actually following these suggestions of the Comintern, or whether they were trying to formulate independently. A detailed study of the activities of the early Indian communists, their relationship with the ongoing nationalist movement and their own clash of interests and ideas reveal a very interesting story. It can be said that until the Sixth Congress of the Comintern in 1928, the communist movement in India was growing mainly on the initiative of the Indian communists themselves. The influence of the Comintern was undoubtedly there, but it was not all encompassing in nature and there was scope for independent development of ideas.

Shashi Joshi has said, "The Indian Communist Movement has given Lenin's colonial theses of 1920 the status of a scriptural source..."[3] She has also said that Lenin was not actually addressing "the issue of colonial revolutions" but that he only "sought to unite all the existing anti-imperialist forces and tendencies in the world"[4]. She has cited the example of Lenin's letter to Bhupendranath Datta to prove that Lenin did not, through his theses, recommend any type of approach that the communists were to follow regarding the bourgeoisie[5]. She has said that Dutta had prepared a thesis "discussing the role of various classes in the Indian society in the making of an Indian revolution". The thesis of Datta however, was on the "Scheme of Organisation of Indian Work"[6] and he did not discuss about "the role of various classes" in it. Hence, the point that Lenin did not recommend an approach for the communists regarding the colonial bourgeoisie is rendered invalid. On the contrary, the Second Congress theses prove that Lenin did believe in supporting the nationalist movements during the first stage of the revolution that he envisaged for the colonies. After his debate with Roy, he also understood that the nationalist movements in the colonies consisted of two classes— the reformist and the revolutionary bourgeoisie. And he propagated that the communists should only support the revolutionary nationalists. His writings of this period also provide an example of an internal tension between the bourgeoisie and the communists, a clear separation of two stages of revolution, and a collapsing of the two stages by urging the formation of soviets from an early stage. Lenin did consider the struggles for national liberation in the colonies as helpful for the routing of capitalism in Europe, but at the same time he understood that such movements had enormous potential for socialist revolution as well. He clearly differentiated between the two layers of exploitation of the colonial masses and devised his strategy accordingly. The reason that the discussion of the history of the communist movement stems generally from the theses at the Second Congress is because it was for the first time that the colonial issue was discussed in details from the communist standpoint. The colonies were not only ascribed a role in fostering the world revolution, but the way in which they too would reach the revolutionary stage had been given due importance at the Second Congress. Colonial liberation had never been so important before.

It can be seen that the emergence of Indian communists began from the early years of the third decade of the twentieth century. This coincided with the withdrawal of the Non-Cooperation movement as well as the Second Congress of the Communist International. The role of the emerging Indian communists in shaping the history of the communist movement in India has to be therefore studied in the context of the role of the Comintern and the early communists in relationship with the contemporary nationalist movement.

THE ÉMIGRÉ COMMUNIST PARTY OF INDIA

The émigré Communist Party of India was established on 17th October 1920 at Tashkent with only seven members consisting of M.N.Roy, Evelyn Trent-Roy, A.N.Mukherjee, Rosa Fitingov, Mohd. Ali(Ahmed Hasan), Mohd. Shafiq Siddiqi and M.P.B.T Acharya. Shafiq was elected as secretary[7]. But what is important is that the minutes of the same day say that "The Indian Communist Party adopts principles proclaimed by the Third International and undertakes to work out a programme suited to the conditions in India."[8] The minutes of 15th December state that "It was unanimously agreed & resolved that the Rev. Party& the Indian Comm. Party will each maintain their respective independence, but will work in co-operation for the Revolution..."[9] These two early minutes of the Indian Communist Party clearly outlines the line that the communists intended to follow from the very beginning. It was to conform to the principles advocated by the Comintern on the one hand, and evolve at the same time, a programme of work that would be effective in Indian conditions. This work was directed towards the achievement of revolution in the colonies. In other words a plan was to be formulated in terms of the Indian situation, but in conformity with the spirit of the Second Congress.

It was perhaps this attitude that was in the minds of Roy and Abani Mukherjee when they jointly wrote a letter to Gandhi on 3rd January 1921[10]. The contents of the letter are also a clear indication of the policy to promote alliance with the bourgeois forces. The tone of the letter is one of enthusiasm and friendliness. It also declared that the Comintern and the Russians were very keen to help the revolutionary cause in the colonies and welcomed the cooperation of the bourgeois forces for its advancement[11]. This was at a time when the Non-Cooperation movement was in its full swing. Gandhi was also invited to join the All-India Central Revolutionary Congress which was to be organised by a Provisional Central All India

Revolutionary Committee. This committee was possibly an organ of the Indian Communist Party at Tashkent. The letter shows clearly that Roy and Abani were making attempts at collaborating with Gandhi, a fact that shows that they were in a way trying to incorporate the strategy of colonial revolution that had been evolved at the Second Congress.

ROY'S AFGHAN PLOT

This was what Roy and Abani were trying to do by conforming themselves to the strategies formulated at the Second Congress. There were moves however, that were at times totally contrary to what was being proposed at the Comintern debates. One such move was Roy's Afghan Plan. Roy submitted to Lenin a detailed "Plan of Military Operation in the Borders and in India"[12] sometime in 1920.

Roy began by saying, "Although the ultimate success of the Proletarian revolution in India greatly depends on the organisation of a strong, well- disciplined Party, which will carry on extensive doctrinarian propaganda among the masses of workers and poor landless peasantry, military operations on a sufficiently large scale are indispensable for the beginning of the work".[13] This was strictly not what had been propagated at the Second Congress of the Comintern, which had laid stress only on propaganda work at the initial stage. In fact, no mention of violent insurrection had been made at all. Roy however, it seems, wanted both propaganda as well as insurrection. He was saying, "Of course a Party of the Proletariat and the Peasantry (distinct from the Nationalist), which will lead the Revolution and assume Revolutionary Dictatorial power, must be formed and adequate propaganda among the workers, peasants and the revolutionary middle class intellectuals must be carried before the military operations are undertaken".[14] This shows that propaganda work was important, but only in so far as it could be used to prepare the minds of the workers and peasants for the imminent insurrection. This insurrection clearly was the goal.

Roy's idea was to occupy an area in the country along the border-line, where "Propaganda and organisation work will be instantly and vigorously started among the masses of the occupied territory", which will be used as the base of operation of the Central Revolutionary Committee, transformed as the Provisional Revolutionary Government".[15] Regarding Afghanistan as the right choice as the centre from where the operation was to be carried out, Roy said, "On account of the close proximity to Russia and the friendly attitude of the Ameer of Afghanistan, the above plan could be best carried out from the North Western Frontiers having in view the province of Punjab, or at least a portion of it, as the territory to be occupied by the Attacking Army."[16] His idea was to utilise the different tribes "inhabiting the frontier regions, from the Pamir to Beluchistan" to "procure the Attacking Army". The army would be a mercenary army and hence "utmost care should be taken in choosing the officers who will lead it"[17]. The commanders of this army were to be "chosen from the young intellectual revolutionaries, hundreds of whom can be brought out of India to be educated and trained in Russian Military Academies of Schools specially established for this purpose"[18]. He said, "The strength of the Attacking Army should be no less than 20,000 men well equipped with modern arms"[19]. Roy felt that in order to keep the army adequately supplied with "arms and other materials will "require large stores in Kushka, Tashkent and other convenient places", and that the supplies should be enough to maintain "at least" 50,000 men for "several months". After unfolding this mammoth plan, Roy went on to remark, "This plan is suggested on the supposition that the imperativeness of the destruction of British Imperialism for the success of the World Revolution, is recognised. A successful revolution in India would mean the crumbling the British Empire".[20]

One cannot help but remark at this point that this adventurous plan had a definite influence of Roy's early life when he was desperately trying to smuggle arms into India in order to facilitate a nationalist insurrection. The plan however was interesting and smart and above all, lined with Roy's sense of spontaneity, which, on the whole, made it quite impressive. Roy has said in his "Memoirs" that Lenin, though interested, was sceptical from the very beginning. He had commented that King Amanullah was not a revolutionary and that he was "shrewd enough" to see that he could gain by "pretending" to be anti-British. This opportunist policy, Lenin had felt, would ultimately lead him to "deal with the highest bidder" and the British could always pay more.[21] Besides, he had more in common with the British rulers than that with the Russian Bolshevik regime. But Roy was not to be put down so easily. He managed to convince Lenin that "all available opportunities" should be exploited and risks taken, without which the success of the Revolution would not be possible.[22] Roy then narrated at length about his journey from Moscow to Tashkent in-charge of two trains, loaded with currency, gold, arms, and ammunition.[23]

Meanwhile the Khilafat Conference was held in Delhi to demonstrate the reaction of the Indian Muslims regarding the usurping of the seat of the Islamic Khilafat. The Conference decided that the Muslims should no longer succumb to British superiority and leave the country to go to Hijrat. And nearly 18,000 Muhajirs joined the Hijrat and left for Afghanistan. Many of them, after facing several debacles on the way, ultimately reached Tashkent in September 1920.

These Muhajirs were picked up by Roy and his colleagues and sent to the newly formed Indian Military School at Tashkent. Apart from the Muhajirins, Indian traders in Central Asia and deserters of the Indian army, stationed in the Khorasan region were also picked up for this training. Much emphasis was placed upon the military training of Indians, while the deserters from the Anglo-Indian army, were soon put into Soviet service— who thus became some sort of an "international brigade"[24] as they joined the Communists from Russia, Persia and even Austria-Hungary. Two of the Muhajirs later became very important— Fazl-I- Ilani Qurban, a leader of the Communist Party of Pakistan and Shaukat Usmani, one of the founders of the Communist Party of India. It can be noted here, from a letter, probably written by Roy himself to one "Lord Byron" that the "Khilafat pilgrims were a terrible lot", who were "…religious fanatics or dirty adventurers without any idealism".[25] Apart from military training of the Indians, other preparations were also being made for the attack. The Soviet government began making inroads into Central Asia, Iran and Chinese Turkestan. General Mohammad Wali Khan, the Afghan ambassador in Moscow was also making arrangements for a treaty between Afghanistan and Soviet Russia, which ultimately materialised in February 1921. Soviet consulates were established in Herat, Jalalabad, Maimana, mazar-i-shaif, Kandahar and Ghazni. A powerful radio station was permitted to be built in Kabul. Russian engineers were also allowed to build a road connecting Turkestan and Afghanistan, in order to facilitate Roy's army. Instructions were also given to build an Afghan air-force.[26] By the summer of 1921, the time became "ripe for a possible Soviet invasion of India through Afghanistan".[27]

Lenin's doubts regarding the credibility of Ameer Amanullah began to surface very soon. It is clear from two letters written by Maulana Barkatullah, one each to Chicherin and Suritz[28]. These letters clearly hint at the fact that Amanullah had already begun asking for money, on the basis of which he proposed to help the Indian revolutionaries. Barkatullah's letters are fervent appeals for money on behalf of the Amir.

The attack on India was however, never made. Why such happened is a matter of debate. Scholars differ in their interpretations. David Druhe has ascribed several reasons behind this failure. He says that the Bolsheviks, "in spite of their efforts, were not so successful in bringing about the formation of a nucleus of Indian revolutionaries in Central Asia as they had desired." Besides, there was "...dissension among the Indian Communists...", many of whom like Acharya and Abdur Rab seem to "have resented Roy's authority in Central Asia..." Another reason for failure, as attributed by Druhe, was the failure of Soviet Russia in Chinese Turkestan, Persia, Iran and "above all" Afghanistan. The Amir, after sometime, refused to co- operate with Soviet Russia and the plan to attack India had to be abandoned[29].

Druhe has emphasised yet another factor that led to the abandonment of the plan. He has said that "the Russo-Afghan treaty resulted in a stern British note to the Russians on March 17th, 1921, which indicated that Great Britain was quite aware of Soviet intrigues in Afghanistan up to the signing of the Russo-Afghan treaty" in which, "intrigues were specially detailed ... The note concluded with the blunt warning that Soviet activities must cease." This, he says, affected the attitude of the Soviet government. Haithcox is of the same opinion. He says that "the Soviet government, not wishing to jeopardise economic relations with Great Britain for the sake of a project with such uncertain prospects, disbanded the school (Indian Military School) in May 1921."[30] Such a situation rendered the Indian revolutionaries practically helpless. There was no way in which they could, at that stage, carry on with their unfinished job without the help and co-operation from Soviet Russia and Afghanistan.

Right wing communist scholars like Ulyanovsky maintain that the "...left communists, led by Roy were in a hurry. The natural course of events, as envisaged by the Second Congress of the Comintern did not suit them at all, and they tried to speed it up. They were more concerned with the actual making of a Socialist revolution than with the painstaking preparations...." He also says that Roy's left "sectarianism" resulted in differences with his comrades and followers. Besides, his "...misunderstanding of the substance of Lenin's Preliminary Draft..."regarding the "united anti- imperialist" front was another reason for his failure[31]. In another incident, he actually challenged the authenticity of Roy's memoirs. He says, "...neither the Political Bureau of the RCP (B) Central Committee, nor the Council of the People's Commissars, nor V.I. Lenin could ever approve of a left sectarian plan of military operations along the border and in India. So, what was it that Druhe based his claim on? His only source was Roy's memoirs.... That source can in no way be considered reliable." He also goes on to say that money, gold, arms and ammunitions that were despatched to Tashkent "were meant principally for Afghanistan, which the government of Amanullah Khan had asked the Soviet government for and was promised... incidentally the mission of military instructors that was going to Kabul at the Amir's request was not led by Roy at all, nor was it under its control. Roy just happened to travel in its train to Tashkent and was going to proceed further on into Afghanistan, where he proposed to organise an Indian revolutionary centre."[32]

This is rather harsh on Roy. He could not simply keep appropriating the funds that were meant for someone else for some other purpose and retain its proximity to the Comintern too at the same time. This is rather farfetched an idea. Moreover Shaukat Usmani has also mentioned about this plan in his memoirs[33]. Moreover, there is nothing to prove that Roy did not have Lenin's consent before proceeding on his plans. In fact, his plans would have actually have amounted to nothing, had he not been offered Russian help. It can also be commented at this point that Lenin, who had not spared Roy in any way in making alterations in his theses, only a few months back at the Second Congress, would have had any problem at contradicting Roy's plan at this juncture. So blaming Roy alone for intending to hasten the pace of policies formulated at the Second Congress would not be accurate.

The Military School was disbanded, the project was undone, and the Central Asiatic Bureau of the Comintern was also abolished. Nothing in fact, remained of the spirit, which had a few months back, marked the initiation of the project. Roy returned to Moscow in

January, leaving behind Abani Mukherjee in charge of "his affairs at Tashkent." It undoubtedly "dispelled" some of Roy's illusions about India and he came to learn that "...the Indian revolution was still a long way off..." and that "...Arms and money would not make a revolution" [34]. He has written in his *Memoirs*, "...So I closed an exciting chapter of my life with the experience of a failure, but without regret" [35]. Meanwhile the Khilafat movement had also abated and the "India House" at Tashkent closed down. Twenty-two of the Muhajirin turned revolutionaries were chosen to go to Moscow and join the Communist University there. Each of the rest was given some money and then asked to leave.

This move by Roy was very revolutionary in nature, but against the policies advocated by the Comintern. This attempt, despite its failure, makes one thing very clear. Roy and other contemporary communists were, at this stage, not always seeking Comintern theories in order to formulate their own policies. They were trying to evolve a theory of their own— one that would provide an answer to the Indian problems. In doing so, their high strung nationalist sentiments often superimposed upon their newly acquired communist principles. Despite the Soviet Russia led Comintern's influence, they remained largely independent of Soviet dictates. This was the main feature that characterised the Indian communists during the first four Congresses of the Comintern.

Roy's manoeuvres in Afghanistan, though a failure, do indicate a very significant point. It shows that the communists were aware from the very beginning that military power was needed, if the British were to be contested with. This notion had been the guiding force behind most of the militant revolutionary organisations that had existed in India, those which had provided the primary impetus to most of these nationalist revolutionaries turned communists during the early parts of their nationalist careers. This feeling that violence was an essential factor that was needed in order to repel the British hence was once again rooted in their nationalist beginnings and was not quite compatible with Comintern strategies that stressed mass mobilization rather than just armed struggle.

The émigré Communist Party formed at Tashkent could not however, unite all the communist factions that existed outside India. In fact, Virendranath Chattopadhyaya and Roy were constantly at loggerheads with each other. Both were fervently trying to capture the attention and favour of the Soviet led Comintern by either criticising or understating the activities of the other. The Home (Political) Department files of this time show clearly that the early communists were not united in their ventures. File No.54 of June 1921 states, "Friction between Roy and Chatto[36] still continues. It appears that Roy has induced the Soviet to despatch 40,000 dollars to the San Francisco Ghadar party. Chatto heard of this from the Soviet representatives in Berlin and tried to stop the funds being despatched but it was too late..."[37] File No. 55 of June 1921 states, "In the third week of March a letter and telegram from Moscow was received by Chatto stating that it would be impossible to send the promised assistance as M.N.Roy stood in the way. Roy, It seems, advised the Soviet that Chatto's group is a Nationalist Party and not a Communist Party...After receiving this news the Indian Committee in Berlin was at a loss how to proceed, discussed innumerable plans which included a scheme for the murder of Roy..."[38] A close reading of these documents however, reveal that Roy was in a better position than the others, especially regarding his relationship with the Comintern, at least during the early 1920's.

THE FORMATION OF THE AITUC

The All India Trade Union Congress was formed around the same time as the Indian Communist Party was formed at Tashkent, that is, October 1920. Although the AITUC at that time was not led or controlled by the Communist Party of India, its significance lay in the fact that it was the first all-Indian organisation of the workers, which was soon to play a leading role in the activities of the CPI. The first Manifesto was issued by the first general secretary of the AITUC, Dewan Chaman Lall. Adhikari has said,

> "It is true that the initiative to form the AITUC was taken by the nationalists and humanitarians, but the real driving forces behind this development were the spontaneous militant mass actions of the industrial workers themselves, which took a qualitatively new form in the post war years of 1918-20, and the activities of those democrats who under the impact of the October Revolution and of the ideas of Lenin in India were seeking new revolutionary paths for our struggle for independence and were turning to the formation of the Communist Party, the class organisation of the workers and peasants."[39]

Adhikari has said that the war had caused several changes in the industrial scenario. The working class population had increased from

5 lakhs in 1910 to 13.4 lakhs in 1922[40]. There was a reason as to why labour population increased to such an extent. "Whatever may have been the situation at the beginning of the twentieth century, or in the few years following the famine and the influenza epidemic of 1918-19, from the middle of the 1920's onwards there was little scarcity of labour—even of a short-term character— in any major industrial centre of India[41]. So there must have been a tremendous exodus of population from the rural areas to urban ones, mainly in search of work. Besides, inflation was on the rise, thereby causing a rise in the living costs of workers. However, the profits of jute and cotton industries rose. But the mill owners refused to increase the wages of workers[42]. On the whole, the atmosphere became very tense. Strikes became rampant. Thirty-nine strikes were registered in the jute mills in Bengal with the involvement of 186,479 workers and the loss of 706,229 working days in 1921 alone. 104 industrial disputes were registered in Bombay in 1921 with the involvement of 131,999 workers and the loss of 1,272,362 working days[43]. Despite these problems and the consequent rise in the number of strikes, there were hardly any organised trade unions in the early 1920's[44]. Hence, when the first Manifesto of the AITUC was issued, the question regarding how many workers could come into contact with it, let alone comprehend it, remains to be answered.

The Manifesto to the Workers of India is a clear indication of the necessity of political involvement of the workers. It starts like this:

"Workers of India!

The time has come for you to assert your rights as arbiters of your country's destiny. You cannot stand aloof from the stream of national life. You cannot refuse to face the events that that are making history today for India. You are the mass of the population. Every movement on the political chessboard, every step in the financial and economic arrangements of your country affects you more than it affects any other class. You must understand your rights. You must prepare yourself to realise your destiny."[45]

But this necessity for political involvement was not in terms of a socialist revolution, it was still limited to the nationalist goal. "...There is nothing in the nature of union membership to prevent you from joining the Indian National Congress..." the Manifesto said. If the nature of leadership is given any notice, this becomes very clear. Dewan Chamanlal's preliminary note written after the fifth meeting of the Executive of the AITUC held on 30 July 1921 stated "the decision to hold the first All India TU Congress with Lala Lajpat Rai as the first President was taken in a meeting of Bombay workers held in Parel on 7th July 1920. Bal Gangadhar Tilak was elected as one of the Vice-Presidents together with Joseph Baptista, S.A.Brelvi, C.F.Andrews and Mrs.Besant."[46]

Adhikari has recorded that the All India Trade Union Congress was attended by "801 delegates from all over India of some 106 trade unions affiliated and sympathising, which together with miners' representatives represented 5 lakhs workers (miners represented being 2 lakhs). But this representation was clearly of the "affiliated and sympathising" workers. Hence not all of them had membership in registered trade unions. This shows that the workers' movement had begun, but like the early communist movement, this too was largely nationalist[47] in nature one the one hand and lacking organisation[48] on the other. Hence the education of the workers on communist lines was still to begin.

ROY'S WORKS ON THE CONTEMPORARY COMMUNIST MOVEMENT

In *India in Transition* M.N.Roy and Abani Mukherjee[49] have analysed the strike movements among the working classes in India. They wrote:

"Unable to drag any longer in their unbearable existence— unorganised, practically leaderless— the workers of the textile industry found the first weapon of the class-war. They instinctively learned to strike...Out of strike movements were born labour organisations. Trade unions were organised by workers in various industries...The government endorsed the attitude of the employers, many of whom were Indians and not a few belonging to the nationalist movement".[50]

Hence they were aware that the trade union movement began under nationalist guidance and support and they considered it as the beginning of the class struggle of the working class. They were saying, "...Suffice to say that, side by side with the national struggle, the class struggle has also been developing"[51]. However, they felt that the nationalists were using the workers' strikes as weapons "to be used for purposes of demonstration" which:

"...led to the disasters of Punjab, Bombay and other places in 1919...Consequently, the leadership of organised labour began to pass into the control of conservative reformists and government agents. Nevertheless, mass action still remains the backbone of the national struggle; and the masses are pushed into the revolutionary ranks not so much by revolutionary enthusiasm, as by the instinct of self-preservation, which is the mother of the struggle for economic emancipation".[52]

The chapter ends with an emotional outburst regarding how the emancipation of the masses would occur.

"...It is the mass awakening that has at last given real potentiality to the movement for national liberation; and it is the organised, class-conscious proletariat aided by the pauperised peasantry, which will lead the national struggle to a successful end. An unconscious ignorant mob, excited by frothy sentiments is no match for the mighty British imperialism. In spite of its growth, the Indian bourgeoisie is still very weak and is bound to be unsteady in its purpose; but before the worker there is nothing but struggle. It is having nothing to lose but his chains, on whom ultimately depends the national freedom; but national freedom does not mean anything to him unless it brings in its train economic and social emancipation. The national liberation of India is a prelude to a greater thing— the social emancipation of the working class. National struggle and class struggle are going on side by side; the noisiness of the former cannot conceal the existence of the latter."

India in Transition does not discuss the means by which this "economic and social emancipation" of the workers would come about. It only outlines the fact that fighting within the aegis of the nationalist movement, the workers were sure to attain their goal. It has also been highlighted that national liberation would comprise only of "a prelude to a greater thing— the social emancipation of the working class", but the strategy has not been worked out.

The strategy becomes somewhat evident in *What Do We Want?*[53] Here Roy said that the Indian workers were gradually developing a consciousness and becoming articulate. They wanted freedom because it would "prove helpful to its economic progress"[54] At the same time, he emphasised:

"To rally the working class under the banner of Swaraj, we must make this economic struggle a part of the political struggle. The redress of the immediate grievances of the Indian workers and peasants should be our object. In case of conflict between the interests of the native capitalist and the worker, we must boldly take the side of the latter if we are sincerely fighting for the majority of the Indian people..."[55]

Labour unions were needed, said Roy, because they would act as "militant organs of the working class struggle"[56]. He said that industrial development was necessary in order to lessen exploitation of the workers. It would "release the workers from the drudgery of primitive production"[57]. The use of machinery would reduce the need for human labour and hence serve as a means to reduce exploitation as well. But all this was impossible unless the social system dependent on private property was changed. And Roy proposed at this stage, "state supervision and workers' control of industry".[58] He then went on to say how this "National State"[59] would be formed, what the role of the workers would be in it, and how it could be used to advance the interests of the workers as against the native capitalists, who would flourish after the imperialists were overthrown. If the strategies that were being proposed by Roy at this stage are compared to those that had been propagated at the Second Congress, it will be seen that Roy was formulating more for the post-liberation scene than for the near future. He was endorsing the dual scale of struggle, but emphasising more on how the second layer of exploitation, that of capitalism regardless of its point of origin, would be eliminated.

In his *The Aftermath of Non-Cooperation*, Roy has said that during the Ahmedabad Congress in 1921, the Non-Cooperation movement had reached its "pinnacle". At such a stage the movement was "...bound to decline if new measures were not adopted to push it forward to a more advanced stage..."[60] In the Manifesto to the Ahmedabad Congress, Roy and Abani Mukherjee had warned about it. They had said, "...Because only by including the redress of their immediate grievances in its programme will the Congress be able to assume the practical leadership of the people...To enlist the conscious support of the masses, it should approach them not with high politics and towering idealism, but with readiness to secure their immediate wants, then gradually to lead them forward..."[61] They were aware from this time that the masses could not be lured into action with mere promises of political independence, that had no bearing on the miseries of their daily existence. Hence what was needed was to be achieved only by making efforts to solve the immediate problems of the masses. Only then could they be educated on political lines. Incidentally Dange too, writing at around the same time after his disillusionment with the Non-Cooperation movement said:

"In Swaraj and out of Swaraj, it is all the same to them. The peasant toiling today is not the master of his corn. He sees no government.

He knows his landlord and his moneylender, who rob him of his fruits. Them he hears crying for Liberty, and the peasant only sighs at the irony in it... With nothing to offer the toiling masses we cannot move forth."[62]

Hence, among the early communists, there was prevalent this consciousness about first solving the immediate problems of the masses so as to enlist their support in future for the cause of attainment of political independence.

The Manifesto to the Ahmedabad Congress criticised strongly the Gandhian tactics of Swadeshi and boycott. It said:

"For the defence and furtherance of the interests of the native manufacturers, the programme of Swadeshi and boycott is plausible. It may succeed in harming the British capitalist class and thus bring an indirect pressure on the British government, though being based on wrong economics, its chances of ultimate success are very problematical. But as a slogan for uniting the people under the banner of the Congress, the boycott is doomed to failure; because it does not correspond, nay it is positively contrary, to the economic condition of the vast majority of the population. If the Congress chooses to base itself on the frantic enthusiasm for burning foreign cloth, it will be building castles on a bed of quick sand. Such enthusiasm cannot last; the time will come when people will feel the scarcity of cloth and as long as there will be cheap foreign cloth in the market there can be no possibility of inducing the poor to go naked rather than to buy it. The Charka has been relegated to its well deserved place in the museum; to expect that in those days of machinery it can be revived and made to supply the need of 320 millions of human beings, is purely visionary..."[63]

The Manifesto also said:

"His personal character may lead the masses to worship the Mahatmaji; strikers engaged in the struggle for securing a few pice increase in wages may shout 'Mahatma-ji-ki-Jai'; the first fury of rebellion may lead them to do many things without any conceivable connection with what they are really fighting for; their newly aroused enthusiasm, choked for ages by starvation, may make them burn their last piece of loin-cloth; but in their sober moments what do they ask for? It is not political autonomy, nor is it the redemption of the Khilafat. It is the petty but imperative necessities of everyday life that egg them on to fight. The workers in the cities demand higher wages, shorter hours, better living conditions; the poor peasantry fight for the possession of land, freedom from excessive rents and taxes, redress of the exorbitant exploitation by the landlord..."[64]

Dange was saying:

"...Politics in the Congress is completely dead. To think ourselves to be forsaken of all wisdom and the power to do better things than we are doing in the absence of the Mahatma is certainly a sign of slavishness and degeneration. Had we rotted down for the want of organising and fighting capacities if the Mahatma had not been given to us at all? Some of us are opposing all change for they would have us do nothing that does not emanate from the High Gadi of the Mahatma. The Maharashtrians who are rationalists first and religious afterwards, find it very difficult to believe in the infallibility of the Gadis."[65]

Considering the fact that there were several early communists who had been initiated to communism from nationalism because of their disillusionment with the Non-Cooperation movement under the leadership of Gandhi, this was only a reflection of such ideas[66]. If freedom from foreign domination was not the goal to be pursued at the initial stage, the question that arises is regarding what the immediate demands would be and how the achievement of these demands would help in securing mass support for the Congress. The early communists said that freedom from foreign domination could not lure the masses to fight the foreigners. It was only a hope for the betterment of their existing condition that would do so. Here too, it can be seen that the early communists were thinking more or less on the same lines.

The Manifesto to the Ahmedabad Congress highlighted the need for the improvement of the "material condition" of the masses. It said in no uncertain terms:

"...The slogan which will correspond to the interest of the majority of the population and consequently will electrify them with enthusiasm to fight consciously, is 'LAND TO THE PEASANT AND BREAD TO THE WORKER'. The abstract doctrine of national self-determination leaves them passive; personal charms create enthusiasm loose and passive."[67]

It further said:

"...If the Congress would lead the revolution which is shaking India to the very foundation, let it not put its faith in mere demonstrations and temporary wild enthusiasm. Let it make immediate demands of the Trade Unions, as summarised by the Cawnpur workers, its own demands; let it make the programme of the Kisan Sabhas its own programme, and the time will soon come when the Congress will

not stop in front of any obstacle; it will not have to lament that Swaraj
cannot be declared on a fixed date because people have not made
enough sacrifice. It will be backed by the irresistible strength of the
entire people fighting for the material interest..."[68]
Dange was once again saying the same thing.
"The peasant worker must have land to himself. The worker must
own that with which to work...The real people of India shall own
the land, capital and instruments of production. Then alone will
people fight for Swaraj and win it, quite a different sort of Swaraj
from the bourgeois raj."[69]

It can be noticed that the Manifesto was putting pressure on the
Congress to adopt policies in order to solve the problems faced by
the masses. It said that the masses' support could not be ensured
until their immediate demands were taken care of, and that without
mass support independence could not be achieved. The Manifesto
was saying:

"Of course it should not be forgotten that with or without the
leadership of the Congress, the workers and peasants will continue
their own economic and social struggle and eventually conquer what
they need...Let not the Congress believe that it has won the
unconditional leadership of the masses without having done anything
to defend their material interests."[70]

The Manifesto of Roy and Mukherjee was in a way trying to
influence the decisions of the Congress. It was warning the Congress
leadership that the mass support on which they had depended during
the Non-Cooperation movement would withdraw itself until they did
something concrete to resolve the immediate problems of the masses.
However, the notion of a separate party for the masses is not evident
in the Manifesto. Hence, despite the pressure that the Manifesto put
on the Congress, yet, it was still advocating a collaborative policy
with the Congress, one that was very much in keeping with the
guidelines of the Comintern. In the absence of a Communist Party in
India, they were attempting to influence the radical minded Congress
members to think in terms of the lines on which they were thinking.
The only way by which this could be done was by widespread
experimentation and propagation. In the absence of any previous
socialist theoretical orientation in India, the proliferation of
communist ideas among the Indian intelligentsia was still a far cry,
one that had to be resolved before any step could actually be taken
towards the formation of the Communist Party of India.

ACTIVITIES OF THE EARLY COMMUNISTS AND ROY'S RELATIONSHIP WITH THEM

Meanwhile organisational work was also going on. In April 1922, Roy and his wife, Evelyn Roy went to Berlin. At that time Berlin was the centre for several Indian revolutionaries. In fact, Roy's rivals, Virendranath Chattopadhyay, Bhupendranath Datta and even Barkatullah were actively functioning there. Chattopadhyay started the "Indian News and Information Bureau" "to carry on propaganda openly and to act as a cover for revolutionary activity..."[71] He even made plans to oust Roy from power. Barkatullah had also organised the Indian Independence Party there. Besides, most of these rival groups were not without Soviet support either. Bhupendranath Datta "...reorganised his Indian Revolutionary Committee and called it the Indian Revolutionary Council: and sent letters to Taraknath Das and S.N.Ghosh in America, to Rashbehari Bose in Japan, and to Barkatullah, Acharya, Dr. Hafiz and Obeidullah in Afghanistan, urging them to join. His main object continued to be to combine all revolutionary Indians abroad and to form them into a central organisation directed from Berlin, in opposition to Roy..."[72] But despite these apparent hindrances, Roy could not be stalled and he actually managed to achieve much during his stay there. The most important of his achievements was the launching of his fortnightly paper, *The Vanguard of Indian Independence*. He regularly wrote in it along with his wife, who wrote under the pseudonym, Santi Devi. The name had often to be changed from *Vanguard* to *Advance Guard* because of British interception. He also began sending copies of *The Vanguard of Indian Independence* and *International Press Correspondence*, better known as *Inprecor*, the organ of the Comintern to India with the help of seamen. *Vanguard* proved to be a source of great inspiration for several Indian papers, both English and vernacular. *Amrita Bazar Patrika, Nava Yuga, Dhumketu, Desher Bani, Vartaman, Atma Shakti, Independent, The Socialist* etc. were some of them. As it is, the withdrawal of the Non Cooperation Movement had disillusioned several of the radical minded nationalists. Roy's writings in the *Vanguard* provided them a greater impetus to think on the lines of communism.

By this time, the relationship between Roy and Abani had also deteriorated. Roy's letter to the Eastern Section of the Communist International of September 11, 1922[73] only proves this. That Roy was pressurised by the activities of his rival groups also becomes very evident from his letter to the Secretary, Eastern Section, Communist International. It began like this,

"Dear Comrade,

The circle of Indian emigrants here is positively vicious. There is not one who can be trusted upon for any revolutionary work. Intrigues and obstructive activities are increasing everyday. Now our ex-comrade Mukherjee has joined it openly..."[74]

This excerpt shows that Abani had joined the anti-Roy group in Berlin. Roy however, did not put in much effort at reconciliation either. A letter of Tivel to the Presidium of the Executive Committee of the Communist International announced:

"On the initiative of Comrade Roy it is proposed to call a conference of Indians in Berlin in the middle of January. The object of this conference is to unite the communist groups in India which hitherto had been working disconnectedly, to draw up a programme of action for the left wing of the Indian National Congress, and the Trade Union Congress and the organisation of the press and the publication of literature in India."[75]

In this letter, when the invitation was made, it was made only for "...the organiser of the Communist groups in Bengal, the editor of the Bombay "Socialist"; the ex-secretary of the Trade Union Congress, representatives of the left Wing of the Congress, of the Bengal Federation of Seamen, the Calcutta Seamen's Union and the Bengal Railwaymen's Union, altogether from six to eight persons..."[76] Considering the fact that the Communist groups in Berlin were highly active at the time, Roy's move can be judged to be more deliberate than anything else.

The plan, like several others, could never be executed. But it shows the attitude of Roy. In his arrogance, he refused to relent to pressure from his rivals, and refused to reconcile with them either.

What is important is that despite disturbed relationships and divergent ideas, all the early communists were putting effort to spread communism in India. Roy's contribution was massive, if compared to that of the others. The fact that Roy did have certain advantages over the others, especially because of his high esteem in the Comintern circles explains this to some extent. At the same time, he was also very active in propaganda work among the Indians. Besides, he had links with almost all the emerging Indian communists like Muzaffar Ahmad, S.A.Dange, Singaravelu and others. He had already completed writing *India in Transition*. The first edition of his *The Vanguard of Indian Independence* came out on May 15th, 1922. It was more or less a reiteration of his thoughts in *India in Transition* and the Manifesto the Ahmedabad Congress, both written in collaboration with Abani Mukherjee. It said:

"...If the very existence of the British government is threatened today, it is not because the people of India has suddenly made up its mind to free itself from foreign thraldom, but because the inexorable forces of progress inherent in the organism of Indian society..."[77]

It was once again very critical of the Congress leadership. It said:

"...Foreign rule has to be overthrown because it has been obstructing our national growth and is detrimental to our social and economic evolution. But if a programme is set up which frankly foregoes all forward movement of the Indian society, it is but logical that the advocates of such a programme are trying to obstruct the progress of the Indian people, and therefore are not capable of leading us in the great historical period of our national life. This was the case with the National Congress ever since it came under the influence of orthodox nationalism..."[78]

The paper also said, "It is a mistake to think that the movement is the creation of great personalities. On the contrary, leaders are created by the movement..."[79] These thoughts of Roy as expressed in his paper are reflected in the writings of Dange in *The Socialist*, thereby clearly proving Roy's influence on him.

Roy's strategy was in no way pacifist in nature. He believed strongly in the need for violence while pursuing the path to his goal— the dictatorship of the proletariat. The Non-Cooperation movement did not endorse violence. Roy considered this fact to be defeatist in itself. And since communist theories sanctioned violence, Roy was only incorporating it into his own formulations. "Roy's writings suggest that the Communist attitude to violence may have been a factor in drawing him into the Comintern orbit. Communist theory endorsed violence, which was compatible with Roy's Bengali terrorist background, but it led him to a far more advanced ideological position since it deprecated individual acts of terrorism and advocated organised, full scale, armed revolt."[80]

ROY'S IDEAS ON VIOLENCE AND MODERATE POLICIES OF THE CONGRESS

The *Vanguard* issue of June 1st elaborates in details on these thoughts.

He was clearly in favour of an "open offensive". He said:

"…We must undermine the strength of the enemy and organise our forces, making them ready to be led straight into an open offensive at the earliest possible opportunity. This is the synthesis of Non Cooperation, if it is to be considered a political weapon. Let us not make out of it a spiritual principle, or a political programme, or abstract pacifism. It is a weapon to be used cleverly and mercilessly in the fight, not to purify our souls, but to cripple the enemy with the express intention of destroying him altogether…"[81]

Roy was repeatedly emphasising the same point. He said:

"Since the day of Non Cooperation was hedged in the cult of non-violence, it has lost all its potentialities; its revolutionary possibilities have been sacrificed on the altar of sentimental pacifism, born of the dread that the interests of the respectable upper class will be equally jeopardised by the systematic development of mass action…"[82]

Roy also said, "We must be realists: let us call a spade a spade. We have to fight an enemy who can rely upon all that modern science can provide. We can be crushed to the dust if we fail to find out first of all an equally unassailable ground…"[83] In an article in the same issue, Roy analysed this attitude to non-violence. He has said that the abandonment of the Non Cooperation movement just when it had turned militant was "not only impractical, but non-revolutionary". He also said, "This reprehensible tendency has of late degenerated into a pseudo-spiritual cult, which makes religion out of politics…"[84]

In *One Year of Non-Cooperation*, the same views were reiterated. It said:

"All honour to Mr. Gandhi, who found a way for his people out of the way for Government censorships and repression; who by his slogans of non-violent Non-Cooperation, Boycott and Civil Disobedience, was able to draw the wide masses into the folds of the Congress Party and make the Indian movement for the first time truly national. But the movement had outgrown its leader. The time had come when the masses were ready to surge ahead in the struggle, and Mr. Gandhi vainly sought to hold them back; they strained and struggled in the leading-strings of Soul Force, Transcendental Love and Non-violence, torn between their crying earthly needs and their real love for this saintly man whose purity gripped their imagination and claimed their loyalty."[85]

Looking at these views of Roy, it can be said that he was totally against the withdrawal of the Non Cooperation movement. Like other disillusioned nationalist counterparts, this undoubtedly proved to be a great source of influence. Dange's *Gandhi vs. Lenin* had already been published. His close associate, C.G.Shah, who was never quite influenced by Gandhian norms of struggle, now found strong grounds to base his theories. His *Hundred Percent Indian*, which came out in 1926, was perhaps an outcome of all these events and influences.

During the first few months of the *Vanguard*, Roy was still continuously trying to influence the policies of the Congress. This was perhaps the only way by which he could win over the radical minded Congress members towards communism. In the absence of any previous ground work of socialist theories in India, this attitude can be explained. In the issue of July 1st, 1922 Roy said:

"The Moderates representing the economic and political interest of the rich industrial and mercantile class, are fighting for a definite object and are well acquainted with the methods needed in their struggle. The congress in spite of its Extremism as against the Moderatism of the Liberals cannot be said to be free from the influence of these economic interests. Consequently its policy has been to utilise the mass-energy for its political purposes...If the Congress wants to represent the interests of the small middle class in the fight for national freedom, it must lose the support of the masses.

"To save the Congress from such an ignominious end, to enable it to lead the struggle of the Indian people further ahead on the road to freedom, the adoption of a fighting programme is indispensable— a programme by which the Congress the leadership of the struggle for existence, in which the masses of the people are involved..."[86]

Roy said in clear terms that the Congress was a body representing the propertied classes. "...All talk of humanitarianism and the crocodile tears shed over the Indian masses could not hide the true social affiliation of the Congress. It is an obvious fact that whenever a choice had to be made between the rich propertied class and the exploited working masses, even the Mahatma did not hesitate to stand by the former."[87] At the same time Roy was, as usual, overestimating the independent and revolutionary role of the working masses in the nationalist struggle. He explained that the Russian Revolution was one of the greatest contemporary events that could be compared in magnificence only to the French Revolution. He then said:

"The Communist International is the greatest outcome of the Russian Revolution. In it is concentrated all the revolutionary forces working for the liberation of humanity from the impasse and the building up of a new civilisation…Consequently the repercussion of the Russian revolution in India or in any other colonial land is not to be felt through the millions of gold coins imported, but through the organic relation that exists between the two revolutionary peoples. This relation will become more and more evident in proportion as the revolutionary forces in India develop…"[88]

Roy felt that since the Congress leadership was intent on supporting the cause of the propertied, and since the Bolshevik regime aimed at the emancipation of the working masses through a revolution that would give them political and economic power, both the goals contradicted each other. The Congress leadership was well aware of this. Hence, even when the Indian press was constantly trying to make propaganda in foreign countries to win foreign support, both moral and material, the Congress leaders were averse to taking the help of Russia. He said "They are so terrified about the Bolshevik gold, because of the apprehension that it may bring Bolshevism in its train. But let them be warned of the fact that an unmixed blessing is a fiction. American aid will be secured only in exchange for supremacy conceded to the Standard Oil Co., or some such other corporation."[89] This was a warning to the Congress leaders. This was also a statement that contained the roots of Roy's future plans, when he advocated a split with the agitation methods of the Congress and proposed instead an independent fight under communist leadership against imperialism and capitalism.

Just before Roy went to attend the Fourth Congress of the Communist International, Roy wrote in the *Vanguard* that the Congress needed to come out of its moderate policies. It should begin to draft a programme for the common people. Besides, it was time that the communists took up "…an increasingly aggressive part in the leadership of the movement. But to be able to do so we must have organic connection with the most revolutionary social elements. We must be their standard bearers. We must become their means of political expression…"[90] Needless to say that the toiling masses were to Roy, "the most revolutionary social elements". According to him, "And since the salvation of this class can and will be worked out by the workers themselves, they are the only relentless and uncompromising revolutionary force…"[91] Roy was saying clearly that all the classes were fighting for swaraj because they felt that the overthrow of foreign rule would cater to their economic interests.

However, the interests of each class were different and often hostile to that of the other. The interests of the upper classes were represented by their party and the same party could not see to the interests of the propertied and the toiling masses at the same time[92].This was what Roy was thinking before he wrote the Message to the Gaya Congress. He continued the article in the next issue, where he said:

> "Therefore *the formation of a Party of the masses has become necessary, at first to support the middle class democrats in their struggle against the alliance of the Liberals and imperialists, and then to assume the leadership of the movement as soon as it will be deserted by the middle class party, unable and unwilling to go any further*... The capture of the Congress by a mass party will have to take place before the goal of national independence can be reached..."[93]

THE GAYA CONGRESS

The thirty-seventh annual session of the Congress was held at Gaya in December 1922. On the occasion of this Congress Roy wrote "A Programme for the Indian National Congress" in *The Advance Guard* of December 1st, 1922[94], which was a summary of the actual separate pamphlet that was enclosed in the paper itself. During this time, he also wrote another pamphlet, *What Do We Want?* which was more or less in line with the ideas of the previous one. *The Advance Guard* of December 1922, along with the enclosed leaflet, "A Programme for the Indian National Congress" reached India on the eve of the Gaya Congress. It happened to create quite a flutter in the Indian press, so much so that "**The Times of India** (Bombay), the organ of the local big business, commented: 'Reuters Agency has been giving to M.N.Roy a publicity which is seldom accorded even to a prime minister's most serious utterance. Why should it have been thought worthwhile to cable three columns of Bolshevik delirium to this country?'..."[95] Adhikari has added, "...The British big business organ knew that such publicity in India has only an opposite effect..."[96]

The earlier pamphlet was divided into two parts. The first part was the address by the Fourth Congress of the Communist International "To the All India National Congress, Gaya, India Representative of the Indian People"[97]. It was written by Humbert Droz, the Secretary, and was quite strong in content and appeal, especially to the radical minded. It began quite dramatically:

"The Fourth Congress of the Communist International sends you its heartiest greetings. We are chiefly interested in the struggle of the Indians to free themselves from British domination. In this historic struggle you have the fullest sympathy and revolutionary proletarian masses of the imperialist countries including Great Britain.

"We communists are quite aware of the predatory nature of Western Imperialism, which brutally exploits the people of the East and has held them forcibly in a backward economic state, in order that the insatiable greed of capitalism can be satisfied...British rule in India was established by force and is maintained by force; therefore it can and will be overthrown by a violent revolution. We are in favour of resorting to violence if it can be helped; but for self-defence the people of India must adopt violent means, without which the foreign domination based upon violence cannot be ended. The people of India are engaged in this great revolutionary struggle. The Communist International is wholeheartedly with them."[98]

This tenor lines heavily the entire text, both that of the Comintern as well as that of Roy. In fact, Roy's writings throughout the year had been similarly aggressive in content and manner.

The document also said that the policy of "liberal imperialism" was a farce and that the National Congress should not have illusions about a "'change of heart' on the part of the British[99]. The Indian people must be free or be crushed to death by British imperialism; there is no middle course. And the people of India will never liberate themselves from the present slavery without a "sanguinary revolutionary struggle." Roy was saying the same thing. He considered the theory of equal partnership "a myth", which could have advantages only for the upper classes of the Indian society. This was because the British, through the theory of joint participation in the government, were actually trying to incur "the support of the native landowning and capitalist classes by means of economic and political concessions allowing them a junior partnership in the exploitation of the country. Such concessions will promote the interests though in a limited way of the upper classes leaving the vast majority of people in political subjugation and economic servitude..."[100] Roy was however, in favour of the Indian National Congress joining the national government as elected representatives of the people, so that it could "boldly challenge" all the steps that were taken by the British "to deceive the people". It should also "...declare in unmistakable terms that its goal is nothing short of a completely independent National Government based on the democratic principle of Universal Suffrage."[101]

Incidentally, Roy had made his attitude clear about opposition to the boycott of the reformed Councils in the *Vanguard*, a few months back. In this issue, he had shown preference for the line that the faction led by C.R.Das wanted to pursue, but remained silent for the sake of unity. Roy said, "...The boycott of the Reformed Councils by the Congress has not in any way injured the government. On the contrary it has provided it with Councils exactly after its desire...What was the motive of introducing these reforms? It was to split the Indian national struggle—to buy the services of the upper and a section of the middle classes. This object has been realised in spite of the boycott of the Councils by the Congress..."[102] Roy however, did realise that the scope of the Reformed Councils was very limited. Besides, if the Indian representatives were chosen from the upper classes, it would tantamount to helping in the strengthening of the British forces. If, on the other hand, "...the Councils are captured entirely by revolutionary Non-cooperators, who will enter the Councils, not with the hope of getting as much benefit as possible out of them, but to use them as a weapon of resolute warfare...This will be a revolutionary act, and participation in the Councils with this object in view, will be the revolutionary tactics. But a revolutionary party is required to carry out this tactic with determination."[103]

The message of the Comintern also said:

> "The relation of the Communist International with the struggle of the oppressed people is inspired by revolutionary idealism and based upon mutual interests. Our sympathy and support are not confined to empty phrases couched in sweet words. We must stand shoulder to shoulder with the people of India in their struggle against imperialism; therefore we will fail in our revolutionary duty if we do not point out to you the mistake that weaken the struggle and harm the cause of Indian independence."[104]

It then suggested to the Indian National Congress that:

"1. The normal development of the people cannot be assured unless imperialist domination is completely destroyed.

2. That no compromise with the British rulers will improve the position of the majority of the nation.

3. That the British domination cannot be overthrown, without a violent revolution.

4. That workers and peasants are alone capable of carrying the revolution to victory."[105]

Once again there is the display of aggressiveness on the part of the Comintern. In Roy's Programme for the Indian National Congress too there was this emphasis on violence. He said, "...a militant Programme of Action has become indispensable in order to mobilise under the banner of the National Congress all the available revolutionary forces..."[106] His programme was divided into three parts, Programme for National Liberation and Reconstruction, Social and Economic Programme and Action Programme. The first programme demanded complete national independence, election of national assembly by universal suffrage and the establishment of the "Federal Republic of India"[107].

The Social and Economic Programme wanted abolition of landlordism, reduction of land rent, introduction of modern methods of agriculture by state aid, abolition of all indirect taxation, nationalisation of public utilities like mines, railways, telegraphs etc., development of modern industries by state aid and under state supervision, fixation of minimum wages, hours of work and other facilities for workers in industries, recognition of the right of workers to organise, declare strikes and enforce demands by direct action, free compulsory education for boys and girls, freedom of religion, recognition of full social, economic and political rights for women, and abolition of standing army and organisation of a National Militia for defending national freedom.[108]

Action Programme included the organisation of militant peasant unions for defending the rights of peasants, organisation of countrywide mass demonstrations, mass resistance and mass strikes etc against high prices, increased railway fares, salt tax etc., organisation of countrywide Volunteer Corps. and participation in Councils with the object of wrecking them.[109]

Cecil Kaye has said that even if Roy's Programme could be called "moderate", the same could not be said for the Message from the Communist International. But the fact was, according to Kaye, that Roy himself had "drawn up" the message.[110] Kaye has said, "...Three typed copies of it, with the space for signature left blank, and with manuscript corrections and alterations in Roy's handwriting, were intercepted enclosed in letters from Roy to Muzaffar Ahmad, Dange and Singaravelu. In each case the letter (dated December 12th, 1922) asked for the publication of the enclosed document..."[111] Kaye's statement proves several things. One, that the Message from the

Communist International to the Gaya Congress was drafted by Roy himself. Secondly, Roy had close connections with Muzaffar Ahmad, Dange and Singaravelu[112]; and thirdly, communist bases however preliminary in nature, had been formed with Roy's influence in the eastern, western and southern parts of India, under the leadership of Muzaffar Ahmad, Dange and Singaravelu respectively.

David Druhe too has characterised Roy's Programme as mild. He said, "...Why was this programme so mild? In the first place it was in line with the Leninist thesis that communists should collaborate with the national bourgeoisie as against the imperialists, and secondly, Roy and his Soviet masters hoped that by this moderation the petty and the middle bourgeoisie of India as represented in the National Congress would become friendly with the Indian Communists."[113]

The question of violence in M.N.Roy's programme has been given much importance by scholars like Overstreet and Windmiller[114]. On the one hand, they have said, "Das was not the only man to be frightened by Roy's emphasis on violence. In his speech at Gaya even Roy's own man, Singaravelu felt obliged to endorse non-violence..."[115] On the other hand, they have also said "It is quite possible, of course, that Singaravelu and C.R. Das were merely shrewd politicians, quick to adjust to the new climate of opinion created by Gandhi's exceptional qualities of leadership. Regardless of their own views of non-violence, they may have decided that for the time being it was poor to oppose it. Roy was at a disadvantage in being far from the scene..."[116] True, Singaravelu did denounce violence[117], although he endorsed all the other points made by Roy[118]. He did say that "...we have to attain swaraj and the method which we, as followers of Mahatma Gandhi, can use in attaining swaraj is non-violent non-cooperation. I have the greatest faith in that method. That method has been disputed by our fellow communists abroad. I need not tell you their names...But we the communists of India differ from our fellow communists abroad in this particular method. We, therefore, send them our message that not only we believe in non-violent non-cooperation but that we are going to use non-violent non-cooperation against the British domination here..."[119]

But Overstreet and Windmiller have made another point too. They have quoted one of Roy's letters to Dange, written on November 2nd, 1922, which shows that he was "confident" that his programme would be rejected by the Congress. They also said, "...He intended this programme to serve as a litmus paper by which he could conclusively show that the Congress was not red. The exposure of reactionary leadership by such methods was an approved communist tactic and had been discussed many times by Zinoviev and others. Though Roy may have hoped that this device would open the way for 'a new party of the masses', his speech at the Fourth Congress a short time later suggests that he also hoped, by exposing the 'true character' of the Congress, to persuade the Comintern to place less emphasis on capturing it."[120]

If the first part of the analysis is considered, it can be inferred that C.R.Das and Singaravelu were either frightened to support Roy's stress on violence, or were merely adjusting to the existing political opinion, or were both frightened and hence adjusting to the existing political opinion. If the question of fear taken up, it can be said that Roy had a terrorist background, which was not the case of either Das or Singaravelu. Both were members of the Congress for quite sometime, without ever following terrorist means in their work. So, a sudden conformation to Roy's principles, as elaborated in the programme was not expected of them, and hence the question of fear did not arise. The opposition was a matter of difference in opinion. If being branded as a Bolshevik was embarrassing, it could be said at least for Singaravelu, that he would never have established links with Roy in such a case. But Kaye has pointed out, that Singaravelu was indeed maintaining links with Roy. In fact, one of his letters to Roy, just preceding the Congress had been intercepted, in which he had said that "...Roy's ideas were 'indestructible and imperishable, and will fructify in time'..."[121] Besides, he was endorsing Roy's views in every other way, was calling himself a representative of the communists and strongly supporting the cause of the proletariat.[122] Hence, after claiming already that he was a communist, it was not necessary for Singaravelu to adjust his opinion to remain at par with the majority opinion in the Congress. Roy too, on the other hand, had known Singaravelu for some time, and was definitely aware that like Dange, he too was still a member of the Congress. As for C.R.Das, Roy was pinning hopes on him and was perhaps even visualising an ally in him, but at the same time, he was also aware that C.R.Das was not clearly walking on the same path with him. He was aware of the contradictions in his appraisal of the problems that were facing India and the tactics to get rid of them[123].

C.R.Das, who on the other hand, was known to have opposed Gandhi before, did not need to adjust his opinions in favour of the Congress majority. But his differences with Gandhi were not on the issue of non-violence, but that on the question of joining the reformed Councils. It was perhaps that he simply did not agree to Roy's formulations, and hence did not comply with them.

The second argument stating that Roy was aware that his programme would be rejected, and that he sent it only to prove that the Congress was not influenced by communism in any way, is also rather farfetched. It may be that the roots of his deviation from the doctrines of the Second Congress lay in the failure of the Non-Cooperation movement, but that he was actually making policies in line with this deviation at this stage itself, cannot be proven. This notion that there was no point in alliance with the bourgeoisie democratic forces, and that an independent struggle of the masses led by the communists was needed, was evolved not before the Fifth Congress of the Comintern. But all the strategies that Roy was feneulating were perhaps only to win over the left-wing Congress members, so as to create a base for the establishment of a Communist Party in India, a fact in which he undoubtedly could not yet make much success. His numerous articles in the *Vanguard* or *The Advance Guard* were criticisms of Congress policies and suggestions for improvement on communist lines. He was never, during this time, talking about coming out of the Congress orbit while struggling to oust the British despite the fact that his suggestions were often quite radical. His emphasis on the necessity for the support of the masses for the attainment of freedom, or his point that the masses could not be ignored as they were the only potentially revolutionary class does not prove that Roy was actually recommending an immediate split. Besides, the readership of the *Vanguard* or *The Advance Guard* was very limited and British repression limited it further. If he was propagating that the masses would ultimately rise and assume leadership to reach socialism, it was only a furtherance of earlier Comintern doctrines. His programme therefore, was possibly intended more to expose the radical minded Congress members and win them over towards communism than anything else.

The argument on whether Roy managed to scare away the radical minded Congress members through his discourses on violence nevertheless brings into consideration a very significant aspect that

Roy was increasingly bringing into focus—his emphasis on violence. Over the year preceding the Congress at Gaya, Roy wrote several articles in his papers that signified the need for violence. He wrote in the *Vanguard*, "...Although it will be stupid to talk of premature violence, we are, nevertheless of the opinion that non-violent revolution is an impossibility..."[124] In the edition of the *Vanguard* of June 1st, he was writing, "Neither Charka, nor Khaddar, nor the cult of non-violence will bring swaraj to India..."[125] he also said, "The domination of one nation over another is established and maintained by brute force; therefore it cannot be shaken an iota by all talks about 'constitutional right', 'justice', 'non-violence', 'non-cooperation', etc. Its very existence gives birth to revolutionary forces and it is by violent revolution that it can be overthrown"[126]. Roy was explaining over and over again that non-violence was futile where the question of liberation from foreign domination was concerned. This feeling emerged mainly out of the withdrawal of the Non-Cooperation movement when it had reached a very high stage. This withdrawal of the movement by Gandhi expressed one extreme form of nationalist politics. Roy, in expounding the futility of non-violence, and asserting the necessity of violence, was advocating the other extreme. Considering the fact that the communism of Marx or Lenin endorsed the need for violence only when it was absolutely necessary, Roy's attitude was not totally in compliance with it. He was in a way glorifying the use of violence in his theoretical analysis of contemporary Indian conditions. This attitude can be said to have had long term consequences for future communist movements in India, whose left wings advocated violence as the only means to achieve the goal of socialist revolution.

It was not just the propagation of theoretical formulations that had been going on in the early 1920's. Roy was trying to enlist support in Europe for the advancement of communism in India. He was seeking the help of both French and British sources. He had written to the Communist Party of Great Britain for two men who would help in propaganda work in Bombay and in Calcutta. Their basic work would be "...to arrange for the reception and distribution of Communist literature..."[127] in India. He also sought assistance from the "Friends of Freedom for India" group in the United States, in answer to which S.N.Kar came to Berlin from America. The Communist Party of Great Britain selected Charles Ashleigh for helping Roy. Roy sent him to India under the name of Ashford. But his departure was detected a few days before he arrived at Bombay. So his passport was cancelled and he was deported. But due to some local problems, he could not leave immediately. He was allowed to stay in a hotel in Bombay for sometime, which somewhat helped him. Originally his plan had been to contact communists of both Bombay and Calcutta. But since his entire plan was cut short, all he could do was to carry verbal messages to some people there[128].

THE INDIAN COMMUNISTS BEFORE THE CHAURI-CHAURA INCIDENT

Roy admitted the failure of the communists in the Congress at Gaya in his "Open Letter to C.R.Das", written from Zurich on 3rd February, 1923. He asserted at the very beginning of the letter that "...The social tendencies that constituted the innate weakness of our movement during the last two years, still reign supreme in the Congress..."[129] He still referred to the Congress led national movement as "our movement". He wanted a change in the organisation of the Congress Party, one, which would actively involve the toiling masses into its sphere. He also said that the time had come when the masses or "the objectively revolutionary elements" needed to be woven into a party of their own, "...which will be the great Peoples' Party of India. The organisation of this party, the future leader of the struggle for national independence,— is the task of those who stand for a change, but for a forward looking change in the Congress Programme."[130] So Roy was still formulating according to the Second Congress doctrines. He was proposing the involvement of the masses as the Peoples' Party of India, in the struggle for national independence, but within the Congress orbit. Only the general attitude since the Second Congress of the Comintern had changed by the time the Fourth Congress had taken place. It can be seen that even after C.R.Das failed to conform to his views at the Gaya Congress, he was still eagerly coaxing him and his followers to aggressively break down the monopoly that was being maintained by Gandhian doctrines. In doing so, Roy's own explanations tended to become rather rigid in content. David Druhe has said, "...But the Congress certainly could not endure the sentiments of an 'open letter' written by Roy to Das on February 4th, 1923, in which the Bolshevik Brahmin[131] averred: 'We Communists stand for the abolition of classes and consequently of class struggle, but classes cannot disappear unless private property is abolished.' No wonder the Communists did not secure the services of Das, although they did find a patron in the Congress in a certain Vithalbhai who was not a very influential Congressman."[132] In comparison to the fame that several of the Congress members like Gandhi had acquired, Vithalbhai is certainly not that well known, especially outside India. But the fact is that he, like Motilal Nehru, had been a supporter of C.R.Das in the Congress in the early 1920's when the Swaraj Party was formed in 1923. C.R.Das, however, could never respond positively to the hope that Roy had in him, and Roy ultimately had to surrender that C.R.Das had indeed undergone a "metamorphosis" since his earlier days when he had openly championed the cause of the masses in the struggle for liberation from foreign rule. Roy criticised the Swarajjya Party's programme which defended the acquisition of private property and said:

> "...But the fact that such a statement was published, far in advance of any other clause of the Party's programme, is an important indication of the true nature of the men who lead it. It is a frank declaration of class-affiliation and class-consciousness on the part of the rising Indian bourgeoisie, whose special interests the Swaraj Party is dedicated to defend.[133]

Roy also said that Das "...is caught upon the horns of a dilemma which corresponds to the poles of his own temperament,— the lawyer in him struggled to escape from the metaphysical toils of orthodox Gandhism and so fell into the meshes of bourgeois Rationalism, against which his poet's soul rebels..."[134]

It was not just Roy's failure to bring C.R.Das into conformity with his ideas that was shaping the contemporary political movements. Several other events were also taking place at the same time—events that determined several moves of the British in the years to come. Among them was the rising discord between Roy and his fellow communists abroad. It remained a parallel factor, unchecked and ever-increasing, throughout the early years of the Indian communist movement. Several documents relating to this rivalry have been unearthed[135]. It is however, very strange that the Comintern did not interfere into this rivalry.

Another factor that needs mention here is that along with Roy others too were trying in their own ways to help in the spread of communism in India. They might have had differences with Roy, they might not have enjoyed the same stature that Roy had in the Comintern circles, but all the same, they too were responsible in spreading ideas of communism in India.

Abani Mukherjee came to India in 1922. By then he had already split with Roy. But after coming to India he began active work. He made propaganda among the so called Indian communists as well as the radical minded Indian revolutionary organisations. He made a detailed report of his work to the Comintern in his "Report on the Indian Situation and my one and a half year's work there"[136] and in "General Indian Situation during my One and Half Year's Stay there"[137] in August 1924. He has mentioned in his reports that he had set up a nucleus of a communist party in India. "The communist group that I organised consists only of fifteen members, of which Comrades U.N Banerjee and N.Chaudhuri are state prisoners now. Two of the comrades, N.Sen and P.Ganguli, who are controlling the Anushilan Samiti, are wanted by the police, and have to be illegal. Three of us are in Europe and the rest are working legally in the Indian labour movement."[138] He also mentioned that they also had good influence over the Swaraj Party mainly through the "...right hand man of C.R.Das, Mr. S. Bose..."[139] But what is noteworthy is that despite his rift with Roy, he did mention that the *Vanguard* had done good work in educating the radical section of the Indian revolutionaries, although the paper being in English failed to reach the masses, who did not know English[140]. He even reported that he had been to Madras and had established contacts with the labour leaders there[141].

Nalini Gupta, another communist, was despatched to India by Roy with the intention to form a party that would be useful in spreading communism in India. He came to India by sea via Colombo. British intelligence however, detected his movements as he had to show his passport at Dhansukodi, and his movements henceforward became recorded[142]. Nalini Gupta had close links with Roy. British intelligence was of the opinion that he was Roy's "most resourceful agent"[143]. Nalini Gupta was basically a technical man, who had "worked in a munitions factory in England during the first world war and was an expert in making bombs and other explosives"[144]. He had been highly influenced by Roy in Germany. He became very close to Roy and came to India to form links with the revolutionary organisations, with which Roy had already made or revived earlier contacts. He actually came to India twice during this time, once in 1921 and again in 1922. The object of his first visit was to enlist cadres for attending the Fourth Congress of the Communist International, which had laid great emphasis on the participation of representatives of the Communist Party of India. He contacted Nazrul Islam and Muzaffar Ahmad and actually influenced the latter to communism during this time. But the intention to secure representatives to attend the Comintern Congress could not quite succeed.

When Nalini Gupta came to India for the second time he was given shelter by the Anushilan group in Dacca. But they were, it seems, more interested in training party cadres in bomb-manufacture, than in communism as such[145]. But Nalini was "more interested in recruiting revolutionary boys for forming a unit of the Communist Party—the job for which the Comintern had sent him to India"[146]. The same point has been reiterated in Gopal Basak's article, "The Face of Nalini Gupta That I did Not See"[147]. But Nalini Gupta, despite these problems, actually set out to replace the traditional revolutionary ideas of the members of the Anushilan group and influence them with new ideas of communism. He even succeeded to some extent, but the conservative leaders "got the scent of what was happening in their underground world and particularly about the undreamt faithlessness of their special group, which fact had not only shocked them rudely but made them nervous about all sections of their cadres, in the face of the rapidly descending sword of the Bengal ordinance..."[148] It has been said in the same article that the conservative Anushilan leaders actually intended to kill him for polluting traditional revolutionaries into "traitors"[149]. But Nalini managed to flee. But his second mission was not a total failure. He did manage to secure some cadres to attend the Fifth Congress of the Communist International apart from indulging in other propaganda efforts. British reports say that "...He also gave financial assistance to several Bengali-Hindu students and sent them to Europe in the hope that they would become useful propagandists, but naturally these Hindus undertook the journey with the main object of completing their studies, and having reached Berlin, the majority of them dissociated themselves from Roy..."[150] If the experiences of the journeys that the newly converted communists undertook in order to reach Europe, and the dangers that they faced subsequently, is given any consideration, it can be said despite British Intelligence reports, their the analysis cannot be simplified to that extent[151].

S.A.Dange too by this time had become quite prominent in the communist circles both in India and abroad. His paper, *The Socialist* had also gained renown and M.N.Roy established close links with him. When Charles Ashleigh halted in Bombay for a few days due to certain local problems, even after his stay was cancelled, he visited Dange and gave him the list of persons who were to be contacted as per Roy's instructions. British documents say, "...He appears to be the directing spirit of communism in India, and the list handed over by Ashleigh—puts him in a position to coordinate work throughout India..."[152] Dange however, had not been much impressed by Ashleigh[153]. He had close contacts with several communist circles in India as well. He maintained regular communication with Singaravelu Chettiar of Madras, with S.Satyabhakta of the Central Provinces, with Ghulam Hussain of Lahore, apart from several important Bengali communists. Both Nalini Gupta and Abani Mukherjee are said to have contacted him during their stay in India. He was the first to organise a communist circle in Bombay, with R.B.Lotwala, C.G.Shah, S.V.Ghate, K.N.Joglekar, R.S.Nimbakar and others. He had formed the Indian Socialist Labour Party in September 1922. Though still a member of the Indian National Congress, he was trying to impress communism upon the radical minded Congressmen.

Singaravelu Chettiar had joined and left the Non-Cooperation movement like several of his contemporaries, and had taken to communism after that. He had made contacts with Roy much before the Gaya Congress. Cecil Kaye has said, "Roy had kept up a voluminous correspondence with Singaravelu, remarkably little of which had been intercepted...."[154] After his outburst on the issue of non-violence, Roy had tried to explain to him that he was not advocating the use of violence because of his "love for it", but that because he was a "realist", and he understood the futility of the "cult of non-violence"[155]. Roy had also made arrangements to send a printing press to him. Roy, to some extent, it seems, depended on him. Even after his denouncing of violent methods of revolution at the Gaya Congress, this dependence remained[156]. Unlike his arrogance in dealing with revolutionary groups in Germany, Roy's dealings with Indian revolutionaries were much more subdued and diplomatic. This was mainly because his entire work depended on their support, one that he could not just let go in favour of the other factions which too were actively working in India at the same time. He had secured an assistant called Velayudham, who was also quite efficient at undertaking difficult tasks. Moreover, he too had established links with Roy which is evident from the correspondence between them.

Ghulam Hussain was a schoolmaster in Peshawar, and was interested in communism. He was associated with Shamsuddin Hasan, the Publicity Secretary of the North Western Railway Union at Lahore. It was perhaps after consultation with him that he visited Kabul in June 1922. In Kabul he came into contact with the communists and managed to secure a grant from them. He returned back to Lahore in July. Soon afterwards, he began preparations to bring out a newspaper with the help of Shamsuddin Hasan. By December his newspaper *Inqilab* began to come out regularly. It published translated versions of Roy's writings. They also distributed communist pamphlets free of charge. However, the publication of the newspaper stopped as the subsidy obtained from Kabul was soon exhausted, and further plans could not be made easily as the Afghan Aamir expelled the Bolsheviks after his agreement with the British.

Ghulam Hussain also managed to start a preliminary communist organisation in Lahore. He made contacts with the labour movement in the west. Apart from Shamsuddin Hasan, he also brought under his wing, M.A.Khan, the well known labour leader of the NW Railway Union and the secretary of the All-India Railwaymen's Federation. British intelligence reports were of the opinion that he was suing the Lahore National College as a centre for propaganda[157]. Ghulam Hussain also established contacts with communists of other regions, mainly with Dange and Singaravelu. Roy too had correspondence with him, who referred to him as Muhammad Siddiqi in his letters.

One of the important agents of Roy was Shaukat Usmani. He was a muhajirin turned communist. He was despatched to India in 1922 via Persia, and he managed to secure more results in the spreading of communist doctrines, unlike his counterpart, Nalini Gupta, one of the reasons for this being the fact that he did not have to contend with his rivals in the region where he was working. After landing in India in mid 1922, from where he set for the United Provinces, he succeeded in forming groups in Benaras and Kanpur. Usmani himself was a native of Bikaner. This helped him to secure several supporters from amongst the students of the Hindu University at Benaras, especially those who belonged to his native place. Imam Uddin Rizvi, one such student, had already been converted to communism. In fact, he had already established links with Roy. He became very close to Usmani. A professor at the university, Sampurnanand, who had "showed Bolshevik tendencies",[158] was also influenced by Usmani.

Usmani's contacts were widespread. Not only did he form connections in India with Dange, Singaravelu and Muzaffar Ahmad; he also had regular links with European communists. Several of his letters that had been intercepted by the British authorities prove this fact[159].

Usmani must have achieved quite a bit of success in his work, because he became a source of constant irritation for the British and was persistently mentioned as a Bolshevik threat in British records. He was wanted by the British for the Peshawar Conspiracy case, but he could not be arrested before the trials began.

It can be seen that by the end of 1922 Roy had achieved much as far as consolidation of forces in India was concerned. Nalini Gupta was unable to secure the support of the Bengal revolutionaries. But here too, Roy, through correspondence managed to win over Bhupati Mazumdar and Bhupen Datta. They found in the Bolsheviks a source for securing arms. Roy also established links with Manilal Maganlal Doctor (Shah) who had been deported from Fiji islands for causing labour unrest. By this time M.N.Roy had quite a few centres from where communist propaganda was being activated in India— Bombay under Dange, Calcutta under Muzaffar Ahmad, Madras under Singaravelu, Punjab and Lahore under Ghulam Hussain, and United Provinces under Shaukat Usmani. M.N.Roy wanted to convene a conference of Indian communist groups in Berlin. He had even sent his emissary, Jatin Mitra to arrange for the journey of the Indian delegation to Berlin. The plan however, like many others, had failed.

Meanwhile Roy's rivals had formed the New India Revolutionary League in August 1922. They too were trying desperately to come into the limelight. They prepared a memorandum on this account and submitted it to N.N.Krestinsky[160], who was then the Soviet Ambassador in Berlin. The memorandum was signed by Bhupendranath Datta, Surendra Karr, Abul Hassan and Pandurang Khankoje. They expected that it would reach the Comintern through him. This group too was quite conversant about the problems that India was facing. Among other things, this group intended to publish literature in Indian languages so as to familiarise the working masses regarding socialist principles and strategies. They also wanted to train young men "in methods of labour organisation on Marxist principles"[161]. They also wanted military training for "a group of young men"[162]. The aims were not in contradiction to the policies advocated by the Comintern, but were in several ways similar to what Roy was propagating. Regarding the work that their members had already begun, they were quite categorical. They enlisted the organisation of a "Workers' and Peasants' Party" under this heading[163]. They said clearly that efforts at creating a federation of the workers' organisations and peasants' organisations too had also begun[164]. In the same memorandum they put forward certain suggestions for the Communist International. The suggestions are very interesting. From the very beginning it was an attempt at reconciliation with Roy's group[165]. This can be understood in the background of the fact that Roy had already incurred much support not only from the Indian communists but also from the Comintern. They had perhaps realised that overriding the progress that Roy's group had already achieved would be unwise and that using his influence would come in more useful.

THE CHAURI-CHAURA SENTENCE

The Indian situation during this time was quite tense as far as the communists were concerned. The prosecution of the accused at Chauri Chaura sentenced one hundred and seventy-two persons to death. The judgement was passed by the Allahabad High Court on 30th April, 1923. This raised a tremendous furore among the communists. M.N.Roy repeatedly wrote in the *Vanguard* about the brutality of the sentence, his main point being that one hundred and seventy-two deaths were too much to pay for the death of twenty-two policemen. Besides, he wrote "An Appeal to the Labour Unions of India" pointing out that "...the crime of these men was that they dared to assert their right to live and challenged the authority which orders them to toil and starve perpetually. Chauri Chaura was the scene of revolt not only against the government but also against the established order of society, against the sacred right of property—of landlordism. Hence the hand of repression has come down there in

its naked brutality..."[166] He also asserted that the apathy of the
Congress regarding these sentences was deplorable. So in order to
save the lives of the victims of the Chauri Chaura judgement, he
appealed to the workers of India. He said:

> "Workers of India, it depends on you to save these men. No idle
> resolutions, no expressions of horror, no criticism of imperialist
> justice will be of any avail. These men stand at the door of death as
> a result of their courage in responding enthusiastically to the call of
> Non-cooperation, and they can be saved only by effective Non-
> cooperation, which no other section of the people but you— the
> producers of everything, the life blood of Society— can declare to
> enforce the demand for the release of your condemned comrades.
>
> "Workingmen and Workingwomen of India! Demand the release of
> the Chauri Chaura victims *under the threat of General Strike*...Such
> an action will on your part will have the sympathy and will be
> supported by the revolutionary proletariat of the world."[167]

The Executive Committee of the Communist International and
the Executive Committee of the Red International of Labour Unions
jointly supported Roy in his propaganda. In the "Manifesto of the
Communist International on the Chauri Chaura Sentence", the
Comintern strongly condemned the imperialists regarding their
activities in the colonies. Regarding the Chauri Chaura sentence, the
Manifesto said:

> "The international proletariat, engaged in a bitter struggle with
> Capitalism in every part of the world, must not let this imperialist
> butchery go unchallenged...The proletariat of the imperialist
> countries cannot remain indifferent. Energetic action must be taken
> on behalf of our Indian comrades fighting bloody battles against the
> imperialist terror.
>
> "Working-men and working-women! Hold protest meetings and
> demonstrations, condemning this act of imperialist butchery and
> demanding the release of the condemned men...."[168]

The Communist International also called upon the proletariat of
Great Britain to take up the case as "...The wild career of Imperialism
gone mad can only be checked under the threat of direct action of
the home proletariat..."[169]

The Communist International was evidently thinking on the lines
of Roy. Here too, like Roy, there is a clear denunciation of nationalist
policies and a rather strong assertion of the fact that the problems of
the toiling classes could be solved by the toiling classes themselves.
As it is, the Chauri Chaura incident had spelt a note of betrayal to the

communists. Now after the judgement was passed, the same conviction became stronger. Roy said, "...Do not permit the upper class leaders to sabotage this urgent action in defence of your class, and in protest against the barbarity of Imperialist justice..."[170] The Comintern Manifesto said, "...If the reformist leaders will not be moved to action even by such a flagrant violation of every moral and legal code which they hold up as a standard for others, you must repudiate their leadership and resort to direct action, in order to uphold the right of the subject peoples to revolt..."[171] The working classes were called upon to act independently, to depend upon the sympathy and support of the world proletariat, and to shirk away from the bourgeois-led movements for the cause of their fellow toilers who were the victims of the Chauri Chaura sentence. This breach of interests between the nationalists and the communists leading to the declaration of repudiation of Congress leadership if necessary, even if only for an isolated incident, was in actuality, a policy that would be further elaborated at the Fifth Congress of the Comintern in 1925.

THE THIRD SESSION OF THE AITUC

The main complaint of the communists regarding the Indian National Congress was that it did not have a definite policy concerning the workers and peasants. Besides, another point that irked the communists was the bourgeois representation in the Trade Union Congress sessions. It disturbed them that the working class representation was still low and that the leadership was being provided by the bourgeoisie, who failed to conform to Marxist ideals. M.A.Khan's article in *The Socialist* of March 1923, was a strong criticism of Dewan Chamanlal's inactivity after each of the two sessions of the Trade Union Congresses. Khan accused Dewan Chamnlal for neglecting the strikes in the Oudh-Rohilkhand Railway and in Jamshedpur. Khan said:

"...The kisan movement and other attempts on the part of the exploited masses of India to get their grievances ventilated or redressed could not draw any inspiration or guidance from the general secretary who has been from the very beginning to this day essaying to retain in himself all the prerogative and all the show of the TUC."[172]

The third session of the AITUC was held on 27th March, 1923, at Lahore, after being postponed from its earlier date in November of the preceding year. C.R.Das was made the president of this session.

The Fourth Congress of the Communist International sent a message to the AITUC on this occasion. It declared its support for the session and said, "...we should like to remind you that your tasks are great and that you must not narrow them down. The working class of India is not only fighting for honourable work, but the economic liberation of the workers and peasants of India depends on the nation's political liberty. No amelioration can be obtained in the framework of imperialist exploitation. Therefore your duty is to play an important role in the framework of imperialist exploitation..."[173] The note clearly attached singular importance to the attainment of freedom from foreign domination before the task of economic liberation of the masses could be achieved.

But M.N.Roy was not at all satisfied with the proceedings of the third session of the AITUC. He was already disturbed at the turn of events at Gaya, and the attitude of the delegates of the AITUC at Lahore disturbed him further. The representation of the workers and peasants was very low, unlike that in the second session at Jharia, where several "...coalminers came to the platform of the AITUC session to narrate their condition of wages and work and to plead for the support of the session to their struggle."[174] The Resolution passed at the Jharia session had been quite significant. It had expressed solidarity with the famine-struck masses of Soviet Russia, it had backed the cause of unemployment of the British workers in Great Britain and Ireland, it had supported the struggle of the workers at Fiji, and had aimed at the creation of strike insurance fund to maintain the strikers in times of strikes lasting for over a month[175]. This session of the AITUC too had not been attended by the Indian communists like Dange and Muzaffar Ahmad. Singaravelu had only sent it a message. Roy compared the third session with this and said, "...But what a long way this Trade Union Congress has gone since those days of 1921 when it came dangerously near to being a real working class organisation...Seventeen month ago its second annual session was attended by six thousand working men and it was defended against the combined attack of the employers and the Government by an army of over fifty thousand rebellious workers, who by the force of mass strike wrested from the reluctant capitalists at least the promise of a 20 per cent wage increase. What a change this interval of seventeen months has wrought in the Trade Union Congress. In the place of ragged men straight from the coal pits, Lahore gaily welcomed a galaxy of bourgeois Nationalists and intellectual dilettantes who rolled luxuriously to the Congress in a 'huge fleet of motor cars'[176] to make speeches and pass resolutions in the name of the poor downtrodden '98 per cent'..."[177] Evelyn Roy more or less reiterated Roy's thoughts. She said that the third session of the AITUC was a "...strange conglomeration of nationalism, utopianism and reformism (to say nothing of more dubious 'isms' such as humanitarianism and opportunism)..."[178] Adhikari has however, said that the resolutions adopted at the third session of the AITUC did have a certain significance. He said that the resolution thanking the Workers' Welfare League for India for its services to the TUC and the anti-war resolution urging the workers not to join any war that was unjustified alarmed the British. He has also said that these resolutions also show that despite the absence of communists in the Trade Union movement, it "...was nevertheless influenced by socialist and communist trends appearing in the country."[179] Communist trends had undoubtedly begun to influence the labour movement, but the leadership was still in the hands of the bourgeoisie, those whom Roy labelled as the "reformist bourgeoisie". Roy wanted the labour movement to free itself from such leadership.

As early as November 1922, much before the session began, Roy wrote:

"So the task of the Trade Union Congress is not reform, but revolution. It is not conservative unionism, based upon the bankrupt theory of 'collective bargaining', but revolutionary mass action involving the pauperised peasantry as well as the city and rural wage earners, who must be organised and led by those who want to see a free India enter upon a period of social progress...The Trade Union Congress, in order to execute the historic task it has undertaken, must free itself from the leadership which believes in piecemeal reform. Such leadership is, consciously or unconsciously, hostile to the interests of the working class.

"To bring about this inevitable union of the two radically evolutionary forces under the banner of national independence and social progress is the task undertaken by us. We believe that you are fighting for the same object. Therefore, let us work together."[180]

M.N.Roy was from the very beginning, it seems, opposed to the Trade Union leadership. He felt that the leadership was reformist in nature, especially after his earlier interaction with C.R.Das. He was therefore refusing to corroborate with the Trade Union leadership and was instead calling upon the working masses to fight for their cause jointly with the communists. He was not yet clearly enunciating the need for communist leadership of the workers, but was hinting at cooperation between the two forces after the Trade Unions could free themselves of the reformist leadership. Now this was in conformity with the Second Congress doctrines[181]. Dange too was thinking on the same lines. In *The Socialist* of March 1923 he said:

"We advise labour leaders and workers not to heed these soft words and philosophic phrases of bourgeois intellectuals. Only by class war, to which the Ahmedabad workers are slowly drifting unconsciously, can labour hope to win. Defeats may come once or twice, but final victory is of the workers."[182]

THE IDEA OF THE PEOPLE'S PARTY EMERGES

Another idea was taking shape at this time, the idea of a mass party composed of the workers and the peasants. Roy called it the Peoples Party and by the 1st October issue of *The Advance Guard*, he had already given a concrete shape to the idea. He felt that such a party would serve the interests of the masses, in both immediate and ultimate aspects; it would represent their class interests and at the same time advocate a programme of national liberation, where the masses were to play an active role. Dange called it the Indian Socialist Labour Party of the Indian National Congress[183]. Another document that mentioned the concept of a mass party was the "The Statement and Memorandum Submitted by the New India Revolutionary League in Regard to the Workers to be Carried on in India"[184] This document said that the New India Revolutionary League had already started to organise "a Workers and Peasants' Party". It also suggested to the Comintern in its list of suggestions that there was the need "...To organise revolutionary party of the workers and peasants in India in order to eliminate the present government. Steps should be taken that this party works in complete co-ordination with the present nationalist revolutionaries for the common, in Overthrow of British Imperialism..."[185] Roy had supported Dange's move. In his letter to Dange in November, 1922, he said, "...we look upon the step taken by you and other comrades working with you as a timely one..."[186] but at the same time, in the very next sentence, he said, "I take it for granted that the Socialist Labour Party of India understands the necessity of international affiliation and believes that the Communist

International is the only revolutionary international body."[187] Roy's insistence on international affiliation led to debates between him and the Indian communists time and again especially on the issue of Bolshevisation. It can also be said at this juncture that when Roy was functioning as an official of the Comintern, Indian communists were being more intent in developing their own understanding of the objective conditions prevalent in India. The discussions undertaken at the level of the Comintern (at least as much of it that reached them despite strict British vigilance) influenced them somewhat, as did the model Bolshevik revolution of 1917. But their formulations were not totally dependent on the policies formulated by the Comintern. They evolved their own notions of tackling with the Indian situation, often much at variance with the strategies of the Comintern. Like Roy, their main focus was on overthrowing the seemingly insurmountable British regime before plunging on to anything else. In doing so alliance with the Russians, or the Bolsheviks, as they preferred to call them, posed uncertainties and fears. Besides, they could not quite conceive of the theory of internationalism at that stage. It is obvious from the letter that the Labour Party of Dange did not develop as an answer to the dictates of the Comintern. It developed independently. Adhikari has said that "...Roy and Dange were the first to arrive at the idea of forming an open legal mass party, and they did so independently of each other..."[188]

It can be discerned from these examples that different views on the necessity of the workers' and peasants' party had already been felt by the early 1920's. Conscious efforts at the organisation of such parties also began during this time. The efforts reflected the policy adopted at the Second Congress. But the significance of these efforts is the fact these were independent efforts by varied individuals from different areas and not as a response to the dictates of the Comintern. The Workers' and Peasants' Parties were formed in different parts of India between 1926 and 1928. But these efforts indicated that the beginning had already been made and made at the initiative of the Indians themselves.

Adhikari has said that the idea of forming a mass party on the lines of the programme proposed by Roy in *The Advance Guard* of 1st December of 1922, had been discussed "...at the time of the Gaya Congress by Dange, Singaravelu, Abani Mukherjee and Manilal

Doctor, who were present there and seemed to have met together. These discussions at Gaya resulted in what is known as 'Dr. Manilal's manifesto' which was produced with the collaboration of Abani Mukherjee"[189]. This manifesto was published on 25th March, 1923, in the English weekly, "Navayuga", which was issued from Madras by G.V.Krishna Rao. Though prepared in collaboration with Abani Mukherjee, the manifesto came out "…as one by 'Dr. Manilal' and purported to be signed by 'the Textile Workers of India and the Kishans of Northern India'. This manifesto, addressed to 'Indian Labourers and Peasants for organising a Party of their own'…"[190] This is probably because Abani Mukherjee came to India in 1922, he had come "…with a warrant over his head…"[191] and therefore his identity could not be disclosed so blatantly. The manifesto proposed "…a Labour and Peasant Party of India…"[192] It endorsed the principle of non-violence but wanted the abolition of the standing army and the police, which it was felt, should be replaced by "voluntary conscription from suitable and willing elements from the people, and arming of the masses and organisation of the militia". It also objected to Bolshevik domination but declared at the same time that it had nothing against "the labour section of the Bolshevik movement"[193].

DETERIORATION IN THE RELATIONSHIP BETWEEN ROY AND ABANI

Cecil Kaye has said that Roy was aware of Abani's presence in India, and he could detect Abani's hand in the manifesto. He had been right too. British Intelligence reports say that Abani was in Gaya with Manilal "…is well known from the intercepted correspondence and my informant corroborates this…"[194] Meanwhile Muzaffar Ahmad communicated to Roy evidence of Abani's connections with Zinoviev even after his expulsion from the Comintern[195]. Moreover, Abani was also having close connections with the communists in South India. British records say that Abani had gone to Madras as Ganga Prasad in a German boat "Warteenfels" and on reaching there, he stayed "…with Velayudham Pillai for some days and then with Chetti and met some of the local extremists and it was during this time that Singaravelu Chetti's manifesto was drawn up"[196]. Singaravelu Chettiar's manifesto undoubtedly indicates the manifesto of the Labour and Kishan Party of Hindustan. Now considering the bitterness that was prevalent in the relationship between Abani and Roy, this must have been quite alarming to Roy. He could not allow Abani to override him in bringing about the formation of the much wanted mass party in India. So he wasted no time and sent notes to all his Indian contacts cautioning them about Abani's underhand dealings. Various documents can be mentioned in this connection. One is Roy's letter to Velayudham[197]. This letter is very interesting. The first part of the letter mentioned that Roy had understood from the very beginning that the manifesto of Manilal was actually an effort of Abani Mukherjee and that Manilal's signature had been forged in the document by Abani. It is probable that Abani sent it to Germany for publication, because Roy said in the letter, "...They would not publish it unless I would investigate into the genesis of the affair...Therefore, I was in a position to inform the German Comrades immediately that the Manuscript was a fake document as a result of Muk's[198] intrigues...."[199] He said that he regretted the fact that he did not know that the same document was in actuality identical to the one "...issued by a bona fide organisation and signed by honest revolutionaries..."[200] Roy's attitude must have estranged Singaravelu, and he might not have responded affably to his subsequent letters. So knowing that Velayudham was his close associate, Roy decided to write to him instead, and explain his position. He said, "...I have nothing against Muk. as an individual as Com. Sing. appears to think..." and that it was certainly not a case of personal jealousy that had facilitated his action. At the same time Roy used the letter to serve also as a warning to the communists sheltering Abani. He said that despite the recent attitude of Singaravelu towards Roy, Roy still maintained "...perfectly friendly relations with you and did not fail to give practical indications in so far as I could give in the limitations put upon me by the International to which I must submit..."[201] The contents of the manifesto regarding its dissociation with the Bolsheviks was strongly criticised in the letter. He said that "...if the International disowns your party, I cannot fulfil my promises to help you. But did my best, notwithstanding, because I hoped that as honest revolutionaries you would such see your mistake as soon as it was pointed out to you..."[202] The last part of the letter highlights the fact that Roy was interested in joining hands with them only if they made a fresh start again. "If you are willing to reconsider the whole position and begin all over again I will be very glad to join hands..."[203] Roy raised the issue of a preliminary conference that would unite all the communist forces working in India through discussions. He said, "All these misunderstandings and political blunders could be avoided, had the party been launched after proper deliberations..."[204] He indicated in the letter that he would be happy if delegates from all over India represented the Conference. Roy also highlighted the issue that Shamsuddin Hassan, a close associate of Ghulam Hussain had already written to him regarding the fact that "...he has 4 men (2 in Bengal and 2 in U.P.) to come as delegates to the Fifth Congress of the C.I..."[205]

Apart from the fact that the letter was serving as a note of regret as well as a warning, it was also proving another thing— there was difference of opinion leading to a rift between Roy on the one hand, and Singaravelu Chettiar on the other, a fact that Roy was trying hard to mend. In all probability, and much to Roy's anguish, Chettiar perhaps had become friendly with Abani. Besides, it was already known to Roy that Abani was maintaining correspondence with Zinoviev despite his expulsion from the Comintern. In such a situation there was every chance that if Abani could actually do some concrete work of organisation of a mass party in India, he would be rendered help by the Comintern, one that could make Roy's position in the Comintern somewhat vulnerable in comparison to his earlier position. Roy could not afford to do that. So Roy tried in every way to stall such a development, and the letter to Velayudham was one such venture.

Among other documents relating to the same problem was a letter from Usmani to Singaravelu Chettiar dated 9.2.23[206] It says that Usmani had been directed by Roy to inform Singaravelu of Abani Mukherjee's expulsion from the Comintern. It says that Abani was not to be trusted as he was only spreading "nuisance" in India[207]. Another document was Roy's letter to Dange in which he advised the latter to remain "...in close touch with Singaravelu and work together for the organisation of a legal party. By associating with him inside an organisation you will be able to control his ideological weaknesses."[208] But at the same time Roy was applauding Singaravelu's capacities. He was saying, "I am convinced he is the best man available to be the figurehead of the legal party..."[209] A warning regarding Abani's moves was issued in this letter too. The letter said quite categorically, "Other efforts are being made to organise a worker' and a peasants' party. If we do not hurry up we will be faced with an accomplished fact in the shape of a socalled workers' party under very questionable leadership... Abani Mukherjee who formerly worked with us is the moving spirit behind this group. I have already warned you against him. He has been expelled from the International as well as from our party. He is a questionable and a dangerous character."[210] Another factor stressed in this letter was the advice regarding joint work by the Indian communists. M.N.Roy wanted some sort of a central organisation of the communists to come up in India, with which he could communicate in a less complicated manner. He said, "...We may accomplish more in every way by centralisation of effort..."[211] though this was said in the context of organisation of the party press, the letter undoubtedly expresses Roy's increasing frustration at the absence of a centralised party. In another letter of Roy to Dange in May, 1923, the same feeling was expressed clearly, "As far as my information goes, there are good elements scattered all over the country and these should be gathered together into one central organising committee. To this end I request you very urgently to get in touch with Singaravelu without delay and to try to convene a preliminary conference to which besides our own comrades, such men as Sampurnanand of Benaras, Manilal of Gaya, the editor of *Vartaman* of Kanpur etc. can be invited. I would also suggest Upendranath Banerjee[212] of *Patrika*...The idea is to have political control of the legal party in the hands of the Communist Party..."[213] These letters to Dange and the letter to Velayudham express the same note throughout.

ATTITUDE OF THE COMMUNISTS REGARDING COMINTERN LEADERSHIP

Dange however, was not quite keen on working under the aegis of the Comintern. He said as much in his "Hunt for Bolsheviks in India" that was published in the Maratha daily, *Lokmanya*. This was what he said:

"A conference of all the communists in the world was held at Moscow in November 1922. The representatives of all the communist and socialist parties all the world over and affiliated to the central body were present at this conference. There is no such party in India as yet. Mr. M.N.Roy sent a friend of his to me hoping that I may be available to act according to the dictation of this (Moscow Central Communist Party) party as I was a socialist though all the time he knew that there was no such party here…But as I was not ready to work under a party in a distant country, I told him that I was not ready to present myself at the congress. I also told him that Indian politics differed vastly from the European one."[214]

He then went on to explain that it was not the help of the Bolsheviks both financially and otherwise, that prompted him to seek the emancipation of the toiling masses of India, and that his labour movement was devoid of Bolshevik influences[215]. Regarding Roy's conference in Berlin, Dange wrote to Singaravelu on 29.2.23:

"You perhaps know that Roy wants to hold a Conference of Indian Communists in Berlin. I think it is a mad venture for the Indians to go hunting communism in European conferences. Whatever has to be done must be done in India. Moreover, there must be less talk of revolution than what Roy indulges in, even when the preliminary rights of labour are not obtained, it is a dream to talk of proletarian revolution. You might differ but that is my view."[216]

These two documents prove that Dange was not working under the influence of the Soviet Russia led Comintern. He might have been influenced by their theories, but his organisation work was being done independently. Singaravelu had also written to Dange:

"…Who are the Indian Communists, has many of them, who are prepared to go to Berlin when Germany is on the throes of starvation! There is a good deal to be done here before one thinks of a Congress. But let him go on if he has resources enough, but it is absolutely impossible to cross our shores at the present…"[217]

Adhikari has said, "The reason why Roy was so insistent on holding a conference of delegates of Indian communist groups in Europe is to be sought in his hostility to and lack of confidence in Abani who was then in India and already in contact with the communist groups. Roy wanted that the launching of the open mass party should take place under his auspices in Europe and not in India where perhaps Abani would get the credit…"[218]

But apart from the fact that Dange and Singaravelu were more keen on working in India than in attending conferences abroad, and apart from the fact that Roy's wariness of Abani Mukherjee's activities prompted him to try and pull the Indian communists more and more to his side, the whole issue raises yet another question. Why, despite assured help from Roy, did Dange and Singaravelu shirk from conferences in Europe? This tacit agreement about not joining conferences in Europe can be explained by a certain similarity in their ideas regarding communism in India. Shashi Joshi has said:

"The essential point that emerged from both Singaravelu's and Dange's ideas and organisational efforts was that of *primarily* overthrowing foreign imperialism while *secondarily* trying to ensure that the interests were represented favourably in the national consolidation, and that social and political power was *tilted* against capitalism...Obviously for them what was on the agenda was not a Communist party but a party that would *create the conditions for its emergence*..."[219]

She has felt that their aims were more in the nature of organisational and preparatory work that would set the conditions for the development of Indian communism, and that the "real life development of the mass movement and its needs would determine the nature of its goals and programmes..."[220] Looking at the ideas of Dange and Singaravelu during this time it can be assumed that they were both trying to groom the Indian communist movement ideologically and indigenously. They both felt that the objective conditions for the emergence of communism in India was different from that in Europe and that its emergence in India could not be superimposed by the experiences of its emergence in the west. Before heading on to revolutionary activities, they therefore wanted to properly prepare the forces that would combat imperialism and native capitalism. In this they differed from Roy and in this they also established once again the fact that independent thinking formed a basic part of the emerging communist movement in India.

ROY'S MEMORANDUM TO THE LUCKNOW CONFE-RENCE AND THE EMERGENCE OF THE WORKERS' AND PEASANTS' PARTY

Meanwhile copies of the Manilal Manifesto had been circulated to Dange, Singaravelu, Ghulam Hussain and others. Cecil Kaye has said, "...Dange, who had schemes of his own in preparation, temporised; but Ghulam Hussain adopted the idea enthusiastically, and, on April 27th, sent out a circular addressed to various 'Comrades' (signed by himself and his assistant S.D.Hasan, the titular editor of the 'Inqilab') calling a meeting at Lucknow for June 30th 'to organise Dr.Manilal's Manifesto Party'. He also sent a copy to Roy..."[221] As an answer to it, Roy sent a Memorandum to the proposed conference, which was, in reality, never held, like so many earlier instances.

The Memorandum in a way was a reiteration of Roy's pronouncements at Gaya. He said that an independent working class party was necessary in order to liberate India from the hands of the foreigners and also for its own emancipation. He said that the working class would not participate in this struggle for liberation if the anti-imperialist struggle had a "programme of bourgeois nationalism". He proposed that the programme "...drafted for the consideration of the National Congress at Gaya be adopted as the programme of our party..."[222] He also said that the party should be called as "...the workers' and peasants' party of India..."and that it was "...advisable to avoid the name *Hindustan* which may not be taken kindly by the Muslim masses..."[223] He was perhaps criticising Singaravelu's Manifesto that proclaimed the name of the workers' and peasants' party as the "Labour and Kishan Party of Hindustan". He opposed the slogan of "labour swaraj", saying that it was vague and that it could not be attained until the nation could be freed from imperialism. He said that the immediate goal that confronted the communists was a "...democratic government based upon universal suffrage with as much protection as possible for the workers and peasants..."[224] Endorsing the points of the Second Congress, he said that the alliance of the Bourgeois forces and the working classes should be sought in the struggle against imperialism[225]. Roy also stressed on the fact that the party of the working classes should comprise of both the trade unions as well as the kisan sabhas. "The political party of the working class must maintain the closest relation with the economic organisation of the workers and the peasants..."[226] Roy also proposed that the central executive committee of the Indian labour movement should have an affiliation with the Communist International as well as the Red International of Labour Unions. This would provide the movement with international affiliation and would help the masses in their ultimate struggle for emancipation[227]. Roy was aware that the establishment of a legal party of the workers and peasants was not enough. He said:

> "While believing firmly that the legal existence is indispensable for the growth of the mass party, I must urge upon you the necessity of an illegal apparatus which should be built as a parallel organisation. Since the party which will be born out of this conference, may not from the beginning adopt a communist programme, it cannot take

the place of the Communist Party of India, therefore the latter should continue as the illegal apparatus of the legal party while, on the other hand, those members of the Workers' and Peasants' Party who fully subscribe to the communist programme will be allowed to join the Communist Party and maintain their membership of the legal party at the same time..."[228]

He felt that this would not lead to any dispute between the two because the programme of the legal party "...will be the minimum programme of the Communist Party and therefore will have the fullest adhesion of the latter..."[229] The Communist Party, said Roy, need not be, on the other hand, liquidated, "...because experience all over the world has proved that the working class can reach final victory only under the banner of the communist programme. In consideration of the situation we have to work in, it may be necessary to have a 'dual organisation'. But the role of the Communist Party cannot be taken by any other organisation."[230] The last part of the Memorandum highlighted once again Roy's insistence on violence. He said, "...It should be remembered that to swear by the term 'non-violence' will not save the party from the penal code...The best way would be to leave out of our propaganda the controversy of violence versus non-violence..."[231] But afterwards however, Roy was saying, "...Economic emancipation of the exploited can only be attained by the expropriation of the expropriators which cannot be done by peaceful and non-violent means. It is ridiculous to say that we are 'non-violent revolutionaries'. Such a breed cannot grow even on the soil of India..."[232] After the sarcasm, he explained in the end, "...The workers and the peasants are to be organised not to face sufferings but to develop the will and power to fight for freedom. Therefore the term non-violence negates all the essential principles upon which our party is based. This will in no way commit us to acts of premature violence nor will it oblige us to indulge in stupid talks which can come under the purview of the penal code..."[233]

One of the basic differences between Roy and Indian communists like Singaravelu was regarding the issue of non-violence. But here, Roy was refusing to bend at all as is obvious from his comments. It could be that he had become somewhat impatient after the withdrawal of the Non-Cooperation movement and the Gandhian tactics of non-violence that was still influencing several of the revolutionary minds in India. Though treading on the principles of the Second Congress,

Roy's tone did suggest a note of this impatience. Once again the explanation can be sought in his earlier revolutionary nationalist background. Adhikari has said that Roy's Memorandum was "...also a constructive criticism of Singaravelu's manifesto, the text of which was now in the hands of Roy..."[234]

Overstreet and Windmiller have said that when Roy attended the third plenum of the enlarged ECCI in Moscow in June 1923, "...he apparently succeeded in getting its (ECCI) agreement that the WPP should exist separately."[235] But, at the same time, the ECCI did not agree to his "view of the bourgeoisie".[236] They then quoted from the message that the Comintern sent "To the First Conference of the Workers' and Peasants' Party of India" to prove these points. O.V.Martyshin has also made a similar observation, "Roy's line ran counter to the Comintern's directives and the ECCI rejected his attitude to the national bourgeoisie..."[237] If Roy's Memorandum and the message of the Comintern are analysed once again, it can be seen, on the contrary, that Roy's policy was in conformity with that propagated in the message from the Comintern.

The Comintern message said:

> "The Indian bourgeoisie is so situated today that at least temporarily its interests will be best served by an agreement rather than a revolutionary struggle with British imperialism...The working class alone can save itself from this dreadful eventuality by snatching from the faltering hands of the bourgeoisie the standard of national revolution...The struggle for national liberation is a revolutionary movement. In leading this movement the political party of the workers and peasants must in co-operation with and give the fullest support to the bourgeois parties so far as they promote the struggle against imperialism in some form or other."[238]

Roy's Memorandum said:

> "...The first and foremost problem that every political party in India must face and solve is the problem of national liberation. The fate of every party depends upon its ability to find a solution of this problem...the mere formulation of this aim obliges us to challenge the political domination of the Indian people by a foreign power. It does not make any difference if this domination will be eventually readjusted to the demands of the native upper classes in order to secure their service for the joint exploitation of the workers and peasants. Our party which stands for the liberation of the producing classes from all sorts of exploitation cannot leave the question of

national liberation out of its programme because national liberation, i.e. the release of all the forces of social production, is the first step towards the ultimate realisation of our programme which is the end of class domination...."[239]

Just because Roy's Memorandum was not spelling out in detail on the issue of co-operation between the working class and the bourgeoisie like the message from the Comintern, there is no reason to presuppose a contradiction between both. The primary aim was national liberation, and the working masses were called upon to struggle for it, as this struggle would be the first step towards their ultimate goal of revolution. In this context, not only were the two similar, but that they also showed conformity to the ideas propagated at the Second Congress of the Comintern.

In 1923, for the first time, as a response to Singaravelu's call, the first of May was celebrated as a proletarian holiday in Madras. Two mass meetings were held in Madras, where the problems of the working classes were discussed. Another important development that took place on the same day was that Singaravelu established a workers' and peasants' party. He even announced its programme that had been previously published in Tamil language. The new party was called Labour and Kishan Party of Hindustan, the word Hindustan being one that Roy wanted to avoid as mentioned previously. Singaravelu sent telegrams to the press of other provinces urging similar celebrations of May Day throughout India. The whole incident was given coverage in the *Vanguard* of June 1923[240].

The Manifesto of Singaravelu had been framed more or less in accordance with Roy's Programme for the Indian National Congress at Gaya, and had been signed by Singaravelu himself and Velayudham. The Manifesto attempted, like Roy, to put forward a programme for the national liberation movement; it emphasised the necessity of the formation of a left-wing party, but within the Congress, and also a party of the workers and peasants, that would cater to their demands[241]. Adhikari has said, "...Roy was putting forward these ideas, as we have seen, more clearly and cogently, and what is important was simultaneously insisting on the formation of a communist party by uniting the four or five groups which had arisen in different parts of India into an all-India centre to guide and implement in practice the abovementioned task."[242]

There were however, some differences between Singaravelu's

Manifesto and that drafted by Roy on the occasion of the Congress at Gaya. One has been mentioned already in Adhikari's quotation— that Roy went a step forward where organisation of a mass base was concerned. He aimed at the establishment of a workers' and peasants' party simultaneously with the establishment of a clandestine Communist Party, one that would take up the task of guiding the mass movement. This point is very significant. Whereas Roy maintained the necessity of a parallel organisation of the Communist Party to complement the mass party, Singaravelu's Manifesto or even that of Chamanlal did not corroborate to it. Their aim was to remain strictly within the folds of the National Congress. Hence, their theory of the emancipation of the working class was limited to the point of liberation from the foreigners and the safeguarding of the interests of the masses. The question of the ultimate revolution that would lead to the dictatorship of the proletariat had been ignored in their respective projects.

Another point of difference between Roy's ideas of the time and those of Singaravelu was regarding the question of violence. Singaravelu pointed out that the Labour and Kishan Party of Hindustan was to act as "...the *Vanguard* of Indian labour and kisans in their struggle for existence. The creed of this party was to achieve labour swaraj by non-violent means..."[243] Roy however, was firmly against such a pronouncement. He said that strict adherence to the principle of non-violence could not be made into a principle. He justified the use of violence if it was necessary for redeeming the cause of the toiling masses.

Chamanlal and Singaravelu, both in their respective Manifestoes, dissociated themselves from the influence of the Bolsheviks, but declared at the same time that they were not averse to joining hands with the "labour section"[244] of the Bolshevik movement. This too had been unacceptable to Roy. Adhikari has said, "...It is quite likely that Abani Mukherjee himself may have suggested to both Manilal and Singaravelu to avoid such a stand to avoid prosecution at the hands of the British government. The arrest and prosecution of the young muhajirs as Bolshevik agents just because they had been trained in communist schools in Tashkent and Moscow was already well known."[245] Abani was staying in India at that time, and it is possible that looking at the existing situation from very close quarters, he had advised such a measure. But what is important is that the movement was still not under the sole control of the Comintern. It was developing on its own, in an indigenous manner, so much so that even Roy's advice was being judged as advice from foreign agents of the Bolsheviks[246].

David Druhe has held that the Indian communist movement was more or less an appendage of the Soviet led Comintern and the moment the Comintern turned its back on it, communism in India also faced a retreat. He said that the Russians submitted to British pressure regarding the proliferation of communism in the east. "Unwilling to submit a break in its de facto relations with England, the Soviets after an exchange of correspondence evinced a disposition to conciliate the British..."[247] Druhe's idea implied that the early communist movement in India was solely dependent on the whims of the Soviet and the Comintern. He has said:

"As a consequence of these British actions there was a marked lessening of Soviet and Comintern interest in India in the second half of 1923 and a corresponding deterioration in the position of the budding Indian Communist movement. Intercepted correspondence between Roy and Indian Red leaders indicated that the latter were becoming disappointed by a lack of interest in Hindustan in the Communist movement (they had apparently felt that once the idea was introduced— Communism would sweep the country), and by the effective surveillance of their movement by the Anglo-Indian authorities and they were disappointed with the work of Roy in Europe. By the end of 1923, the Indian Communists who earlier in that year had been so intent on launching their all-Indian Workers' and Peasants' Party were now begging Roy to have the Comintern in Moscow send them funds to keep their two publications 'The Socialist' and 'Inqilab' going..."[248]

It can be asserted at this point that the Comintern had not lost interest in the Indian communist movement. It was constantly sending notes that promised support to the burgeoning communist movement in India[249]. Secondly, intercepted correspondence between Roy and the Indian leaders do not show that the latter were becoming disappointed by the "lack of interest in Hindustan in the Communist movement". On the contrary, they showed that they were taking several steps for the advancement of communism in India. Chamanlal Manifesto and the All India Labour and Kishan Party of Singaravelu are examples. Another point that needs mention is that the correspondence between Indian communists like Singaravelu and

Dange reflected that they did not want much interference from Roy while they formulated their ideas. They even disagreed with him on certain points. Regarding "begging" Roy for funds from the Comintern to keep their publications going, it can be said that the Comintern funding in India was meagre when compared to that in China. Besides, the multiplicity of languages necessitated publication of communist literature in different languages, a fact that was proving to be too expensive for the nascent communist movement in India.

Gautam Chattopadhyay has said that "...the Comintern and M.N.Roy had built up an extensive contact among Indians both in India and abroad and the imperialist ruling circles were becoming frankly panicky. They now determined to bring down the heavy hand of repression on all shades of Indian communists and all contacts of M.N.Roy..."[250]

THE KANPUR CONSPIRACY CASE

The British meanwhile had already started adopting drastic measures to curb communist influence in India. The muhajirins who were returning to India after the petering out of the Khilafat movement were arrested by the British from the middle of 1922 and tried in the Peshawar Conspiracy cases over the next few years. Gautam Chattopadhyay has further said, "...The Secretary of State for India had been demanding action ever since the end of 1922, but the head of the intelligence service in India, Colonel Kaye, had been holding back. But in July 1923, Kaye yielded and agreed to prompt action against the Indian communists..."[251] An attempt to track down Roy's connections in India hence began. His contacts were diverse, but a "...statement of cases against Roy, Muzaffar Ahmad, Usmani, Ghulam Hussain, Dange, Singaravelu, Sharma, Nalini Gupta, S.D.Hasan, M.P.T.Velayudham, Sampurnanand, Manilal and Satyabhakta was submitted to Counsel for opinion. Counsel reported in favour of proceeding against the first eight, and not against the remaining five: and this recommendation was approved by the Government of India..."[252]

Shaukat Usmani, Ghulam Hussain and Muzaffar Ahmad were all arrested in May 1923. Nalini Gupta was also arrested by January 1924. The arrest of Dange however, came later and Singaravelu, on account of ill health, could avoid the arrest. The arrested communists were tried in the Kanpur Conspiracy Case. Shaukat Usmani had been operating at Kanpur as a schoolmaster called Habib Ahmad. Cecil Kaye has said that it had been decided that the intention was to try Usmani in the Peshawar Conspiracy Case trials[253], "...but he was too late for this as the trial had already concluded..."[254] Ghulam Hussain too managed to avoid the prosecution by appealing to the government that he had understood the "impropriety of his writings" and that he would give up politics on the pretext of his ailing health[255]. Cecil Kaye has however maintained that Ghulam Hussain was released not just because of his appeal, but also because he consented to give evidence against Shafiq, who was one of Roy's agents, and had been arrested in Baluchistan and sent to Peshawar for trial[256]. Those who were left to face the trial were Shaukat Usmani, Muzaffar Ahmad, Nalini Gupta and Dange.

Roy had by now fled to Zurich from Berlin and had set up his headquarters there. He reacted sharply to the arrests. It was obvious that the arrest of all the prominent communists would prove to be a setback to the progress of communism in India. Before the trials began, he wrote an "Open Letter from the Communist Party of India" to Ramsay Macdonald, the labour prime minister of Great Britain, the secretary of state for India, Lord Oliver, the Labour Government and the British working class. Roy called the Kanpur Conspiracy case, "...an attempt to throttle the constitutional right of agitation, organisation and association which exists unchallenged in every other part of the British empire, and throughout the world..."[257] Roy said that if working class propaganda was not illegal in Great Britain and her dominions, "...Then why should it be illegal in British India? Have socialist and communist parties, that is to say working-class parties, been denied the right to exist in any other part of the British empire? Then why should Indians be denied the right? Does affiliation to the Third International constitute a crime on the part of the Communist Party of Great Britain, of Australia, New Zealand, Canada and South Africa? Then why does such affiliation on the part of the Communist Party of India constitute 'seditious conspiracy'?"[258] Roy's letter bore a pointed criticism of the labour government in Britain. But as usual, it failed to arouse any reaction in this regard. The Kanpur Conspiracy Case was not affected in any way.

The accused were tried under section 121-A, that is they endeavoured "to deprive the King-Emperor of his sovereignty in India" by securing a complete separation of India from imperialistic

Britain through a violent revolution[259]. The trial began in Kanpur on 22nd April 1924 before the British judge, H.C.Holme, the same person who had only a year before, "tried the Chauri Chaura case and sentenced 172 peasants to death by hanging"[260]. The accused communists made an appeal to the government for the transfer of the case, but it was ignored. Documents say that "In the lower court all the accused were undefended. In the session court they were defended by three lawyers— Dr. Manilal of Gaya appeared on behalf of Shaukat Usmani and Muzaffar Ahmad, while the other two (Dange and Nalini Gupta— G.A.) were defended by Pandit Kapildeo Malaviya of Allahabad and Mussadilal Rahtagi of Kanpur."[261] The trial continued for four weeks and "...on 20th May 1924 the judgement was pronounced sentencing the four accused to four years' RI..."[262]

Evelyn Roy wrote an article in the *Inprecor* of 17th April, 1924, titled, "Will the British Labour Government Stand for this?"[263] She too, like Roy, defended the cause of the accused, saying that all of them were being wrongly convicted under the "vulgar charge of 'conspiracy' for having committed the "...crime of having studied, thought and written about the conditions of the Indian masses and for having advocated a means for their emancipation from political and economic exploitation..."[264] Another point that she raised was, "What was the real meaning of this trial at Kanpur, so suddenly sprung at this moment on evidence that was allowed to accumulate for several years?..."[265] She said that the answer to this lay in the fact that the British wanted to "crush the steadily growing mass movement"; it aimed to "terrorise" all those who sought to study the spirit of "the mighty social revolution" in Russia and the "national revolutions in other eastern countries" and then tried to apply to India the lessons that they learnt as a consequence; and lastly, "to prejudice the impending Anglo-Russian conference" on trade[266].

A pointed reference to the Peshawar trial was made by M.N.Roy in the *Vanguard*, a few months later. He said that the Peshawar Conspiracy Case "...was the first real communist trial in India; the Kanpur trial that followed it two years later, was the second..."[267] M.N.Roy had obviously realised like several other contemporaries that these two trials would affect the Indian communist movement very adversely. He said that the seven prisoners at Peshawar and the four at Kanpur constituted the backbone of the Indian communist movement, and that their sentences would be shattering to the communist movement in general. Roy knew that in order to keep communism alive in India new leaders were needed to replace those who had been arrested, at least temporarily. The concluding part of his article hence said:

> "Where are the leaders to replace those rendered silent and impotent by governmental tyranny? Let them come forward in their hundreds to perform the vast and fruitful work that lies waiting to their hands. The effective alliance of labour fighting under its own class programme with the nationalist cause will spell death to imperialist domination and early freedom to the Indian nation."[268]

All these details point out to one major factor— the growing role of the communists, which had by now alarmed the British greatly, hence resulting in their repeated attempts to crush the emerging communist movement with a very strong hand[269]. It also proved another point once again— "...the weakness of native communism in India..."[270] However, even though the movement was vulnerable to British attacks, and despite the measures that they took to crush it, they could not quite undo totally the work done by the communists. Even after the Peshawar and the Kanpur Conspiracy cases shook the very foundations of the communist movement in India, work still continued. Many new figures made appearance after the arrest of the prominent communist leaders. They could not often conceive of communist theories as their predecessors did, nor did their views match always with them, but they tried to carry on the movement further as new entrants to the communist movement in India.

THE ESTABLISHMENT OF THE COMMUNIST PARTY OF INDIA AT KANPUR UNDER SATYABHAKTA

One of the major events of that time was the First Communist Conference in Kanpur. It was held in December 1924, and organised by Satyabhakta, a face that was so long quite insignificant in the communist circles. He belonged to a national revolutionary group in the United Provinces and had been attracted by the communist ideology of the Bolshevik Revolution. All communist groups that were in function, had been invited to the conference. Adhikari has said, "...The conference became the instrument of bringing together all the genuine communist groups in the country, thus creating the first Central Committee of the CPI and framing its first constitution. It is this all-India centre of the CPI which during the next 3-4 years organised military mass trade-union and kisan movement, formed workers' and peasants' parties in various provinces which in December 1928 united in an All India Workers' and Peasants' Party at its conference in Calcutta. Thus it created a new mass force for the country's independence struggle—a mass force which under the leadership of the working class fought for the acceptance and implementation of an anti-imperialist anti-feudal national revolutionary programme by the country's liberation movement. It is against this mass force that the imperialists struck hard by launching the Meerut Conspiracy Case in March 1929."[271]

Shapurji Saklatwala, a member of the Communist Party of Great Britain, had been asked to preside over the conference. But he did not come "owing to the pressure of business on this side"[272]. Singaravelu was hence made the president. Saklatwala however, understood that the conference, despite its origin, did have a significance. This is reflected in the text of his message. Singaravelu's presidential address was in total consonance with his Manifesto to the Hindustan Labour and Kishan Party. But two points ought to be mentioned in this context. One is that he was still refuting the need to ally with the Bolsheviks. He said:

"...We are not Russian Bolsheviks and bolshevism may not be needed in India. Bolshevism literally means the doctrine of the majority. And this Russian majority are men in power in Russia with the peculiar method of their rule, administration and propaganda...We are one with the world communists but not with Bolsheviks..."[273]

This anathema about the Bolsheviks made his remark rather contradictory. There was no way in which he could be "one" with the world communists without uniting with the Bolsheviks because of the fact that the Bolsheviks not only formed a very important portion of the world communists, but also provided leadership to them. This notion had been there in his message to the Hindustan Labour and Kishan Party as well, much to Roy's wrath. The second point regarding Singaravelu's address was that he was propagating the need for the workers' party. But his conception of a peasants' party was still quite vague. In his "Appeal to the Peasants" in the same address, he said with a flourish:

"...You are, like the Cinderella of our eastern tradition, ceaselessly catering to our wants, and supplying all our comforts and needs, while the landowners have been keeping you in the background. But the denouement is fast approaching, while your haughty masters will sink into merited neglect, you the peasants will be proclaimed alike worthy and beautiful and you will become supreme..."[274]

How this was to come about remained unexplained. While he was on the one hand, calling upon the workers to form unions, he displayed a glaring discrepancy on the other, by not similarly formulating on the need for peasant unions.

Although Adhikari has highlighted the fact that the conference organised by Satyabhakta at Kanpur had lasting consequences in the field of the Indian communist movement, yet at the same time, he has definitely made sure that there should remain no doubt that the ideas of Satyabhakta were still quite immature in comparison with his contemporaries like Roy and Dange. He said that Satyabhakta had denounced the need for any link with the Comintern out of fear that it was this link that was leading to the prosecution of the Indian communists. In doing so, he was also imposing the idea of national communism over the Marxist concept of internationalism[275]. Satyabhakta did say that connections with the Comintern could not be established "...owing to the fact that the government will at once try to suppress our activities on the slightest move towards that direction..."[276] Another reason that Satyabhakta admitted, regarding his disinclination to ally with foreign organisations was the question of violence. He felt that communist revolutions in the west were necessarily the outcome of violent actions, a fact with which he was very unwilling to conform to. He hence said, "...It should be admitted that we are not in a position to employ violent methods in the pursuit of our propaganda as is the case with the communist parties of other countries..."[277] He also felt that without national independence the opinion of the Indians in the international sphere would not tantamount to anything serious. Hence, what was needed was the achievement of national independence, before any collaboration could be made. He was so averse to foreign connections that he simply shirked the idea of financial help from outside, considering it to be degrading. "...Even if we succeed in getting financial help from across the seas, it is much more likely to corrupt and degrade us than to be of some real service to the country in the present state of India..."[278] His attitude was rather strange when compared to his contemporaries, and he formulated equally strangely the future work of the communists in India, when he said, "...For us the way is plainly chalked out— the way of self-denial and suffering. Through these alone we can be able of any service to the masses of India."[279] He criticised the Congress for having become an organisation of the elite classes in India, but refused to break away from it at the same time. "...After all the Congress is a well-established and influential institution and the best interests of the country require us to reform it and not to go against it. We appeal to all members of the party to become also members and delegates of the Congress with the intention of changing it into an instrument of service to our people."[280] Adhikari has said, "His 'national communism' was not even national because it failed to formulate a national revolutionary programme for the country's independence struggle in which organisations and struggles of workers and peasants had a revolutionary role to play. Such a programme had already been put forward by the communists already before the Gaya Congress in December 1922. Satyabhakta was blissfully ignorant of this..."[281]

The ideas of Satyabhakta were rejected at the conference. The resolutions taken at the conference clearly indicated this. It said among other things:

"...This conference of the Indian communists resolves that a party be formed for the purpose of emancipation of the workers and peasants of India. This party shall be known as the COMMUNIST PARTY OF INDIA and the ultimate aim of the party shall be the establishment of a republican swaraj of workers and peasants, and the immediate object of the party shall be the securing of a living wage to the workers and peasants by means of nationalisation and municipalisation of public services namely land, mines, factories, houses, telegraphs and telephones, and railways and such other public utilities which require public ownership.

"For the purpose of achieving these objectives, the party shall form labour and peasants' unions in rural and urban areas, enter district and taluk boards, municipalities and assemblies, and by such other means and methods carry out the ideal and immediate programme of the party with or without the cooperation of the existing political bodies in India."[282]

It can be seen that this was a clear reiteration of Roy's thoughts on council entry and the ultimate objective of the Indian communists.

Satyabhakta actually wanted to establish a legal Communist Party of India. Adhikari has said that this was the consequence of a statement by Ross Alston, the prosecution counsel in the Kanpur Conspiracy Case which said that "...the accused in the case are not tried only because they held communist doctrines…"[283] Satyabhakta reacted to this statement and organised his 'legal' Indian Communist Party. Dange too during the same time, in reaction to the same statement, had felt the need to hold an open conference of the communists in India. His idea however, could not be implemented. But the idea of an open conference was gaining grounds among the founders of the communist movement in India. This was reflected in the articles in the *Socialist* in early 1924[284]. Roy was, at this time, undoubtedly advocating the need for uniting all the communist groups into a central all-India organisation, but he was still in favour of Communist Party of India to function as an illegal apparatus, whose work would parallel the work done by the emergent workers' and peasants' parties. This was certainly a new development that reflected that the ideas of the Indian communists had progressed a step further. The British too were apparently aware of this and Satyabhakta was being watched closely by them. But that Satyabhakta was not the member of a genuine communist group, and that his activities would not have any serious consequence, also became evident to them in no time. Cecil Kaye said in his report to the Indian government in September 1924 that "Satyabhakta and his associates, are men of no weight whatever: and as is certain, as anything can be, that the 'Communist Party of India' will be nothing but a name" and that it will "not embarrass the G.O.I. in the least"[285].

It can be seen that despite the non-coherent trends that formed a constant feature of the early Indian communist movement, an effort was being made to unite all the existing forces. This initiative was not the result of foreign directives. It originated indigenously. The Kanpur Conspiracy case revealed the problems of practising communism illegally and efforts were made to form a legal communist party in India, one that would unite all the diverse opinions and groups into a single central organisation. This idea was not at variance with the doctrines of the Second Congress of the Communist International, but at the same time, it did not develop as a product of its sole influence. This formed one of the basic features of the early Indian communist movement.

The British wanted to cripple the communist movement in India by arresting the most important communist leaders. However, the years that followed showed a different trend altogether. Not only was the establishment of the 'legal' communist party facilitated by

Satyabhakta, there was also the rise and development of the workers' and peasants' parties— a fact that played a significant role in the advancement of communism in India, especially among the toiling masses. On the other hand, the Comintern too began to show more interest in the Indian affairs and in the process, sent help both in the form of money and agents for the cause of communism in India. The communist movement too, on the other hand, still kept on maturing on its own, exhibiting thereby, a parallel amalgamation of ideas that developed indigenously and independently of Comintern dictates— that is till the Sixth Congress of the Comintern, when all parallel views were stifled by the Stalinist regime both in the Comintern and the Soviet Union.

The communist movement in India was faced with a situation that was very different from that in other Asian countries like China. The dearth of funds was phenomenal and help from the Comintern was intermittent. This was not only because of British surveillance but also because of the distance between Soviet Russia and India. Besides, the multiplicity of languages was another hindering factor in the spread of communism as this necessitated the publication and translation of communist literature in several Indian languages, a fact that raised expenses very high. All these factors proved to be immensely detrimental to the cause of communist propaganda. But despite these obstacles, communism in India continued moving forward on its own initiative and with whatever help it could gather from the Comintern for the next few years.

ROLE OF THE COMINTERN IN SHAPING THE COMMUNIST MOVEMENT IN INDIA IN THE MID-1920s

The Comintern too by this time began to take an active interest in the Indian events. It realised that some amount of help to the Indian revolutionaries would come in useful at a time when its communist movement had been thrown to shambles after the arrest of its most powerful leaders. By the end of March 1924, the Comintern had stated the process of allocating funds for the Indian cause. In June-July 1924, the Fifth Congress of the Comintern had already taken place. The Fifth Congress raised much controversy on the issue of supporting the bourgeois led movements that had been in vogue in the colonies since the Second Congress. Besides, the question regarding the dissatisfactory role of the peasantry in the communist movement had been raised by Zinoviev. An organ of the Comintern, the Red Peasants' International or the Krestintern, led by A.Voznecienski, was also increasingly becoming involved in the happenings in India. It endeavoured mainly to help the peasant organisations and assist them in their struggle against oppression and realisation of their rights[286]. Regarding the peasantry, the Resolution said:

> "The peasantry is a very important social factor in India. The attitude of the peasantry will decide the outcome of the revolution in India. To penetrate the peasant movement and to assume its leadership, therefore, should be one of the most important tasks of the CP in India. An agrarian programme (of action) should be carefully drawn up with a view to leading the peasant movement in the country and uniting the various peasant organisations into a national body under Communist influence."[287]

In July 1925, at a conference in Baku, it was resolved that a special Strike Fund would be made in order to foment strikes in India. The Comintern actually aimed at supporting the labour organisations in the eastern countries and bring them into close contact with the movement of the international proletariat. The question of Indian communism had assumed a significant role by this time this was because the Indian situation was making the rise of the working classes both as an imminent as well as an indispensable factor for the improvement of the condition of the masses. The Indian working classes had by now acquired a very important position, one that was felt to be vital for the overthrow of imperialism and the achievement of the World Revolution. In its Resolution on the Indian Question, the Comintern said:

> "Much preparatory work for the organisation of the Communist Party has been accomplished by the ideological and political propaganda carried on from the centre abroad. As a result of this propaganda a series of Communist groups and nuclei have come into existence. These are active in the trade unions, peasant movement and Left Nationalist parties, exercising a considerable influence upon the general political life of the country. Repeated efforts to unite these groups have been so far frustrated by imperialist terror. Nevertheless, the growth of the revolutionary movement is creating the possibility of a struggle for the legalisation of the Communist Party. The Communist groups are coming forward to lead this fight for legalisation."[288]

That Satyabhakta's Communist Party could not make any gateway regarding the uniting of various communist groups, and that this fact was known to the Comintern, becomes obvious from the above excerpt. It becomes more apparent in the next point, where the Resolution said:

"In view of these facts the Enlarged Executive of the CI resolves that the most important task in India is to build a strong CP on the basis of the existing groups. The creation of a cadre of Party leadership is of supreme importance. For this an ideological and political centre abroad will be indispensable for a considerable time to come. Particular attention will be given to strengthening the existing centre abroad and to improve its contact with the party in India."[289]

The Comintern was hence aware that in the advancement of communism in India unity of different communist factions was very important, a fact that was not very keenly followed by the existing communist factions in India. Even if ideas merged at times, efforts towards bringing about unity of ideas were still inadequate.

THE FIFTH SESSION OF THE AITUC

The fifth session of the AITUC was held in Bombay on 14th-16th February 1925.This session had been presided over by D.N.Thengdi, a trade union leader of Nagpur. One important question that emerged from this session was the need to organise the labour party. In the presidential speech however, no mention was made on these lines. Sarojini Naidu, member of the Bombay Provincial Congress Committee, had attended the session. She had commented that "Labour's aloofness from politics was fatal."[290] *The Masses* issue of April 1925, however, mentioned that preliminary meetings regarding the formation of the labour party in India had already been held by nationalist leaders earlier. The launching of the labour party has also been recorded in the *Indian Annual Register*, Volume 1, 1925, though no documents can be found regarding it. Adhikari has said:

"The AITUC session, it appears, passed no resolution on the organisation of the labour party for India though, as stated in the article, one was launched and formally announced during the session...The chief among the sponsors of this new venture were militant nationalists like Lala Lajpat Rai and Dewan Chamanlal from Punjab, Davaki Prasad Sinha from Bihar, N.M.Joshi from Bombay— long associated with welfare among textile workers of Bombay on behalf of the Servants of India Society and was connected with the AITUC from the very beginning, and Sir Sankaran Nair from Madras. 'Labour Party' was a discredited name in India because in 1924 the

Labour Party came to power in Great Britain its performance both on the question of India's demand for national independence and on the question of the wages and working conditions of Indian labour was hardly different from the imperialist Tory party of Britain."[291]

This shows that the labour party was, from the very beginning, associated with the nationalist leaders of India. Adhikari has said that in naming the Labour Party so, "...its sponsors were obviously wishing to demarcate themselves from the above trend (that of the Labour Party of Britain)."[292] Yet, at the same time Adhikari was also saying albeit sarcastically, "...That is why in their preliminary speeches they emphasised moderation and caution, wanted to eschew class struggle and, above all, wanted that organised labour should not jeopardise the interests and the profits of the Indian capitalists."[293] Adhikari was more or less repeating the thoughts of Roy. In the article, "A Labour Party for India", Roy said:

"...it is considered undesirable by these new found champions of the Indian working class to introduce into India the doctrine of class struggle, or to create such a party which will in any way jeopardise the interests and ambitions of Indian capitalism.

"In such hands the new Labour Party will not go very far. The birth of a political organisation of the Indian workers is a still-birth, and no amount of theoretical schemes on paper will succeed in breathing the breath of life into this defunct embryo.

"Yet the growth of an Indian Labour Party is an historical necessity, already long overdue. The position of India as the seventh on the list of industrialised countries of the world and her aggregate total of 20,000,000 proletarian workers prove that some organisation to express the economic and political needs of this vast mass of workers must come into being sooner or later."[294]

Roy's distrust of the bourgeoisie had surfaced at the Fifth Congress already. Now the same feeling consolidated itself even more. Roy understood that though it was the reformist leadership that vouched for the necessity of a labour party, one that would perhaps bear no consequence for the cause of the toiling masses; nevertheless he realised simultaneously that a party of the masses was of utmost necessity amidst Indian conditions. "...What is needed is a People's Party, embracing the vast masses of India, led by men and women with a revolutionary vision, who can bring the Indian movement for social, economic and political emancipation into line with the world movement for social revolution."[295]

USE OF AGENTS BY THE COMINTERN IN INDIA AND THE GROWING ROLE OF THE CPGB IN THE INDIAN COMMUNIST MOVEMENT

One factor that needs mention is the use of agents in the spread of communism in India. The concept of using agents as the mode to regulate communist activities in the countries of the east was not new to the Comintern. It had already used agents in Indonesia and China to further the cause of communism there as well as to keep a close contact with the Soviet led Comintern circles. This had often helped in the field of organisation of the communist movement. Besides, it helped the Comintern to understand clearly the objective conditions prevalent in these nations and then work accordingly. But the problem was that it sometimes created for these communist movements, a total dependence on the Comintern, which at times proved to be detrimental to their interests. This became all the more pronounced after the advent of the Stalinist regime, which sought to choke all independent opinions that did not conform to its policies. Another problem was that these agents, mostly educated in the western view of communism, tended to mould the emerging communist movements in these countries totally according to the dictates of the Comintern.

Besides, the Indian case was somewhat different too. The communist movement here had already made a fair progress before the Comintern began to send its agents. M.N.Roy too, as a member of the Comintern, tried again and again to communicate closely with the Indian communists still holding divergent opinions about national liberation and communism, and bring them under his sway, one that had somewhat faded after the Kanpur Conspiracy case. It was perhaps with this purpose, that he too sent one of his agents to India, just as he had sent Nalini Gupta or Charles Ashleigh before. A new factor could be noticed in this context, one that became very prominent in the post 1928 era, after the Sixth Congress of the Comintern had taken place. This was the direct involvement of the Communist Party of Great Britain in the communist movement in India.

The involvement of the Communist Party of Great Britain in the spread of communism in India had begun even before the Fifth Congress had taken place. It had a Colonial Bureau to look after the affairs of working class organisations in its colonies. The Comintern too facilitated this involvement by incorporating the members of the CPGB in the work it wanted to carry out in the colonies. A document has shown clearly that the decision to form an International Colonial Bureau to supervise colonial work had been taken by the Comintern as early as March 13, 1924[296]. The members of this organisation were to consist of M.N.Roy, Somai, a member of the Eastern Section of the Comintern and one member each from Britain, France and other countries which were concerned with colonial work. Each of these members was referred to as "comrade". It also said that the members were to carry out "the directives of I.C.B. and also the Eastern Section of the C.I." as well as their "own Colonial Work"[297] By the time the Fifth Congress took place in June-July, 1924, the Comintern found that the work done in the colonies by the CPGB was not quite satisfactory. And since the Fifth Comintern Congress giving special attention to colonial work, it was decided to from an International Colonial Bureau in Paris, one that was to be independent of the CPGB. A document relating to it said, "After the Fifth World Congress it was decided to set up an International Colonial Bureau in Paris. The object was on the one hand to establish closer contact with the movement in the French and British colonies and on the other hand to strengthen the colonial activities particularly of the British and French parties. The Bureau had to meet a series of difficulties before it could begin practical work. One of the difficulties was the attitude of the British party."[298] This document has further related that the work done by the Bureau in the British colonies was less because of the "reluctance of the British Party to co-operate with the Bureau." It also said the difficulties could eventually be overcome and some work could actually be done. But soon afterwards, Roy, who happened to be the chairman of the Bureau, was expelled from France and the work of the Bureau had to be suspended.

The next known organisation that was formed under the aegis of the Comintern for doing organisational work in the colonies was The Indian Foreign Bureau[299]. This was set up in 1925 itself, and was composed of three members, Mohammad Ali, C.P.Dutt and M.N.Roy. C.P.Dutt was representing the CPGB and Mohammad Ali alias Sepassi was from Paris. This Bureau began the publication of *The Masses* that had already stated coming out since January 1925 under the editorship of Roy. What is significant that the Comintern directed the CPGB to "...give all assistance possible in the production and distribution of *The Masses* and other literature, the political direction of which will rest with the Indian Bureau."[300] It can be seen that the Comintern was not only controlling the appointment of such organisations which were necessarily composed of members of the CPGB, but was also, at the same time, instructing the CPGB to get actively involved in the working of the organisation. It was perhaps more because of this pressure than its own initiative, that the CPGB too began showing some interest in colonial affairs, though its full fledged involvement came a few years later in the post Sixth Congress years when it began to control the advancement of the communist movement in India.

However, as early as March 1925, the Colonial Committee Report[301] outlined a detailed plan concerning its work in the colonies. Regarding it work in India, certain points were made among which one was to send P.Glading to India. Meanwhile, in the same year, another organisation called the Indian Bureau was formed by the Indian communists in Britain[302]. This group maintained close contact with Roy and was at the same time, "acting in conjunction with, but independently of, the Communist Party of Great Britain."[303] Associated with this group were some very eminent personalities like N.J.Upadhyaya, C.P.Dutt, A.C. Banerjee, P.C.Nandi and M.A.Khan[304]. But when the same group comprising of a total of nine persons sought membership with the Indian Communist Party from the Indian Foreign Bureau, after listing the work it would do for the advancement of communism in India[305], it was denied affiliation. The reply from Moscow said:

"The programme outlined in the communication is generally acceptable. According to the Statutes of the Communist International, all the Indian communists resident in Britain should have their party membership transferred to the CPGB during their sojourn in Britain. This rule applies to all communists living outside their native countries.

"The Indian Communist Group in Britain will, therefore, carry on the programme outlined in your communication in conjunction with the Colonial Commission of the CPGB. It will be politically guided by the European Bureau of the CP of India as well as the Colonial Commission of the CPGB."[306]

These documents prove that the domination of the CPGB over the Indian communist movement in the post Sixth Congress era was the result of the constant attempts made by the Comintern to assign it a significant role in the Indian communist movement since 1924-1925. In other words the seeds of the CPGB's domination over the Indian communist movement were sown during this time. M.N.Roy wrote a letter to Petrov in which he expressed concern over this factor. He said:

> "...Our Bureau is not working well. Particularly the British part of the work is very unsatisfactory. Contrary to the letter received from you, we are informed by the British party that the representative there has come back from Moscow with new instructions which reject entirely the line we have been following up till now. According to these new instructions, the Colonial Commission of the British party assumes supreme political responsibility for the work in India, Egypt and other colonies...Com. Dutt, who has so far been acting as the representative of the bureau is not liked by the party owing to internal conflict, and has been practically pushed out of the work. So we have absolutely no control over what is done in and from London. It will be necessary to go over the whole situation during the plenum. Till then, things must remain in present state."[307]

Stalin's growing authoritarian control over the Comintern, and his way of smothering voices against his own were perhaps responsible for this new development, which was soon to gain a very big shape in the Indian communist movement. For not only was the CPGB gaining more and more control over Indian affairs, it was also affecting the position of Roy in the Comintern. Considering Roy's attitude about the strategy of alliance with the bourgeois movement and his total distrust of the nationalist bourgeoisie in the Fifth Congress and even later, as expressed through his writings in different papers, this was not surprising. Roy perhaps realised this. The tone of his letter did not have the same strength as before. Besides, his future plans for India often displayed actions counteracting those of the CPGB.

For example, The Communist Party of Great Britain sent George Allison alias Donald Campbell to India at the end of April 1926 to work under their instructions for the development of communism in India. M.N.Roy too, in a few months time, sent Fazl Ilahi alias Kurban to India. David Petrie has said that this was "...arranged primarily by M.N. Roy's group with the cognisance of the Communist Party of Great Britain..."[308] Now why suddenly, a Comintern member, as powerful as Roy, should need to send his agents to India "with the cognisance of the Communist Party of Great Britain"? Besides, this was not the first time either. Roy had sent plenty of men to India before ever since 1921. It can be seen that the Communist Party of Great Britain was showing much interest in the progress of communism in India, as envisaged by the Comintern. It sent two more of its members to India soon afterwards with the same purpose, that is to help in building "a militant trade union movement..."[309] These two members were Philip Spratt and Ben Bradley. Many of these foreign agents however, could not achieve much as they were detected easily and then either arrested or sent back. But some, like Spratt, did manage to rise to prominence as labour leaders and organisers of the early communist movement in India. The British trade unionists were not sent without the approval of the Comintern. In the Resolution to the Indian Commission in March 1926, it was clearly said, "...Every effort should be made to obtain a closer contact between the Indian trade union movement and the British trade union movement in their common struggle against imperialism. The attempts of the British labour imperialists to bring the young Indian trade unions under reformist influence should be energetically fought..."[310] If the attitude of the Comintern regarding the CPGB is juxtaposed with that for Roy, it can be said that Roy was certainly not gaining the same favour that he used to gain from the Comintern a few years back.

RISE IN STRIKE MOVEMENTS AND THE SIXTH SESSION OF THE AITUC

Meanwhile, there was an increase in the number of strikes in 1925. In fact some of them had been quite protracted and managed to draw the attention of the European trade unionists. Some of them were the North Western Railway workers' strike, the BN Railway strike, the Bombay textile workers' strike and the strike of the Tata Works workers. Of them the two most long lasting strikes were the North West Railway workers' strike and the Bombay textile workers' strike. Adhikari has discussed at length both these strikes. He has said that these strikes "...form a transition between the spontaneous strike wave of 1918-1924 and the consciously led strike upsurge of 1927-1929 out of which the militant trade union movement is born. These strikes of 1925 were transitional in the sense that though essentially spontaneous outbursts, they at the same time, had some features of the consciously led strike upsurge of 1927-29..."[311] Adhikari has also said, "...These strikes were the precursors of the historic red-flag workers' movement which was to appear in the political arena in 1927-1929..."[312]

The North West Railway workers strike saw the appearance of the red flag "...for the first time in a big way..."[313] The strike began with the dismissal of an important member of the North West Railwaymen's Union. The management retaliated by declaring a lockout on 28th March. When all forms of negotiations failed, the union declared a general strike on 10th April 1925. Adhikari has recorded that out of a total staff of 100,000 about 40,000 workers joined the strike, demanding recognition of their union, all-round 25 per cent wage rise, abolition of arbitrary funds and punishments and investigation of other grievances. The strike continued till June, when the "...AIRF appealed to the chief commissioner of railways for the appointment of a conciliation board. The AITUC executive committee also made a similar effort and appointed C.F.Andrews to mediate. But the railway authorities remained adamant and by the end of June the strike was called off..."[314] Adhikari has said that the strike though defeated, was significant in the sense that it was able to hold out for two months without "help from any quarter, because of the militancy and unity of the striking workers and also because a large number of them went away to their village homes."[315] Another significance of the strike lay in the fact that the involvement of the AITUC came very late, when the workers had already held out for very long.

The Bombay textile workers' strike began in September 1925. The main issue that led to the strike was the government decision to impose cotton excise duty from January 1926. This led the mill owners to resort to wage cut by reducing the dear food allowance given to the workers from 70 and 80 per cent to 50 and 60 per cent, so as to maintain their earlier profit levels. The strike had been tremendous. By the end of September, nearly 1,25,000 workers had joined the strike. But this strike saw the involvement of the AITUC from the beginning. Adhikari however, has said, "It is the solidarity and determination of the workers which finally compelled the labour leaders to take steps to render concrete assistance to the striking workers..."[316] What is perhaps the most significant is that this strike received help from several quarters, both national and international. In fact, this was the first time that international support and assistance found its way to India in the face of a prolonged strike. Adhikari has recorded:

"...Towards the end of the strike, over 5000 workers in Bombay were being given grain allowance daily from 19 different distributing centres. The total expenditure per day was Rs.800. Donations came almost entirely from the trade-union movement in western countries, in the Soviet Union and the labour leaders organising relief got a small amount from the nationalist or Congress sources."[317]

Support from international organisations was also forthcoming. "...'A message of greetings' was sent by the central committee of the Textile Workers' Union of the USSR to the textile workers on strike in India and a donation to the strike fund..."[318] Another factor was that both the labour organisations of the west, namely, the Red International of Labour Unions and the International Federation of Trade Unions rendered their support and assistance. The British Trades Union Congress also assisted the striking workers. The strike was called of only after the government announced the suspension of the cotton excise duty on 30th November and the notices of wage reduction were withdrawn and the on 1st December. This event proved that the Indian working class movement had made a definite beginning in getting itself linked to the movement of the world proletariat in general.

By 1926 it could be seen that strikes had greatly increased in both the Bengal and the Bombay presidencies. Though the number of strikes in the jute mills of Bengal was much less in comparison to the textile mills of Bombay, yet it cannot be denied that there had been a definite rise in strikes. The reason might have been the homogeneity of the workers in Bombay in contrast to those of Bengal where the majority of the workers came from the surrounding states that resulted in a linguistic separation among them[319]. These strikes nevertheless saw the involvement of several thousands of workers each year. This was despite the absence of proper trade unions. Amiya Bagchi has said that "...before 1926, trade unions did not have much legal protection, and the registered trade unions were more in the nature of friendly societies or welfare societies for workers..."[320] Here too, it could be noticed, as in the case of the strikes, that the number of workers organised in trade unions in Bengal was negligible to that compared to Bombay[321]. The Comintern was aware of all the developments in India and began to make policies accordingly[322]. Another point was that the nationalist leaders like Gandhi often idealised the relationship between the workers and the capitalist mill owners. Adhikari has said that considering the tremendous influence that emanated from his mere presence on the common masses, it was often used at an advantage by the capitalists to resolve differences with the workers. He has cited two examples regarding such a situation. One was the reconciliation of the workers of the Tata Iron Works, who wanted an independent Labour Association, which was being conceded on the ground that membership subscription to the union fund would be deducted from the wages of the workers, and that the fund would remain under the control of the Company. Gandhi had considered this a generous offer by the Company and one that should be accepted wholeheartedly by the workers. The second example was the friction between the textile mill owners and the workers in Ahmedabad. Here Gandhi had said that the workers were to cooperate with the mill owners in their moments of crisis and not ask for more pay.[323]

It was in against such a background that the sixth session of the AITUC took place in Madras on 9th-10th January, 1926. The sixth session of the AITUC was presided over by V.V.Giri, the head of the Bengal-Nagpur Railway Union. Certain things were very significant about this session of the AITUC. One was that it received messages of greetings from the Red International of Labour Unions, the British Trade Union Congress, the British Minority movement, the Central Council of Russian Trade Unions and the International Federation of Trade Unions. This shows that the labour movement in India was drawing much support at the international level. The reformist leaders like N.M.Joshi and the British Trade Union representative Graham Pole wanted affiliation with the IFTU (the International Federation of Trade Unions). But when the question of affiliation to an international organisation arose, it became clear that the AITUC, despite pressure from its reformist leaders to join the IFTU, could not come to a decision. Adhikari has said that this inability to adopt a decision on affiliation "...meant in fact, the rejection of affiliation to the reformist IFTU..."[324]

Another point was that the presidential address was rather soft on certain issues like the peasant movements. Regarding the peasants' organisations Giri said, "These organisations are not against the landed interests of the landlords in any form, and this should be made abundantly clear. If they are properly organised, they will form a happy medium in bringing about peace and harmony to both landlord and tenant..."[325] Roy's comments on the AITUC was much the same as before. He was disgusted about the reformist leadership in the Trade Union Congresses. He felt that the Congresses should be chaired by the workers themselves and drew the example of the previous president Thengdi, who was a railway employee[326] and how he was reduced to oblivion by the reformist or "respectable" leadership[327]. Roy also felt that the AITUC had failed to draw any lessons from the North Western Railway strike and the Bombay lockout, both of which faced acute problems because of non-affiliation to any international organisation. Yet, the issue had been averted at the AITUC Congress. He felt that the reformist leadership in the Trade Union Congress was actually impeding its normal progress and that the left wing in the trade union movement was still "...too weak organisationally and too immature politically to meet the situation..."[328] In another article in *The Masses of India* Roy said that the reformist leadership of the trade union movement in India "... did not represent the interests of the Indian proletariat..."[329] He felt that the failure to lead the workers to an offensive in the Bombay Lockouts established the temperament of the leaders of the movement who were more in favour of the mill owners than the workers who had undertaken and suffered the strikes themselves[330]. Roy's criticism was harsh, but it established one point. He felt that the leadership of the workers in the hands of the reformist nationalist leaders would be practically the same as working within the folds of the nationalist wing itself. Such leadership would always attempt to preserve the interests of its own class before that of the workers, a fact that was highly detrimental to the cause of communism[331]. These ideas of Roy conformed to his ideas at the Fifth Congress—ideas, that were to an extent taken to be a deviation from earlier communist principles. Even in the Comintern circles, similar ideas were gaining grounds during this time[332]. The sixth session of the AITUC established once again that sharp differences existed between the reformists and the communists in the leadership of the trade union movement which became all the more pronounced on issues of policy making. Whereas the former was bent upon securing only the welfare of the workers from the trade unions, the latter were seeking much more. Mere welfare activities were not enough for them. They wanted to establish the rule of the proletariat, and in order to achieve it they wanted the active participation of the workers. This was possible only if the trade unions could work in strengthening the working class movement so as to enable the working class to usurp power into their own hands from the classes that aimed to control them. This notion unquestionably clashed with the reformist idea of using the trade unions merely to facilitate the well being of the proletariat within the existing situation itself.

Considering the fact that communism in India was still a long way from maturity, and considering the fact that it had to constantly contend with reformism at the same time, made the development of communism in India quite difficult. But nevertheless, the situation was not unprecedented and tactics to combat such a situation had been evolved as early as the Second Congress of the Comintern. The only problem was that the Second Congress sanctioned a split between the communists and the nationalist bourgeoisie, only after the imperialists were overthrown and the native bourgeoisie took their place. But there was no time frame that could bind these strategies, nor was it possible to do so as an element of hypothesis outlined them along with varied characteristics and terms of progress in different nations. Besides, although the situation had progressed over the years, no systematic analysis had been made at the Comintern about the role of the communists in India; their relationship with the native as well as the foreign capitalist classes; the progress of working class movement in India; and the relationship between the native capitalists and the imperialists. Added to it was the Stalinist line that strictly believed in alliance with the bourgeois led nationalist movement. The ECCI Resolution of 1925 clearly stated:

"The watchword of the People's Party in the programme of which the points of emphasis should be the total separation from the Empire, a democratic Republic, the universal right to franchise and the abolition of feudalism is one which was proclaimed by the Communists and continues to be adhered to, and is correct. The organisation of such a Party will provide an appropriate form to a repressed a majority of the nationalist forces, namely, the progressive section of the bourgeoisie, the revolutionary intellectuals belonging to the petty bourgeoisie, the workers and the masses. It will also strengthen the position of the Indian bourgeoisie, which, till now, has remained confined to skirmishes over timid legislature, so that it will contribute to a strengthening of every resistance against imperialism, the underlying principle being a united nationalist form...Only as a well organised, class conscious advanced detachment of the working class, equipped with a clear understanding of the meaning of national liberation movement and acting in close cooperation with the world proletariat (namely, that of England) it will be possible for the Indian Communists to play an active role in the organisation of a revolutionary, anti-imperialist, united-front. The victory on this front will lead to the 2 stage of the struggle, towards the struggle for emancipation of the working class from all exploitation."[333]

This point regarding this alliance with the bourgeois led movements in the colonies was especially a source of great debate between Roy on the one hand and Comintern leadership on the other[334]. Even the Indian communists varied with Roy on several counts. For example, when Roy was thinking that the time had become ripe for the revolution, Dange and Singaravelu felt that organisation work was still to be done. The objective situation, as it presented itself to different individuals, differed. The attempts to unite all the different communist factions under one central organisation had only just begun, and still had a long way to go before a logical and systematic evaluation of the situation was made, and coherent policies taken accordingly. Roy was also involved in a fight for power over the members of the CPGB, especially because the Comintern was ascribing it with much importance in the Indian issues[335]. The Comintern, in fact, was trying to associate the Indian working class movement with that of the British, much to Roy's annoyance. These were the major causes of strife in the early communist movement.

THE ALL BENGAL PEASANTS' CONFERENCE

On 6th-7th February, 1926, the All Bengal Peasants' Conference was held at Krishnanagar. It was at this conference that the Bengal Peasants' and Workers' Party was formed. This Bengal Peasants' and Workers' Party created for its functioning, an executive body, which was to remain valid for one year. Dr. Nareshchandra Sengupta was its president. Among other members were Soumyendranath Tagore, Qazi Nazrul Islam, Muzaffar Ahmad, and others. The party was represented from all parts of Bengal. Its foremost aim was "...the attainment of swaraj in the sense of complete independence of India based on the political, social and economic equality of women and men."[336] The party also laid much stress on agriculture. It said that agriculture being the mainstay of the Indian economy, the peasants deserved much attention. It was said in this context that "…the most important and desired right so that those who till the land also own it…" and that without this one right, all other rights would tantamount to nothing where the tiller of the soil was concerned[337]. This programme too, like several others, retained a similarity of content and approach with Roy's Gaya Manifesto.

But what is particularly noteworthy about the programme of the Bengal Peasants' and Workers Party was its approach towards the peasantry. It was, perhaps for the first time that singular importance was attached to the peasant question in India. All this long the primary concern had been for the workers, peasants received only sporadic glances. But after the formation of the Bengal Peasants' and Workers Party, and the emergence soon afterwards of the Workers' and Peasants' Parties in other parts of India, the peasantry began to gain importance. This was also in consonance with Zinoviev's speech in the Fifth Congress where he had said that the Comintern was dissatisfied at the turn of the events in the colonies in the east, and that this was primarily because the peasant question had been neglected and the development of peasant movements in the colonies were weak and insignificant. It was perhaps because of the same reason that the August issue of *The Masses* also ascribed an important role to the peasantry. It said:

"…The rural programme of the left wing should be the programme of the agrarian revolution. The revolutionary intellectuals seek their way to the masses. They want to place the nationalist movement on a broad basis of mass action. They should then voice the objective demands of the peasantry. The interest of the peasant masses demands lower rent, security of tenure and freedom from the usurer's greed. The left wing should go to the villages, with a programme based on these three demands of the peasantry. If they can have the courage to do this, they will be the vanguard of a revolutionary peoples' party leading the battle from freedom to victory.

"The peasantry is a very important factor in the struggle for national freedom. Without a revolutionary agrarian programme the nationalist movement will remain powerless…"[338]

But at the same time Roy had refused to budge from his earlier stand regarding the importance of the proletariat. He said in no uncertain terms,

"…But there is another social factor that is still more important than the peasantry. It is the urban proletariat. Without minimising the importance of work among the peasantry, the middle class revolutionaries should make a united front with the proletariat..."[339]

This proved once again that the Indian communists often harboured their own ideas, those which they retained, without always going in line with the policies taken at the Comintern's Congresses. It is also to be noted that two more articles dealing with the peasantry were published in the same year. One was "Agricultural Policy of British Imperialism in India"[340] by G.A.K.Luhani, and the other was "Punjab Moneylenders Bill"[341] by Roy both written on the rural question during this time. These two articles dealt with the problems faced by the peasantry and their relationship with other rural factors like the landlords and the moneylenders.

The central point emphasised in the policies and demands of the Bengal Peasants' and Workers' Party however, was that since all previous attempts to achieve freedom from the British had failed, what was needed was a new approach. This purpose could be served only by organising the workers and the peasants who formed eighty per cent of the country's population. The programme hence said:

"Whereas it has been seen that efforts to snatch freedom from unwilling hands with the help of force and terrorism have not succeeded in the past; whereas it is not possible to bring about an improvement in the condition of the masses by flattering the bureaucracy; or whereas the freedom of the unarmed masses, who have been tied down by a thousand bonds with the help of the native army (?), cannot be won by means of secretly collected weapons, and whereas it is proved that the only effective way of winning freedom for an unarmed nation is the use of the dynamic force of a militant mass movement, which is many times more powerful than bombs and pistols."[342]

This was in a way, a reiteration of Marxist principles which acknowledged without glorification the use violence on the basis of need. Therefore, the militancy that was being criticised was one that was being used by one section of the nationalists, a section that was as elite in its outlook as its moderate counterpart, and which functioned as the leaders of the vast and ignorant masses, instead of educating the masses themselves so that they could come forward and assume leadership in their own hands, as the communists envisaged.

The Bengal Peasants' and Workers' Party also felt that the

"declassed" educated youth needed to join the workers and peasants, so as to "...make them more conscious of their political rights so that they will be able to snatch freedom out of the hands of a few aggressive and selfish individuals, who work only for their own self interest and aggrandisement..."[343] This idea reflected once again that the Indian communists were trying to imbibe the Bolshevik model since 1905 and situate it in terms of Indian conditions. The petty bourgeois factor was also gaining importance. Their interests were often at variance with those of the big bourgeoisie, a fact that was causing a split within the bourgeoisie. It was perhaps a call to the petty bourgeois intellectuals to assume the leadership of the mass movement. Besides it also proved that the nascent communist party was trying to unite a majority of the people in its immediate struggle against imperialism. This becomes evident a little later in the draft where it was said:

> "The party will cooperate wherever possible with all other parties engaged in national activities...The party will assist those who fight for the undermentioned demands of the workers and peasants, in their election campaign for legislative bodies and other representative institutions and when elected they will be recognised as representatives of the party in the legislative bodies..."(the undermentioned demands were the formulation of their own rules of conduct and opposition to all measures that were detrimental to the interests of the working classes and supporting those which upheld them.)[344]

It shows clearly that though the draft expressed its misgivings about all the bourgeois nationalist parties that were struggling for the cause of national liberation, yet, at the same time it could not just do away with the strategy of alliance with the bourgeois led nationalist movement that had been formulated by the Comintern during the Second Congress. This emphasis on the strategy of supporting the bourgeois led movements in the colonies was very much in line with what was being advocated by the Comintern under Stalin. Despite Trotsky's opposition to the Stalinist line of action in China, and the problems faced by the communist parties of Germany, Poland, America and Bulgaria, nothing could be done in the way of change or even modification of the tactic of supporting the bourgeois movements. As Stalin's authoritarianism increased, along with the growing authoritarianism of the CPSU in the Comintern, bitter opposition in the Comintern order against Stalin also surfaced. But

Stalin suffocated all opposition. Even Zinoviev, who had supported Stalin till March 1926 by drafting the Theses on Current Question of the International Communist Movement, a document that strongly favoured an alliance with the bourgeois led nationalist movements, left Stalin soon afterwards. Roy's ideas, already perched in opposition to Stalin and his strategy that envisaged a lasting alliance between bourgeoisie and the communists, too made themselves clear in his pronouncements about the nationalist movement in India.

M.N.Roy had been aware of the impending All Bengal Peasants' Conference. He in fact sent a letter to the Central Committee Communist Party of India which enclosed a draft on "How to Organise a Working Class Party", one which he had wanted to despatch before the Conference was convened. Roy said that the post-war discontent saw the welling up of mass energy against the imperialist order. It only lacked a proper leadership. He felt, "...And it was but a question of time. Such a gigantic fermentation of mass energy was sure to throw up a conscious vanguard—the revolutionary party of the working class...Indian working class had become the backbone of a great political movement. It must develop its own political organ..."[345] He also felt that the imperialists were aware of the power of the working class and hence

"...all the forces of imperialism were put into action in order to prevent the growth of a working class party...The nationalist movement as a whole remained indifferent to that struggle between two apparently unequal forces—the pioneers of the Indian proletariat and the agencies of imperialist repression. Worse than that: in critical moments leading sections of the nationalist movement joined the imperialist cry against the 'Bolshevik menace' as the call for the organisation of the working class party was depleted to be..."[346]

These problems however, could not deter the working class movement. Roy said, "The small proletarian vanguard, however, survived all vicissitudes. Imperialist oppression could not kill it..."[347] In such a situation, said Roy,

"...The frontal attack of the enemy— fierce repression of the vanguard— is now supplemented by clever stratagems of flank attack...Instead of being opposed as before, the idea of forming a working class party receives patronage from unexpected quarters, and in many instances the sinister hand of imperialism is perceptible behind the scene..."[348]

It can be noted that Roy's distrust of the nationalist bourgeoisie was a reflection of his ideas at the Fifth Congress. He simply felt that there was a need to re-examine the policies of the Comintern.

Roy's distrust of the bourgeois order was so deep seated that he felt that even the middle class was unable to grasp the true situation in India. Instead of acting as the "ideological spokesmen" of the masses, they suffered from class prejudice and wanted to "...uplift the downtrodden, not to lead the expropriated and exploited in the revolt against class domination...They do not admit that the working class is the backbone of society...these leaders have only been forced to see that the that the movement for national freedom will never succeed without active participation of the masses. Hence their wish to capture the masses, in other words, to use the masses as so many pawns in the struggle."[349]

Roy said that the bourgeois order wanted to keep the proletariat away from class-consciousness and national politics. He was also aware of the fact that the pioneers of the working class movement, educated on European lines, would tend to move ahead without quite matching its pace with the workers themselves. He warned the communists against such tendencies. He said:

"While the counter-revolutionary bourgeois politicians and agents of imperialism, in deceptive garbs, are seeking to divert the growing class-consciousness of the young Indian proletariat into wrong channels, the revolutionary vanguard of the working class must know how to accomplish its task— how to organise the working class party. One essential thing to be kept always in mind is that the party is the vanguard of the class and that the strength of the vanguard lies in its close and constant contact with the army it leads. The vanguard should be careful not to go too fast and too far ahead of the entire working class. The party as the political organ of the class must grow out of the class. It should not be formed as the so called labour parties, far away from the working class to be imposed upon it, or even to ignore it. Ideological pioneer of the working class party may come from the declassed intellectuals (it is bound to be so particularly in India where the middle class intellectuals are proletarianised and the proletariat culturally backward), but the bulk of the membership should be recruited from the proletariat."[350]

That more and more workers needed to be brought into the movement and that the movement should be one of the workers and not one which did not involve them properly, were thoughts that Roy had been entertaining ever since the Third All India Trade Union

Congress was held in Lahore from 27th March, 1923.
M.N.Roy said in the same article:

"...The programme of a working class party, therefore, is the programme of Socialism...But the road to Socialism passes through successive stages of social development. The working class in countries, which have had these stages of social development, is engaged in the final stage of class struggle— struggle for the immediate realisation of Socialism. The situation in India is different. India is engaged in the revolutionary struggle for democratic freedom. This would be realised through the overthrow of foreign domination and the liquidation of medieval socio-economic institutions. The working class must actively participate and lead this struggle for democratic freedom. The working class party, therefore, must fight under two programmes: minimum programme to be realised in the immediate future and the maximum programme the realisation of which will depend upon the carrying out of the minimum programme. The minimum programme will contain immediate demands of the working class party and will be broad enough to rally around the working class and all the other social elements whose interests demand national independence... the maximum programme of the working class party is the programme of the victorious class-struggle— of Social Revolution, of Socialism. The minimum programme should be fitted into the maximum programme. It is but means to the end..."[351].

So far, Roy showed adherence to the Second Congress policies. But the moment he began to analyse the role of the bourgeoisie in the struggle for freedom, he revealed the same deviation that he had made in the Fifth Congress of the Comintern. He felt that the native bourgeoisie aspired for political power, was not ready to fight the British despite the fact that their interests were antagonistic to imperialist monopoly capital. Roy said:

"...The British domination cannot be overthrown without a revolutionary fight. This depends on the mobilisation of the mass energy. The native bourgeoisie is afraid of a revolution. They would rather share power with imperialist overlords and grow economically under their protection. Thus, the struggle for national freedom under bourgeois leadership and with a capitalist programme has ended in compromise. The nationalist bourgeoisie would be satisfied with self-government within the Empire. This means the bourgeoisie have abandoned the fight for the complete democratisation of the country. The task of carrying through the bourgeois revolution, which began with British conquest, therefore, devolves upon the working class and other exploited sections of the society. The working class must carry on a determined fight against compromise with imperialism, because this compromise will intensify capitalist exploitation of India. Greed of native capitalism will be satisfied not by diminishing imperialist plunder, but by intensifying exploitation of the Indian working class."[352]

The idea of the masses carrying on struggle against compromise with imperialism as the native capitalists tended to do, made very obvious the notion of a breach between the proletariat and the bourgeoisie. This had been the main issue of argument with the Stalinist line of thought since the Fifth Congress. Roy demonstrated it once more.

The last part of Roy's article deals with the factors like trade unions, press etc. that were needed to build up a successful working class party. But this working class party, according to Roy, was not the Communist Party or the peoples' party, as he preferred to call it. Adhikari has said, "...He makes it quite clear that the meeting is for organising an open forum of the Communist Party, i.e. the workers' and the peasants' party, and not the people's party. He points out: 'They are entirely two different things. One is a veiled communist party while the other is a revolutionary nationalist party.'..."[353] The same idea of the working class party being an organ of the vanguard party also becomes clear in Roy's concluding paragraph:

"Lastly, ideological clarity on the part of the vanguard is indispensable for the organisation of a real working class party. Otherwise we may repeat the story of blind leading the blind. Only a clear sighted revolutionary vanguard with faith in the masses, fully conversant with the role of the proletariat is destined to play, closely connected with the entire working class will organise the working class party in India. In short, there cannot be real working class party without a Marxian leadership."[354]

It is clear from the above excerpt that the vanguard was to organise and lead the working class party in India, and that without the existence of a Marxian vanguard, there could be no "real working class party".

THE INDIAN SITUATION AND ROY'S ATTITUDE TOWARDS CONGRESS POLICIES

One major problem that the Indians were facing at this time was the constant communal strife between the two major religious groups, the Hindus and the Muslims. Roy wrote a series of articles in different papers during this time, his focus being on the fact regarding how the imperialists were using the communal differences between the two groups to further their own policies. He also said that the bourgeois leaders had had failed to solve the problem. He said, "The reason of this deplorable failure is the inordinate importance given to religion in nationalist agitation. It is also due to the fact that the bourgeois-nationalist leaders only searched for a basis of compromise."[355] In another article Roy said:

"The mixing of religion with politics is another factor which leads to the resuscitation of communal bickerings. A political movement based on religion cannot but lead to religious aggressiveness and thus defeat its own purpose...The movement for national liberation must be divorced uncompromisingly from religion, otherwise it will bring ruin and disaster in its wake. There lies the only hope for the success of the struggle."[356]

Roy however, was optimistic that the time had come when all these problems would be resolved. He felt that once a party based on "mass action" was formed, one which had a programme that catered to the interests of the masses along with national liberation, "...that the wide masses of the people can be united, their dynamic energy employed for the liberation and not for cutting each other's throats as at present...Mass civil disobedience, the discarded weapon of the bourgeois nationalism, would crown the programme of action and Hindus and Muslims would march shoulder to shoulder as brothers in the fight."[357] Roy's feelings were best expressed in an article by Safdar:

"The present period of development of the national-revolutionary movement in India brings with it the chance to solve the Hindu-Mussalman problem. The modern Indian big bourgeoisie is allied with British imperialism. The driving forces of the revolution today are the proletariat, the peasantry and the petty bourgeoisie (the artisans, small traders, and the petty bourgeois intelligentsia). The economic conditions of these classes are becoming worse and worse, for the compromise between the British and Indian capitalism is based upon intensified exploitation of these classes. The struggle of the latter against imperialism therefore is a historically necessary struggle. In this struggle the proletariat will assume the leadership. This means that the basis of the national struggle will become wider. This will lead to the dying out of group and religious distinctions, for common problems will take supreme place above all others. We see therefore that the solution of the Hindu-Mussalman problem is a function of the social struggle of the workers and peasants."[358]

The Gauhati Congress of 1926 was another very significant event that took place during this time. Just before the Congress, Roy wrote an article, "From Gaya to Gauhati" in *The Masses*. He said in this article:

"...The national programme is meaningless if the goal is not national freedom, national freedom is meaningless if it does not bring democracy, education and rights for the workers and peasants...The leftwing nationalist movement should in all sincerity and earnestness ally itself with the struggle of the workers for the organisation of industrial labour, for the establishment for the full rights for trade-unionism, for the eight-hour day, minimum wage, workers' compensation, adequate factory legislation and other needs for a healthy and vigorous labour movement...At present the programme of the official leadership of the Congress is discredited, the left wing stands disorganised and the masses are waiting for a lead. There has never been a better opportunity for settling the nationalist movement on a new path. It is for the sincere fighters in the nationalist movement to see that the opportunity is not missed and that preparations are made well in time that Gauhati will witness the inception of a new phase in the nationalist struggle."[359]

It is clear that Roy was creating pressure on the Congress leadership just before it began, regarding the attitude that it would subsequently take towards the masses. This used to be one of the major tactics of the early communists. They understood that without the Congress, they would not be able to reach the masses in a short time. This was because the Congress under Gandhi had established links with the masses and they in a way identified themselves with him. Hence, proceeding without the help of the Congress in such a direction would amount to wastage of time and energy. So they often tried to use the Congress and its resources, which were immense as compared to their meagre funds, to make contacts with the masses at the grass root level. This had also been one of the policies of the Comintern. But with the passage of time, the situation had changed. The bourgeois leadership that dominated the Congress could not quite satisfy the communist leadership any more. So they began to seek the help of the left wing revolutionary elements within the Congress. This step would not only help in propaganda work, but also reduce to some extent the power of the dominating bourgeois leadership.

Roy's growing distrust of the bourgeoisie in India, his misgivings about their vacillating nature between the imperialists and the masses in terms of their material interests, was expressed in this article.

Another very important document of this time was *A Manifesto the Indian National Congress*[360] by the Communist Party of India. The Gauhati Congress was attended by two important communist personalities, R.S.Nimbakar and K.N.Joglekar. Both were members of the central executive of the Communist Party of India elected at the Kanpur Congress. Their presence might have added more weight to the Manifesto. The Manifesto was very significant in the sense that it criticised is no uncertain terms, the Congress policies that in general did not cater to the interests of the workers and peasants. It said clearly that "The Legislatures Do Not Represent the People"[361]. In this context the Manifesto also said, "...the nationalist movement as represented by the existing political parties is divorced from the popular masses. It has neither the power nor the will to fight for freedom. The general desire is to reach a compromise with imperialism without losing face. Mutual recriminations and loud protestations of patriotism do not change the essentials of the situation."[362] The Manifesto also said that despite the nationalist movement breaking into factions, they all subscribed to the same programme of "self-government within the British empire"[363]. This was something that the communists never corroborated to. They wanted complete liberation from the British rule. Their loss of confidence in bourgeois leadership was also expressed in the Manifesto. While speaking of the "Contradictions inside the Swaraj Party", the Manifesto said that the bourgeois leaders of the Swaraj Party "...deceived the party. Actually, however, they have betrayed the party and the nation. Their insistence upon the staking the future of the party on the verdict of the electorate is a violation of the sovereignty of the people. They would make not only the Swaraj Party, but the National Congress, an instrument to be used in the interests of the small minority—enfranchised by the grace of Britain."[364] The influence of Roy on the Indian communists becomes evident from this excerpt. It becomes even more transparent in the analysis of "National Interest and Class Interest". Under this heading the Manifesto said:

"...The quarrel between imperialism and the upper classes of the Indian society is a quarrel over booty. Native landlords and the capitalists also live at the expense of the producing masses. But the monopolist policy of imperialism did not permit them an unrestricted economic development which would increase their capacity to exploit the working class. The major portion of the values produced by the Indian workers and peasants go to swell the pockets of imperialism. The Indian bourgeoisie were allowed only a modest middlemen's share. In course of time they have become dissatisfied with this small portion of the booty. They wanted an ever increasing share and finally the prior right over the entire resources of labour-power of the Indian masses.

"The Indian bourgeoisie, however, could not realise their aspirations for the mastery of the country without challenging the monopoly of imperialism. This again they cannot do by themselves. India cannot become free from foreign domination except through the revolutionary action of the entire people. But the popular revolt against imperialism is not caused by the grievances of the nationalist bourgeoisie. It has its own causes. The popular masses rise against exploitation as such. Consequently, the nationalist bourgeoisie, who would like to be the sole masters and rulers of the country, do not dare to use the weapon which alone can seriously threaten the imperialist hold on the country. National interests— the interests of the 98 per cent—are thus sacrificed for class interests. The attempts to conquer sole mastery over the country being fraught with possible danger of immense gravity, the nationalist bourgeoisie enter into an agreement with imperialism to exploit the Indian people jointly."[365]

The Manifesto also said that despite the fact that the bourgeoisie were allying with the imperialists, yet, the struggle for national liberation should be carried out in the interests of the majority of the masses represented by the workers and the peasantry. The peasantry was given a special importance because they formed 70 per cent of the population and was the mainstay of Indian economy. The communists gave much importance to the need of the majority of the masses and felt that the Congress should demand the betterment of the condition of the masses. "*National independence and complete democratisation of the national life in every respect*— these are the main planks of the nationalist platform. The battle to realise this programme must be fought with the slogan: '*Land, Bread and Education*' "[366]

Roy wrote a series of articles during this time regarding the Indian situation. He felt the political outlook of the Congress had always been reformist in nature and its social ideology reactionary. Moreover, it had always represented the bourgeoisie who tried to use the mass movement to "further reformist demands of native capitalism"[367]. He felt that the Swaraj Party too was led by the same bourgeois class, who were incapable of leading the mass struggle against imperialism, and who would reconcile with the British only "if a few grievances of theirs were removed". However, he felt at the same time, that the revolutionary elements of the Swaraj Party, belonging mainly to the petty-bourgeois class, were tending to get "closer to the masses not as agents of capitalist exploitation and feudal domination, but as a revolutionary factor irresistibly drawn to a mightier revolutionary force."[368]

Roy also felt that the Gauhati Congress was indecisive about its future policies. He said, "The Gauhati session of the National Congress was the most uneventful of recent years...The chief characteristics of the congress are all negative; it took no momentous decisions, it settled no vexed questions, it excited no heated debate."[369] He attributed two reasons for this failure. The first reason was that the Congress "...was no longer 'national' except in a geographical sense, and hardly even in that. The Congress had become the appendage of a single section, it has become practically synonymous with a single comparatively narrow political party..."[370] By the 'single comparatively narrow political party, Roy obviously meant the bourgeoisie, a fact that he elaborated in the same theme. The second reason for the "...indecisive character of the Gauhati Congress is to be found in the equilibrium of forces within the comparatively homogenous representation of congressmen..."[371] Roy felt that the right wing leaders, representing the middle bourgeoisie and "drawn towards compromise, were balanced equally by the left wing "...that feels the pressure of the masses for whom the bourgeois leadership holds out no hope..."[372] In such a situation, it was very difficult to arrive at a particular decision as both sides would try to impose their own demands. The independence resolution that was moved by the Communist Party of India was defeated at the Congress. Roy admitted the failure. He said, "The left wing scored no victory again this year. The reason for this is that there is no common programme, no common platform on which they could unite. Besides they are lacking in initiative. So Roy was aware that the petty-bourgeois classes needed to be organised for the cause of the revolution. His later writings proved this attitude.

Another very important event of this time was the Political Sufferers' Conference that was presided over by Bhupendranath Datta. In can be recalled here that Bhupendranath Datta with Ebul Hasan and Abul Hasan had written a thesis regarding the scheme of organisation of Indian work and had submitted it to the Mali Bureau on August 9th, 1921. It can also be recalled that Lenin, after reading it, answered to him that he should be more involved in organising peasant leagues in India[373]. Bhupendranath had taken Lenin's advice in his stride and had done some work in this connection after he returned to India in 1925. *The Masses of India* gave coverage to this Conference, and the presidential speech of Bhupendranath was appreciated in it. The conference was one of "political sufferers or political ex-prisoners"[374]. *The Masses* of February 1927, in its characteristic critical tone, called Bhupendranath Datta's speech a courageous one, which did not try to make "...a sentimental appeal on behalf of those who have suffered at the hands of British imperialism...His speech is like a breath of fresh air blowing away the shibboleths of congress oratory and enabling his hearers to see clearly, perhaps for the first time, the realities of Indian social development."[375] He divided the so called political sufferers of the Non-Cooperation movement into two groups, those who had suffered for the "cause of revolutionary nationalism and those who had suffered for the noncooperation movement" he said that though the former group was opposed to the party of "so-called constitutional method" and were regarded as a "party of violent action", they too had been a part of the bourgeois order and could not do anything effective as they "never reached out to the masses"[376]. He also analysed the class character of the Congress as being predominantly bourgeois, who, of course, were "treacherous"[377]. He felt the need for organising the workers and the peasants on the basis of a socio-economic programme and called upon the petty bourgeois class to give up their bourgeois identity and join the toilers in their struggle for emancipation[378]. He also emphasised the necessity of bringing the mass movement in India into contact with the world proletarian movement against world imperialism and also the British proletariat[379].

Roy's attitude about Datta, as expressed in *The Masses*, proved another thing. It showed that the earlier bitterness between the two had lessened to a great extent, so much so that not only was the former applauding the latter, but that the latter was also revealing the influence of the former. It can also be noted that several of the earlier rivals of Roy like Bhupendranath Datta and Virendranath Chattopadhyaya later on reconciled with him. This was either because they had understood that the need for a united effort at mass organisation was necessary or because they had also felt that challenging Roy's power and his position in the Comintern would be detrimental for the advancement of their own work. Whatever the case, it was certainly one of the basic features of the emerging communist movement in India, where ideological and other rivalries were very common because of the absence of one particular organisation that could act as a disciplining factor for the various communist groups and factions.

By this time the British trade unionists like Spratt and Bradley, who had been despatched to India, had become quite active in building up a revolutionary trade union movement in India. In other words, the role of the CPGB (Communist Party of Great Britain) in the Indian communist movement was growing. Adhikari however, has said that "...it is not true that after 1925, the CI kept in touch with India not through Roy but through the CPGB. In fact, after the first Communist Conference, when a constitution of the party was framed, Roy suggested a clause which provided for a foreign bureau of Indian communists abroad who were unable to return to India, but who were to do ideological work for the party and also to maintain contact of the party with the CI. This foreign bureau consisted of M.N.Roy, Clemens Dutt and Muhammad Ali Sipassi. This arrangement functioned up to the beginning of 1928. On the eve and after the Sixth Congress of the CI, M.N.Roy ceased to be in charge of India on behalf of the CI but even thereafter in the early thirties, the contact was direct and not through the CPGB."[380] The contact with the Indian situation was undoubtedly "direct" as Adhikari pointed out. The significance of the growing authority of the CPGB established the point that Roy was rapidly losing favour in the Comintern. In his place, the CPGB under C.P.Dutt was gradually assuming an all encompassing role. The Comintern too was involved in facilitating this change. On the other hand, the Comintern was also in its own way, trying to help the cause of Indian communism directly as it had been doing earlier. H.G.Haig, the Secretary to the Government of India, Home Department, was writing to the India Office in February

1927:

> "A well placed source at the end of November stated that at the instigation of DEBITSKY, who is in charge of recently organised information bureau for Indian Affairs, the Eastern Department of the IKKI has instructed the Baku section to detail 28 extra pupils to join the Higher Military School of Eastern Studies in Tashkent. 2. The object of this was the rapid preparation of agitator propagandists for work in India, and particularly, if possible, for work in Indian military units, for which it was considered essential that pupils should have military and political instructions..."[381]

The Baku Council of Action and Propaganda had also been founded and it was sending its agents to India to carry on propaganda work[382]. The British were, as usual, keeping a watchful eye on the activities of the communists. The were intercepting their letters, copying them, and then forwarding them to the addressees, as they had been doing all along to keep the correspondence going. This intercepted correspondence and the reports from British sources reveal the nature of the communist movement in India as well as the attitude of the British towards it. Among them, the fortnightly reports were very detailed. Most of these documents of the post Kanpur Conspiracy days, became exhibits of the Meerut trial, and they form an important source for the study of the history of communism in India.

Meanwhile, Shapurji Saklatwala, member of the British parliament and a British communist at the same time, also visited India in January1927 with the intention to help in building up the trade union movement in India. On the other hand preparations had begun since the end of the previous year for holding the second conference of the Communist Party of India at Lahore. This was the same party that Satyabhakta had created. The impending arrival of Saklatwala added more life to the communist movement. Many of them assembled at Bombay to welcome him. They in fact, even wanted him to preside over the coming conference at Lahore. At this point however, a note of discord arose between the Indian communists on the one hand and Saklatwala on the other. This is because Saklatwala refused to preside over the conference of the Communist Party of India since it was not affiliated to the CPGB or the Communist International[383]. He felt that his main task was to organise the militant working class movement. Therefore, he contacted his English comrades, George Allison alias Donald Campbell and Philip

Spratt. Campbell was arrested soon afterwards, but Spratt continued to function effectively for the next few years. The differences between Saklatwala and the members of Communist Party of India were however, later resolved, but Saklatwala could not preside over the conference, as the conference had to be called off.

EMERGENCE OF THE WORKERS' AND PEASANTS' PARTY IN BOMBAY

The Workers' and Peasants' Party emerged in Bombay from the earlier Congress Labour Party that had been formed in November 1926. "...Subsequently, however, it was decided to take the name of the Workers and Peasants' Party (13 February 1927)"[384]. Like in Bengal, the Workers' and Peasants' Party in Bombay too was formed by communists and left wing nationalists. Adhikari has said, "...It was a small group of left-wing radicals and communists who took the initiative for the formation of the party..."[385] Like the Peasants' and Workers' Party of Bengal, this party too adopted a programme representing the demands of the workers and the peasants. Like the previous party in Bengal, this party too realised the futility of the nationalist organisations in facilitating the well-being of the workers and peasants, and though the core of the party was formed by members of the Congress, yet the aim of the party was to capture the Congress and establish a federated republic of India based on adult suffrage. The party felt that mere welfare activities for the peasants and workers, as the Congress was demanding, was not enough because they were entitled to political, social and economic rights as well[386]. Its programme clearly enumerated its objectives. Firstly, it would be a "...political party of workers and peasants..."[387] Secondly, it would be one that would function within the National Congress so as to "...promote the organisation of trade unions, wrest them from their present alien control, to advance the organisation of the peasants on the basis of their economic and social requirements, and to present a determined and pertinent opposition to the government and thus secure a social, economic and political emancipation of these classes..."[388] Thirdly, the programme aimed at the "...attainment of complete national independence..." and that it would "...cooperate for that end with other organisations which profess to desire it and are willing to struggle for its realisation."[389] Its last aim was to "...obtain swaraj wherein the means of production, distribution and exchange are publicly owned and socially controlled…"[390] Among the office bearers of the Workers' and Peasants' Party, S.V.Ghate, R.S. Nimbakar and K.S.Joglekar belonged to the Central Executive Committee of the Communist Party of India that had been formed at the Kanpur conference in 1925. S.S Mirajkar joined the Communist Party of India by the end of 1927. The rest were all Congress members, some with earlier or later associations with the trade union movement and some without any such influence whatsoever. This shows clearly that the Workers' and Peasants' Party was closely tied to the greatest nationalist party of India, the National Congress.

Soon after its formation in February 1927, the Bombay Workers' and Peasants' Party put a programme before the AICC through its members, Nimbakar and Joglekar. It started with a criticism of the Congress activities: "The present Congress activity and programme are completely divorced from the everyday life of the masses, and in consequence the bulk of the population, the disenfranchised 98 per cent, have lost all interest and sympathy for the congress, which has become a feeble body. The present leadership of the congress has tied itself and the congress machinery to a programme of work which is of benefit only to an insignificant section of the people, the big capitalists and their allies, the intellectual and professional upper classes…In the interest of the vast majority of the people it is now urgently necessary to free the congress from the narrow shackles of class interests, and to yoke it to the task of attaining national freedom from imperialist bondage, as a step towards complete emancipation of the masses from exploitation and oppression."[391] It then enumerated the demands that the Congress was supposed to meet with. These demands were more or less the same as those enumerated in the programme of the Workers' and Peasants' Party. But the significant part of these demands is that pressure was mounting on the Congress because of them. Not only was the Congress to be involved in helping the mass movements, but adding on to this pressure was the demand that the Congress members in the Councils were expected to help in the execution of the programme as well. The programme said in this context:

"…In the elementary and the initial stages of the above work all legal protection and conditions of direct help will have to be created under the existing political machinery and with this definite purpose alone the councils and all other political bodies will be utilised by all congressmen whenever and wherever possible.

Congressmen will go into the councils, local boards, municipalities, village organisations and occupy all points of vantage and will use them to the fullest extent for the furtherance of the abovementioned programme an to bring more and more power in the hands of the people. For this purpose of the utmost democratisation of the whole machinery of government, congressmen will make use and exploit all existing laws and statutes and will further try to introduce new statutes by moving bills, resolutions, amendments, etc., in furtherance of this cause. While thus utilising the existing machinery for the furtherance of the cause of the control of the masses over the same, congressmen will continue the policy of continuous, consistent and uniform obstruction to all government measures whereby the bureaucracy intends to or is likely to strengthen its position. All possible tactics will be used by congressmen to foil government interest, as opposed to above aims, whenever and wherever possible."[392]

Adhikari has said that the significance of the resolution lay in the fact that it "…put forward the slogan of complete independence with the concrete socioeconomic programme before the Indian National Congress, when it still stood for dominion status and when pressure was being built up for the acceptance of the goal of complete independence at the Madras congress which was to take place six months later."[393]

This point about the Congress taking up an active role in the Councils for furthering the interests of the masses had already been made by M.N.Roy a few years back. But the activities of the Congress had come against searing criticism from the communist members. They were visibly dissatisfied by the turn of events in the Congress which catered to the interests of the propertied class as against those of the masses. The communists still sought to remain within its folds perhaps because their movement was still weak, perhaps because of the dictates of the Comintern regarding rendering total support to the bourgeois led movements, or perhaps because they had not yet thought in terms of an alternative movement. Most of the members of the Workers' and Peasants' Party of Bombay were still members of the Congress to which they adhered and propagated adherence. Their nationalist pasts perhaps had still not been totally superimposed by their later communist orientation and living as they did within the realm of imperialist oppression such a thought was still a far cry. But a beginning had been made. They had at least begun the task of influencing the left-wing Congress members on the notions of liberation from foreign yoke and the attainment of a socialist order, or "swaraj" as they preferred to call it.

Roy however, had his own ideas about the tasks of the Workers' and Peasants' Parties. In his article, "The Workers' and Peasants' Party", in *The Masses of India*, he said:

> "At the present stage, the fight for a militant nationalist and labour movement is the immediate requirement in India. The fight for militancy needs to be waged both in the field of nationalist organisation and the field of workers' and peasants' organisations. This is the special function that can be fulfilled by the Workers' and Peasants' Parties. It is not itself the party of national revolution aiming at leadership of national struggle, nor is it the international class party of the proletariat. It is somewhat in the nature of an organised left-wing which will endeavour to secure the adoption of a militant programme of mass action by the existing organisation and to build up the mass movement in an organised manner on that basis... The Workers' and Peasant Party will, on the one hand, strengthen the forces of the left in the national movement and on the other hand it will prepare the way for a powerful class leadership of the revolutionary workers and peasants. It must have a mass following or it will be of no avail."[394]

Adhikari has commented:

> "M.N.Roy's journal correctly formulates the twofold task of the newly formed Workers' and Peasants' Party, but he was simultaneously putting forward the perspective of building the national revolutionary party as a parallel to or in place of the Indian National Congress which he thinks is practically politically dead. The Indian comrades working in the practical field, as well as George Allison (Donald Campbell) and the newly arrived Philip Spratt who were working with them do not seem to have accepted the perspective. The Workers' and Peasants' Party, as we have seen , both in Bengal and in Bombay, was by constitution and programme working both inside the Indian National Congress, to form a revolutionary left wing within it, as well as outside it as an independent party to build class organisations of workers and peasants and to lead their struggles."[395]

The bourgeois question and the problems regarding the tactic of alliance between the bourgeoisie and the communists had already been going on for quite sometime when the Workers and Peasants' Party was set up at Bombay. And Roy, it can be said, was thinking more in terms of the National Congress being a party of the bourgeoisie that catered only to the interests of the bourgeoisie and that in the process of doing so, was not only neglecting the interests of the working masses, but also trying to suppress their movement against the existing order. He also felt that the Indian bourgeoisie was in alliance with the British imperialists, and hence their organisations were useless from the point of view of the masses. He had already said so in his earlier articles.[396]

LEAGUE AGAINST IMPERIALISM

During this time, it could be seen that the left-wing nationalist leaders of the Congress were trying to voice their problems in western conferences. The Brussels Congress of the League Against Imperialism was one such endeavour. The first meeting of this Congress was held between 10th and 14th February 1927 and was attended by leaders of the trade union and labour movements of the imperialist countries of Europe and America along with eminent representatives of the national liberation movements of Asia, Africa and South America. Adhikari has said, "The idea of holding such a world congress against imperialism and national oppression arose out of the massive anti-imperialist upsurge and struggles in China, India and Egypt in the mid-twenties..."[397] Apart from discussing the problems and goals of the Indian nationalist movement, another very important aspect that could be noticed in this Congress was the support that the Indians were openly lending to the Chinese cause.

From the very beginning the League was in favour of complete emancipation from foreign domination. It said:

"This congress accords its warm support to the Indian movement for the complete freedom of India from foreign domination and all kinds of exploitation is an essential step in the full emancipation of the peoples of the world... This congress further trusts that the Indian national movement will base its programme on the full emancipation of the peasants and workers of India, without which there can be no real freedom, and will co-operate with the movements for emancipation in other parts of the world."[398]

This excerpt shows that the League was also advocating the need for the emancipation of the workers and peasants without which there could be no "real freedom". Though there was no mention of the term "socialism", yet, the spirit of the resolution did hint at something similar.

Regarding the Chinese question, the Indian, Chinese and even the British delegations were quite vocal. They said that the time had come for the Indians and the Chinese to join hands in the overthrow of British rule. The Joint Resolution of the Indian and Chinese Delegations said "...British imperialism, which in the past has kept us apart and done so much injury, is now the very force that is uniting us in a common endeavour to overthrow it."[399] The Indian members of the league repeatedly expressed their concern about the use of Indian troops in China by the British, and resolved to prevent it in future[400].

The concept of complete independence was not new. The Indian communists had already been harping on the issue for quite sometime. After the Fifth Congress of the Comintern, M.N.Roy too had constantly been writing on it. He had felt that complete independence was necessary before any concrete step could be taken towards the emancipation of the masses, and that alliance with the reformist nationalist leadership as represented by the Congress would deter not only the liberation from the British, but also the development of a true mass movement set towards the achievement of the final goal of socialism. The Indian National Congress was represented in the League, initially by Jawaharlal Nehru and later by Motilal Nehru. Saklatwala did attend one meeting, but that was on invitation. Jawaharlal Nehru was trying to impress upon the left-wing Congress leaders the need for complete independence for the Indians. The League too endorsed this idea as its "Resolution on India" clearly showed. Another fact was that these ideas were in tune with those being propagated by the Comintern. But at the same time, the significance of these Resolutions was that they failed to consider the already existing ideas on complete independence in India. The Indian delegates were undoubtedly prominent members of the Indian National Congress, a fact, with which they managed to influence the Congress enough to get their views endorsed. Yet, at the same time, they displayed ignorance regarding contemporary parallel organisations that had already begun formulating on issues like complete freedom, those on which the League Against Imperialism had only just begun to think. In the meeting of the League executive in Cologne on August 20th-21st Jawaharlal Nehru had said that there was no party in India with a "...definite objective of 'complete independence'."[401] Saklatwala had been invited to this meeting and he was present in it. Virendranath Chattopadhyaya also attended the meeting. Now they were both aware of the establishment of the Workers' and Peasants' Parties in Bengal and Bombay along with the emphasis that these parties were laying on the need for complete independence. Hence both of them challenged Nehru, to which he had replied that "...'I said there is no organised party which has a definite or an indefinite name, saying that we want complete independence...'..."[402] At this point there was again an interruption, "...'What about the Workers' and Peasants' Parties in India?'..."[403] This time Nehru had answered that there was "...no such thing as the Workers' and Peasants' Party of India. There is a section which calls itself Communist Party of India. Mr. Saklatwala can tell you more about it than I can.'"[404] This shows that the leaders of the Indian National Congress, as represented by Nehru, were either not aware of the activities of the communists, or were deliberately being ignorant so as to enhance the role of the Congress in the bringing about of Indian freedom in the eyes of the European representatives[405].

ATTITUDE OF THE COMMUNISTS TOWARDS THE CHINESE PROBLEM AND THE POLICY OF ALLIANCE WITH THE BOURGEOIS LED NATIONALIST MOVEMENT IN THE COLONIES

While dealing with the colonial issues the League was reiterating what the Comintern had advocated in the Second Congress. It was strongly in support of the anti-imperialist movements that were surging in the colonies. It even went to the extent of supporting the issue of emancipation of the masses. But what it failed to discuss or even consider, was the rise of divergent opinions among the communists. These opinions were contradicting those that the Comintern was advocating, or for that matter, what the League was reiterating. The communists were advocating a split with the nationalist parties in the struggle for liberation from the imperialists. They had total mistrust for the bourgeois led nationalist organisations, and felt that they were only strengthening the hands of the imperialists in the face of the ever increasing mass movements that would, they realised, prove to be much more damaging to the advancement of their vested interests. M.N.Roy and Chen Tu hsiu were some of the major protagonists of this line of thought in India and China respectively. The Communist Party of India or that of China were not discussed even though there was plenty of discussion and deliberation on the question of working class movement. Native exploitation in the colonies was also not given much consideration. The League formulated on the lines of the Comintern without bringing the Comintern, the communist movements and their theories into consideration. It was more as a means to reinvigorate the leftist wing in the nationalist parties against imperialism than anything else.

The Indian communists discussed the Chinese problem from two angles— one regarding the role of British imperialists in China, and the other regarding the role of the Chinese bourgeoisie. Regarding the first point, Indian communists were highly critical of the policies that the British were applying to China. Philip Spratt wrote a series of articles on the Chinese question in the Indian National Herald in January-February 1927. These articles were later reprinted by S.S. Mirajkar under the title, *India and China— by an Internationalist.* In these articles Spratt said that despite a few exceptions like Jawaharlal Nehru, the Indian nationalist leaders as a whole were being rather indifferent to the Chinese cause. He said, "...Our perhaps rather bitter comments on this inaction seem to us still to be justified, since, although some protest has been made, it was of a very formal lifeless character, and was directed purely against nationalist grounds against the use of Indian troops without the consent of the Indian people. There is still shown a complete lack of understanding on the one hand of the importance of the Chinese movement in itself, and on the other of its importance to India, and the response which it should call forth in India."[406] He also said that there were lessons that could be learnt from the Chinese experience. Elaborating on the theme, he said:

> "How can this be done? China here gives us the lead. It is not merely a question of propaganda, of spreading of opinions, but of organisation. The National Congress, the acknowledged representative of the Indian nation, corresponding roughly to the Kuomintang, must take up the concrete demands and needs of the workers and peasants...and with these as a basis it must use its unique authority and resources to build up the workers' militant trade union movement and the peasant unions, as has been done in China. Such an organisation can attack the government and the whole capitalist oppression, as no other weapon can.
>
> "But on this point we can get a further lesson. These tasks, imperative as they were, were only taken up in China actually under the pressure

from the masses themselves, led by their representatives in the 'left-wing' of the Kuomintang. Similarly, here we require a party in the Congress to represent the working class and the peasantry, and to urge and force upon the Congress generally the realisation of its duty in this matter. Such a project has been in the air for sometime. It must be realised as quickly as possible."[407]

Regarding these articles Adhikari has said, "...The pamphlet as a whole was so effective in transmitting to the Indian readers the rich and exhilarating experience and achievements of the contemporary Chinese revolution that the British imperialists immediately banned it."[408] Spratt was arrested in August 1927 and Mirajkar himself was arrested in September. However, both were acquitted soon afterwards.[409]

When Spratt was writing it was 1927. By then Chiang had already begun his attacks on the communists and the latter restive though they were, remained quiet in the name of maintaining party discipline. By then, the workers who had so fervently supported Chiang's Northern Expedition were suppressed and their movement fiercely stemmed. Chen Tu hsiu and Peng Shu tse put forward a resolution in the party central committee that demanded a reorganisation of the Kuomintang and the granting of independence to the communists who were to carry on independent work among the workers and the peasants. But this was opposed not only by the Chinese communists, but also by the Comintern leadership[410]. Considering the fact that the Kuomintang had assumed tremendous powers under its leader, Chiang Kai shek, and considering also the fact that his rise to power coincided with the brutal suppression of the communists in China, this was rather a blind reiteration of the policies of the Comintern.

Regarding the role of the bourgeoisie in China, a very important fact was that Trotsky had begun to understand the problems that the Chinese communists were facing by being bound to the Kuomintang. He supported the Resolution of Peng and Chen. He said, "The revolutionary struggle in China has, since 1925, entered a new phase..."[411] in which the peasants and the proletariat had assumed much prominence. The bourgeoisie too were breaking off "to the right", he had said. He also added:

"...This very fact confronts the CCP with the task of graduating from the preparatory class it now finds itself, into a higher grade. Its immediate political task must now be to fight for direct independent leadership of the awakened working class— not of course, in order to remove the working class from the framework of the national revolutionary struggle, but to assure it the role of not only the most resolute fighter, but also of a political leader with hegemony in the struggle of the Chinese masses."[412]

Besides, Stalin's increasing authoritarianism was also being felt in the Comintern circles. His close associates, Zinoviev and Kamenev also broke up with him and joined Trotsky. Even Radek, "galling"[413] though it was to him, joined Trotsky and Zinoviev. At first, he kept away from openly attacking the Comintern for the cause of maintenance of party discipline. But by March 1927, he realised that "...salvaging the Chinese Revolution took precedence over observing party discipline..." In a debate in the Communist Academy, he sharply criticised Stalin for his "lack of policy in China"[414]. However, he was not totally in favour of the Chinese communists taking power into their own hands. He only wanted them to join the left forces of the Kuomintang to forcefully snatch power from the hands of Chiang Kai shek. Even Bukharin in a speech in the Indian Commission in August 1927, said that a comparison should be made between the Chinese and the Indian situations without blindly repeating the Chinese policies in India[415]. He said that apart from economic differences or differences in the methods of imperialist exploitation, another major difference was there. He analysed it as follows:

"2. Another big difference consists in the role of the bourgeoisie of the two countries. Here we must analyse whatever special features are presented by the development of the Indian bourgeoisie in comparison with the former role of the Chinese bourgeoisie. Are these points in common, are there differences, to what extent are they weighty, to what extent do they modify the role of the Indian bourgeoisie, etc.? It is clear that the Indian bourgeoisie stands in closer relationship than did formerly the Chinese bourgeoisie. This is a weighty question and here we must have an exact appraisal of the Indian bourgeoisie.

"3. In comparison to the Chinese problem we have, in India, a greater class differentiation. In my opinion it is fundamental here to distinguish that which is specifically Indian, in order not to carry over once more the Chinese results in India. This would be a big mistake. Though India is a Colonial country the class situation must be appraised differently there than in China."[416]

This excerpt from Bukharin's speech clearly indicates the doubts that the Comintern leadership was facing about its policy of alliance with the bourgeois led movements in the colonies. But all these doubts amounted to nothing as Stalin had assumed leadership and was in favour of supporting the bourgeois led movements in the colonies. He choked all arguments that differed from his own and asserted the domination of the CPSU in the Comintern. Bordiga, an Italian communist differed with him regarding his increasing domination, but nothing resulted from his criticisms as Stalin did not even bother to give it any consideration. Rethinking of the strategy of alliance with the bourgeois forces was therefore rendered virtually impossible in the Comintern.

Roy was also propagating fiercely against the attitude of the bourgeois class. He said:

"The first line of cleavage from the Indian bourgeoisie has been conveniently provided by British imperialism itself. When the British imperialists determined to widen the social basis of their support in India, they were well aware of how far they could go with safety, and fixed the limit to 2-3 per cent of the population. Experience has already demonstrated that it is vain to expect any resolute struggle against imperialism from this section taken as a whole. The two per cent of the Country are now closely tied to the Imperial power. Their leaders have received concessions in the shape of tariff, subsidies, appointments etc. and are more and more conscious of the desire for harmonious co-operation with the ruling imperialist power, to whom they look for protection against the rising tide of revolt among the masses."[417]

In the same article Roy emphasised the point the petty bourgeois elements were also being increasingly drawn into the struggle against the big bourgeoisie. This was because they did not gain anything from allying with the imperialists. Their living standards were low and were going lower day to day because of the rise in the cost of living. They could, as a result, identify more with the proletariat than with the rich bourgeois classes. Roy said that "...a revolt is growing against the bourgeois domination of the Congress and nationalist movement. It is the task of the revolutionary left wing to bring the cleavage into the open to mobilise the revolutionary section and to unite them with the workers and the peasants. The immediate demands should be so framed that they represent the needs of these classes and are such as mark their distinction from the upper strata."[418] Roy was on the one hand criticising the actions of the bourgeoisie in stemming the rise of the mass movement, while on the other hand, he was showing how the bourgeoisie themselves were divided broadly into two sections, where the interests of one section contradicted that of the other. This was a repetition of his earlier thought on how the bourgeois class would wane in the face of rising mass movement.

Roy's concept of not collaborating any longer with the bourgeois forces in facilitating the working class movement was further emphasised in the June 1927 issue of *The Masses*. He felt that policies regarding the bourgeoisie needed to be changed because of the rise of a severing tendency of the petty bourgeois elements from their richer counterparts. He wrote:

"...it can be said that the Programme of Action put forward by the Workers' and Peasants' Party for the consideration of the All India Congress Committee comes at an opportune moment. The plea has been put forward that the programme is opportune because it provides a basis on which the country can unite, because it suggests a method by which the present "unfortunate" divisions in the movement can be healed. This is not the case. The disunity in the movement is the inevitable result of the progress of class differentiation accompanying the development of capitalism in India. We should not be concerned to create an artificial unity by proclamation of empty high sounding phrases under cover of which the bourgeoisie can continue to delude the poverty stricken masses while they bargain with the imperialists for concessions which will enable them to feather their own nests. We need not be concerned to find a programme on which the dissident sections can agree. We must put forward the special interests of the workers and peasants which have been so shamefully neglected and betrayed, and we can rest assured that in doing so we are performing the best service to the national movement because these interests are those of 98 per cent of the nation."[419]

This shows that M.N.Roy's position at the Fifth Congress regarding the role of the bourgeoisie in the national struggle for liberation and the necessity of giving a second thought to the earlier tactic of supporting the nationalist movements in the colonies had not undergone any change. He was against the alliance of the bourgeoisie and the working masses just as he had been in 1924. Roy was of the opinion that since the masses were not just fighting for political liberation but that since their main interests lay in economic and social emancipation, the bourgeoisie would never ally with them. For the economic and social emancipation of the masses would mean ruin for the imperialists and the rich Indian bourgeoisie. He had said at the Fifth Congress that the national movement was split by class struggle and the time had come when a choice had to be made between the masses and the bourgeoisie[420]. The same views were repeated again in 1927. In fact he had become quite vocal on this issue by the time he had been despatched to China as the Comintern in 1926. The Chinese events perhaps proved to be more of an eye opener to him than he had envisaged, and he became even more opposed to the cause of supporting the nationalist movements in the colonies. He realised once again that the class interests of the bourgeoisie were opposed to those of the common masses and that the time had come when a breach had to be made between the communist led movements on the one hand, and the bourgeois led nationalist movements on the other. In *The Masses* of May 1927, he wrote an article that criticised strongly the role of the bourgeoisie in China.[421] His Chinese experiences possibly added further strength to his arguments about the Indian bourgeoisie. In November 1927, he wrote:

> "There are historical reasons for the remarkably non-revolutionary character of the Indian bourgeoisie. The growth of Indian bourgeoisie has been such that they are bound on the one hand, with reactionary feudal economy and, on the other, with imperialist trade and finance. Therefore, without hurting their own class interest, they cannot lead a revolutionary struggle for the destruction of native reaction and foreign imperialism, which is the programme of national revolution. For these objective reasons, Indian revolution (overthrow of imperialist domination) cannot be a bourgeois revolution."[422]

Roy was of the opinion that the Indian bourgeoisie was functioning more as an appendage to British imperialism than as its enemy. He felt that the British were using the native imperialists to further their own interests. It became easier for them to do so as the Indian bourgeoisie were split into factions depending on their economic attributes. The British used the upper bourgeois classes for furthering their purpose. He said in this context:

> "Imperialism is obliged to bribe the Indian bourgeoisie not only to broaden its base in India, not only as the corollary to the policy of increasing colonial plunder by the introduction of changed methods and forms of exploitations to meet the changed world conditions. The collaboration of the Indian bourgeoisie is necessary for the defence of the position of British Imperialism in the entire East and in the case of the projected war against the U.S.S.R."[423]

Roy wanted to develop a militant mass movement in India that would come to the forefront, usurp the British and then proceed to bring about socialism by destroying the power that was being wielded by the native bourgeoisie in the exploitation of the toiling masses. Roy was convinced that the bourgeoisie would be of no use where the overthrowing of the British was concerned. He felt that the bourgeoisie were aware that opposition to the British rule would be harmful to their vested interests. This was because the overthrow of the British was likely to generate the rise of the masses, a fact that would ultimately lead to the fall of the native bourgeoisie. Supporting the British, on the other hand, would mean the subordination of their interests to those of the British, but at the same time, it would also guarantee their preservation against the rising tide of the militant mass movement that sought to exterminate all forms of exploitation and to bring about the emancipation of the masses.

PROGRESS OF THE INDIAN COMMUNIST MOVEMENT

By this time the relationship between Roy and the CPGB had deteriorated further. In fact even the Indian communists did not like the high handedness of the British communists like Saklatwala. They had already proved that they valued their independent way of thinking while dealing with Saklatwala. It can be recalled that Saklatwala came to India in January 1927. The Indian communists had invited him to preside over their conference that was to be held at Lahore. But Saklatwala had refused because the Communist Party of India was not affiliated to the Communist International or to the CPGB. The joint secretaries of the Party, Ghate and Bagerhatta had answered, "We in India have every right to form a communist Party and to contribute in our way to the cause of Indian communism. The question of international affiliation comes later. This is what we understand from the opinion expressed by the communist leaders of international reputation..."[424] At the same time, once their problems were resolved, they made him chair their AITUC session at Delhi. They even went to the extent of shifting the venue to Delhi for his convenience. It can be said that the Indian communist movement was progressing, though not quite steadily, under Indian leadership. These Indian leaders welcomed foreign support, but shirked away from foreign guidance or forced imposition of their ideas and policies. This was evident even in their dealings with Roy.

A document of March 1927 also made a reference to the growing problems between the CPGB and the Indian communists. It said, "The leaders of the CPI bring a number of charges against the British comrades. Some of these are imaginary or based on simple misunderstanding but others indicate a real difference of opinion and call for correction or frank discussion."[425] It seems from the Report that the main charges that the Indians were having against them was "...that of 'bossing' or attempting to domineer over the Party."[426] This question of domination arose on several issues that Campbell and Saklatwala seemed to be fostering. Among these issues, one was to substantially cut off Roy's powers and another was to affiliate the Workers' and Peasants' Party to the British Communist Party. Regarding the point of reducing the powers of Roy, no comment can be traced in the Report. But the problems regarding the Workers' and Peasants' Party was given due consideration by Dutt and Mohammad Ali. This part of the Report is very enlightening. It said,

"The inauguration of the Workers' and Peasants' Party has taken place in Bombay and Calcutta, but it has not begun under very happy circumstances because:

a) The CPI does not look upon it as any organisation of theirs, but as a fad of the Britishers which they have promised to humour.

b) The CPI help given to the Workers' and Peasants' Party is only like that given to an external auxiliary, the leaders of the CPI refusing to give up the legal CP.

c) There is a feeling of suspicion on the part of the CPI towards the British comrades. They suspect a conspiracy against them to take away their party and to drive them into a British organisation.

The relation of the CPI and the Comintern also needs to be cleared up. The CPI leaders do not see any reason why they should accept instructions from any outside body. At the same time they claim to be as good a Communist Party as any other. The activities of the legal party are very small. Yet in event of attack there is no illegal apparatus which could take up the work."[427]

Regarding the first point about the CPI not looking upon the Workers' and the Peasants' Parties as their organisations, but as "a fad" of the British, certain points need to be re-examined. First, the office bearers of the Workers' and Peasants' Parties were composed entirely of Indian delegates, comprising of communists, non-communist trade unionists and nationalists. This was evident in both the cases. Besides, the Workers' and Peasants' Party began in Bengal in early 1926 when the British agents had hardly begun to function. In such a case, the point that the Indian communists should consider these parties as British fads that "they had promised to humour" cannot be accepted. It appears from this note that the members of the CPGB too were at a loss where understanding of the Indian conditions was concerned. The second point about the CPI helping the Workers and Peasants' Parties as if they were "external auxiliaries" too cannot be accepted. The amount of work that the members of the CPI were doing among the peasantry and the proletariat was certainly not like that which is given to external auxiliaries. They were active members of the Workers' and Peasants' Parties and were doing much organisational work among the masses. Mass movement was clearly on the rise during this time. Another point that needs mention is that Campbell who was supposed to be one of those who were antagonising the Indian communists against the CPGB could not function for long. He was arrested not long after he came to India. On the other hand, no documents can be found that prove that Spratt was not on good terms with the Indian communists. On the contrary, documents actually show that he was functioning at par with the Indians in facilitating the organisation of the working classes. Taking into account all these factors, it can be said that the conflict with the CPGB was more with Roy than with the Indian communists as such. The third point regarding the suspicious attitude of the Indian communists regarding the role of the CPGB is acceptable. Coming from nationalist backgrounds they looked with suspicion at any help that came from abroad. Considering once again the fact that they began to emerge only a decade ago, primarily as a result of frustration with nationalist policies and the consequent influence of the Russian way of life, this immaturity was only to be expected. Communists like Dange and Singaravelu belonged to this genre of Indian communists. They wanted to advance their work in India on their own terms, even when help was assured from other sources. In fact, alliance with the Bolsheviks too was considered with caution, when invitations came for attending conferences abroad. They felt that bolshevisation of the Indian communist movement would not come of use as the Indians still had a long way to go. Besides the Indian situation was very different from that of the west, and hence it had to develop accordingly so as to address its own problems.

THE SEVENTH SESSION OF THE AITUC

The seventh session of the AITUC was held in Delhi on 12th-13th March 1927. It had originally been decided to hold the session at Calcutta in April but the venue was shifted to "suit the convenience of Saklatwala"[428], who was on a visit to India, wanted to attend it. Rai Saheb Chandrika Prasad was the president of the session. His attitude had perhaps been quite meek. Philip Spratt sent a Report on this session to Robin Page Arnot in which he said, "...the rule of the chairman Prasad, who is a benevolent old man, was extremely weak, and very frequently the proceedings had to be almost forcibly quietened..."[429] Spratt also said that during his speech "everyone slept"[430]. Adhikari's comment too was no less unflattering. He said, "The presidential address was that of a benevolent humanist and nationalist, to whom a trade union was not an organ of class struggle. He made the stupid remark that trade unions existed in India from ancient times and referred to *chaturvarnya* and *caste-guilds* of artisans as precursors of trade unions!..."[431] These remarks show that the AITUC was still being dominated by members who considered the movement a welfare movement for the workers and nothing more than that, despite the fact that several important issues were also debated at these congresses.

The same attitude about following the path of moderation was reflected again and again in the seventh session of the AITUC Congress. Adhikari has cited two examples in this connection, both of which need mention in order to comprehend the actual working of the trade union movement.

One resolution was brought forward by Dewan Chamanlal on the issue of despatch of Indian troops to China after which Thengdi proposed a more general resolution that said:

"(a) This congress puts on record its wholehearted approval of the magnificent advance made by the people of China towards self-determination. Congress warmly appreciates the valuable work that has been done by the trade unions and peasants' organisations, which under the leadership of the Kuomintang have frustrated the aggressive designs of the united imperialistic powers. Congress while pledging its full support to the movement of liberation in China, expresses its firm conviction that the cause of Indian nationalism and the struggle of the working classes against exploitation should profit from the example of solidarity of the national movement and the workers' and the peasants' organisations as set in China.

(b) This congress vehemently protests against the action of the Indian government in furthering the aims of imperialism by sending Indian troops to China and calls upon the government of India to recall all such troops."[432]

This resolution had led to a great debate as reformist leaders like Joshi and Shiva Rao objected because they felt that the resolution was committing the Congress to a policy of violence. The resolution however remained unaltered as Spratt has mentioned.[433]

Thengdi moved another resolution as well on international unity. This too was worded strongly. It said, as Spratt had said,

"This congress deplores its lack of effective organised connection with the world trade union movement, and at the same time the absence of a single all-inclusive international of trade unions...It pledges itself to support such efforts in the future and to affiliate to an international which shall unite these two organisations and strive to embrace the whole trade-union forces of the world."[434]

Again there had been a heated debate and amendments made in the proposed resolution. The result was,

"This congress views with approval the efforts which have been made by the Anglo-Russian unity committee to bring about unity between the International Federation of Trade Unions and the Red International of Labour Unions and expresses hope that the international unity will soon be achieved and regrets its inability to consider joining the international movement till such unity is achieved."[435]

Saklatwala in his speech made quite a few important points on the standing committee for international negotiations, labour research bureau, district organisations, a permanent office of the trade union congress, and stricter rules for affiliation to the trade union congresses, a central fund to enable the delegates to attend the trade union congresses, and so on.

These incidents prove that despite the discussions, there was always a note of restraint in the policies that the AITUC adopted, and no outright breach with nationalist policies was ever attempted to be made or even supported. The leaders were mostly in acquiescence with the nationalist movement that saw the trade unions as mere welfare organisations for the workers.

Adhikari has cited yet another example of how the leadership of the trade union movement was averse to the militancy of the workers in any form. He has said that Philip Spratt recorded in his report "...a resolution declaring the paramount need for the establishment of a workers' and peasants' party and the congress pledging to work for the creation of such a party on an all- India basis was unanimously accepted..."[436] In Spratt's own words the same was noted as:

"A resolution was then moved as follows, and accepted unanimously, without amendment.

"This session of the AITUC deplores the fact that the industrial working class, despite its immense importance, has not yet found expression for its political aspirations through the medium of an independent working class political party. Similarly, congress notes the plight of the peasantry who form the basis of Indian society, is exploited by other political creeds and organisations, while their material condition remains unaltered. Congress therefore declares that the paramount need of the working classes, industrial or agricultural, is the establishment of a workers' and peasants' party that shall fight insistently against the exploitation of those classes, strive to secure for them full rights of citizenship, political, social and educational, and achieve the complete liberation of India from all alien domination. Finally this session of the congress pledges itself to work for the creation of such a party on an all-India basis."[437]

The May 1927 issue of *The Masses* also recorded the same text as represented in Spratt's report. It also added further that such a labour party was not to be organised on the lines of the British Labour Party that functioned only in bargaining in the parliament. It was to be a militant political party that would lead the workers and peasants against exploitation and complete liberation from foreign domination.[438]

There was a third document, Spratt's "Labour and Swaraj" of October 1928, which too mentioned that the "The Workers' and Peasants' Party now developing in different parts of the country, fulfils the requirements of a genuine working-class political party and must receive the support of the Trade Union Congress, as was decided at the 7th congress, Delhi, March 1927, and of the individual unions."[439]

Now this resolution was not mentioned in the text of the resolutions that were published later as a printed pamphlet by N.M.Joshi. Adhikari has said the proposal had come up at the sixth session of the AITUC in Madras, and was as a consequence put forward at the seventh session. But the president of the seventh session of the AITUC, Raisaheb Chandrika Prasad, was totally against considering the question of the Workers' and Peasants' Party.

Adhikari quoted from his presidential address:

"Should the labour movement in India have a labour party independent and separate from the Trade Union Congress? So long as the majority of the workers of India have no vote for sending members to its legislatures, it is needless to talk of having a labour party in India. So far this congress has refrained from identifying itself with any of the political parties in India, but it gratefully appreciates the services of those members in Indian legislatures who have taken interest on behalf of the workers."[440]

Adhikari has scorned this attitude. He has said, "So Raisaheb Chandrika Prasad did not want even a reformist labour party because the workers have no vote. For him the only purpose of a political party of the working class was to get some bigwig elected to the imperialist legislature to plead for workers' grievances therein!"[441]

The proposal however, could not be easily rejected as it had been a recommendation by a sub-committee appointed by the AITUC itself. And by the time the resolution was adopted at the seventh session of the AITUC, Workers' and Peasants' Parties had already come up in Bengal and Bombay. Adhikari has commented:

"...At the time these parties were not headed by communists. Neither Nareshchandra Sengupta and Hemantakumar Sarkar of Bengal nor D.R.Thengdi of Bombay were communists. But later it became clear that these parties were sponsored by communists and N.M.Joshi, whose own view was that trade union movement should not be mixed with politics, was not happy about the resolution. He probably took the view that it was not a resolution but the presentation of a report of the sub-committee on the question and its implementation is yet a matter for further consideration. That is why he did not put the resolution in the official report..."[442]

This led to another question regarding why the communists did not object to the non-inclusion of the resolution. Adhikari has said, "...The communists and left-wingers on whose strength the resolution was adopted, did not question its non-inclusion in the official resolutions published later. Their two main objectives were achieved, viz. (1) the scotching of the formation of the reformist labour party, and (2) general recognition to the workers' and peasants' party by the AITUC."[443] Despite these controversies it can be said that the trade union movement was for the first time, given a militant profile, though weak, by the communists and the left-wing nationalists. Adhikari has commented that the seventh session of the AITUC "...registered the beginning of the entry of the communists and the militant leftists into the trade union movement..."[444] The presence of prominent leaders like Saklatwala perhaps made itself felt and strong and radical resolutions could be adopted without much controversy. The event did not go unnoticed abroad. Both *The Masses* and the *Inprecor* recorded it. *The Masses* said that the left-wing National Congress members were coming closer to the true revolutionary struggle of the masses and that it was a sign of progress where the trade union movement was concerned. It also said that Saklatwala had a strong influence on the members of the AITUC that was proved by the election of several leftist members as office bearers[445]. The *Inprecor* however, said that the incident did not show any major advancement as the trade union leadership was still primarily in the hands of reformist leaders who had been forced to make some changes in their policies due to pressure from workers, movements and Saklatwala's influence; and who still believed in class-collaboration and not class struggle as such[446].

STRIKE MOVEMENTS IN 1927-1928

Some of the most important strikes took place in 1927-1928. Although the strikes during this time were not many in number, yet it can be said that those that took place had a tremendous significance in the Indian trade union movement and among the working classes as a whole. The Bengal-Nagpur Railway strike or the BNR strike was one of them. It occurred in two phases— one in early 1927, just before the seventh session of the AITUC and again in September of the same year, just before the commencement of the eighth session of the AITUC.

The first BNR strike began on 11th February, 1927. The workers were becoming antagonistic because their wages were low and on top of that there was continuous retrenchment of the workers. But the strike began when a transfer order was served on the branch secretary of the B.N. Railway Indian Labour union, W.R.Naidu. Several meetings were held at Kharagpur, which were attended by Mukundalal Sarkar, Santosh Kumari Gupta, Aftab Ali, W.R.Naidu, V.V.Giri and others. V.V.Giri was the president of the union. During the middle of the first week of the strike, the striking workers were shot down by the railway auxiliary force.

This incident raised a tremendous controversy. Not only did the working class movement get a boost from it, even the national movement was influenced. An adjournment motion was moved by V.V.Jogiah that demanded enquiry into the grievances of the workers and the indiscriminate shooting down of the workers by the railway auxiliary force. N.M.Joshi, Dewan Chamanlal, all enquired into the shooting incident, apart from the grievances of the workers. The British government remained firm and said that there were no grievances, and in case any had arisen they would look into it. In fact the government tried to justify the incident saying that the striking workers had stopped the Puri Express and lay down in front of it. David Petrie has totally ignored the issue of firing in his narrative. He has simply said:

> "...The grievances of the workshop people included the dismissal of some workers from the wagon shops, the dismissal of station committee chowkidars, the ejection of the people living in a village on railway land and the demolition of their houses and lastly the alleged overbearing conduct of two European foremen..."[447]

In three weeks the strike became general. About 40,000[448] workers went on strike from among the 60,000 that the company employed. The BN Railway agent, who had so far remained very arrogant on the issue, retained the same attitude. The only thing that he offered was to cancel the fine that had been imposed on W.R.Naidu and to make his transfer order temporary, only on the condition that the workers returned to work. Nothing however, was said about the grievances of the workers regarding low wages or retrenchment. It was at this point of time, when the strike was in its strongest position that V.V.Giri, the president of the union, decided to call off the strike, which hence ended on 10th March 1927.

K.N.Joglekar has criticised this compromise made by the TUC president, V.V.Giri, and other union leaders. He said that it was because of the withdrawal of the strike that the workers did not benefit anything from it. The dismissed workers were not reinstated, and retrenchment also continued, a fact that led to another strike in the same year. *The Masses* reported the incident in three consecutive issues of March April and May, 1927. This paper also criticised the compromising attitude of the union leadership. It felt that the strikers had been betrayed by their leaders when the strike was at its height. *The Masses* also said that the time was suitable to organise militant action among the workers, which the union leaders failed to do. This resulted in the fact that the workers hardly received any concession from the authorities[449].

The breach between the reformist and the communist factions within the AITUC that had appeared in the sixth session of the AITUC now began to widen further. The communists criticised the role played by the reformist members in limiting the strikes to a certain level and then vouching for compromise. As a result the British employers often did nothing to satisfy the demands of the striking workers once the strikes were withdrawn and the workers returned to work.

The second BNR strike was one such instance. Soon after the first strike of the BNR workers was called off, the railway authorities launched their policy of suppression again. Large scale retrenchment of the workers began on the pretext of lack of enough work. V.V.Giri and other union leaders sent representations to the railway agent, but it did not help. In August notices were put in the Kharagpur Workshop regarding the intention of the Company to reduce the number of workers, and on 7th September individual notices were served on 1700 men regarding termination of their work. Joglekar said in his statement at the Meerut court that 90 per cent of these men were "those who had been active union members and who had been prominent in the February strike."[450] The workers, of their own accord, resorted to passive resistance after the notices were served. They went to the workshop, remained peaceful and refused to do any work until the notices were withdrawn. This continued for two days and on the 12th of September the Company declared a lockout. V.V.Giri, the president of the union and W.R.Naidu, the branch secretary, however did not support the workers, and Giri made a public statement about his feeling. Joglekar has severely criticised this attitude of the union leadership.

The workers continued to remain firm and refused to withdraw the strike. Meanwhile relief centres for the striking workers had been opened "as some remittances have been received from abroad."[451] The BNR union was pressurised by the workers to call a meeting of the central council, which met on 26th September and which decided to prepare the entire BNR line for a general strike and "commanded Giri to tour on the line for the purpose."[452] Giri however, did not obey the orders of the central council.

The secretary of the All India Railwaymen's Federation, who was at Kharagpur at this time, became involved as he understood that the BNR union leaders were rather passive. On 29th October 1927, the

All India Railwaymen's Federation met at a special convention in Kharagpur. It resolved despite bitter opposition from Giri, Joshi and others that it would prepare for an all-India railwaymen's strike, if the minimum demands of the BNR union were not satisfied within a week[453]. But when the secretary of the AIRF attempted to send telegrams to other railway centres asking the unions to prepare for a general strike if necessary, the telegraph officials refused its transmission as the contents of the telegram were objectionable[454].

The strike continued unabated. On 5th November Giri, Joshi and Chamanlal had an interview with Sir George Rainy and Sir Clement Hindley, the chief commissioner of railways. They offered to call off the strike if lockout wages were granted to the workers, but the railway board agreed to grant only a subsistence allowance for the lockout period. By December 1927, "...the rumblings of strike on SIR had already started..."[455], and fearing combined action, the authorities decided to end the strike. They agreed to pay full lockout wages to the striking workers on the condition that they resumed work unconditionally and accepted the retrenchment of the two thousand men. On 8th December, the union called off the strike which had continued for more than three months, without resolving the very issue on which the strike had begun— the retrenchment of workers.

It was not just Joglekar who criticised the attitude of Giri. *The Masses of India* of January and February1928 also made scathing criticism of the BNR union leadership[456]. *The Masses* also said that the only demand of full lockout wages that were granted by the government to the workers was because they had used their most effective weapon, that of unity and solidarity against the capitalist system[457]. *The Masses* reiterated once again, what it had been harping for quite some time— the replacement of the reformist leadership in the AITUC. It said, "Once more the Kharagpur betrayal brings home the lesson that an immediate end should be made of the false leaders of the unions and only those who are loyal to the interests of the working class should be trusted to lead them in their class struggle."[458]

Adhikari has said that the government policy of retrenchment of the railway workers, however continued, a fact that resulted in more railway strikes in the coming years[459]. What is important about the second BNR strike was that it displayed the rise of militancy in the workers, who without much guidance from their union leaders could actually continue the strike for more than three months. Another factor that needs mention is that the Workers and Peasants' Parties too became involved in the strike, with the presence of Muzaffar Ahmad, Bhupendranath Datta, Abdul Halim, M.Singaravelu, Dange and Mirajkar in the convention of the All India Railwaymen's Federation at Kharagpur in October 1927. None of them were connected with any railway union, but all were active members of the Workers' and Peasants' Parties of Bengal and Bombay[460]. The significance of the second BNR strike lay in the fact that the way it was brought to an end showed the communist and leftist TUC members that a reformulation of strategies regarding workers movements had become necessary, one that they were soon to formulate after the eighth session of the AITUC.

Another important strike of this period was the strike of textile workers of Apollo and Manchester mills of Bombay. The strike was very significant in the sense that the red flag, which had been used earlier during the May Day celebrations in Bombay, was brought into use again by the striking workers during a procession. Adhikari has said that it was for the first time that the flag appeared at the "...head of a striking workers' procession in Bombay..."[461] Important leaders like Joglekar, Mayekar, Alve etc. were involved in the strike. Mirajkar too participated, but in a restrained manner as he disagreed on certain tactics that were being employed in the strike. Besides, he found it a suitable time for uniting the two unions, viz. the Girni Kamgar Mahamandal and the Bombay Textile Labour Union, a point that was not being looked into[462].

The strike resulted because of several reasons, the most important being the introduction of the three loom system in the place of the prevailing two loom. This would increase work pressure on the one hand, and result in retrenchment of several workers, on the other. The workers who would be working at the three loom system would get more wages, but that would be mere eye wash as they would have to work much more than the rise in wages would actually compensate for. The Manchester Mill workers broke down after a few days but the Apollo mill workers, under the leadership of the Girni Kamgar Mahamandal, held on for over a month and actually met with partial success with the mill owners assenting to hold back the scheme and consider its consequences before implementation. The Marathi daily, *Kranti*, and *The Masses* of September-October reported about the strike. Another reference to the strike was made in the Eastern and Colonial Bulletin of the Red International of Labour Unions dated 15th January 1298. It was highly appreciative of the trade union activity that had spurted in Bombay. It said:

> "…A big textile strike was conducted by the Bombay Workers' and Peasants' Party in August 1927 ending in complete victory for workers. In 1927 the party organised enormous demonstrations on May Day and on the 10th anniversary of the October revolution drawing in these large number of workers. In conclusion it is not too much to say that the young workers' and peasants' parties of India (especially in Bombay) have accomplished great work during their short period of existence. A definite programme of national revolution has been drawn up and extensive work developed among the toiling masses of India. With the cooperation of the Communist Party, left revolutionary groups have been formed in the All India National Congress and the Indian Congress of Trade Unions."[463]

The Madras Oil Company workers struck work in early 1927. These workers had been fighting for their right to organise their union. The strike began when 115 workers were dismissed without citing any reason for it. The union sent five representatives to the employers to voice their grievances, but they refused to recognise the union. The workers then went on strike. They even tried to persuade the men working in the Company's transport to stop work. While doing this, it was said that the workers threw stones on some of their lorries. This made the authorities furious and they themselves started firing at the workers. Seventeen men were consequently injured. The July issue of *The Masses* said that this incident resulted in consequences that the Company officials had not anticipated. "…Instead of breaking the ranks, the workers stood firmer than ever. The very next day the strike extended to two other oil companies. During the following week, scarcity of petrol caused a big rise in Madras…"[464] This alarmed the authorities. They negotiated with the workers and agreed to take back the dismissed men and address to the other grievances of the workers. *The Masses* reported that the workers won "…because of their solidarity and because of their resolute spirit of resistance."[465]

EIGHTH SESSION OF THE AITUC

It can be seen that working class movements, though gradually, were on the rise during this time. They were not only getting organised while voicing their demands, they were also resolutely fighting to get them met. But at the same time, it can be said that the reformist nationalist leaders of the trade union movement were trying desperately to check the rise of mass movements. It was at this time that the eighth session of the AITUC was held in Kanpur from 25th to 28th November 1927. The *Labour Monthly* of April 1928 reported, "...Out of fifty-seven affiliated trade unions, with a total membership of 125,000, only twenty-seven were represented at the congress by about 100 delegates...Out of the 57 affiliated trade unions, 13 were railway unions, 11 textile, 10 general labour, 7 transport (other than rail), and 4 seamen's unions."[466] The RILU also sent a message to the eighth AITUC, which said at the outset, "The Executive Bureau of the RILU, on behalf of the revolutionary trade union movement of all countries, sends cordial and fraternal greetings to the eighth trade union congress and the whole working class of India and wishes for success in the struggle against alien and native oppressors..."[467]

The *Labour Monthly* also reported "...the presence of an active left-wing group, mainly representatives of the Workers' and Peasants' Party, who succeeded in getting discussed in the Simon Commission, the threat of war, the League Against Imperialism and Colonial Oppression, etc..."[468] This left-wing was still being opposed by the reformist right wing of the AITUC who found support in Purcell and Hallsworth, delegates from the British Trades Union Congress. They refused to accept the resolutions taken on the League against Imperialism, on war danger and on Pan-Pacific conference. At the same time, they too failed to secure vote in support of the IFTU as the Congress stuck to its earlier decision "...to press for unity between the IFTU and the RILU."[469]

Regarding China, the AITUC showed its appreciation for the "...magnificent advance made by the people of China towards the attainment of national freedom and in pursuit of the principle of self-determination..."[470] What is significant in this regard is that the AITUC was only appreciating the anti-imperialist efforts made by the Chinese trades unions and peasants' organisations under the leadership of the Kuomintang. It failed to analyse the role that was being played at the same time by the bourgeois faction under the leadership of Chiang Kai shek. It did not discuss how the counterrevolution that the Chinese masses were facing, would help in shaping the future strategies of the Indian communists. This was perhaps because the AITUC members, even those who belonged to the left wing, did not have detailed information about the Chinese counterrevolution, considering the hindrances involved in the inflow of communist literature from abroad.

The RILU however, had a definite stand on the Chinese question, especially when it was comparing its own role with that of the IFTU. It said in the message to the AITUC:

> "In this struggle against the alien oppressors and the national exploiters the working class of India and the trade unions must always count on the aid of the Red International of Labour Unions and its sections. This constitutes the very distinction between the RILU and the reformist Amsterdam international which is permeated with the imperialist spirit whilst the former has at all times supported the struggle of the colonial and semi-colonial peoples for independence. "There was particularly clearly revealed the distinction between the imperialist policy of the Amsterdam International and the revolutionary policy of the RILU in the course of the bitter struggle of the Chinese proletariat against imperialism and the internal counterrevolution. Whilst the RILU did all in its power to help the Chinese revolution, the Amsterdam International did not lift a finger to help the Chinese proletariat in its hard struggle. The denial of aid to the Chinese workers and peasants was tantamount to helping the world imperialists and the Chinese counterrevolution."[471]

The eighth AITUC saw the emergence of a radical left wing. This wing had been present in the TUC for quite sometime, but it was at this particular session that they decided to amend certain policies of the TUC. Their aim was to "…lay out a plan of a cohesive group and plan for future work in order to foster real trade union-activity amongst the workers."[472] They even lay out a comprehensive plan of action that would promote a spurt in union activity.

This was one side of the picture. The other side was clearly revealed in Philip Spratt's review on the Indian trade union movement[473]. In this article Spratt said that the Indian labour organisation had not reached its maturity and was poor by western standards. But he asserted at the same time that "…Indian unionism is in its second stage, in which it will remain until there come into being the conditions necessary for the next stage. That these conditions will ripen fairly soon is also expected, and indeed the beginnings are already to be seen."[474] Spratt said that the trade union movement in India was not of a homogenous kind and that the union movement could be graded according to their activities, their membership, their financial status and also their aims and objectives.

The level of maturity attained by the trade unions varied from union to union and also from region to region. "Interunion organisation is not of importance..."[475], said Spratt. This was because "...Owing to the great distances and the general poverty of the movement, meetings can seldom be held between congresses, and the work done is mainly of a routine character..."[476] Spratt made another significant observation. He said that the trade unions in their early stages needed the help of outside leadership "...because of general illiteracy and risk of victimisation..."[477] But the outside leadership, he commented, often proved to be detrimental to the interests of the workers. This was because "...Many enter the movement with interested motives, and though they may promote efficiency they are not to be relied upon...Even if, as is often the case, their motives are purely unselfish, they generally strengthen the sectarian and otherwise reactionary tendencies to which the movement is so prone..."[478] He cited the examples of the BNR leadership, the leadership of the Ahmedabad Union and the TUC leadership as a whole to prove his point. After presenting this bleak picture of the trade union movement in India, Spratt said that the picture would soon change as the British colonies especially those in Asia had begun to assert themselves. He said, "...It seems in any case safe to prophesy that the decades of peaceful progress, which many Indian leaders apparently on the example of Britain appear to expect, will not materialise. But it is even safer to predict that the present political quiescence in the country will not last for more than a year or two..."[479] Spratt felt that the struggle between the petty bourgeoisie and the bourgeois leadership had begun. Several bourgeois leaders belonging to the upper bourgeois classes had already turned to the imperialist rulers for support. Those who remained were rapidly moving over to the same camp. The imperialist British rulers of India too gave them certain concessions that the bourgeois leadership readily accepted. In the process the nationalist opposition to British rule was being weakened. Spratt was of the opinion, "...the mantle of nationalism will fall upon the shoulders of the petty bourgeoisie, who will be forced to seek the assistance of the labour movement..."[480] They would be aided by the Workers' and the Peasants' parties that were forming in different parts of the country. Meanwhile the upper bourgeoisie could not let go of the situation so easily. They were aware that the rising mass movement had to be stemmed and brought under control without which their social and economic status would be threatened. They would also hence try to bring the labour movement under their own control. It was in this development that Spratt foresaw the future of the Indian labour movement. He said, "...The struggle between nationalism and imperialism for the possession of the labour movement has begun. When it has fully opened out, the next stage in the history of Indian labour will have commenced."[481]

It can be said that though Spratt differed with Roy in his appraisal of the development of the labour movement in India, one that Roy considered to be sufficiently mature, yet, in his analysis of the imminent split between the higher and the petty bourgeoisie, he was very much in tune with what Roy was thinking during the same time[482].

CONTEMPORARY EVENTS AND THE INDIAN COMMUNISTS

The communists meanwhile began to exhibit an independent train of thought, very different from that of the nationalists, while analysing the Indian political situation. They started to criticise the imperialist attempts at partial appeasement of the Indians through reforms. They had begun to comprehend the true nature of the British imperialists who were insisting on reforms in order to stall the mass upsurge against them. The British could carry on this policy of reforms with the help of another class whose vested interests would also be threatened with the rising mass movement. This was the upper bourgeois class, which gave leadership to the nationalist movement in India. This class, alarmed by the rising movement of the workers and peasants, began to seek shelter within the imperialist camp that would on the one hand preserve their social status in return for allegiance and prevention of mass upheaval. The opposition to the Simon Commission was one such gesture. The Manifesto issued by the Workers' and Peasants' Party of Bombay on the Royal Commission said:

> "The Workers' and Peasants' Party as the political representative of millions of exploited masses of India universally stands for a universal and really effective boycott of the royal commission. Besides cooperating with the other political parties, Congress and non-Congress, in organising a concrete method of boycott it will utilise all its resources and influence among trade unions and other mass

organisations in the country to carry out the said boycott in more effective and concrete terms than mere abstinence from tendering evidences before the royal commission or partaking in any formal or informal gatherings where the members of the royal commission might possibly attend with a view to gauge public opinion in any direct or indirect form."[483]

Considering the fact that the Congress members had also protested, but that their means of protest was through "mere abstinence from tendering evidences before the royal commission or partaking in any formal or informal gatherings" this Manifesto certainly spoke of an altogether different spirit.

It can be said that the Congress was divided in opinion where their demands were concerned. The protest came about in the Congress primarily because the Indian Statutory Commission, better known as the Simon Commission was made up of only British representatives. No Indian found any representation in the commission. "...That no Indian should be fit to serve on a body that claimed the right to decide the political future of India was an insult that no Indian of even the most moderate political opinion was willing to swallow..."[484] The left wing Congress members like Jawaharlal Nehru and Subhas Bose demanded complete independence or "purna swaraj". But the Nehru Report[485], to which the right wing Congress leaders endorsed, advocated Dominion Status. When the left wing Congress members objected to it and kept pressing for complete independence, Gandhi and other leaders decided to stick to the Nehru Report for a year at the end of which, if it was not accepted, they would adopt the principle of complete independence and resort to civil disobedience to achieve it. They even had a resolution passed in this regard in the Congress after defeating the idea of immediate adoption of complete independence[486].

When this was what the right wing and the left-wing members of the Congress were debating upon, the communists struck a very different note. The Manifesto issued by the Workers' and Peasants' Party of Bombay on the Royal Commission said:

"...the party challenges the very right of British imperialism to sit in judgement over the political destiny of this land and emphatically condemns the short sighted policy and compromising tendencies of other political groups who quibble over the personnel of the commission and thereby fundamentally forsake the principle of self-determination— the inherent right of every nation."[487]

This was the basic difference in policy between the nationalist leaders, both right wing and left wing, and the communists. When the nationalists were protesting, demanding dominion status or even complete independence, they were in a way recognising the right of the British in deciding the future of India. The communists challenged that very right with which the British formulated policies after policies that shaped the socio-economic and political future of India. They rejected the very role that the British were playing while controlling the Indian body politic. Roy was highly critical of the bourgeois led nationalist movement in India, which he said was too suppliant to the control of the British, a fact that put the national interests at stake. He wanted the masses to come out of their folds and bring about a revolution that would put an end to imperialism in India once and for all, and then proceed to the ultimate task of emancipating themselves. An article "The Role of the National Revolution" in *The Masses* expresses his thoughts clearly. That conforming to the British policies was not necessary and that it was only a ploy that the bourgeoisie employed to maintain their own stronghold, a point that the British used to serve their own vested interests were the basic things that the article said. The article was very sarcastic about the reform programme that the British were to set for India's future. It said at the very outset:

> "The dominant topic of Indian politics at the present moment is the Royal Commission on Constitutional Reform which is due to be set next year. Speculation and canvassing are rampant as regards the composition of the Commission. The pastime of constitution making is indulged in on all sides. Indian has served her apprenticeship. The time of promotion is drawing near. The question is how far will she be promoted on the scale of self government within the Empire?"[488]

Shapurji Saklatwala commented in an article that the British were only "reforming the reforms". He said:

> "India readily sees in the Simon Commission all the elements of danger attendant upon reforming the 'reforms', which in effect would be strengthening imperialist power, or the tightening of the empire...The Indian leaders, like the German social-democrats and British labour leaders whom they criticise now so freely, must make up their minds on the future course. World events and world politics leave to them also the same choice as to others: they must imperialise themselves and share with their erstwhile opponents what spoils are secured from exploiting and governing the masses, or they must

bolshevise themselves and lead their masses to a programme of common ownership, control and administration of all land, industries and state departments. There is no middle course and there are no different nationalist ways to settle such large human problems, which are common to all nationalities."[489]

G.A.K.Luhani was saying much the same thing. In his opinion:

"The situation created in India now is certainly rich with revolutionary possibilities. The only safeguard against their degeneration into reformist compromise is an energetic and concerted action by the nationalist left wing and the Workers' and Peasants' Party to orient the whole anti-imperialist movement towards the vast exploited masses and find in their revolutionary organisation their sure 'sanction' for coercing British imperialism into submission to the fundamental demands of the national revolutionary movement."[490]

It can be seen that communist opinion was in favour of a mass upheaval against the imperialist order. In it the communists had no place for a so called "middle course". It had to be either the overthrow of the imperialists or a compromise with them. The former would help in mass emancipation while the latter would serve just the opposite— that was the maintenance of the upper classes at the expense of the masses. While advocating such a policy with vigour they undoubtedly expressed yearnings of their revolutionary pasts only there had been a metamorphosis of thought and ideas, thos that had been acquired through communist influence. The new policies, though depicting the convergence of communist ideas, were not however, strategies that were forced upon them by the Communist International, they did not even merge with those being proposed by it. They emerged independently, as a consequence of repulsion to nationalist policies that conformed to moderate tactics favouring the bourgeois order while at the same time, shunning the interests of the masses.

The year 1927, and especially its closing months has found a special place in Adhikari's introductory notes on the last section of Volume 3B of the *Documents of the History of the Communist Party of India*. He has said:

"The year 1927, it is true, was darkened in its early months by the recrudescence of communal tension, particularly in the north, by the agitation against the provocative pamphlet *Rangila Rasool*, by the assassination of Swami Shraddhanand, by the clash in Delhi over the body of the assassin after his execution. But as we have seen, the

year as a whole was packed with the events and developments of the
left wing and national revolutionary movement."[491]

Adhikari appreciated the rise in the activities of the Workers'
and Peasants' parties, the strikes that took place and displayed militant
trends in the railways and other sectors in different parts of India, the
publication of communist journals in different vernaculars (*Kirti,
Langal, Ganavani, Kranti* etc.) which aimed to propagate doctrines
of scientific socialism and the achievements of the Russian Revolution
among the masses. He also praised the role of the Workers' and
Peasants' parties which tried hard to imbibe the masses with the idea
that the struggle for national liberation and mass emancipation was
not an isolated event in India. It was a part of the "...worldwide anti-
imperialist anticapitalist movement for freedom, peace, democracy
and social progress at the head of which stood the socialist Soviet
Union."[492]

But what is most significant in what Adhikari has shown is that
the year 1927 saw not merely a spurt in communist activities. It also
saw the emergence of a powerful left wing within the Congress, led
by Jawaharlal Nehru, Subhas Bose and others. How much they
succeeded in convincing the Congress members regarding their
notions of independence or that of British rule is doubtful. What is
important is that they made themselves heard in the Congress, so
much so that the moderate section had to pull itself up when it faced
a reasonable amount of opposition while it formulated strategies that
conformed to British dictates. The presence of Nehru in the League
Against Imperialism and later in the celebrations of the 10th
anniversary of the Russian Revolution, were events that influenced
the resolutions of the Congress session at Madras[493].

The year 1928 began with the anti Simon commission protests.
In this the National Congress and the communists remained united
in approach. Though the Congress move stemmed from the exclusion
of Indian members in the Commission and though the communists
were more intent in challenging the right of the British in deciding
India's future, yet, at this point, both these issues converged and the
protests became total. The Simon Commission landed in Bombay
on 3rd February and on that day all major towns and cities observed a
complete hartal. There were mass rallies, processions and
demonstrations against the Simon Commission. Wherever the Simon
Commission went, it was greeted with black flags and slogans of
"Go Back Simon".

But the bourgeoisie could not win over the communists by this gesture and the communists still remained highly sceptical of their intentions. Several statements on this accord can be found in the Meerut Records. The Workers' and Peasants' Party of Bombay adopted a resolution on the Simon Commission which said clearly that though they welcomed the support that the Congress was rendering in the way of opposition to the Simon Commission, yet, they were wary of the dangers that it imposed at the same time. "…But we desire to warn the nation in general against the dangers to be expected from the participation and leadership of a certain section of the bourgeoisie. This class has shown in the past, and many of its representatives are showing now, that they are not desirous of independence or even of democracy and freedom…"[494] This was not only the general trend among the communists, but that it also reflected the feelings of their sympathisers. Adhikari has said that this resolution had been passed by the enlarged meeting of the executive of the WPP of Bombay on 29th January 1928, which had been attended by thirty-six sympathisers, apart from the members of the executive. These sympathisers belonged to the labour movement in various spheres, the peasantry and the intellectuals.[495] This shows that communist strategies, though gradually, were making definite positive impressions on other classes.

Nimbakar's statement in the Meerut Record too belies the same notion— that of the "…vacillating character of the bourgeois opposition to British imperialism…"[496] S.S.Mirajkar's statement in the Meerut Record was yet another example of criticism, aimed at the bourgeois class. It said, "The Indian bourgeois politicians were, no doubt, at that time very much displeased with British imperialists because they expected to get a few seats on this royal commission; and had that happened the Indian bourgeoisie would surely have cooperated with the said commission…"[497] It was then explained in detail:

"It must be made quite clear that although the WPP of Bombay cooperated with the other political parties, our differences were quite distinct. The extent of the 'opposition' of these political parties to British imperialism was very limited, and they were quite willing to submit to the parliamentary commissions and committees which the British imperialists might appoint from time to time. It is because this commission was an 'all-white commission', as they termed it, they opposed and boycotted it. Whereas the WPP the party of the complete independence of India, vigorously contented the claim of British imperialism and having pointed out that the British parliament had no right whatever to appoint such commissions any longer and that the Indian masses must rise in revolt and be completely independent. This difference in the political outlook was very distinctly maintained in the whole boycott agitation by the WPP of Bombay..."[498]

The strongly worded telegram that Mirajkar intended to send to John Simon, one which he later sent by post as the telegraph office had refused to transmit it, shows the true spirit of the communists regarding the Simon Commission. It said:

"REVOLUTIONARY INDIAN MASSES ARE DETERMINED ACHIEVE COMPLETE INDEPENDENCE. THEY NO LONGER NEED EXPLOITING BRITISHERS IN THIS LAND. NO INQUIRY THEREFORE NEEDED. PLEASE STOP THE FARCE AND GO BACK TO ENGLAND. ALL THOSE THAT HAVE COME FORWARD TO COOPERATE WITH YOU ARE TRAITORS AND ENEMIES OF THE MASSES AND THEY SHALL BE PROPERLY DEALT WITH WHEN THE TIME COMES..."[499]

He signed off as "S.S.MIRAJKAR, COMMUNIST", a fact which shows that his thoughts were primarily an outcome of communist theories than anything else.

This anti–bourgeois outlook nurtured by the communists becomes further evident from some more documents. An All Parties' Conference was held in Delhi on 12th February 1928. Its main objective was the drafting of a Swaraj constitution, as had been resolved at the Madras Congress. It was attended among other parties, by the subcommittee to formulate a labour constitution for India of the All India Trade Union Congress. S.S Mirajkar, on behalf of the Workers' and Peasants' Party of Bombay, sent an open letter to the conference. This letter reflected the same anti-bourgeois spirit as expressed before both in tone and in content. It said at the beginning itself:

"...The nation has shown by its reception of the Simon commission that it wants swaraj and is able and willing to fight for it. It has fought the first engagement, and won. It now waits expectantly for the next step. What that step is to be, whether it will lead us on to victory, or defeat, or worse, to an ignoble compromise, depends upon you."[500]

The letter also said:

> "We shall raise a further question. Your conference consists of representatives of political parties, communal, commercial and similar organisations, and elected members of legislatures. We venture to say that it is no fit body to draft the nation's constitution or to lead its campaign for freedom. It is almost as unrepresentative as the legislatures, which speak for 2 per cent in the name of the whole. Your conference will not even be able to achieve unity among the national institutions. The National Congress has voted for complete independence. If the decision is a serious one, how is agreement possible with those who will not demand separation from the British empire?"[501]

Regarding the election of the constituent assembly it said:

> "The national constituent assembly must be elected by universal adult suffrage. No other basis will satisfy the people as a whole. It is deplorable that some of the draft constitutions already prepared contemplate a far more limited suffrage..."[502]

It can be seen that the entire concept about the present and the future political structure of India had undergone a metamorphosis where the communists were concerned. From earlier strategies of moderation and unity with the bourgeois parties in the struggle against imperialism, the communists now began to venture on more radical lines— lines on which Roy had already been propagating for quite sometime. However, a total breach with the policy of supporting the bourgeois led nationalist movement had still not been made. Communist leaders, especially those who belonged to the CPGB, and had been sent to India with the mission to organise the working class movement, still clung, although the ties had loosened considerably, to the Comintern strategy of supporting the bourgeois led nationalist movement in India.

It was perhaps in the later part of January 1928 that Philip Spratt drafted the principles on which the labour constitution was to be based. He justified himself for not drafting the constitution itself by saying,

> "It is to be taken for granted that the ultimate object of the labour movement here, as elsewhere, must be the establishment of an independent democratic socialist republic, and the only kind of constitution it can agree to is that of such a state. The attainment of this ideal is only possible through the strength of mass union organisations, primarily of the industrial working class, and secondly

of the peasants, acting together, and a political party representing these sections. And it will obviously be attained against the will, rather than in agreement with, a large proportion of those represented by the existing nationalist parties. The time when this is likely to be brought about is manifestly yet distant...

"It is also useless to put forward a constitution from our side with a view to modify the constitution which will now be produced by the nationalist parties. The gulf between the two, which is a gulf between the working class and the capitalist class, is in principle unbridgeable, and though working agreements on the basis of an anti-imperialist policy may be arrived at, no compromise as to ultimate aims is possible. We should not attempt to bring about minor modifications of their drafts, at the price of our political independence..."[503]

Spratt was attaching primary importance to the necessity for independence, before any further formulations were made. He felt that the labour constitution would certainly be one that would raise objections among the bourgeois classes in India. Besides, he also felt that the labour movement in India was still not yet in a position to demand such a radical constitution. So it would be best to achieve independence first, by toeing with the wishes of the other classes and then advance the mass movement to a level from where it would be able to demand a constitution for the working classes. This idea was very much in tune with what the Comintern was propagating.

Spratt said in his draft of "Labour and Swaraj", the principles on which the labour constitution was to be made, that "...the function of the working class in history is the realisation of socialism...Socialism must be the aim of the working class, and all its efforts and policies must be subordinated to that aim..."[504] He said at the same time:

"In this struggle the working class must ally itself with all forces and sections which will unite for the overthrow of imperialism...It will also find alliance in the National Congress, the anti-imperialist organ of the middle classes. In so far as the National Congress conducts a real struggle against imperialism it must be helped by the working class."[505]

It can be seen that Spratt was following the lines of the Comintern when he was advocating his own theories on how socialism was to be arrived at in India. But at the same time, he could not do away with the developments that had already taken place. It could be that perhaps the influence of the Indian communists was also, in a small way contributing to the shaping of his ideas. This is evident from certain excerpts in his draft, where the tone reflects somewhat the influence of radical notions that were being preached by communists like Roy. For example, his draft said, "...The working class must openly and avowedly adopt a political programme, the essence of which must be the establishment of socialism through the destruction of imperialism and capitalism, and the assumption of state power."[506] In another place it said, "...A definitely political organ must be created, with the policy and programme here outlined. The Workers' and Peasants' Party, now developing in different parts of the country, fulfils the requirements of a genuine working class political party, and must receive the support of the Trade Union Congress, as was decided at 7th congress, Delhi, March 1927, and of individual unions."[507] These examples show that some amount of radical thinking about the development of working class movements had seeped into his thoughts, like many of his Indian counterparts. But he was still rather bound by the dictates of the Comintern.

The significant result of the All Parties Conference of February 1928 was the Nehru Report, known so because Motilal Nehru was its principal author. This report prepared a draft constitution for India, which demanded among other things a Dominion Status for India. This became a major issue of debate among the left wing Congress members and the veteran right wingers. The left wing radical members refused to accept Dominion Status and wished complete independence instead. The communists too criticised the Nehru Report as one that catered to the interests to the upper classes. They also felt that the demand for Dominion Status would tantamount to a farce because foreign domination would prevail, and the situation that would precipitate as a result could never be equated with genuine independence. They also felt that the British would never want to let go of their powers in India without an armed insurrection. Hence the army had to be brought under control unlike what the Report said, and at a time when the masses were already in a militant mood after the Simon Commission protests, endorsing the Nehru Report would only mean wasting it[508]. M.N.Roy reiterated the same feelings in his article, "The Indian Constitution" in the *Inprecor*[509]. It is clear from the reactions of the communists to the Nehru Report that a feeling, very contrary to that being proposed by the Comintern was emerging. The communists were not making any bones about it either. They refused to cooperate with the Congress if their own theories of mass emancipation and socialism clashed with that of theirs. But before any concrete steps could be taken on developing a stand on these lines, the Meerut arrests had begun and the party consequently faced a tremendous setback, from which they began to recover after a long span of time.

THE ASSEMBLY LETTER

Meanwhile, another development that needs mention is the Assembly Letter of M.N.Roy and the furore it raised among the imperialist circles. This letter was published in *The Statesman* of Calcutta on 18th August 1928 and as an excerpt in the London *Times* on the 26th of the same month. The British claimed that it had been addressed to the CCs of the CPI and WPP, and was sent to Muzaffar Ahmad at Calcutta. It was made an issue in the Legislative Assembly and was later produced as a prosecution exhibit in the Meerut Conspiracy Case. So far as the debate goes, regarding the authenticity of the letter, it hardly has any bearing on the development of the communist movement. Starting from Roy on the one hand, to Muzaffar Ahmad and Ghate representing the CPI and the WPP on the other, all denied that the letter was actually written by Roy and sent to them. Besides, the letter was intercepted much before they received it and could actually make use of the instructions forwarded in it. Another point was that the Meerut arrests began not long afterwards, thereby making it impossible for the communists to adopt strategies on the lines prescribed in the letter.

Adhikari however, has said that the during the Meerut Conspiracy Case, Muzaffar Ahmad, Ghate, Spratt and Bradley examined the letter and the covering letters connected with it, evaluated the evidence, and then came to the conclusion that the letter was undoubtedly authentic[510]. This is why a discussion about some of its contents becomes necessary. Apart from theories and strategies regarding the working class movement under the Workers' and the Peasants' Parties, and the organisation and activities of the Communist Party, the letter gave much emphasis on international affiliation. What is significant is that Roy was once again exhibiting a note of distrust for the Congress members, even the left wing ones. He said in the letter,

"...As far as the WPP is concerned, the question is answered; it should affiliate itself against the League Against Imperialism. That will serve our purpose. Through that you will have the relations and the aid you need; but you will not be condemned for having connections with M. it is politically important also. Up till now the League has its connections with India through Jawaharlal Nehru. The connection with the League has done him some good as indicated by his actions in the Madras congress. But we need not entertain much illusion about him. The League must have relations with revolutionary organisations. Comrade Jhabwala is already in correspondence with the League. The WPP can become a recognised organ of the League in India..."[511].

For the Communist Party however, he recommended the Comintern. He said clearly, "The CP must unquestionably be a section of the CI. It is practically treated as such, but no formal request to this effect has as yet come from our party in India."[512]

These two excerpts reveal certain points. First, Roy was not in favour of the Congress members taking up the platform in the League. His apprehensions about them were growing. Meanwhile his relation with Virendranath Chattopadhyaya had improved considerably and he wanted to use him as a communist contact in Berlin. Chattopadhyaya too had become the Secretary of the League Against Imperialism, which had its headquarter in Berlin.[513] Roy must have felt that if Jawaharlal Nehru, a member of the National Congress, represented India in a communist frontal organisation like the League Against Imperialism, there was a danger that in case he vacillated, as Roy always warned about the bourgeois leadership, it would prove detrimental to the interests of communism in India.

Secondly, despite the fact that he was losing favour among Comintern leadership, he still felt that the Communist Party ought to have affiliation with it. This was perhaps because Roy had come to realise in all these years that the Comintern was the most powerful organisation where the advancement of communism to other countries was concerned and that alliance with it would help in the development of communism in India.

ESTABLISHMENT OF WORKERS' AND PEASANTS' PARTIES IN SEVERAL PARTS OF INDIA

By 1928, the Workers' and Peasants' Parties had become quite powerful and were doing much work in the sphere of mass emancipation. They also began to spread to other parts of the country.

In Punjab, the Workers' and Peasants' Party was established on 12th April 1928. Sohan Singh Josh said in his statement in the Meerut Case:

"...The need for this party for the workers and the peasants was shown in the Gurumukhi Kirti as far back as April 1927...The Hindu-Muslim fights were going on and it was the peasants and workers who were suffering most in the communal fight. In order to put a stop to this fratricidal strife and make people realise that, be they Hindus or Muslims, Sikhs or Parsees, their interests were identical, some Hindu, Sikh and Muslim workers who detested these communal strife and wanted to put an end to them by organising the masses without any differentiation of creed or religion and by putting forward common demands, gathered together at my initiative, in the Jalianwala Bagh, Amritsar, and founded this party. The formation of this party came about not because of the wire-pulling of somebody but because there was in Punjab no organisation based on economic realism to represent the interests of the workers and peasants. I was thinking of forming some party that would put forward an economic programme of the workers and peasants when my attention was drawn towards the workers and peasants parties of Bombay and Calcutta. I, along with some other friends, therefore, made up my mind to form a party approximately on the lines of those parties. This is the history of the birth of the Punjab Workers and Peasants Party."[514]

This lengthy excerpt shows that the Workers' and Peasants' Party did not originate only out of the inspiration of the communists. Nor was it intended only to serve the interests of the masses on the path of socialism. It had other goals too— goals that served the immediate interests of the masses in their daily lives. The issue of communalism too formed one of the major issues around which the Party evolved. What is important is that the awareness regarding the condition of the workers and peasants was spreading not only in communist circles, but also among others. This was evident in other places too. However, the main intention was to form a party of the workers and the peasants that would fight for a militant policy in the struggle for freedom.

The second conference of the Punjab Workers' and Peasants' Party took place at Lyallpur from 28th to 30th September 1928. It becomes clear from Sohan Singh's statement that he was in touch with the communists in other parts of India. He had invited Lala Kedarnath Sehgal, Muzaffar Ahmad, Mirajkar, Dange and Spratt to the second conference but only Kedarnath was able to attend it. His statement also says that the second conference was "deliberately"[515]

held at Lyallpur. This was the place where the influence of the
Zamindara League was very strong. It was dominated by the landlords
and shaukars and it had the peasantry completely under its control.
The conference, according to Sohan Singh, "was a great success"[516].
He explained in his statement:

> "Our object of holding the conference there was to free the peasants
> from the leadership of the landlords and the shaukars and to show
> the Zamindara League in its true colours...As the general secretary
> of the party I can claim that we did succeed to a great degree in our
> object. The peasants came in large numbers to attend the conference.
> The Punjab provincial political congress which was holding its
> session at that time refused to give us the use of their pandal. We
> were therefore forced to hold the conference in the open, the result
> was that after a short time of our starting the conference, the congress
> pandal became empty because the peasants left the conference of
> the Congress and came to us. The congress people became very
> furious with us over this affair..."[517]

The same spirit prevailed in the third conference that was held at
Rohtak. Here too Sohan Singh Josh said that "unless the land hunger
of the peasants was satisfied"[518] the condition of the peasants could
not be improved. The WPP of Punjab also formed some small
workers' unions like the Press Workers' Union in Amritsar, the Motor
Drivers' Union and so on.

The significance of the Punjab Workers' and Peasants' Party lay
in the fact that they gave tremendous importance to the peasantry,
unlike those in Bengal and Bombay, which were more involved in
the emancipation and education of the workers on communist lines.
The Party set up its branches in Ludhiana, Rohtak and even Calcutta.
It succeeded because the peasantry had already become somewhat
disillusioned by the Zamindara League and the "defeatist policies of
the congress"[519]. At least that is what Sohan Singh has claimed.
The new party, that of the workers and the peasants, on the other
hand, offered new and encouraging prospects, that the peasants
accepted. Sohan Singh Josh called the WPP of Punjab, "...an
independence party in the real and full meaning of the term...The
party aimed at the establishment of national democratic
independence through revolution. It was openly a revolutionary
body of the workers and peasants..."[520] Another party that came
into existence in Punjab during this time was the Kirti Kisan Sabha.
The communists were active in this party too, and the party aimed

at organising the workers and the peasants.

After the sudden withdrawal of the Non-Cooperation movement, several disillusioned leaders had shifted away from the Congress, and inspired by socialist ideas, began to work for the organisation of the workers and peasants that would lead them on the road to socialism. This gave rise to different communist groups in Bengal, Bombay, Madras, Punjab and even Delhi and the United Provinces. Similarly, as an outcome of their efforts, the Workers' and Peasants' Parties or similar organisations were established in different parts of India. The Workers' and Peasants' Party of Delhi and UP was formed at a conference held at Meerut from 14th to 16th October 1928. This meeting was attended by several prominent leaders like Spratt, Muzaffar Ahmad, Kedarnath Sehgal, Abdul Majid, Sohan Singh Josh and others. It set up its branches at the same time in Delhi, Meerut, Jhansi and Gorakhpur. The Hindi paper *Krantikari* became its main organ and reported its resolutions in its issue of 24th November, 1928. The aim of the party was the "Attainment of complete independence from British imperialism through democratisation of India based on economic and social emancipation and political freedom of men and women."[521] This Party was also averse to the proposals made by the Nehru Report and it said so in its political resolutions.[522] This Party, like its counterparts in other parts of India, was based primarily on socialist principles and aimed at the economic emancipation of the masses from exploitation by the imperialists and the native bourgeoisie. It aimed at curtailing all forms of differences "...between black and white, caste and creed, Hindu and Muslim, men and women..."[523] The proposals were concrete and the party received the guidance of prominent leaders of communism in India.

Meanwhile youth leagues associated with the freedom movement were coming up in many parts of India. Most of them arose because their leaders were dissatisfied with the turn of events that were being precipitated by the policies of the National Congress. They did not want to endorse with the Congress policy making and wanted to evolve by themselves, a more revolutionary approach towards the achievement of freedom. Among them, most were broad based parties, functioning independently of the WPP's. However, the Young Comrades League (Tarun Bandhu Dal in Bengali) was closely connected with the WPP of Bengal. In fact four of the seven members of the executive committee of the League were leading members of the WPP, and the "...documents seized in the Meerut Case searches in Calcutta give proof of the intensive work the WPP conducted among the youth..."[524] This helped the Bengal WPP to secure young men and women to help in active organisational work like selling papers, organising meetings etc.

SPURT IN STRIKE MOVEMENTS IN 1928

A very significant development that occurred during this time was the rise in strike activity among the working classes in several parts of India. Its significance lay in the fact that the workers were given leadership in their struggle primarily by the communists and that their movement had already started reflecting their influence. The red flag spirit that had been somewhat amiss in the earlier movements now made a strong appearance. The strikes were now more organised than ever before and the leadership too showed a capability that had been lacking so long. The communists plunged wholeheartedly into the movement, the Workers' and Peasants' Parties too became involved and the total effect was quite tremendous. The major strikes of this period were the strikes of the textile workers of Bombay, the East Indian railway workers' strike in Lilooah, jute mill workers' strike in Bengal and the strike of the workers of South Indian Railway union.

The strike in Bombay resulted because of the usual problems like wage cut, workload and retrenchment that were being enforced by the British mill owners so as to increase their own profit margin. The trouble started when the owners of the Sasoon group of mills introduced a system of three looms instead of two and two spinning frames instead of one per worker. The intention was to increase production by increasing the workload of the workers and at the same time, cutting the piece rate in the weaving section with the excuse of increased production, a fact that would in a way justify the wage cuts and retrenchment of the workers. The new system was not introduced all at once but in groups. The workers were very dissatisfied with the new measures. At that time the textile workers of Bombay were led by two unions. One was the N.M.Joshi and R.R.Bakhale led Bombay Textile Labour Union and the other was the Girni Kamgar Mahamandal under Mayakar and Alve, both being textile workers themselves. The workers struck work in the beginning of January 1928, and they were given leadership by the Girni Kamgar

Mahamandal. The strike however, could not last long and within two months the workers called back the strike. K.N.Joglekar had been quite active in this strike and helped to organise the workers.

The failure of this strike led the communists to believe that only a general strike could actually help in stalling the mill owners from executing measures at the detriment of the workers. The Workers' and the Peasants' Party had already issued a statement on this accord. Meanwhile the failure of about 20,000 workers in their resistance to the new system lured the mill owners to pursue their policy further and by March and April more and more mills were brought under it. Alve, at this time, began to issue handbills which called for a general strike of the textile workers as a step to curtail the mill owners from resorting to more forms of exploitation. The Bombay Textile Labour Union, the Girni Kamgar Mahamandal and the Workers' and Peasants' Party joined efforts to launch a general strike and by mid April more than 20,000 workers went on strike. The British government at the behest of the mill owners now started taking drastic actions against the striking workers. Meanwhile Alve had started having differences with Mayekar on the issue of militant trade unionism. Whereas Alve wanted militancy in the workers' movement, Mayekar was favoured towards a more moderate policy and by May 1928, the Girni Kamgar Mahamandal had split and Alve registered his union under the name of Girni Kamgar Union.

Another event gave a sharp impetus to the rising strike movement among the textile workers of Bombay. The British had by now taken strict measures to curb the movement and when a procession of workers was returning home from the British police fired at them with the object of dispersing them. In the process, one worker, Parsuram Yadav was killed. The strike then started spreading rapidly. By the end of April the strike was complete and more than 40,000 workers went on strike. The movement was given leadership primarily by the Girni Kamgar Union under Alve whereas the WPP and the Bombay Textile Labour Union gave full support to the strike movement. A joint strike committee was also formed soon afterwards. By May nearly one and a half lakh workers were on strike. An important development during this time was that the women for the first time participated actively in the industrial dispute. Bradley said in his statement in the Meerut Case that "...Women pickets were placed on the mills and vigorous picketing was carried on."[525]

The funds that were available with the joint strike committee were meagre and highly insufficient for the maintenance of so many workers. Grants poured in from abroad from the Red International of Labour Unions and the International Federation of Trade Unions. The Textile Workers' Union of USSR also sent some money to the strike committee. But even these proved to be insufficient. Reconciliation too was not being possible as the mill owners were refusing to relent to the workers demand against standardisation. Several workers began to leave for their village homes. By October it could be noted that though the workers were still fighting, they had become exhausted. On 4th October a meeting was called that was attended by both the workers and the mill owners. It was decided in this meeting that the standardisation scheme would be dropped for the moment and that the workers would join work. The six month strike hence ended. Bradley said:

> "The workers consider it only a truce to give them time to prepare for when the owners again attempt to force this scheme on them. A very important point of this struggle is the wonderful consciousness that has awakened among them, and they realise now that they have always waited to be attacked by the employer. But now the workers are organising to alter this and fight for better conditions."[526]

The Sasoon workers, the first victims of the standardisation scheme however felt betrayed as they had to join work under the previous conditions. They did not want to end the strike. Dange said that the leaders stayed with them until they too realised that after fighting for nearly one year, they too had become exhausted and they decided to end the strike[527].

The East Indian Railway strike at Lilooah was another very important strike of 1928. The circumstances of this strike were similar to that of the textile strike of Bombay, only this was less organised and unplanned to a great extent. Discontent had been spreading among the railway workers of the East Indian Railway ever since the EIR workers union was established in 1927, after the Oudh-Rohilkhand railway merged with the East Indian Railway. The main grievances were regarding low wages, housing and dismissal of workers without proper reason. The British refused to concede to any of the demands and dismissed two workers instead. The workers resorted to strike and the workshop was locked out after a day's strike. This lockout eventually turned into the strike.

The president of the Union of the EIR was K.C.Mitra. When he and the President of the EIR Union met the agent of the British to represent the demands of the workers, all the demands were rejected. The workers then wanted to extend the strike to the whole line. But K.C.Mitra stalled them for sometime. But the strike wave kept on rising. On 28th March 10,000 workers, led by Mitra demonstrated in front of the agent's office. But their demands were once again rejected. When the disgruntled workers were returning, they were fired at by the British police at a place called Bamangachi. Two workers died as a result. After this incident the strike began to rise and 40,000 workers became involved in it. The strike continued for two months. Meanwhile the funds of the Union had been exhausted. The fund that had been sent by the Red International of Labour Union was also nearly gone. Besides, a strike committee had also not been formed and K.C.Mitra himself was leading the movement. The WPP had for sometime been pressing to spread the strike along the whole line, but this was done only after two months had already passed. When the workers of Ondal and Asansol joined in, along with Spratt and Dharani Goswami as representatives of the WPP, the workers had already become quite exhausted. The strike continued for six more weeks before it had to be called off unconditionally and unsuccessfully. Both Dharani Goswami and Spratt criticised K.C.Mitra for his moderate tactics during the initial days of the strike. They felt that the lack of militancy and organisation led to the failure of the strike[528].

Both Spratt and Dharani regretted the plight that the workers had to face during the strike. They also regretted the failure that was brought about as a result of moderation and faulty tactics. Yet, at the same time, both their statements in the Meerut Conspiracy Case end on a positive note that said that despite the failure, the workers had gained solidarity and class consciousness that had to be preserved and nurtured for future movements. They also felt that working class movements had to overcome many defeats before final victory could be achieved[529].

The South Indian Railway Strike resulted primarily because of the retrenchment policy of the British, who were doing so in order to combat their losses that arose because of the imminent economic depression. 17,000 workers were involved in the strike and it lasted for ten days between 20th and 30th July 1928. The leadership was given mainly by Singaravelu Chettiar and Mukundalal Sarkar. The British resorted to repression and the strike was brought to an end.

The condition of the jute mill workers in Bengal was very miserable when they resorted to strike in 1928. Strikes occurred in jute mills in Chengail, Bauria and Rishra. The jute mill workers had gone into strike in 1926 too, but the 1928 strikes showed a definite tendency towards militancy. Moreover the 1928 jute mill workers' strikes were led by members of the WPP. This involvement of the WPP not only made the strikes stronger, but also more planned and organised. The Bengal Jute Workers Union was also formed for the entire industry. All this brought the consciousness that the oppression of the jute mill owners could be restricted only by general strikes of the workers of all the mills instead of individual attempts. A militant cadre of working class leaders also emerged out of these strikes.

THE NINTH SESSION OF THE AITUC

When the ninth session of the AITUC was held at Jharia, it was against this background of the rising strike movements across the country, and the clear expression of British fear for them through their policy of repression of the communists and trade unionists. The session began on 18th December 1928 with 200 delegates representing 98,600 organised workers and several political figures like Jawaharlal Nehru, Dr. Bhupendranath Datta, Ramananda Chatterjee and so on. Two foreign delegates, F.W.Johnstone from the League Against Imperialism and Jack Ryan from Australia representing the Pan Pacific Trade Union Secretariat also attended the Congress. M.Daud was the president of the session[530].

What is important as Bradley pointed out in his statement in the Meerut Record that despite the continuous strike wave across the country not much could be actually achieved out of it. He said, "In my opinion sufficient consideration was not given by the TUC to these most important struggles that took place during the year and the different aspects of them, in its failure to do this it failed to produce a definite policy for its relationship with the workers in their struggle against capitalism."[531] Bradley also said, "The main reason for this was the fact that the reformists were there in majority, unfortunately several of the new trade unions were unable to affiliate to the Congress owing to the rule that a union had to be in existence for one year. Under this rule the Girni Kamgar Union were unable to send delegates."[532] This reformist leadership, as can be seen from Bradley's statement, was clearly dominating the policies of the AITUC even as late as 1928. This was one of the basic reasons that the trade union movement could not progress rapidly on communist lines as the communist leadership in the TUC had to constantly contend with reformism while formulating their strategies. Reformist leadership in the trade union movement disfavoured militancy. Intent on spooning out policies of moderation, it managed to restrain the spontaneous development of the working class movement on communist lines. Bradley advocated that reformism should be fought in the TUC at all costs. He said, "The trade union movement of India is young and weak and the attempts that were made at Jharia to lead it on to reformist lines must be vigorously fought"[533].

One such reformist strategy that was fought by the communists was affiliation to the International Federation of Trade Unions. Dange said that "....The International Federation of Trade Unions is the labour mask worn by imperialism to hoodwink the unwary..."[534] The Workers' and Peasants' Party of Bombay sent a circular to the AITUC on the question of affiliation. It said in no uncertain terms, "The IFTU is in close relations with the International Labour Office of the League of Nations, an institution run by the capitalists of Europe in their own interests."[535]

Workers' organisations from abroad sent messages to the ninth session of the AITUC. These messages were, as usual, greetings to the proletariat, recognition to the movement that they were carrying on, and encouragement for future movements. These messages too spoke in the same tenor as the Indian communists. They were in favour of militant movement of the workers against imperialism and capitalism and they strongly denounced reformism and moderation of every kind.

The message from the Red International of Labour Unions said: "...despite their weak organisation, the broad masses of the workers and women-workers chose the right road when they came out on a wide front, setting up strike organs in the process of the struggle, and, lastly, (5) that for victory over the capitalists, strong mass trade unions are necessary imbued with the implacable spirit of the class struggle, trade unions that will struggle resolutely against the capitalists and against the adherents of class-collaboration in the ranks of the workers themselves."[536]

The All-Russian Trade Union's Central Council too was

thoroughly against the reformist tendencies that were prevalent in the trade union movement. It said that the reformists were actually "agents of British capital"[537] and that they were pursuing policies in the interests of the imperialists and capitalists.

The All China Labour Federation also sent a message to the AITUC. It described the plight that the Chinese workers were facing under the oppression of the British, Japanese, American and French capitalists along with the terror that the Kuomintang itself wielded under the leadership of Chiang-Kai-shek. It wanted to join hands with the Indian proletariat in its struggle against oppression of the masses. It read:

"Of course, not only our own and your struggles but also the revolutionary movement of all other colonial and semi-colonial peoples, and that of the workers and peasants in particular, will be greatly accelerated as soon as a revolutionary united mass front of all the oppressed and exploited against the capitalists and landlords, the militarists and imperialists as well as against the working class traitors will be set up and coordinated..."[538]

The Chinese communists were, like their Indian and Russian counterparts, against joining the International Federation of Labour Unions. They were also against collaboration with the reformists in the trade union movement and the nationalist led independence movement. The message said clearly, "Evidently Mr. Joshi and his like are preparing to betray your Trade Union Congress as Mr. Nehru and his like did it recently in your national independence movement or, as was the case with the Chiang Kai shek in our country last year..."[539] This is very significant in the sense that the Chinese communists were also following a policy of non collaboration with the nationalist movement. And this time it was in line with the principles of the Comintern. By this time an ultra left line had been imposed by Stalin on the Chinese Communist party, the same ultra left line that would be adopted by the Sixth Congress. In October 1929 the ECCI said that a new revolutionary wave had appeared in China. It also laid down a programme of insurrection for the Chinese communists to follow. But even in doing so, the Comintern that was being led by Stalin, was actually calling for adventurist lines of armed struggle. The Red armies of 1928-1929, those that were scattered in the mountain districts of the Central provinces of China were not even "primarily peasant forces"[540]. They composed of dispossessed peasants, jobless agricultural labourers, mutinous soldiers, local bandits, none of them playing a direct role in agricultural production. They had obviously learnt their lessons from the revolution that failed in China because the Comintern refused to interfere when Chiang Kai-shek brutally suppressed the communists and rose to power. Kunal Chattopadhyay has said that this policy of the Comintern also served as an answer to the Trotsky led opposition in the Comintern which was continuously criticising the role of Stalin in guiding the course of the Chinese revolution of 1925-1927[541]. This was also in line with what M.N.Roy had been propagating at the Comintern since the Fifth Congress, one that the Comintern refused to endorse or even consider under the increasing domination of Stalin.

THE INDIAN COMMUNIST MOVEMENT BEFORE THE MEERUT ARRESTS

Meanwhile the Comintern, it can be noted, was still following the policy of bringing the Indian communist movement increasingly under the control of the CPGB. The Indian communists, however, often expressed their disregard for it[542]. But that was not enough to deter the Comintern from future formulations on the same line. In its Resolution on Organisational Work in regard to India, it said clearly, "The Communist Party of Great Britain must support the revolutionary movement in India and particularly the organisation of the Communist Party in every possible way."[543] In fact the adherence of the Comintern to its policy of pushing the CPGB and also its frontal organisations like the Young Communist League into assumption of control of the Indian communist movement was starkly expressed in the same resolution. It said, "The CPGB and the YCL GB should cooperate with the Communist Party of India in the organisation of Young Communist Leagues. The Young Communist League of Great Britain should send one of its members with this object to India to work there under the same conditions as the Party members going to India for that purpose."[544] The entire resolution was in fact an instruction on how the CPGB was to make inroads into the communist movement that was developing in India indigenously and often, even without the ideological support of the Comintern. Although the Comintern wanted to bring the Indian communist movement under the control of the CPGB, it was also asserting simultaneously that the Indian communist movement had developed greatly from where it began. This is evident from another resolution on India passed only two days later[545]. This resolution was also directing the Indian communists regarding their future course of action. Here however, the CBGB was not mentioned at all. This was perhaps because the Stalinist led Comintern, through the CPGB, wanted to bring the Indian communist movement under its absolute control, one that was not possible if the movement developed and gained grounds without the interference of the Comintern. It would also not be possible if the communists like Roy kept on opposing the strategies of the Comintern in India, a reason that can be clearly attributed to his expulsion from its folds. This attitude of the Comintern however, alarmed the British.

On the whole, the situation was rapidly going out of control of the British rule. The strikes actually shook the foundations of the British stronghold in India. They had been aware of the rise of a new anti-imperialist force, that of the communists in India. British records show clearly that they kept themselves abreast of this new tendency and tried to keep it under control. But the events of 1928 clearly showed them that the communist movement had gained a momentum that needed to be curbed immediately or it would prove to be very fatal to their interests. The first Conference of the All India Workers' and Peasants' Party had also taken place by the end of December. It was another step at forging unity between the different communist factions in India. This movement was not just based on notions of freedom that were entertained by the rich and educated Indian intelligentsia. It was based on an economic premise that promised the toiling masses a freedom not just from foreign rulers but also from economic exploitation of all kinds. It had a political orientation that was very alarming to the British. They hence set forth immediately to crush the rising tide of the communist movement in India. Large scale arrests were made in this connection and the trials took place under the famous Meerut Conspiracy Case in 1931. The Meerut Case arrests crushed the communist movement in India for the time being. It closed the chapter of the first phase of the communist movement in India. When, after a couple of years, the communists once again raised their heads, their policies had undergone a sea change and that denoted the beginning of a new chapter in the progress of the communist movement of India.

NOTES AND REFERENCES

1   "There are to be found in the dependent countries two distinct movements which everyday grow further apart from each other. One is the bourgeoisie democratic nationalist movement, with a programme of political independence under the bourgeois order, and the other is the mass action of the poor and ignorant peasants and workers for their liberation from all sorts of exploitation.... For the overthrow of foreign capitalism which is the first step toward revolution in the colonies the cooperation of the bourgeois nationalist revolutionary elements is useful.
    But the foremost and necessary task is the formation of communist parties which will organise the peasants and workers and lead them to the revolution and to the establishment of Soviet republics. Thus the masses in the backward countries may reach communism, not through the capitalistic development, but led by the class conscious proletariat of the advanced capitalist countries." See thesis 7 of the Adopted Text of the Supplementary Theses, G.Adhikari, Documents of the History of the Communist Party of India, *Volume 1, New Delhi, 1971, p.185.*

2   See Chapter 3.

3   Shashi Joshi, *Struggle for Hegemony in India, The Colonial State, the Left and the National Movement*, Volume 1, New Delhi, 1992, p.42.

4   Ibid. pp.42-43.

5   Ibid. p.44.

6   Signed Memorandum to the Indian Commission: Scheme of Organisation of the Indian Work, submitted to the Mali Bureau (Small Bureau) by Bhupendranath Datta, Ebul Hasan and Abul Hasan on the Occasion of the Comintern's Third Congress. For details see Purabi Roy, Sobhanlal Dattagupta and Hari Vasudevan eds. *Indo-Russian Relations*, Part 1, 1917-1928, Calcutta, 1999, pp.133-139.

7   Minutes of the Meeting Held on 17 October 1920, G. Adhikari, *Documents of the History of the Communist Party of India*, Vol.1, 1917-1922, New Delhi, 1971, p.231.

8   Ibid.

9   Handwritten Minutes of meetings concerning the formation of the Indian Communist Party at Tashkent between 18.10.20 and 26.12.20. See Purabi Roy, Sobhanlal Dattagupta and Hari

Vasudevan eds. *Indo-Russian Relations*, Part 1, op.cit. p.40.

10   Ibid. pp.51-52.

11   "As a result of this Congress, the International, and the Russian Government which forms a part of that International, stand pledged to give every help, moral and material, to the cause of the oppressed colonial peoples, and it is stated definitely in the theses that every revolutionary nationalist movements in the countries dominated by foreign imperialism will receive such help." Ibid. p.51.

12   Plan of Military Operation in the Borders of India (presumably sometime in the 20's). See Purabi Roy, Sobhanlal Dattagupta and Hari Vasudevan ed. Indo- Russian Relations1917-1947, Select Documents from the Archives of the Russian Federation, Vol.I. The Asiatic Society, Calcutta, pp. 7-10. (Hereafter referred to as *Indo-Russian Relations*).

13   Ibid.p.7

14   Ibid.

15   Ibid. p.8.

16   Ibid. p.8-9.

17   Ibid. p.8.

18   Ibid. p.9.

19   Ibid.

20   Ibid.

21   M.N.Roy's *Memoirs*, Allied Publishers, Bombay, 1964, p.417

22   Ibid.

23   Ibid.

24   David Druhe, op.cit. p.34.

25   Ibid.

26   Letter from (?) to Lord Byron dated 5.2.20. See Purabi Roy, Sobhanlal Dattagupta and Hari Vasudevan ed..*Indo-Russian Relations,1917-1947*, op. cit. p.12.

27   David Druhe, op. cit. pp38.

28   Letter from (?) to Y.A.Suritz dated 1.6.20. See Purabi Roy, Sobhanlal Dattagupta and Hari Vasudevan ed. *Indo- Russian Relations, 1917-1947*, pp. 14-17 and pp.18-20. In the letter to Suritz it was stated, "...I deem it incumbent upon the Soviet Government to stand by His Majesty (Amir) through thick and thin. As a practical measure and readily effective one, I promise that a certain sum of money— say a million pound sterling be presented to His majesty by two instalments for propaganda work in Afghanistan in favour of alliance between Soviet Russia and Afghanistan.Thus His

Majesty would be able to convert the whole country into staunch supporters of the said policy, to gradually get rid of the Anglophile Ministers and officials and to prepare the nation for a tussle once more with the British..." (See p.14.). In the letter to Chicherin, Barkatullah said, "...Through overwhelming evidences I am convinced of Ameer Amanullah Khan's being a staunch partisan of the Soviet Russian Republic and an irreconcilable foe of the British. But, however, owing to the late British Afghan war of 1919, interruption of trade between Afghanistan and India thereby, stoppage of annual British subsidy and loss of millions of rupees due to Afghanistan from the British Govt. of India, there has scarcity of money being sensibly felt in the country and resulted in discontent among the people....It is, therefore, high time the Soviet Govt should fulfil their often repeated promises and assist the Ameer financially and embrace the extraordinary opportunity for bringing about a revolution in India..."(See p.19.) These two references clearly show that the Ameer was putting pressure on the Indians for money in return for his cooperation.

29   David Druhe, op. cit. p.38.

30   John Patrick Haithcox, *Communism and Nationalism in India*, p.23.

31   R.A. Ulyanovsky ed. *Revolutionaries of India in Soviet Russia: Mainspring of the Communist Movement in the East*, Progress Publishers, Moscow pp. 177-178.

32   R.A.Ulyanovsky ed. *The Comintern and the East: a Critique of the Critique*, Moscow, 1978, p.146.

33   See Shaukat Usmani, *Historic Trips of a Revolutionary*, New Delhi, 1977.

34   M.N.Roy's *Memoirs*, op. cit. p.529.

35   Ibid.

36   Virendranath Chattopadhyaya is referred to as Chatto.

37   See Subodh Roy ed. *Communism in India, Unpublished Documents, 1919-1924*, Calcutta, 1997, p.45.

38   Ibid. p.51.

39   G.Adhikari, *Documents of the History of the Communist Party of India*, Volume 1, New Delhi, 1971, p.206.

40   Ibid. p.207.

41   Amiya Bagchi, *Private Investment in India*, 1900-1939, New Delhi, 1972, p.138.

42   G.Adhikari, *Documents of the History of the Communist Party of India*, Volume 1, op.cit. p.207.

43 Amiya Bagchi, *Private Investment in India*, op.cit. pp. 142-143.

44 Ibid. p.140.

45 D.Chamanlal, Manifesto to the Workers of India, G.Adhikari, *Documents of the History of the Communist Party of India*, Volume 1, op.cit. p.212.

46 Ibid. p.208.

47 The "Manifesto to the Workers of India" by Dewan Chaman Lall clearly reflects a nationalist anti-imperialist attitude. That the influence of the communists had not yet pervaded into the trade union scene is very evident from its tone. See G.Adhikari, *Documents of the History of the Communist Party of India*, Volume 1, op.cit. pp.212-213.

48 If the statistics on trade union organization in 1920-21 are studied, they will show that apart from Bombay cotton mills, where 42.50 % of the operatives were organized in trade unions, the other sections of India had either very meagre or even no organised trade union movement. "Affiliation" to the AITUC therefore, was still very low. See Amiya Bagchi, Private Investment in India, op.cit. pp. 140-142.

49 Both M.N Roy and Abani Mukherjee are being considered because both authored *India in Transition*. The statistics on the other hand, by Roy's own admission, were collected by Abani (See M.N.Roy, Memoirs, Bombay, 1964, p.300), without which the analysis of Indian conditions would be impossible.

50 M.N.Roy in collaboration with Abani Mukherjee, *India in Transition*, Geneva, 1922, pp.135-136.

51 Ibid.

52 Ibid.

53 M.N.Roy, *What Do We Want?* Geneva,1922.

54 Ibid. p.276.

55 Ibid. pp.276-277.

56 Ibid. p.277.

57 Ibid.

58 Ibid.

59 Ibid.

60 M.N.Roy, *The Aftermath of Non-Cooperation*, London, 1926, p.18.

61 Manifesto to the Delegates of the XXXVI Indian National Congress, Subodh Roy ed. *Communism in India, Unpublished Documents, 1919-1924*, Calcutta, 1997, p.54 and p.62.

62 S.A Dange, Probing at the Root, Editorial from *The Socialist* dated

August 5,1922, *Selected Writings*, Volume 1, Bombay, 1974, p.139.

63   Manifesto to the Delegates of the XXXVI Indian National Congress, Subodh Roy, op.cit. p.57.

64   Ibid. p.61.

65   S.A.Dange, Maharashtra Treacherous! Editorial from *The Socialist* dated August 26,1922, *Selected Writings*, Volume 1, op.cit. p.153.

66   See Chapter 3.

67   Manifesto to the Delegates of the XXXVI Indian National Congress, Subodh Roy, op.cit. p.54.

68   Ibid. p.62.

69   S.A Dange, Probing at the Root, Editorial from *The Socialist* dated August 5,1922, *Selected Writings*, Volume 1, op.cit. p.139.

70   Manifesto to the Delegates of the XXXVI Indian National Congress, Subodh Roy, op.cit. p.61.

71   Cecil Kaye, *Communism in India*, Calcutta, 1971, p.11.

72   Ibid.

73   M.N.Roy's Letter dated 11.9— to Secretary, Eastern Section, Comintern, criticising Abani Mukherjee's activities (presumably sometime in 1922). See Purabi Roy, Sobhanlal Dattagupta and Hari Vasudevan ed..*Indo-Russian Relations,1917-1947*, p.170.

74   Ibid.

75   Letter of Tivel dated 7.12- to the Presidium of the ECCI regarding M.N.Roy's proposal to convene a conference of the Indian Communist groups in Berlin (presumably in 1922), Ibid. pp. 171-172.

76   Ibid. p.172

77   *The Vanguard of Indian Independence*, Volume 1, No.1, May 15 1922, p.1.

78   Ibid.

79   Ibid.

80   Gene. D. Overstreet and Marshall Windmiller, *Communism in India*, Bombay, 1960, p.55.

81   *The Vanguard of Indian Independence*, Volume 1, No.2, June 1st, 1922, p.1

82   Ibid.

83   Ibid.

84   Ibid. p.2.

85   M.N.Roy and Evelyn Roy, *One Year of Non-Cooperation, From Ahmedabad to Gaya*, Calcutta, 1923, p.43. It is to be noted that the same thoughts have been expressed Evelyn Roy as Santi Devi in

The Van guard of Indian Independence of June 15th, 1922. It had been said here in more or less the same tenor, with minor differences, "...All honour to Mr. Gandhi had he found a way for his people out of the barbed-wire entanglements of government-vigilance; that by his slogans of Non-violent Non-cooperation, Boycott and Civil Disobedience, he was able to draw the wide masses into the folds of the Congress Party and to make the Indian movement for the first time truly a nation-wide. But the movement has outgrown its leaders. *The Masses of India* sought to forge ahead in the struggle, and their leaders vainly tried to hold them back..."

86   *The Vanguard of Indian Independence*, Volume 1, No.4, July 1st, 1922, p.1.
87   *The Vanguard of Indian Independence*, Volume 1, No.7, August 15th, 1922, p.1.
88   Ibid. p.2.
89   Ibid.
90   *The Advance Guard*, Volume 1, No.3, November 1st, 1922, p.1.
91   Ibid. (It can be noted that Roy reproduced this article in "*The Aftermath of Non- Co-Operation*", pp.19-23, as late as 1926. It is strange since many of the earlier articles were reproduced earlier in *One Year of Non Co-operation* which was published in 1923. The reason may be that he did not want to alarm the moderate leadership of the Congress with the extra aggressiveness that the tone belied in this particular article.) Did all Congress members get to read his Books?
92   M.N.Roy, What is a Programme? Part II, Ibid. pp.2-3.
93   M.N.Roy, What is a Programme? Part III, *The Advance Guard*, Volume 1, No.5, December 1st, 1922, pp.3-4. (The italics have been used by M.N.Roy).
94   The Programme was later published in *The Aftermath of Non Co-operation*, 1926.
95   G.Adhikari, *Documents of the History of the Communist Party of India*, Volume 1, p.562.
96   Ibid.
97   Subodh Roy ed. *Communism in India, Unpublished Documents, 1919-1924*, Calcutta, 1997, p.65.
98   Ibid.
99   The Government of India Act of 1919, very much in the line of the Morley-Mito reforms, declared the setting up of a bicameral system at the centre, with a certain number of elected Indian representatives.

But a close appreciation of the Act shows that several measures had been taken to curb the wishes of the Indians than allowing them a voice in the functioning of the government. See Sumit Sarkar, *Modern India*, 1885-1947,Madras, 1992.

100 Ibid. pp.66-67 and p.70.

101 Ibid. p.70.

102 *The Vanguard of Indian Independence*, Volume 1, No.5, July 15th, 1922, p.1.

103 Ibid. p.2.

104 Ibid. p.67.

105 Ibid. pp.67-68.

106 Ibid. p.69.

107 The Advance-Guard, Volume 1, No. 5, December 1st, 1922, p.1.

108 Ibid.

109 Ibid.

110 Cecil Kaye, *Communism in India*, p.43.

111 Ibid.

112 Dange and Singaravelu had still not left the Congress.

113 David Druhe, *Soviet Russia and Indian Communism*, New York, 1959, p.57.

114 Gene. D. Overstreet and Marshall Windmiller, *Communism in India*, pp.55-58.

115 Ibid. p.57.

116 Ibid.

117 Overstreet and Windmiller have quoted excerpts from Singaravelu's speech, Ibid.

118 Singaravelu's Speech in Support of Labour Resolution, Labour Kishan Gazette, Volume 1, No.4, 31 January, 1924. See G.Adhikari, *Documents of the History of the Communist Party of India*, Volume 1, pp.588-591.

119 Ibid. p.589.

120 Gene. D. Overstreet and Marshall Windmiller, *Communism in India*, pp.49-50.

121 Cecil Kaye, Communism in India, p.20.

122 G.Adhikari, *Documents of the History of the Communist Party of India*, Volume 1, pp.588-591.

123 M.N.Roy and Evelyn Roy, One Year of Non-Cooperation, From Ahmedabad to Gaya, pp.100-102.

124 *The Vanguard of Indian Independence*, Volume 1, No.1, May 15th, 1922.

125 *The Vanguard of Indian Independence*, Volume 1, No.2, June 1st, 1922.

126 *The Vanguard of Indian Independence*, Volume 1, No.4, July 1st, 1922.

127 Cecil Kaye, Communism in India, p.16.

128 Ibid.p.17.

129 M.N.Roy, *Open Letter to Chittaranjan Das and His Followers*, February, 1923.

130 Ibid.

131 To call Roy a Bolshevik Brahmin is rather suggestive perhaps of the author's intention to expose the overriding nature of Soviet communism where India was concerned.

132 David Druhe, *Soviet Russia and Indian Communism*, p.59.

133 M.N.Roy and Evelyn Roy, *One Year of Non-Cooperation, From Ahmedabad to Gaya*, p,169.

134 Ibid. p.170.

135 See Subodh Roy ed. *Communism in India, Unpublished Documents, 1919-1924* and   Purabi Roy, Sobhanlal Dattagupta and Hari Vasudevan ed..*Indo-Russian Relations,1917-1947*.

136 Abani Mukherjee, Report on the Indian Situation and My One and a Half Year's Work There. See Purabi Roy, Sobhanlal Dattagupta and Hari Vasudevan ed..*Indo-Russian Relations,1917-1947*, *pp. 185-189.*

137 Ibid. pp.189-191.

138 Ibid. p.187.

139 Ibid.

140 Ibid. (Roy however, always remained wary of Abani Mukherjee, and he wasted no time in cautioning the Indian revolutionaries about him).

141 Ibid. p190.

142 Subodh Roy ed. *Communism in India, Unpublished Documents, 1919-1924*, p.89.

143 Ibid. p.92.

144 Gautam Chattopadhyay, *Communism and Bengal's Freedom Movement*, p.59.

145 See Gopen Chakravarty's interview, Appendix A, Ibid. p.128.

146 Ibid.

147 See Ibid, Appendix B, p.160.

148 Ibid. p.161.

149 Ibid.

150   Subodh Roy ed. *Communism in India, Unpublished Documents, 1919-1924*, p.199.

151   See Gopen Chakravarty's interview, Appendix A, Ibid. p.129.

152   Subodh Roy ed. Communism in India, Unpublished Documents, 1919-1924, p.85.

153   See Dange's article in the Lokamnya, G. Adhikari, *Documents of the History of the Communist Party of India*, Volume 2, pp. 131-133.

154   Cecil Kaye, *Communism in India*, p.78.

155   See The *Vanguard*, Volume 2 No.8, June 1st, 1923.

156   A letter from Shaukat Usmani to Singaravelu dated 9.2.23 says, "I have been directed by Com. Roy to be in connection with you and it is a long time…If you have not already known it, let me inform you that Abani Mukherjee has been expelled from our party from the order of the Comintern. DO not trust him please…" See Subodh Roy ed. *Communism in India, Unpublished Documents, 1919-1924*, p.168.

157   Home. Pol. F. 103/IV, 1923, Subodh Roy ed. Communism in India, Unpublished Documents, 1919-1924, p.106.

158   Ibid. p.199.

159   Ibid. p.97.

160   Statement and Memorandum of New India Revolutionary League signed by Bhupendranath Datta, Surendra Karr, Abul Hasan and Pandurang Khankoje. See Purabi Roy, Sobhanlal Dattagupta and Hari Vasudevan ed..*Indo-Russian Relations,1917-1947*, *pp.163-169.*

161   Ibid. p.166.

162   Ibid.(Whether this group was the same as the group that was supposed to receive training on labour organization is not clear from the document).

163   Ibid.

164   Ibid.

165   Ibid.pp.167-168.

166   The *Vanguard*, Volume 2, No.2, March 1st, 1923, p.3.

167   Ibid.

168   The *Vanguard*, Volume 2, No.3, March 15th, 1923,p.3.

169   Ibid.

170   The *Vanguard*, Volume 2, No.2, March 1st, 1923, p.3.

171   The *Vanguard*, Volume 2, No.3, March 15th, 1923,p.3.

172   M.A.Khan, D. Chamanlal on Trial. Quoted from G. Adhikari,

Documents of the History of the Communist Party of India, Volume 2, p. 83.

173   Ibid.

174   See G. Adhikari, *Documents of the History of the Communist Party of India*, Volume 1, p.311.

175   Resolution Passes at the Jharia Session, Ibid. p.319.

176   This excerpt is from the "Nation" of March 27th, which gave a vivid description of the gathering at Lahore. "A huge fleet of motor cars drove up to the gate of Bradlaugh Hall, and vociferous cheers greeted the arrival of the leaders. The hall was gaily decorated with wreaths of flowers. Several parties of musicians were present who sang national songs until the arrival of the President-elect. As soon as the Deshbandhu's car drove up, shouts of 'Bande Mataram' and 'Deshbandhu Das ki jai' went up from all quarters... Deshbandhu Das's speech created a sensation in so far as it was a brilliant and passionate exposition of the case for the labour movement in India. Mr. Kanhaya Lal's speech was like a string of pearls, a fine performance, finely delivered." See article Where are *The Masses of India*? by Evelyn Roy in Inprecor, Volume 3, No.36, 9th May, 1923. Quoted from G. Adhikari, *Documents of the History of the Communist Party of India*, Volume 2, p.89.

177   M.N.Roy and Evelyn Roy, The Aftermath of Non-Cooperation, London, 1926, p.40.

178   Evelyn Roy in Inprecor, Volume 3, No.36, 9th May, 1923 Quoted from G. Adhikari, *Documents of the History of the Communist Party of India*, Volume 2, p.93.

179   G. Adhikari, *Documents of the History of the Communist Party of India*, Volume 2, p.75.

180   M.N.Roy, Political Letters, 20th November, 1922. Quoted from G.Adhikari, *Documents of the History of the Communist Party of India*, Volume 2, pp.78-79.

181   Thesis 7 of the Supplementary Theses adopted at the Second Congress of the Comintern says, "There are to be found in the dependent countries two distinct movements which grow further apart from each other. One id the bourgeois democratic nationalist movement, with a programme of political independence under the bourgeois order, and the other is mass action of the poor and ignorant peasants and workers for their liberation from all sorts of exploitation. The former endeavour to control the latter, and often succeed to a certain extent, but the CI and the parties affected must

struggle against such control and help to develop class consciousness in the working masses of the colonies..." See G.Adhikari, *Documents of the History of the Communist Party of India*, Volume 1, p.185.

182   S.A.Dange, The Capitalist Offensive in India, See G.Adhikari, *Documents of the History of the Communist Party of India*, Volume 2, p.80.

183   The Socialist, Volume 1, No.8, 16th September, 1922.

184   Statement and Memorandum of New India Revolutionary League signed by Bhupendranath Datta, Surendra Karr, Abul Hasan and Pandurang Khankoje. See Purabi Roy, Sobhanlal Dattagupta and Hari Vasudevan ed..*Indo-Russian Relations,1917-1947*, *pp.163-169.*

185   Ibid. p.167.

186   G.Adhikari, *Documents of the History of the Communist Party of India*, Volume 2, p.98.

187   Ibid.

188   Ibid.

189   Ibid. p.101.

190   Cecil Kaye, Communism in India, pp.58-59.

191   Gautam Chattopadhyay, Communism and Bengal's Freedom Movement, New Delhi, 1970, p.27.

192   Cecil Kaye, Communism in India, p.59.

193   Ibid.

194   Home Pol. F 261 K.W.1, 1924, Subodh Roy ed. Communism in India, Unpublished Documents, 1919-1924, p.177.

195   Muzaffar Ahmad wrote to Roy, enclosing an original letter from Abani to Zinoviev that accused Roy, Muzaffar Ahmad himself, Nalini Gupta, Jotin Mitter and others as swindlers. See Cecil Kaye, Communism in India, p.59 and Subodh Roy ed. Communism in India, Unpublished Documents, 1919-1924, pp.191-192.

196   Home Pol. F 261 K.W.1, 1924, Subodh Roy ed. Communism in India, Unpublished Documents, 1919-1924, p.177.

197   Ibid. pp.179-186.

198   Muk. Apparently referred to Abani Mukherjee.

199   Home Pol. F 261 K.W.1, 1924, Subodh Roy ed. Communism in India, Unpublished Documents, 1919-1924, p.180.

200   Ibid.

201   Ibid. p.182.

202   Ibid. p.182.

203 Ibid. p.184.

204 Ibid. [The conference never took place. But even if it did, it is really a matter of hypotheses regarding whether it would actually be able to solve the problem of misunderstandings and political blunders. If the list of those who were to be invited is taken into consideration, it can be seen that the Berlin group of revolutionaries and the revolutionaries based in the United States were excluded. See "Letter of Tivel dated 7.12— to the Presidium of the ECCI regarding M.N.Roy's proposal to convene a conference of the Indian communist groups in Berlin (presumably in 1922), Purabi Roy, Sobhanlal Dattagupta and Hari Vasudevan ed..*Indo-Russian Relations,1917-1947*, pp.171-172.]

205 Ibid. p.186.

206 Ibid. p. 168.

207 Ibid. p.168.

208 M.N.Roy's Letter to Dange dated 7 May 1923, G.Adhikari, *Documents of the History of the Communist Party of India*, Volume 2, pp.136-137.

209 Ibid. p.136.

210 Ibid. p.137.

211 Ibid.

212 Abani had made close contacts with Upendranath Banerjee.

213 M.N.Roy's Letter to Dange dated 7 May 1923, G.Adhikari, *Documents of the History of the Communist Party of India*, Volume 2, p.136.

214 Ibid. pp.131-132.

215 Ibid. pp.132-133.

216 Home Pol. F 261 K.W.1, 1924, Subodh Roy ed. Communism in India, Unpublished Documents, 1919-1924, p.167.

217 Ibid. pp.167-168.

218 G.Adhikari, *Documents of the History of the Communist Party of India*, Volume 2, pp.104-105.

219 Shashi Joshi, Struggle for Hegemony in India, 1920-1947, Volume 1: 1920-1934, p.68.

220 Ibid. pp.68-69.

221 Cecil Kaye, Communism in India, p.60.

222 M.N.Roy, Memorandum to the Conference for Organising a Working-Class Party in India, Kanpur Case Exhibit No.12 B, G.Adhikari, *Documents of the History of the Communist Party of India*, Volume 2, p.144.

223 Ibid. p.143.

224 Ibid. p.146.

225 Ibid. p.147.

226 Ibid. P.148.

227 Ibid. pp.149-150.

228 Ibid. p.150.

229 Ibid.

230 Ibid. pp.150-151.

231 Ibid. pp.151-152.

232 Ibid. p.152.

233 Ibid.

234 Ibid. p.111.

235 Overstreet and Windmiller, Communism in India, p.65.

236 Ibid.

237 The Comintern and the Problem of a United Anti-Imperialist Front in India, Article by O.V.Martyshin, R.A.Ulyanovsky ed. The Comintern and the East, Progress Publishers, Moscow, 1978.

238 G.Adhikari, *Documents of the History of the Communist Party of India*, Volume 2, pp.154-155.

239 Ibid. pp.144-145.

240 The *Vanguard*, Volume 2, No. 9, 15th June, 1923.

241 G.Adhikari, *Documents of the History of the Communist Party of India*, Volume 2, pp. 114-129.

242 Ibid. p.108.

243 M. Singaravelu Chettiar and M.P.S.Velayudham, Manifesto to the Hindustan Labourers and Kisans for Organising a Political Party of their Own, Ibid. p.118.

244 Ibid. p.117.

245 Ibid. p.108.

246 Ibid. p.117.

247 David Druhe, Soviet Russia and Indian Communism, p.62.

248 Ibid. pp.62-63.

249 Manifesto of the Fourth Congress of the CI to AITUC session at Lahore, Message to the First Conference for Organising a Working-class Party in India. See G.Adhikari, *Documents of the History of the Communist Party of India*, Volume 2.

250 Gautam Chattopadhyay, Communism and Bengal's Freedom Movement, p.74.

251 Ibid. p.75.

252 Cecil Kaye, Communism in India, p.94.

253 These trials took place just before the Kanpur Conspiracy Case trials.

254 Cecil Kaye, Communism in India p.65.

255 Home Pol. F.261, KW, 1924, G.Adhikari, *Documents of the History of the Communist Party of India*, Volume 2, p.279.

256 Cecil Kaye, Communism in India, p.66.

257 M.N.Roy, Open Letter from the Communist Party of India, Inprecor, Volume 4, No. 22, 27th March, 1924. See G.Adhikari, *Documents of the History of the Communist Party of India*, Volume 2, p.301.

258 Ibid. p.303.

259 G.Adhikari, *Documents of the History of the Communist Party of India*, Volume 2, p.281.

260 Ibid. p.286.

261 Bengalee, 23rd April and 11th May, 1924. Quoted from G.Adhikari, *Documents of the History of the Communist Party of India*, Volume 2, p.290.

262 G.Adhikari, *Documents of the History of the Communist Party of India*, Volume 2, pp.286-287.

263 Inprecor Volume 4 No.25, 17th April, 1924, Ibid. pp.304-310.

264 Ibid. pp.308-309.

265 Ibid. p.309.

266 Ibid.

267 See "Condemned", M.N.Roy, *Vanguard*, Volume5, No.6, 15th October, 1924.

268 Ibid.

269 For more details on the Kanpur Conspiracy Case, see G.Adhikari, *Documents of the History of the Communist Party of India*, Volume 2.

270 David Druhe, Soviet Russia and Indian Communism, p.67.

271 G.Adhikari, *Documents of the History of the Communist Party of India*, Volume 2, p.592.

272 Saklatwalas' Message, G.Adhikari, *Documents of the History of the Communist Party of India*, Volume2, p.639.

273 G.Adhikari, *Documents of the History of the Communist Party of India*, Volume 2, p.656.

274 Ibid. p.667.

275 Ibid. p.592.

276 Satyabhakta, The First Indian Communist Conference, 12th October, 1925, Meerut Case Records, P 1796 (a), Ibid. p.637.

277 Ibid.

278   Ibid.

279   Ibid. p.638.

280   Ibid.

281   G.Adhikari, *Documents of the History of the Communist Party of India*, Volume 2, p.592.

282   Ibid. p.665.

283   Ibid. p.593.

284   Ibid. p.595.

285   Home. Pol. F. 6/IX, 1924, Subodh Roy ed. Communism in India, Unpublished Documents, 1919-1924, p.140.

286   For more details see David Petrie, Communism in India, Editions Indian, Calcutta, 1972, Chapter 3.

287   Resolution of the Indian Commission dated 9.3.26. Purabi Roy, Sobhanlal Dattagupta and Hari Vasudevan eds. *Indo-Russian Relations*, 1917-1947, p.215.

288   Ibid, p.214.

289   Ibid. pp.214-215.

290   See Working Class Struggles of 1925, G.Adhikari, *Documents of the History of the Communist Party of India*, Volume 2, p.523.

291   Ibid. pp.524-525.

292   Ibid. p.525.

293   Ibid. Also see M.N.Roy, A Labour Party for India, *The Masses of India*, Volume 1, No.5, May 1925.

294   M.N.Roy, A Labour Party for India, *The Masses of India*, Volume 1, No.5, May 1925.

295   Ibid.

296   Suggested Organisational Basis of International Bureau adopted at a meeting in Eastern Department, March 13 (presumably in 1924), Purabi Roy, Sobhanlal Dattagupta and Hari Vasudevan eds. *Indo-Russian Relations*, 1917-1947, pp.198-199.

297   Ibid.

298   The Colonial Bureau (A Note kept in the Archive dated Moscow, 3.5.25.), Ibid. p.199.

299   The Indian Foreign Bureau (presumably sometime in 1925), Ibid. pp.200-201.

300   Ibid. p. 200.

301   Colonial Committee Report dated 5.3.25. relating to India, Ibid. pp.201-202.

302   An undated , unsigned Note "Suggestions of Indian Comrades in London" regarding the formation of a Colonial Bureau (presumably

sometime in 1925), Ibid. pp.202-203.

303   Ibid. p.202.

304   Ibid. p.203.

305   Signed letter of nine persons dated 6.7.25. to CPI, European Bureau, seeking affiliation with the CPI in Moscow, Ibid. p.203-204. (The Indian Foreign Bureau was originally known as the European Bureau. It had been renamed at the initiative of Roy, Purabi Roy, Sobhanlal Dattagupta and Hari Vasudevan eds. *Indo-Russian Relations*, 1917-1947, p.201.)

306   Copy of reply from Moscow dated 15.9.25,(?) to the letter of C.P.Dutt and eight others dated 6.7.25. Ibid. pp.204-205.

307   M.N.Roy's letter to Petrov dated 30.12—expressing concern about CPGB's growing control over Indian affairs (presumably in 1925), Purabi Roy, Sobhanlal Dattagupta and Hari Vasudevan eds. *Indo-Russian Relations*, 1917-1947, pp. 205-206.

308   David Petrie, Communism in India, pp. 105-106.

309   G.Adhikari, *Documents of the History of the Communist Party of India*, Volume 2, p. 563.

310   Resolution of the Indian Commission dated 9.3.26. Purabi Roy, Sobhanlal Dattagupta and Hari Vasudevan eds. *Indo-Russian Relations*, 1917-1947, p.215.

311   Working Class Struggles of 1925, G.Adhikari, *Documents of the History of the Communist Party of India*, Volume 2, p.525.

312   G.Adhikari, *Documents of the History of the Communist Party of India*, Volume3A, p.2.

313   Ibid.

314   Ibid. p.526.

315   Ibid.

316   Ibid. p.529.

317   Ibid.

318   Ibid.

319   Amiya Kumar Bagchi, Private Investment in India 1900-1939, pp.142-143.

320   Ibid. p.139.

321   Ibid. pp.139-140.

322   See Resolution of the Indian Commission dated 9.3.26. Purabi Roy, Sobhanlal Dattagupta and Hari Vasudevan eds. *Indo-Russian Relations*, 1917-1947, pp.214-217.

323   For details see G.Adhikari, *Documents of the History of the Communist Party of India*, Volume2, pp.530-532.

324   G.Adhikari, *Documents of the History of the Communist Party of India*, Volume3A, p.4.

325   Excerpts from the Presidential Address of V.V.Giri were published in the Labour Monthly, March 1926. For details see G.Adhikari, *Documents of the History of the Communist Party of India*, Volume 3A, p.51.

326   M.N.Roy has referred to Thengdi as a "railway employee, who to the great discomfiture of the respectable gathering talked about class struggle." The spirit in which Roy has referred to him seemed to be as if he was a worker at the railways in contrast to the respectable leadership. It can be mentioned here that Thengdi had gone to England in 1897 to study engineering. It was there that he was influenced by socialist ideas. So how much of disparity he had in terms of respectability with the reformist nationalist leaders present at the Congress is very doubtful. The disparity was more in terms of thoughts and ideas than in terms of physical status.

327   M.N.Roy, The Indian Trade Union Congress, International Press Correspondence, Volume 6, No.1 3, February 18, 1926, G. Adhikari, *Documents of the History of the Communist Party of India*, Volume 3A, p.59. Roy had said, "By some mysterious means the worker Thengdi was replaced by the English christian missionary, Andrews, who had broken and sabotaged no a few strikes in his highly christian way." Now it is very strange that Roy said, "Nothing more was heard of Thengdi, who had startled the country with his speech as the president of the Trade Union Congress in Bombay" is not known because Thengdi kept on appearing and holding important post in the subsequent trade union congresses.

328   Ibid. p.59.

329   M.N.Roy, Point of View of *The Masses of India*, *The Masses of India* of India, Volume2, No.3, March 1926, G. Adhikari, *Documents of the History of the Communist Party of India*, Volume 3A, p. 64.

330   Ibid. p.62.

331   During the time when Roy was fighting against the reformist leadership in the working class movement in India, another communist, G.A.K. Luhani was saying in support, "The political party of Indian Labour cannot be the type represented by the British Labour Party. Indian labour has to organize itself into a mass party of workers and peasants—a party which, while carrying on the day-to-day fight against the capitalist and the landlord, will adapt itself

more and more as an instrument for the revolutionary overthrow of imperialist domination and class exploitation. The reformist illusion of 'constitutional' advance will have no place in its tactics… The national bourgeoisie have abdicated the leadership of the struggle for political liberation. They have given up the fight against imperialism for imperious reasons of class-interest, and are now ready for 'responsive co-operation' with it. But the economic process of imperialism not only create an industrial proletariat out of the labouring masses of India but also perpetually pauperise the middle classes. It is the historical role of the revolutionary political party of the Indian proletariat to lead all these forces to the battle for freedom…." International Press Correspondence, Volume 6, No. 12, February 11, 1926, Ibid. pp. 71-72.

332   See Chapter 2, pp.28-37.

333   ECCI's Resolution on India dated 6.4.25. Purabi Roy, Sobhanlal Dattagupta and Hari Vasudevan eds. *Indo-Russian Relations*, 1917-1947, p.211.

334   The Resolution of Indian Commission on India dated said clearly in March 1926, "The Enlarged Executive of the CI resolves that the CI of India shall enter into such a broad revolutionary nationalist party…The Enlarged Executive of the CI also resolves that the organisation questions concerning the building of the CP and nationalist revolutionary party in India should be very carefully considered. It recommends the Presidium to take up the matter immediately." This alliance of the Communist Party with the nationalist revolutionary party was the main cause of difference between Roy and the Comintern, and between Trotsky and Stalin. See Resolution of the Indian Commission on India dated 9.3.26. Ibid. p.216.

335   The Resolution of the Indian Commission said, "…Every effort should be made to obtain a closer contact between the Indian trade union movement and the British trade union movement in their common struggle against imperialism." Ibid. p.215.

336   Objects and Rules of the All Bengal Peasants' Conference, February, 1926, Ibid. pp. 155-156.

337   Policy and Demands of the All Bengal Peasants' Conference, February 1926, Ibid, p.158.

338   M.N.Roy , Crystallisation of the Left Wing, *The Masses of India*, Volume 2, No.8, p.7.

339   Ibid.

340 G.A.K.Luhani, Agricultural Policy of British Imperialism in India, Inprecorr, Volume 6, No.33, April 22 1926

341 M.N.Roy, Punjab Moneylenders Bill, *The Masses of India* of India, Volume 2, No.6, June 1926.

342 Policy and Demands of the All Bengal Peasants' Conference, February 1926, G. Adhikari, *Documents of the History of the Communist Party of India*, Volume 3A, p.158.

343 Ibid.

344 Ibid. p.159.

345 M.N.Roy, How to Organise a Working Class Party, *The Masses of India*, Volume 2, No.11, p.6.

346 Ibid.

347 Ibid.

348 Ibid.

349 Ibid. p.7.

350 Ibid. p.8.

351 Ibid. p.9.

352 Ibid.

353 G. Adhikari, *Documents of the History of the Communist Party of India*, Volume 3A, p.31.

354 *The Masses of India*, Volume 2, No.11, p.10.

355 M.N.Roy, The Calcutta Riot, Inprecorr, No.33, 22 April, 1926.

356 M.N.Roy, the Communal Strife, *The Masses of India*, Volume 2, October, 1926.

357 Ibid.

358 Hindu-Mussalman Strife, The Communist International, 30 March 1927.

359 M.N.Roy, From Gaya to Gauhati, *The Masses of India* of India, Volume 2, No.11, November 1926.

360 A Manifesto to the All-India National Congress, G. Adhikari, *Documents of the History of the Communist Party of India*, Volume 3 B, pp.231-247

361 Ibid. p.232.

362 Ibid. p.233.

363 Ibid.

364 Ibid. p.326.

365 Ibid. p.241.

366 Ibid. p.247.

367 M.N.Roy, The Indian National Congress, Inprecorr, Volume 7. No.5, 13 January 1927.

368 M.N.Roy, The End of Swarajism, *The Masses of India* of India, Volume 3, No.1, January 1927.

369 M.N.Roy, The Gauhati Congress, *The Masses of India* of India, Volume 3, No.2, February 1927.

370 Ibid.

371 Ibid.

372 Ibid.

373 See Chapter 3.

374 The Political Sufferers' Conference, *The Masses of India* of India, Volume 3, No.2, February 1927.

375 Ibid.

376 Ibid.

377 Ibid.

378 Ibid.

379 Ibid. (It can be said here that his earlier thesis on the scheme of Indian work too laid much emphasis on the alliance of the Indian mass movement and the world movement of the proletariat against imperialism. See Chapter 3 for details.)

380 G. Adhikari, *Documents of the History of the Communist Party of India*, Volume 2, pp.563-564.

381 Home/Political/1927 F.93, See Subodh Roy ed. *Communism in India, Unpublished Documents*, 1925-1934, p.14.

382 Ibid. Home/Political P&J (5) 436/1927, p.16.

383 "PUNJAB: For the last two months the local communists have been trying to stage an all-India Communist Conference at Lahore. It was originally confidentially announced that SAKLATWALA would preside, and a reception committee was appointed and invitations issued. The organizers, however, met with a cold reception from Saklatwala who pointed out that their party had no standing and advised them to get it affiliated to the British Communist Party or the Third International. The rebuff resulted in the abandonment of the proposed Conference at Lahore, but delegates are to attend the A.I.T.U.C. at Delhi this month. The failure to hold the Conference in Lahore exposed the weakness of the Communist movement in the Province." Fortnightly reports on the internal political situation in India for the month of MARCH, Home/Political/1927 F.32/March, Ibid. p.9.

384 Meerut Record, p.826.

385 G.Adhikari, *Documents of the History of the Communist Party of India*, Volume 3B, p.31.

386   The Workers and Peasants' Party, Ibid. p.166.

387   Ibid. p.167.

388   Ibid.

389   Ibid.

390   Ibid. (It can be noted here that the concept of swaraj to the Workers' and Peasants' Party meant the achievement of socialism, and not just self-government that would result with the liberation from foreign yoke.)

391   WPP Programme for AICC, Ibid. p.169.

392   Ibid. p.171.

393   Introduction, Ibid. p.37.

394   M.N.Roy, The Workers' and Peasants' Party, *The Masses of India*, Volume 3, No.4, April 1927.

395   G.Adhikari, *Documents of the History of the Communist Party of India*, Volume 3B, p.35.

396   See M.N.Roy's article, "How to Organise a Working Class Party", *The Masses of India*, Volume 2, No.11.

397   G.Adhikari, *Documents of the History of the Communist Party of India*, Volume 3 B, p. 9.

398   Resolution on India, Indian Quarterly Register, 1927, Volume 2, pp.155-156, Quoted from Adhikari, *Documents of the History of the Communist Party of India,* Volume 3 B, p.141.

399   Joint Resolution of the Indian and Chinese Delegations, *Modern Review*, Ibid. pp.142-143.

400   Joint Declaration of the British, Indian and Chinese Delegates, Ibid. pp.143-144.

401   Cited from G.Adhikari, *Documents of the History of the Communist Party of India.* Volume 3 B, p. 25.

402   Ibid.

403   Ibid.

404   Ibid.

405   It is rather strange that he was not aware of the Workers' and Peasants' Parties that were slowly spreading in India. In Bengal, it had already been formed by 1926 and in Bombay it was formed by February 1927, around the time the League Against Imperialism was holding its first Congress. The Bombay Workers' and Peasants' Party also submitted to the AICC a programme of action by May 1927. Besides, prominent members of this party like Nimbakar and Joglekar were also members of the Congress.

406   Philip Spratt, *India and China—by an Internationalist*, Cited from

G.Adhikari, *Documents of the History of the Communist Party of India*, Volume 3 B, p.229.

407 Ibid. p.236.

408 G.Adhikari, *Documents of the History of the Communist Party of India*, Volume 3 B, p.71.

409 Regarding the case of Spratt, Muzaffar Ahmad has written how his acquittal came about. He has said that the communists of Bombay went to Sarojini Naidu and "...pressed her to persuade Mr. M.A.Jinnah to look after the case, but he declined the brief. However, he gave a valuable piece of advice to Mrs. Naidu. His advice was that we should make an application to get the case transferred to the high court sessions, where Philip would give up the demand for trial by a European jury: and then the case would be tried by a majority of Indian jurors, who would be naturally sympathetic to an Englishman being tried for treason in India. The Bombay comrades acted according to Mr. Jinnah's advice. The case was committed to the high court sessions and the jury, consisting of one European and eight Indians was selected for the trial. At the end of the trial, the eight Indian jurors returned a verdict of 'not guilty'. Agreeing with the majority verdict, the judge aquitted the accused. The 'India-China' case ended in this manner." See Muzaffar Ahmad, *Myself and the Communist Party of India*, pp.465-466.

410 Les Evans and Block Russel eds. *Leon Trotsky on China*, Monad Press, New York, 1976, p.54.

411 Ibid. p.114.

412 Ibid.

413 Warren Lerner, *Karl Radek, the Last Internationalist*, Stanford University Press, California, 1970, p.140.

414 Ibid. pp.140-147.

415 See Nikolai Bukharin's speech in a meeting of the Indian Commission of the ECCI dated 17.8.27,Purabi Roy, Sobhanlal Dattagupta and Hari Vaudevan eds. *Indo-Russian Relations, 1917-1947*, pp.238-239.

416 Ibid. p. 239.

417 The Congress Rank and File, *The Masses of India*, Volume 3, No.5, May 1927.

418 Ibid. p. 15.

419 The National Congress Programme, *The Masses of India*, Volume 3, No.6, June 1927, pp.7-8.

420   National Question in the Communist International, *Vanguard*, Volume 5, No.2, 15 August 1924, G.Adhikari, *Documents of the History of the Communist Party of India,* Volume 2. p. 358

421   The Split in the Kuomintang, *The Masses of India*, Volume 3, No.5, May 1927, pp.15-16.

442   The Role of the Bourgeoisie in the National Revolution, *The Masses of India,* Volume 3, No.11, November 1927, p.7.

423   Ibid. p.8.

424   Quoted from G.Adhikari, *Documents of the History of the Communist Party of India,* Volume 3 B, p.4.

425   Copy of Report dated 16.3.27. On Organisational Work in India by C.P.Dutt and Mohammad Ali, Purabi Roy, Sobhanlal Dattagupta and Hari Vasudevan eds. *Indo-Russian Relations, 1917-1947*, p.234.

426   Ibid.

427   Ibid. p.235.

428   G.Adhikari, *Documents of the History of the Communist Party of India,* Volume 3 B, p. 45.

429   Philip Spratt, AITUC Delhi Session, 1927. See G.Adhikari, *Documents of the History of the Communist Party of India,* Volume 3 B, p.182.

430   Ibid. p.184.

431   Ibid. p.46.

432   All India Trade Union Congress (7th Session) Resolutions, Ibid. pp.189-190.

433   Philip Spratt, AITUC Delhi Session, 1927, Ibid. p.184.

434   Ibid. p.185.

435   Philip Spratt, All India Trade Union Congress (7th Session) Resolutions, Ibid. p.190.

436   G.Adhikari, *Documents of the History of the Communist Party of India,* Volume 3 B, p.47.

437   Philip Spratt, AITUC Delhi Session, 1927, Ibid. p.187.

438   The All India Trade Union Congress, *The Masses of India,* Volume 3, No.5, May, 1927, pp.9-11.

439   Philip Spratt, Draft of "Labour and Swaraj", cited in G.Adhikari, *Documents of the History of the Communist Party of India,* Volume 3C, p.203.

440   Raisaheb Chandrika Prasad's Presidential Address, cited from G.Adhikari, *Documents of the History of the Communist Party of India,* Volume 3 B, p.49.

441 G.Adhikari, *Documents of the History of the Communist Party of India,* Volume 3 B, pp.49-50.

442 Ibid. p.50.

443 Ibid.

444 Ibid. p.51.

445 The All India Trade Union Congress, *The Masses of India* Volume 3, No.5, May, 1927, pp.9-11.

446 Indian Trade Unions Hold Seventh Congress, *Inprecor*, Volume 7, Number 34, 9th June 1927, pp.713-714. Cited in G.Adhikari, *Documents of the History of the Communist Party of India,* Volume 3 B, p.51.

447 David Petrie, *Communism in India*, Editions Indian Calcutta, 1972, p.274.

448 David Petrie refers to this figure as 26,000, Ibid.

449 *The Masses of India*, Volume 3, Number 3, March 1927, Number 4, April 1927 and Number 5, May 1927.

450 K.N.Joglekar, The Second BNR Struggle, Cited in G.Adhikari, *Documents of the History of the Communist Party of India,* Volume 3 B, p.267.

451 *Labour Monthly*, December 1927, Cited from G.Adhikari, *Documents of the History of the Communist Party of India,* Volume 3 B, p.84.

452 K.N.Joglekar, The Second BNR Struggle, Cited in G.Adhikari, *Documents of the History of the Communist Party of India,* Volume 3 B, p.267.

453 Ibid. pp.270-271.

454 *Labour Monthly*, December 1927, Cited from G.Adhikari, *Documents of the History of the Communist Party of India,* Volume 3 B, pp.84-85.

455 K.N.Joglekar, The Second BNR Struggle, Cited in G.Adhikari, *Documents of the History of the Communist Party of India,* Volume 3 B, p.272.

456 See Kharagpur Betrayed, *The Masses of India,* Volume 4, Number1, January 1928 and Lessons of Kharagpur, *The Masses of India,* Volume 4, Number 2, February 1928.

457 Lessons of Kharagpur, *The Masses of India,* Volume 4, Number 2, February 1928.

458 Kharagpur Betrayed, *The Masses of India,* Volume 4, Number1, January 1928.

459 G.Adhikari, *Documents of the History of the Communist Party of*

India, Volume 3 B, p.83.

460   Ibid. p.85.

461   Ibid. p.87.

462   Letter of Mirajkar to Philip Spratt, Meerut Record, P 1010:Letter dated 21st August 1927, Cited in G.Adhikari, *Documents of the History of the Communist Party of India,* Volume 3 B, pp.86-87.

463   *Eastern and Colonial Bulletin,* 15th January 1928, Meerut Record, P.1201, Cited in G.Adhikari, *Documents of the History of the Communist Party of India,* Volume 3 B, pp.89-90.

464   *The Masses of India,* Volume 3, No.7, July 1927.

465   Ibid.

466   *Labour Monthly,* April 1928, Cited in Cited in G.Adhikari, *Documents of the History of the Communist Party of India,* Volume 3 B, p.273.

467   The RILU to the Eighth All India Congress of Trade Unions, *International Press Correspondence,* Volume 7, Number 68, December 1st, 1927.

468   *Labour Monthly,* April 1928, Cited in G.Adhikari, *Documents of the History of the Communist Party of India,* Volume 3 B, pp.273-274.

469   Ibid. p.274.

470   Ibid. p.276.

471   The RILU to the Eighth All India Congress of Trade Unions, *International Press Correspondence,* Volume 7, Number 68, December 1st, 1927.

472   Meerut Record, p.1878 (1) (c), quoted from G.Adhikari, *Documents of the History of the Communist Party of India,* Volume 3 B, p.278.

473   Philip Spratt, The Indian Trade Union Movement, *Labour Monthly,* October 1927, Cited in G.Adhikari, *Documents of the History of the Communist Party of India,* Volume 3 B, pp.250-266.

474   Ibid. p.250.

475   Ibid. p.260.

476   Ibid.

477   Ibid. p.262.

478   Ibid.

479   Ibid. p.264.

480   Ibid.

481   Ibid. pp.265-266.

482   See The Congress Rank and File, *The Masses of India,* Volume 3, No.5, May 1927, pp. 12-15 and The Role of the Bourgeoisie in the

National Revolution, *The Masses of India,* Volume 3, No.11, November 1927, pp. 5-8.

483   S.S.Mirajkar, Manifesto issued by the Executive Committee of the Workers' and Peasants' Party of Bombay on the Royal Commission, Meerut Record, p.1348(49), Cited in G.Adhikari, *Documents of the History of the Communist Party of India,* Volume 3 B, p.281.

484   Bipan Chandra, *India's Struggle for Independence*, Penguin Books, New Delhi, 1989, p.261.

485   The principal author of this report was Motilal Nehru, who prepared a scheme that outlined the future constitutional structure of India. This scheme considered Dominion Status as the form of government desired by India among other points like universal adult suffrage, equal rights for women etc. For details see Bipan Chandra, *India's Struggle for Independence*, p.263.

486   Bipan Chandra, *India's Struggle for Independence*, pp.263-264.

487   S.S.Mirajkar, Manifesto issued by the Executive Committee of the Workers' and Peasants' Party of Bombay on the Royal Commission, Meerut Record, p.1348(49), Cited in G.Adhikari, *Documents of the History of the Communist Party of India,* Volume 3 B, p.282.

488   The Role of the Bourgeois in the National Revolution, *The Masses of India*, Volume 3, No.11, November 1927,p.5.

489   S. Saklatwala, The Simon Commission, *Labour Monthly*, Cited in G.Adhikari, *Documents of the History of the Communist Party of India,* Volume 3 B, p.296.

490   G.A.K.Luhani, The British Commission on Constitutional Reform in India, *International Press Correspondence*, Volume 7, Number 71, 15th December 1927, Cited in G.Adhikari, *Documents of the History of the Communist Party of India,* Volume 3 B, pp.299-300.

491   G.Adhikari, *Documents of the History of the Communist Party of India,* Volume 3 B, p.106.

492   Ibid. p.108.

493   Ibid.

494   Resolution of the WPP of Bombay, 29th January 1928, quoted from G.Adhikari, *Documents of the History of the Communist Party of India,* Volume 3 C, p.183.

495   G.Adhikari, *Documents of the History of the Communist Party of India,* Volume 3 C, p.11.

496   Statement of R.S.Nimbakar, Meerut Record, Ibid. p.187.

497   Statement of S.S.Mirajkar, Meerut Record, Ibid.

498 Ibid. p.188.

499 Mirajkar's Protest Telegram, Ibid. p.191.

500 WPP(Bombay) Open Letter to All Parties Conference, ibid. p.195.

501 Ibid. p.196.

502 Ibid.p.197.

503 Spratt's Letter to Sub Committee Members, Meerut Record, p545(1), Ibid. pp.198-199.

504 Philip Spratt, Draft of Labour and Swaraj, Ibid. pp.200-201.

505 Ibid. p.202.

506 Ibid.

507 Ibid. p.203.

508 For details see Draft of Statement by the Trade Union Congress on the Nehru Committee's Report and Constitution and Statement of the WPP Bengal to the All Parties' Conference on the Report of the Nehru Committee and the Draft Principles of the Constitution for India, G.Adhikari, *Documents of the History of the Communist Party of India,* Volume 3 C, pp.207-223.

509 M.N.Roy, The Indian Constitution, *Inprecor*, Volume 8, No.64, 24th August, 1928.

510 G.Adhikari, *Documents of the History of the Communist Party of India,* Volume 3 C, p.43.

511 M.N.Roy, Assembly Letter, Quoted from G.Adhikari, *Documents of the History of the Communist Party of India,* Volume 3 C, pp 237-238.

512 Ibid. p.237.

513 Subodh Roy ed., *Communism in India, Unpublished Documents, 1925-1934,* p.55.

514 Workers and Peasants Party in Punjab, Extracts form Sohan Singh Josh's statement in the Meerut Case delivered between 18th May and 4th June 1931 before the sessions judge. Cited from G.Adhikari, *Documents of the History of the Communist Party of India,* Volume 3 C, pp.282-283.

515 Ibid. p.284.

516 Ibid.

517 Ibid.

518 Ibid.

519 Ibid. p.286.

520 Ibid. pp.285-286.

521 The Workers' and Peasants' Party of Delhi and UP, *Krantikari*, No.2, 24th November 1928. Cited from G.Adhikari, *Documents*

of the History of the Communist Party of India, Volume 3 C, p.288.

522 Ibid. p.289.

523 Ibid. p.290.

524 G.Adhikari, *Documents of the History of the Communist Party of India,* Volume 3 C, p.100.

525 B.F.Bradley, Bombay Mill Strike, Cited from G.Adhikari, *Documents of the History of the Communist Party of India,* Volume 3 C, p.330.

524 Ibid. p.332.

527 S.A.Dange, The Strike Upsurge of 1928 and the Emergence of Militant TU Movement, Cited from G.Adhikari, *Documents of the History of the Communist Party of India,* Volume 3 C, pp.320-321.

528 Dharani Kanta Goswami, On Lilooah Strike and Philip Spratt, EIR Dispute, See G.Adhikari, *Documents of the History of the Communist Party of India,* Volume 3 C, pp.332-340.

529 Ibid. p.334 and p.340.

530 See G.Adhikari, *Documents of the History of the Communist Party of India,* Volume 3 C, p.156.

531 B.F.Bradley, The All-India Trade Union Congress, 1928, Statement in the Meerut Case, Cited from G.Adhikari, *Documents of the History of the Communist Party of India,* Volume 3 C, p.367.

532 Ibid. p.156.

533 Ibid. p.368.

534 S.A.Dange, Conspiracy of Imperialism in the All-India Trade Union Congress, *Kirti,* May 1928, Meerut Record, p.545 (8), Cited from G.Adhikari, *Documents of the History of the Communist Party of India,* Volume 3 C, p.371.

535 WPP Circular on Affiliation, Meerut Record, p.87, Cited from G.Adhikari, *Documents of the History of the Communist Party of India,* Volume 3 C, p.375.

536 A.Lozovsky, General Secretary, Executive Bureau, Red International of Labour Unions, Message from Red International of Labour Unions, 27th October 1928, Meerut Record, p.1662, Cited from G.Adhikari, *Documents of the History of the Communist Party of India,* Volume 3 C, p.383.

537 Dogadev, Secretary, Presidium of the USSR Central Council of trade Unions, Inprecorr, Volume 8, No.77, 12th December 1928, Cited from G.Adhikari, *Documents of the History of the Communist Party of India,* Volume 3 C, pp.387-389.

538 Son Chao-jen, Chairman, Lou Tan-hsian, Secretary, All China Labour Federation, Shanghai, 10th October 1928, Message from the All China Labour Federation, Inprecorr, Volume 8, No.77, 2nd November 1928, Cited from G.Adhikari, *Documents of the History of the Communist Party of India,* Volume 3 C, p.390.

539 Ibid. p.393.

540 Harold. R. Isaacs, *The Tragedy of the Chinese Revolution,* Stanford University Press, Stanford, California, 1961, p.328.

541 Kunal Chattopadhyay, *The Marxism of Leon Trotsky,* Kolkata, 2006, pp.160-168.

542 'Abani Mukherjee called the CPGB agents in India "spies and adventurers" who were responsible for "overburdening the communist movement in India to its peril". See Abani Mukherjee's letter dated 7.6.28. from the Institute of Red Professors to Comrade P.Shubin, Indian Commission, Comintern, Purabi Roy, Sobhanlal Dattagupta and Hari Vasudevan eds. *Indo-Russian Relations,* 1917-1947, p.324.

543 Resolution dated 13.2.28. on Organisational Work in regard to India, Ibid. p.265.

544 Ibid. p.267 (It can be noted that youth organizations of the communists had already been formed in Bengal under the guidance of the WPP and independently of the efforts of the CPGB)

545 Resolution on India dated 15.2.28. Ibid. pp.268-269.

CONCLUSION

Work on this thesis had begun with the re-examination of earlier historiography on early Indian communism and its relationship with the Comintern. Traditional historiography, it was found, depended heavily on the police records and the writings of erstwhile British police officials posted in India in the 1920's[1]. The problem that arise from the records of the police officials is that they display a certain bias— a sort of superiority over the emerging communist movement, that they were supposed to keep under control. This can perhaps be explained by the fact that after the Russian Revolution and the setting up of the socialist state in Russia, the Russians began making certain demands regarding Afghanistan and Iraq, those that were at par with their socialist principles, but at the same time, very contradictory to the interests of the British capitalists. In fact socialist doctrines were actually aimed to overthrow imperialism. Hence they were bound to clash with the interests of the capitalists. The moment the capitalist countries realised this, they became conscious about the socialist advent in other countries, one that they needed desperately to keep under control. The police records and consequently the writings of earlier British police officials reflect just this. They can only explain how far the British were able to control the progress of communism in India and with it, the encroachment of the Soviet Russia into their realms. The autonomous development of Indian communism and its nature can be read within the lines but they remain unexplained in earlier historiography, which has considered the development of Indian communism as a Moscow rendered policy of communist expansion in the world. This flaw in earlier historiography was also in a way facilitated by the beginning of the cold-war era which deliberately viewed the evolution of communism and other under-developed countries of the world as a creation of Moscow.

Another point that needs to be mentioned here is that due to the dearth of documents, certain points could not be given due consideration in earlier writings on early Indian communism. The Baku Congress of the Toilers of the East, for example, had been ignored for a long time. It was only after the opening up of the Russian archives after the fall of the Soviet Union and the publication of several documents that had been suppressed for years that the process of evolution of ideas on Indian communism in the Comintern could be interpreted more clearly. John Riddell's collection of documents has been of great value in the analysis of the Baku Congress[2]. John Riddell's collection of documents has also helped in analysing the Marxist attitude towards the colonies of the east during the tenure of the Second International and that of the Third International or the Comintern.

Internal squabbles were rife among the early Indian communists, especially among the factions that were operating abroad. These factions were broadly represented by Virendranath Chattopadhyaya, Bhupendranath Datta and M.N.Roy. Among them, Roy was by far the most powerful and could manage to hold his own in the Comintern circles, a fact which the others could not manage to achieve during their careers. The power struggle that hence ensued between these factions were mainly directed against Roy and his coveted position in the Comintern that existed for a long time to come. Here too, new documents in Purabi Roy, Sobhanlal Dattagupta and Hari Vasudevan ed. Indo-Russian Relations 1917-1947, have thrown much light on the nature of this rivalry[3]. The same set of documents has been of much use throughout the thesis. It was not just the internal rivalry among different communist factions, but also the theories formulated by each faction that these documents have unravelled. All this long only Lenin's reaction to their theories could be known from Lenin's Collected Works. But now this reaction can be properly explained. Another factor that these documents have greatly helped in understanding is the Comintern fostered growing interference of the Communist Party of Great Britain in India since 1926. This part of the story too had remained ignored in the past due to dearth of documents.

However, what is important about the earlier writings is that though sketchy about certain aspects, they do provide a narrative about the contemporary happenings. They are also full of documents to show how well informed the British intelligence was regarding the growth of communism in India, the reason why the movement could be crushed so easily when the British attempted it. Another aspect about earlier writings like "Communism in India" by Gene.

D. Overstreet and Marshall Windmiller[4], is that a detailed analysis about M.N.Roy's thoughts has been made. Roy's writings were made use of quite extensively in order to do this. In fact discrepancies in facts that are evident in these works of Roy have also been pointed out.

It can be concluded that the development of Indian communism was not totally dependent on support from the Comintern. Ideologically and financially, it functioned primarily independently. This can be explained by several factors— distance, ideological education, nationalist background etc. A fundamental difference however remained. The Comintern at first let it develop on its own, at least as long as Lenin was alive. After the advent of Stalin, the situation changed. The Indian communists emerged mainly from nationalist backgrounds, where the guiding principle was the overthrow of British rule. Unlike that in Europe, socialist ideas had not made any progress in India, when the Indians started moving towards communist doctrines. The shift towards communism between 1915 and 1925 began as a search for a better alternative to the nationalist led anti-British movement that was based on the principle of moderation, one that was failing to satisfy the revolutionary minded nationalists. Slowly, as communist principles seeped in and communist doctrines began to offer more challenging theories and solutions to the Indian problems, more and more people began to get attracted towards communism. The theories that hence developed reflected two very different perspectives— one was the influence of nationalism while the other was a tendency to equate the Indian situation with that of the West. Lenin had tried to bring about a balance between the two. Ever since the Second Congress of the Communist International, he had tried to apply Marxist principles to rout imperialism from the colonies of the east by developing strategies that would cater to their specific situations. The united-front strategy was hence evolved. The Comintern had, in this manner, tried to guide the development of communism in the colonies of the east. But after his death and the consequent advent of Stalin, the situation changed enormously. The Comintern, which had so long tried to formulate on the basis of debates and discussions, rapidly became an organ of the Communist Party of the Soviet Union. It suffocated all dissenting voices and imposed its own principles without considering the needs of specific moments or conditions. Kunal Chattopadhyay has summed it up quite aptly, "…From the Seventh World Congress down to the dissolution of the Comintern and beyond, the basic thrust of Stalinism and 'post-Stalinist' official communism has been variants of the same theory, sometimes more 'left', sometimes 'right' but at all times oppose to the seizure of power by the working class."[5] This had a damaging effect on the development of communism in the east. The Chinese revolution failed as a result of it. M.N.Roy, who was sure that the time to make a final breach with the bourgeois led nationalist movement had arrived, entered into debate with the Comintern leadership for which he was expelled from the Comintern. The agents of the Communist Party of Great Britain were used to foster the cause of communism in India. Soon afterwards, the Meerut arrests began. The Meerut Conspiracy Case crushed the communist movement in India for the time being, and when it revived again, a new dimension was added to it. But that is another story altogether.

NOTES AND REFERENCES

1   Cecil Kaye and David Petrie.
2   John Riddell ed., *To See the Dawn, Baku 1920, First Congress of the Peoples of the East*, New York, 1998.
3   Purabi Roy, Sobhanlal Dattagupta and Hari Vasudevan ed. *Indo-Russian Relations 1917-1947*, Part 1.
4   Gene. D. Overstreet and Marshall Windmiller, *Communism in India*, Bombay, 1960.
5   Kunal Chattopadhyay, *The Marxism of Leon Trotsky*, pp.167-168.

BIBLIOGRAPHY

Primary Sources

1. Allan Adler ed. *Theses, Resolutions and Manifestoes of the First Four Congresses of the Comintern*, London, 1981.
2. Gangadhar Adhikari ed. *Documents of the History of the Communist Party of India, Volumes 1,2, 3A,3B, 3C,* New Delhi, 1971.
3. Jane Degras, *The Communist International 1919-1943 Documents, Volumes 1,2,* London, 1960.
4. John Riddell ed. *Lenin's Struggle for a Revolutionary International, Documents: 1907- 1916, The Preparatory Years,* New York, London, Sydney, 1986.
5. John Riddell ed. *Lenin's Struggle for a Revolutionary International, The Communist International in Lenin's Time,* New York, 1986.
6. John Riddell ed. *The German Revolution and the Debate on Soviet Power, The Communist International in Lenin's Time,* New York, 1986.
7. John Riddell ed. *To See the Dawn, Baku 1920, First Congress of the Peoples of the East,* New York, 1998.
8. John Riddell ed., *Workers of the World and Oppressed Peoples Unite! The Communist International in Lenin's Time: proceedings and documents of the Second Congress, 1920, Vol. I,* New York, 1991.
9. Programme of the Social-Democratic Workers' Party, adopted at the Second Congress of the Party, *1903,* Minutes of the Second Congress of the RSDLP, London, 1978.
10. Purabi Roy, Sobhanlal Dattagupta and Hari Vasudevan ed. *Indo-Russian Relations 1917-1947, Select Documents from the Archives of the Russian Federation, Part 1 and 2,* Kolkata, 1999.
11. Subodh Roy ed. *Communism in India, Unpublished Documents, 1919-1924,* Calcutta, 1997.
12. Subodh Roy ed. *Communism in India, Unpublished Documents,* 1925-1934.
13. The General Council of the First International, 1864- 1866, *The London Conference 1865 Minutes,* Moscow, 1964.

14. Home Political Files: Home/Political/1923F.No.103/IV, Home/Political/1923 F.No.5/II/23/K.W., Home/Political/1923F.No.11/1923, Home/Political/1924F.No.6/IX, Home/Political/1928F.No.18/VIIK.W.I., Home/Political/1928F.No.443-S,Home/Political/1928 F.No. 562-S, Home/Political/1928 F.18/7 K.W.2, Home/Political/1928 F.No.18/VII K.W.XI, National Archives of India, New Delhi.

Secondary Sources

1. Aijaz Ahmad ed. *Karl Marx and Frederick Engels on the National and Colonial Questions,* New Delhi, 2001.

2. Allen. S. Whiting, *Soviet Policies in China, 1917-1924*, New York, 1954.

3. Amiya Kumar Bagchi, *Private Investment in India 1900-1939*, New Delhi, 1980.

4. Bhupendranath Datta, *Aprakashito Rajnaitik Itihas* (Bengali), Calcutta, 1953.

5. Bipan Chandra, *India's Struggle for Independence*, New Delhi, 1989.

6. C.G.Shah, *Ends and Means*, Bombay, 1972.

7. C.G.Shah, *Marxism, Gandhism, Stalinism*, Bombay, 1963.

8. Cecil Kaye, *Communism in India*, Calcutta, 1971.

9. Conrad Brandt, *Stalin's Failure in China*, Cambridge, Massachusetts, 1958.

10. David McLellan, *The Thought of Karl Marx: an introduction*, London, 1971.

11. David Petrie, *Communism in India*, Calcutta, 1972.

12. David.N.Druhe, *Soviet Russia and Indian Communism, 1917-1947*, New York, 1959.

13. Duncan Hallas, *The Comintern*, Bookmarks, London, 1985.

14. Edward W. Said, *Orientalism*, New Delhi, 2001.

15. Ellen Meiksins Wood and John Bellamy Foster eds. *In Defense of History, Marxism and the Postmodern Agenda*, Delhi, 2006.

16. G.I.Shirokov, *Industrialisation of India*, New Delhi, 1980.

17. Gautam Chattopadhyay, Rus *Biplab o Banglar Mukti Andolan* (Bengali), Calcutta, 1967.

18. Gautam Chattopadhyay, Abani Mukherjee: A Dauntless Revolutionary and a Pioneering Communist, New Delhi, 1976.

19. Gautam Chattopadhyay, *Communism and Bengal's Freedom Movement, 1917-1929, Volume 1*, New Delhi, 1970.

20. Gene. D. Overstreet and Marshall Windmiller, *Communism in*

India, Bombay, 1960.

21. Harold. R. Isaacs, *The Tragedy of the Chinese Revolution*, Stanford University Press, Stanford, California, 1961.

22. Henry Collins and Chimen Abramsky, *Karl Marx and the British Labour Movement: years of the First International,* London, New York, 1965.

23. Horace. B. Davis ed. *Rosa Luxemburg, The National Question and Autonomy, The National Question; selected writings*, London, NewYork, 1976.

24. Hauce. B. Davis, *Nationalism and Socialism : navxist and labour theories of nationalism to 1917*, New York, Monthlt Review Press, 1973.

24. Irfan Habib, *Essays in Indian History, Towards a Marxist Perception*, New Delhi, 1995.

25. James Joll, *The Second International: 1889-1914*, London, 1955.

26. John Patrick Haithcox, *Communism and Nationalism in India, M.N.Roy and Comintern Policy, 1920-1939*, Bombay, 1971.

27. John.H.Kautsky, Communism and the Politics of Development, New York, 1968.

28. John.H.Kautsky, Moscow and the Communist Party of India, London, 1956.

29. John.H.Kautsky, Political Changes in the Underdeveloped Countries, London/New York, 1962.

30. Karl Marx, The British Rule in India, New York Daily Tribune, No. 3805, 25 June, 1853, *Collected Works*, Moscow, 1979,Vol.12.

31. Karl Marx, The East India Question, July, 25, 1853, New York Daily Tribune, No. 3828, *Collected Works*, Vol.12.

32. Karl Marx, The Indian Revolt, September 4, 1857, New American Cyclopedia, Vol. 1, 1858, *Collected Works*, Vol. 15.

33. Kunal Chattopadhyay, *The Marxism of Leon Trotsky,* Kolkata, 2006.

34. L.P.Sinha, *The Left Wing in India*, 1919-1947, Muzaffarpur, Bihar, 1965.

35. Les Evans and Block Russel eds. *Leon Trotsky on China*, New York, 1976.

36. M.A.Persits, *Revolutionaries of India in Soviet Russia: Mainspring of the Communist Movement in the East*, Moscow, 1983.

37. M.N.Roy and Evelyn Roy, *One Year of Non-Cooperation, From Ahmedabad to Gaya*, Calcutta, 1923.

38. M.N.Roy and Evelyn Roy, *The Aftermath of Non-Cooperation*, London, 1926.

39. M.N.Roy, *India in Transition*, Bombay, 1971 (The book was first

published in Geneva in 1922).

40. M.N.Roy, *Memoirs*, Bombay, 1964.

41. M.N.Roy, *The Future of Indian Politics*, London.

42. M.N.Roy, *What Do We Want?* Geneva, 1922.

43. Muzaffar Ahmad, *Amar Jibon o Bharoter Communist Party (Bengali)*, Calcutta, 1969.

44. Muzaffar Ahmad, *Myself and the Communist Party of India*, 1920-1929, Calcutta, 1970.

45. Panchanan Saha, *Dictionary of Labour Biography*, Calcutta, 1995.

46. Peter Nettl, *Rosa Luxemburg,* London, Oxford, New York, 1969.

47. Philip Spratt, *Blowing Up India; reminiscences and reflections of a former Comintern emissary*, Calcutta, 1955.

48. R.A.Ulyanovsky ed. *The Comintern and the East*, Progress Publishers, Moscow, 1978.

49. R.A.Ulyanovsky ed. *The Comintern and the East: a Critique of the Critique*, Moscow, 1978.

50. Rajat Kanta Ray ed., *Entrepreneurship and Industry in India 1800-1947*, New Delhi, 1992.

51. S. A. Dange, *Gandhi vs. Lenin*, Bombay, 1921.

52. S.A.Dange, *Selected Works, Volume 1*, Bombay, 1974.

53. Samaren Roy, *The Restless Brahmin*, Calcutta, 1970.

54. Samaren Roy, *The Twice Born Heretic*, Calcutta, 1986.

55. Sanjay Seth, *Marxist Theory and Nationalist Politics: The Case of Colonial India*, New Delhi, 1995.

56. Saumyendrananth Tagore, *Against the Stream*, New Delhi, 1977.

57. Shashi Joshi, *Struggle for Hegemony in India 1920-1947*, Vol.1, New Delhi, 1992.

58. Shashi Vairathi, *Communism and Nationalism in India, a study in inter-relationship, 1919-1947*, New Delhi, 1987.

59. Shaukat Usmani, *Historic Trips of a Revolutionary*, New Delhi, 1977.

60. Sobhanlal DattaGupta, *Comintern, India and the Colonial Question, 1920-1937*, Calcutta, 1980.

61. Sobhanlal DattaGupta, - *Comintern and the Destiny of Communism in India 1919-1943. Dialeclics of Real and a Possible History,* Sevibaan, Kolkata - 2006.

61. Sibnarayan Ray ed. *Selected Works of M.N.Roy, Volume 1,* 1917-1922, New Delhi, 1987

62. Sohan Singh Josh, *My Tryst With Secularism, an Autobiography*, New Delhi,1991.

63. Solomon. Frank. Bloom, *The World of Nations*, New York, 1941.

64. Stuart Schramm and Carrere d' Encausse Helene, *Marxism and Asia: an introduction with readings*, London, 1969.

65. Sumit Sarkar, *Modern India*, 1885-1947, Madras, 1992.

66. V.I.Lenin, *Collected Works*, Volumes 15, 20, 22, 23, 30, 31, 32, 33, 45, Moscow, 1977.

67. V.I.Lenin, *The National and Liberation Movement in the East*, Moscow 1969.

68. Leon Trotsky, *The First Five Years of the Communist International*, Volume 1, New York, 1972.

69. Warren Lerner, *Karl Radek, the Last Internationalist*, California, 1970.

JOURNALS AND ARTICLES

1. Dipak Kumar Das, article, "The Colonial Question: Lenin-Roy Debate, An Overview", *Society and Change*, Vol. 5, No. 2 and 3, January – June, 1988,p. 114.

2. *Inprecorrr*, Volume 4 No.25, 17th April, 1924.

3. *Inprecorr*, Volume 4, No. 22, 27th March, 1924.

4. *Inprecorr*, Volume 6, No.33, 22 April, 1926.

5. *Inprecorr*, Volume 6, No.33, April 22 1926

6. *Inprecorr,* Volume 7, Number 68, December 1st, 1927.

7. *Inprecorr*, Volume 7. No.5, 13th January 1927.

8. *Inprecorr*, Volume 8, No.64, 24th August, 1928.

9. M.N.Roy, *Open Letter to Chittaranjan Das and His Followers*, February, 1923.

10. M.N.Roy, *The Way to Durable Peace*, Calcutta, 1986. This essay was originally written in English and published in New York by the Indian Nationalist Party, as "An Open Letter to His Excellency Woodrow Wilson" soon after Roy fled to Mexico in 1917. Later on in Mexico, he rewrote the essay in Spanish and titled it "El Camino Para la Paz Duradera del Mundo" meaning "The Way to Durable Peace".

11. Michael Lowy, Mavxists and the Nationalist Question, *New Left Review 96*.

11. Suchetana Chattopadhyay, Talking Bolshevism: Muzaffar Ahmad and the first socialist nucleus among the urban intelligentsia in the early nineteen-twenties, *Jadavpur University Journal of History, Volume XXI*, 2003-2004.

12. *The Advance Guard*, Volume 1, No.3, November 1st, 1922, p.1.

13. *The Advance-Guard*, Volume 1, No. 5, December 1st, 1922.
14. *The Communist International*, 30 March 1927.
15. *The Masses of India*, Volume 1, No.5, May 1925.
16. *The Masses of India*, Volume 2, No.10, October, 1926.
17. *The Masses of India*, Volume 2, No.11, November 1926.
18. *The Masses of India*, Volume 2, No.3, March 1926.
19. *The Masses of India*, Volume 2, No.6, June 1926.
20. *The Masses of India*, Volume 2, No.8, August 1926.
21. *The Masses of India*, Volume 3, No. 3, March 1927.
22. *The Masses of India*, Volume 3, No.1, January 1927.
23. *The Masses of India*, Volume 3, No.11, November 1927.
24. *The Masses of India*, Volume 3, No.2, February 1927.
25. *The Masses of India*, Volume 3, No.4, April 1927.
26. *The Masses of India*, Volume 3, No.5, May 1927.
27. *The Masses of India*, Volume 3, No.6, June 1927.
28. *The Masses of India*, Volume 3, No.7, July 1927.
29. *The Masses of India*, Volume 4, No. 2, February 1928.
30. *The Masses of India*, Volume 4, No.1, January 1928.
31. *The Vanguard of Indian Independence*, Volume 1, No.1, May 15th 1922.
32. *The Vanguard of Indian Independence*, Volume 1, No.2, June 1st, 1922.
33. *The Vanguard of Indian Independence,* Volume 1, No.3, June 15th, 1922.
34. *The Vanguard of Indian Independence*, Volume 1, No.4, July 1st, 1922.
35. *The Vanguard of Indian Independence*, Volume 1, No.5, July 15th, 1922.
36. *The Vanguard of Indian Independence*, Volume 1, No.7, August 15th, 1922.
37. *The Vanguard*, Volume 2 No.8, June 1st, 1923.
38. *The Vanguard*, Volume 2, No. 9, June 15th, 1923.
39. *The Vanguard*, Volume 2, No.2, March 1st, 1923.
40. *The Vanguard*, Volume 2, No.3, March 15th, 1923.
41. *Vanguard*, Volume 5, No.2, 15th August 1924.
42. *Vanguard*, Volume5, No.6, 15th October, 1924.

INDEX